Economics Education
Research and Development Issues

Economics Education

Research and Development Issues

Papers presented at the
International Research Seminar
held at the University of London
Institute of Education
30 JULY–1 AUGUST 1985
Edited for
the Economics Association by
Steve Hodkinson and
David J. Whitehead

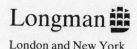

Longman

London and New York

LONGMAN GROUP LIMITED
Longman House, Burnt Mill, Harlow, Essex CM20 2JE, England
and Associated Companies throughout the World

Published in the United States by Longman Inc,
The Longman Building, 95 Church Street, White Plains, New York 10601

First published 1986
ISBN 0 582 36214 8

Set in 10pt Times

Printed in Great Britain
by Butler and Tanner, Frome

British Library Cataloguing in Publication Data
Economics education: research and development
    issues: papers presented at the international
    research seminar held at the University of
    London Institute of Education. 30 July – 1 August
    1985.
    1. Economics——Study and teaching
    I. Hodkinson, Steve   II. Whitehead, David J.
    330'.07'1   HB74.5

    ISBN 0–582–36214–8

Library of Congress Cataloging-in-Publication Data
Main entry under title:

Economics education.

    Bibliography: p.
    Includes index.
    1. Economics——Study and teaching——Congresses.
I. Hodkinson, Steve. I. Whitehead, David J.
HB74.5.E27   1986   330'.07'1   85-24098
ISBN 0–582–36214–8

Contents

Participants and their posts at the time of the seminar

Anna Maria Ajello   *Researcher, Department of Psychology of Developmental and Socialization Processes, University of Rome 'La Sapienza'*

William Baird   *Lecturer in Economics, University of Dundee*

Ronald Banaszak   *Vice-President, Foundation for Teaching Economics, San Francisco*

Mark Blaug   *Professor Emeritus of the University of London Institute of Education and Consultant Professor of Economics at the University of Buckingham*

David Butler   *Senior Teacher, Hailsham School, East Sussex*

John Chizmar   *Professor of Economics and Acting Associate Provost, Illinois State University*

Paul Clarke   *Field Officer, Economics Education 14–16 Project*

Lindsey Collings   *Head of Economics and Politics, Coopers' Company and Coburn School, London*

Ann Cotterrell   *Lecturer in Economics, Waltham Forest College of Further and Higher Education, London*

Margaret Cuthbert   *Consultant in application of quantitative methods to business*

Graham Dawson   *Head of Economics, Birkenhead School*

Kenneth Ferguson   *Principal Professional Officer, Secondary Examinations Council*

Barry Finlayson   *Lecturer in Business Studies and Economics, Jordanhill College of Education, Glasgow*

Alan Gregory   *Senior Lecturer in Education, Monash University, Melbourne*

Tony Halil   *Lecturer in Statistics, University of London Institute of Education*

Suzanne Helburn   *Professor of Economics, University of Colorado, Denver*

Steve Hodkinson   *Lecturer in Education (Economics), University of Manchester*

Steve Hurd   *Senior Lecturer in Economics Education, North Staffordshire Polytechnic*

Barry King   *Her Majesty's Inspectorate for Schools*

Marilyn Kourilsky   *Professor and Director of Teacher Education, University of California at Los Angeles*

Frank Livesey   *Professor and Head of School of Economics, Lancashire Polytechnic*

William Luker   *Professor of Economic Education and Dean of the School of Community Service, North Texas State University, Denton, Texas*

Chris Marsden   *Manager, Educational Liaison, BP plc*

Peter Maunder   *Senior Lecturer in Economics, University of Loughborough*

Barry McCormick   *Lecturer in Economics, University of Southampton*

Richard Powell   *Advisory Teacher, London Borough of Bromley*

Keith Robinson   *Director, Glasgow Centre of the Scottish Curriculum Development Service*

Robert Smith   *Director, Center for Economic Education, University of Nevada, Las Vegas*

John Sumansky   *Program Director, Joint Council on Economic Education, New York*

Angus Taylor   *Headmaster, Cramlington High School, Northumberland*

Linda Thomas   *Lecturer in Education (Economics), University of London Institute of Education*

Michael Tighe   *Head of Economics and Business Studies, Gateway Sixth Form College, Leicester*

Robert van Oosten   *Staff member, Dutch National Institute for Curriculum Development*

Michael Watts   *Director, Center for Economic Education; Associate Director, Indiana Council for Economic Education and Assistant Professor of Economics, Purdue University*

David Whitehead   *Senior Lecturer in Education (Economics), University of London Institute of Education*

Ron Wilkes   *Lecturer in Education, University of Queensland*

Marie Wilson   *Director, Economic Education Resource Centre, Fraser Institute, Vancouver*

Robert Wilson   *Head of Economics and Business Studies, Aberdeen College of Education*

Keith Wood   *Lecturer in Education (Economics), University of Hong Kong*

Invited guests

Denis Lawton *Professor and Director, University of London Institute of Education*

Fred Hankins *General Secretary, Economics Association*

Andrew Ransom *Longman Group Limited*

Maurice Williams *Chair, Department of Education, University of Melbourne*

Other contributors who did not attend the seminar

Anna Silvia Bombi *Department of Psychology of Development and Socialization, University of Padua*

Richard Dunnill *Department of Trade and Industry Fellow, Economics Research and Curriculum Unit, University of London Institute of Education*

Edna Graff *Princeton School District, Cincinnati, Ohio*

Keith Lumsden *Esmée Fairbairn Research Centre, Heriot-Watt University, Edinburgh*

Alphons Moret *Dutch National Institute for Curriculum Development*

Alex Scott *Esmée Fairbairn Research Centre, Heriot-Watt University, Edinburgh*

Walton Sharp *Assistant Professor of Labor and Industrial Relations and Director of Labor Studies, North Texas State University, Denton, Texas*

William Witter *Assistant Professor of Economic Education and Director of the Center for Economic Education, North Texas State University, Denton, Texas*

Cristina Zucchermaglio *Department of Psychology of Developmental and Socialization Processes, University of Rome 'La Sapienza'*

Preface

The joint academic sponsors of the seminar which elicited the papers published in this volume were the Economics Association and London University Institute of Education. Thanks are due to both organizations for their encouragement during the two and a half years' preparation for the seminar. The seminar was funded by grants from our publisher, the Banking Information Service, BP plc, the Institute of Education and the Economics Association: without the support of these bodies the seminar could not have taken place.

The success of this first international seminar on economics education was principally due to the commitment of its participants, and to their willingness to listen as much as to talk. Special acknowledgement is made to our publisher, Andrew Ransom of Longman Group Limited, and to his very efficient editor, Laurice Suess: it has been a pleasure to work with them. For our secretarial support we are indebted to Rosemary Williams, whose global correspondence and distribution of papers was equally effected.

The Organizing Committee, which comprised the editors and Dr Linda Thomas, was responsible for deciding who should be invited to the seminar and what papers should be commissioned. Some hard choices had to be made, and we were unable to invite a number of distinguished figures in the field of economics education. The editors are responsible for the inclusion of the papers published here, though the responsibility for the views, methods and results of the papers rests with their authors.

Steve Hodkinson
David J. Whitehead

Publisher's acknowledgement

We are indebted to the Netherlands Stichting voor de Leerplanontwikkeling for permission to reproduce an extract from Part II, p. 31, of *An Elaborated Illustration of the Economics 13–16 Project of the SLO* by A. L. A. Moret and R. N. J. van Oosten.

Introduction

Background

Interest in the development of economics education in the UK has never been higher. In England and Wales, successive government publications and statements have recognized the important potential role of economics education in citizenship and in adult working life. This has helped to create a climate in which the long-term goal of achieving an economically literate population is realizable. In Northern Ireland, where economics education is less well established in schools, economic awareness has been identified as a major focus for the Department of Education's secondary school curriculum review. In Scotland, with its central impetus, recent curriculum reform has ensured that opportunities exist for all young people to receive an economics education at secondary school.

It is, therefore, hardly surprising that the Council of the Economics Association should have judged the time to be right to organize a seminar which would take stock of current research and development in economics education and attempt to pinpoint the major issues of the day. It had, after all, shrewdly sponsored seminars in 1973 and in 1975 both to record and debate achievements at O and A level and to consider the differing viewpoints within UK economics education on the desirability of extending the teaching of economics in schools to younger and less academically able young people.* Nor is it surprising that the Economics Association should work jointly to organize its seminar with one of the UK's pioneering centres of excellence in economics education, the University of London Institute of Education.

What may be surprising to some is that for its third major seminar the Economics Association should

1 draw participants from the international economics education community and

2 seek funding for and participation in the seminar by industry and commerce

The decision to organize the seminar on an international basis was crucial and one which could influence the nature of future research and development programmes in a number of countries. It involved recognizing the importance of setting current UK research and development issues alongside those of other countries; recognizing the value to be gained from putting faces and

*The collections of papers from the seminars held in Manchester (June 1973) and Worcester (September 1975) were published as follows:

Whitehead, D. J. (ed.) 1974 *Curriculum Development in Economics,* Heinemann Educational
Robinson, T. K. and Wilson, R. D. (eds.) 1977 *Extending Economics within the Curriculum* Routledge and Kegan Paul

voices to names and writings and of engaging in dialogue; recognizing the insights to be derived from experiences in other school systems and cultures; and recognizing the paucity of UK research programmes in relation to the demands currently being placed upon them. Seeking the active involvement of industry and commerce in the seminar was to recognize the role that industry and commerce can play in new initiatives and to welcome its potential contribution to the improvement of education.

The decision to organize the seminar in this way was thus a bold one – language barriers had to be transcended; different traditions and school systems explained and understood; research methods and instruments comprehended; and national boundaries and allegiances set aside in the search for common experiences, problems and issues.

Objectives and scope

The purpose of the seminar was to provide an opportunity for those involved in economics education to consider the implications of current international research and curriculum development work. It was intended to:

1 challenge the economics education community to develop a sound theoretical base from which economics teachers will be able to work

2 stimulate further research in particular areas

3 make a practical contribution to economics teaching

4 encourage the development of coherent and appropriate courses at all levels

The scope of the seminar was therefore not restricted to any particular issue or age level of student. Rather, the encouragement of a wide variety of issues was seen as desirable if progress in general was to be evaluated and future needs assessed. However, two issues were dominant in the organizers' minds:

1 the fact that, despite obvious advances in our understanding of the nature of economic knowledge, of the significance of that understanding for economics education, of the purposes/objectives of economics education and of the kind of economic understanding achieved by students, inconsistencies still exist, research and development initiatives remain largely unco-ordinated and their implications are not fully explored.

2 the need for the economics education community to facilitate the development and implementation of courses designed to meet an entitlement curriculum in economics by addressing itself to the question of defining terms such as economic literacy, economic understanding and economic competence

The seminar provided a unique opportunity for these broad issues to be raised and for participants from four continents with their different perspectives, hopes and fears, to share a common experience.

Participants and papers

The seminar was held at the University of London Institute of Education on 30 July – 1 August 1985. It was attended by university economists, researchers, HMI, lecturers in economics education and teachers from schools and colleges. There were 26 participants from the UK and 13 from overseas.

The 17 papers prepared for the seminar and the response papers relating to them are included in this publication. Circulation of papers prior to the seminar obviated the need for them to be read out at the seminar and instead allowed them to be used as an information base and source of questions for debate and discussion.* What cannot be represented in this book, however, is the wealth of classroom materials which form the practical outcomes of the research and development work highlighted in the papers and which were sampled at the seminar. Viewing Marilyn Kourilsky's film of primary grade children participating in her Mini-Society programme, for example, was to move into a world of communication, problem solving and negotiation set in an economics context far removed from the dispassionate outcomes of statistical evaluation. Similarly, sampling the film series 'The People on Market Street' was to view the problems associated with teaching mainstream demand/supply economics to young people in a new light.

To summarize the contents of each paper in this introduction would be superfluous, for each has its own summary. However, what might be useful would be to signpost themes and to point readers in the direction of papers appropriate to these themes.

Two papers, Whitehead and Luker *et alia*, are concerned with the measurement of economic attitudes and highlight not only the problems for current researchers in this area but also indicate possible ways forward in the future.

Papers by Dawson, Helburn, Sumansky and Wilkes are broadly concerned with the nature of economic knowledge. Dawson argues that advances in economic knowledge are best achieved if the 'meaning' problem is separated from the 'value' problem. Helburn forcefully advocates the need to demonstrate to students the 'tentativeness of knowledge' through an awareness of alternative versions of economic 'truths', an argument at odds with the mainstream of US thought as illustrated in Sumansky's description of the development of the Joint Council on Economic Education's *Master Curriculum Guide*. Wilkes' concern is to devise a practical framework for teaching which will give young people access to 'the economy' (rather than economics). His paper proposes the use of national income accounting procedures to give insights into relationships and variables.

Papers by Ajello *et alia*, Moret and van Oosten, and Kourilsky and Graff are partly concerned with young people's understanding of economics. The experiences at primary school level described by Ajello *et alia* and Kourilsky and Graff are timely for UK readers, given renewed interest in the teaching of

*This was made possible only by the willingness of writers to observe deadlines, the efficiency of our publisher and the tireless and painstaking editorial work of David Whitehead.

economics to very young students. Their realistic but different appraisals of problems, content, teaching approaches and achievements should act as an encouragement to teachers in this country. At the secondary level, Moret and van Oosten report on aspects of a major curriculum development project for lower stream 13–16 year olds in the Netherlands. They argue that their three-level model provides the theoretical base from which experiential learning activities can be devised, students motivated and economic understanding achieved.

A number of papers reflect the greater interest (and perhaps greater number of researchers in the field) in North America in devising instruments to evaluate the effects of instruction. Papers by Chizmar, Kourilsky and Graff, Luker *et alia*, Lumsden *et alia* and Watts reveal the intricacies and problems associated with the application of statistical techniques to explain educational phenomena. Many of these problems are focused for readers in Halil's discussion paper. These descriptions provide important examples for advanced students and others who are interested in research design.

Many of the papers touched on the notion of economic literacy and its application across whole school populations, and this concern was reflected in considerable discussion during the seminar. Is economic literacy, as Hodkinson and Thomas suggest, a way of looking at the world which reflects the unique contribution of the economics discipline to knowledge, or is it simply a question of getting pupils to describe economic concepts? Can the ability to read and understand the economics content of a major national newspaper be considered a sufficient description of economic literacy, as Gregory tentatively proposes? Must economic literacy be confined to mainstream Western economic thinking or can it be reconciled with Helburn's notion of the 'tentativeness of knowledge'? Is economic literacy about teaching economics or is it, as Wilkes advocates, teaching about the economy? Where in the school curriculum can and should economic literacy components be placed? Does the development of economics education for all depend upon whole curriculum review, as Finlayson implies has been the case in Scotland? And can economic literacy programmes be successfully taught, as Wilson suggests, by non-specialist teachers with a minimum of training?

Emerging priorities

It would be tempting to draw out of the seminar and its papers a shopping list of research and development problems which would keep the relatively small economics education community busy for many years to come. Equally tempting would be to declare that all objectives were met and anticipated outcomes achieved. Both approaches would, however, ignore the reality of the educational systems of which we are a part.

Australian participants, for example, pointed to students disillusioned with economics teaching and an oversupply of economics teachers. Their problems are to gain the commitment of those responsible for decisions in schools to long-term community objectives and student-centred approaches and to devise an economics curriculum to meet that commitment.

In the US and Canada, state and provincial control of educational matters may lead to mandatory economics education in schools, but does not guarantee a coherent approach free of political intrusion or that worthwhile educational programmes devised for schools will reach intended audiences. Perhaps, above all, it does not guarantee that the teaching force is sufficiently motivated and 'economics-wise' to implement such programmes.

In the Netherlands, where central control over the curriculum is more obvious, fine streaming at the secondary stage puts innovative curriculum development into apparent conflict with traditional views about the place of economics in schools and the teaching of it. Italy too has its difficulties in transmitting educational reform through the school system.

In the UK, economics education is on the crest of a wave. However, it is not a time to rest on past achievements or to claim territorial rights for specialist teachers. Rather it is a time when economics teachers in general must lead or be led.

The outcomes of the seminar, then, should be seen against these national backcloths. However, the relevance of experiences in other countries to our own UK situation has been demonstrated. Language and communication barriers in economics education, if not removed, have been lowered, and a new dimension to international co-operation created. For the participants it was perhaps a unique experience, but one which new-found colleagues and their subject associations may wish to renew on another occasion.

Steve Hodkinson

Economics and economics education: the selective use of discipline structures in economics curricula

Suzanne Wiggins Helburn

Professor of Economics, University of Colorado at Denver

This paper assesses the use of the structure of the discipline as the content basis for secondary school economics curricula in the United States in order to evaluate the relevance of the thesis articulated by Thomas Popkewitz in 'The latent values of the discipline-centered curriculum' (1977). Popkewitz criticizes discipline-centred curricula because (1) they tend to give a false view of science; and (2) they ignore the multiplicity of perspectives in any given discipline, thereby promoting a consensual view of the world and teaching students to rely on expert opinion as the basis of knowledge and truth. The paper provides a clearer picture of the meaning/nature of a discipline structure and the reasons why school curricula are invariably organized around mainstream structures despite the existence of multiple schools of thought, illustrating three important structures in economics. It then summarizes a content analysis of nine high school economics texts to support Popkewitz's argument. Finally it briefly discusses the consequences of so limiting economics education and suggests strategies to combat these tendencies.

Using the structure of the discipline in curriculum design

In the 1960s I was one of many of the New Social Studies curriculum developers in the US to follow the advice of biologist Joseph Schwab at the University of Chicago, to organize innovative high school curricula around the 'structure' of a discipline. Schwab (1962) defined structure as follows:

> The structure of a discipline consists, in part, of the body of imposed conceptions which define the investigated subject matter of that discipline and control its inquiries. . . . By the syntax of a discipline, I mean the pattern of its procedure, its method, how it goes about using its conceptions to attain its goals. . . . The conceptual structure of a discipline determines what we shall seek the truth about and in what terms that truth shall be couched. The syntactical

structure of a discipline is concerned with the operations that distinguish the true, the verified, and the warranted in that discipline from the unverified and unwarranted.

In 1961 a report by the National Task Force on Economic Education condemned the sorry state of high school texts in economics, which were mainly descriptive, inaccurate or misleading, devoid of any coherent organization around basic economic principles. The Task Force outlined a set of organizing concepts which it considered the basic principles around which high school texts should be built, and called for a new generation of texts.

This was also the period of curriculum reform which took seriously Jerome Bruner's call for more intellectually challenging curriculum content and the use of methods of inquiry as a way to empower and engage students in developing their intellectual powers. Most of us agreed with Bruner's contention that any concept could be taught at any level with some degree of integrity (Bruner, 1960).

In the case of the ECON 12 project (published as *Economics in Society*), which I helped design, our strategy was to conceptualize the 'structure' of the economics discipline not as a list of concepts, but as two relatively simple models, one that described the field of economics in terms of the study of want satisfaction and one that depicted an economy as a system of want satisfaction (Helburn *et alia*, 1974, pp. 36–7). The course introduced the major concepts in the discipline structure and the problems-oriented learning activities required students to use the conceptual structure to discover the meaning of the basic concepts and gradually discover interrelationships inherent in the structure. We wanted to develop students' intellectual powers by providing them with organizing principles which were widely applicable to everyday life and to economics as a science. We were also interested in giving students insight into abstract reasoning by teaching them to use a major tool used in economics – model building. Finally, we tried to impress students with the tentativeness of scientific knowledge, the fact that 'knowledge' represents an abstraction or mental image, a person's view of the world. We wanted to imbue in them some sense of the relativeness of knowledge, and the legitimacy of different and conflicting viewpoints. We took seriously Schwab's warning of the revisionary nature of scientific knowledge, the continuing modification of substantive structures:

> The revisionary character of knowledge assumes curriculum significance because revisions now take place so rapidly that they will probably occur not once but several times in the lives of our students. If they have been taught their physics, chemistry, or biology dogmatically, their discovery that revision has occurred can lead only to bewilderment and disaffection. Again, the alternative is the teaching of scientific knowledge in the light of the enquiry that produced it. If students discover how one body of knowledge succeeds another, if they are aware of the substantive structures that underlie our current knowledge, if they are given a little freedom to speculate on the possible changes in structures which the future may bring, they will not only be prepared to meet future revisions with intelligence but will better understand the knowledge they are currently being taught. (1964, pp. 29–30)

During the 1960s reform movement, many social studies educators opposed focusing content on social science disciplines, because they placed a lower value on the usefulness of discipline knowledge. As a firm believer in the importance of teaching students to use powerful ideas I tended to deprecate these objections until the position was forcefully articulated and given a political analysis by Thomas Popkewitz in 'The latent values of the discipline-centered curriculum' (1977).

Popkewitz criticizes the discipline-centred approach to curriculum design on these basic grounds:

1 This approach tends to give a false view of science by focusing on the logical elements of enquiry and ignoring the social nature of science.

2 The approach ignores the multiplicity of perspectives in any one social science discipline.

3 It promotes the consensual view of the world and teaches students to rely on expert opinion as the basis of knowledge and truth.

Popkewitz points out that in organizing discipline-centred curricula, the designers abstract from scientific practice to develop a reconstructed model of the discipline, identifying some basic structure of knowledge comprising the dominant concepts or generalizations, and/or identifying a standardized set of procedures representing the scientific method. These curricula, he claims, confuse the reconstructed model with actual scientific activity. Students learn the logical structure of the discipline as a fixed, static body of knowledge as if it were a catechism, and in the process they never learn about the tentativeness of knowledge.

Focusing learning on using the correct specialized 'words' from the discipline, according to Popkewitz, detaches students from everyday experience and from a sense that they themselves may be able to affect social change. In addition, this orientation tends to legitimize professional definitions of social affairs and to teach students to rely on recognized 'experts'. Social problems become defined by the experts who become the final arbitrators of what is true and what is important. Popkewitz quotes Apple's argument that these curricula provide children with

> a consensual 'lens' by which individuals are expected to adjust to established authority and to officially defined interpretations of reality. . . . Unquestioned and hidden, the vision of society in curriculum is one in which individuals are functionally related to maintaining the ongoing system and its institutional arrangements. . . . The fact that these consensual orientations remain tacit makes them psychologically compelling in the construction of meaning. That is, [the] consensual view is taken for granted as part of our definitions of what is reasonable and normal in our daily affairs. (1977, p. 46)

The purpose of this paper is to assess the use of the structure of the discipline in the economics curriculum and to evaluate Popkewitz's critique, which I believe to be basically accurate. The next section provides a clearer picture of the meaning/nature of the structure of the discipline, the reasons

why school curricula are invariably organized around the mainstream viewpoint despite the existence of multiple schools of thought in economics, and
illustrations of three important structures in economics. Next follows a
summary of my content analysis of nine high school economics texts to
support Popkewitz's argument. In the final section, I discuss briefly the
consequences of this kind of economics education, and what can be done to
combat these tendencies.

'The' structure of a discipline versus diversity of structures

In the phraseology of the modern philosophy of science debate (Popper,
1963; Kuhn, 1970; Lakatos, 1970; Katouzian, 1980; Blaug, 1980), Popkewitz's argument can be restated to say that the problem with organizing
economics curricula around the structure of the discipline is that in economics
there are other schools of thought with political orientations differing from
those presented in the economics discipline's paradigm. The discipline
structure approach limits economics education to teaching students to see the
world through the concepts accepted by the academic profession of economists. Restricting economics education to 'the paradigm' limits the diversity of
opinion about the functioning of the economy and therefore limits political
debate about government intervention in economic matters to controversies
identified by mainstream economists. In fact, science is not static, and
scientific work is accomplished in scientific communities with diverse and
changing views of the world. At any time there are always unexplained or not
well explained anomalies between theory and observed behaviour. Teaching
students the paradigm as unquestioned truth is unscientific and glosses over
what we cannot explain and what we do not know.

But teaching 'the paradigm' has an important function in scientific professions. In the economics profession it is through control of the education of
aspiring economists and of the general public that the profession creates
discipline, (defines scientific practice) and extends its influence. There is an
additional complication in economics (and in the other social sciences as well)
because economic theory is based on a value-laden world view, what
Schumpeter called 'social vision'. In economics, for every political view of the
viability of capitalism there is also a scientific school of thought. Scientific
theories are more rigorous and falsifiable formulations of the different world
views held by non-scientists.

Because economics is a mature scientific discipline, what Katouzian calls a
normal academic profession, it is organized around the teaching and scientific
development of a single paradigm (Kuhn, 1970; Katouzian, 1980). Through
hierarchically organized professional associations, academic departments and
research institutes, the profession controls journal policy, hiring and

retention decisions, and funding. It disciplines members through control of education and through a highly developed reward system, and discourages work on alternative research programmes by defining 'scientific' activity in terms of 'the' paradigm. It establishes the limits of what is considered scientific and polices the boundaries of economics as science.

Dissidents in economics – minorities – have always known this truth first hand. However, the outcome of the debate initiated by Popper over the nature of science and scientific progress now legitimizes this view. It provides theories which describe the relation between metaphysical/epistemological belief and scientific activity, and explains the political economy of scientific communities. Lakatos has developed a useful model which provides a more comprehensive and precise definition of discipline structure, showing the relation between metaphysical/epistemological presuppositions (ideology) and the scientific theory built on these beliefs. Katouzian's synthesis of Popper's theory of the logic of scientific progress and of Kuhn's theory of the sociology of scientific progress links the development of scientific enterprise to the development of modern industrialized society and provides a theoretical explanation for conventionalism and intolerance in science.

The debate over the structuring of science

One question raised in the debate about the nature of and progress in science started by Popper was whether there can be more than one structure of a discipline. While I do not think that Popper was specifically addressing this question, his work can be used to foster the view that there is only one 'scientific' structure of a discipline.

Popper's main objective was to criticize positivism and historicism as forms of empiricism, the view that theories are scientific because they are corroborated, because they *describe* reality. Instead, he proved that science is based on 'falsifiable theory', furthermore, that science is fundamentally theory based. It starts with theory which describes the *logic* of a situation or process; the function of empirical work is mainly to test the theory by trying to falsify it. According to Popper, thinkers became scientific when they disassociated themselves from metaphysical speculation and began to pursue the logic of discovery. This pursuit of the 'logic' inherent in the phenomena under investigation means that as a whole scientists build on corroborated, logically consistent theory, so that scientific progress involves the gradual development of theory which more closely describes reality; scientists are motivated by the search for verisimilitude.

Popper's theory is both a theory of the logic of the situation – of scientific activity – and a normative theory. He claims that his theory *does* predict scientific behaviour, and that it also describes how science *should* progress.

Kuhn, on the other hand, proceeded to develop his theory described in *The Structure of Scientific Revolutions* in the empiricist tradition. To refute Popper, he looked at the historical record of scientific activity, in physics for instance, and from a sociological rather than logical perspective. He started out with observable *facts*. First, mature science is carried out in scientific communities which study a particular set of problems/puzzles based on a shared 'paradigm', what Kuhn eventually called a disciplinary matrix of beliefs about the world and about scientific procedure, and exemplars of good science which the scientists learn in school or in the literature. Second, while scientific activity seems quite productive of puzzle solutions within the paradigm, 'normal science' is *not* characterized by the pursuit of 'bold conjectures and refutations', Popper's colourful and hopeful description of scientific progress. Rather, normal science is quite lack-lustre and scientists are very conventional; they don't normally or mostly question the paradigm, even after the appearance of anomalies between fact and theory which call into question the validity of the theory. Finally, Kuhn contended that fundamental change in science has come only after a crisis develops and a new paradigm representing a fundamental *'gestalt* switch' becomes accepted in the scientific community. Fundamental change represents a revolution in scientific thinking, a replacement of an old paradigm by a new one which focuses on new scientific puzzles. Because of the conventional behaviour of scientists working in a scientific community disciplined by the paradigm, scientific progress does not progress via the logic of discovery.

Kuhn's concept of paradigm, though not well developed by him, was an important contribution, because it emphasized the necessity that scientific activity be organized around certain presuppositions. Lakatos ignored Kuhn's sociological/historical perspective but developed his notion of discipline paradigm. He amended Popper's theory to recognize that scientific theories are not disjointed and separate, rather they develop as part of a 'scientific research programme' based on an underlying hard core of belief.

Lakatos characterizes the history of science as the history of 'scientific research programmes' (SRPs), a structure of interdependent scientific theories developed over time to which many people contribute. He contends that the most important theoretical structures display considerable continuity because they evolve from a 'genuine research programme', a set of methodological rules which describe the subject of study, and research strategies and procedures. Lakatos retains Kuhn's notion that the basis of the SRP is a set of metaphysical beliefs which are not scientific. He characterizes an SRP as being composed of a 'hard core' of irrefutable theory and a 'protective belt' of scientific theory.

The hard core is the essential first principles which are considered irrefutable, non-problematic, and off limits in terms of attempts to falsify. These propositions are not subject to criticism and they are not designed to be testable. They are metaphysical principles and propositions which consist of unproblematic background knowledge. The 'negative heuristic' forbids testing this theory. The 'protective belt' is the body of scientific theory which is developed from the hard core; it is designed to be subject to refutation and, at the same time, to protect the hard core from criticism. The research programme is organized around a 'positive heuristic' which describes the theoretical problems to be studied scientifically, and indicates how to construct the protective belt theory. Even the positive heuristic can be stated as a metaphysical proposition, viz. Newton's programme that the planets are gravitating spinning tops of roughly spherical shape. However, such a statement implies a research programme involving the development of a theoretical programme which might eventually lead to changing the statement.

Lakatos maintains that an objective appraisal of scientific growth can be provided in terms of 'progressive and degenerating problemshifts' in scientific research programmes. Focusing on historical continuity of scientific work, he limits mature science to those activities which are organized as scientific research programmes. He recognizes, however, that in a mature science more than one research programme can exist at the same time, and he contends that 'budding research programmes' need to be protected, because competition between SRPs is healthy.

Lakatos' characterization of an SRP, or a discipline structure, includes both the 'prescientific' and the 'scientific' parts of the programme. In economics, a crucial part of the 'prescientific' theory is the 'social vision': a view of the nature of the economy (in particular, of capitalism and its viability), therefore of the nature of 'the economic problem', of what is important to study about economic organization and behaviour. This means that preceding any development of economic theory there is a presumption about how economic organization works and how well it works, therefore about what problems are crucial. Given this viewpoint, it is not possible to separate values from science by distinguishing between 'positive economics' and 'normative economics'. There is only the hope that through scientific practice the economics profession can weed out scientific research programmes which turn out to degenerate into *ad hoc* rationalization of its hard core.

Lakatos strengthened the view of scientific progress as pursuit of the logic of the phenomena under study while recognizing the possibility of different approaches to studying the same phenomena based on different hard core presuppositions. However, Lakatos ignored Kuhn's insights into the actual sociology of academic communities and the tendency towards conventionalism – the unwillingness to permit diversity in theoretical perspectives. Katouzian (1980) develops a political economy of science in advanced industrial societies to explain conventionalism and intolerance of competing paradigms/research programmes.

Katouzian analyses the impact of increased specialization and of dispersal of power in mass participation democracies on the organization of science. Increasingly, he contends, science is carried out by 'normal academic professions'. Science is becoming specialized, professionalized and intolerant as scientists pursue the logic of career advancement, and this explains why scientists in normal academic professions practise 'normal science' organized around a single paradigm.

We can now state more precisely what is wrong with the practice of developing curricula around the structure of the discipline. Invariably the structure chosen will be the ruling paradigm. Furthermore, as we shall see, in developing the 'structure', curriculum developers adopt the profession's view of the hard core, the metaphysical and value presuppositions. Either they don't exist – there *are* no value positions inherent in the discipline viewpoint – or they are accepted as background knowledge, i.e. they are taken as unproblematic. No distinction is made between hard core belief and scientific theory. In fact, it will become apparent in this paper that most of what is taught in the school curriculum is the hard core belief.

Alternative scientific research programmes in economics

It is quite fashionable these days to talk about the crisis in the economics profession. Kuttner's 'The poverty of economics' published in *The Atlantic Monthly* (1985) is the most recent broadside. It documents the multiplication of alternative SRPs alongside the continuing power of the neoclassical/ Keynesian synthesis to hold sway as the discipline paradigm. There are the Austrians, the New Classicals, the post-Keynesians, the neo-Keynesians/ Ricardians, the fundamentalist Marxists, the structuralist Marxists, the underconsumptionist Marxists, etc. But teaching a science completely from the point of view of the ruling paradigm is one of Kuhn's indicators of maturity of a science, and economics is a good case in point. None of these alternatives are included in any meaningful way in university-level economic education except by their adherents, although there are a growing number of textbooks available, for instance, in the Marxist tradition. None appear in the school curriculum, as my analysis in the next section will show.

To illustrate the impact on subject matter of alternative scientific research programmes, Table 1 summarizes the focus and the hard core background information for the three most influential programmes today: the neoclassical/Keynesian synthesis, Keynes and Marx. The focus and hard core of the neoclassical/Keynesian SRP shows its micro orientation and origins in the neoclassical economics of Walras and Marshall. The programme is devoted to the study of individual market exchange decisions and the effects of such decisions when aggregated to the market level and to the economy as a whole. For purposes of model building it is assumed that decisions are always based on constrained optimization; the theory is limited to predicting individual reactions to a given state of affairs. Keynes's concern for modelling the macro economy has been incorporated into the older tradition, but his social vision has not had much effect on the hard core. Furthermore, through the development of micro foundations, his macro theory has been thoroughly revised.

Keynes built on to and revised the Marshallian neoclassical model which, as Robinson pointed out, included two separate bodies of theory – principles and money (1975, p. 123). Kahn depicts Keynes's decade or more of theoretical work prior to *The General Theory* as a long struggle to escape from the principles doctrine, which held that money has no effect on the real operation of the economy, and the quantity theory doctrine, which holds that the price level is determined by the quantity of money (1978, p. 547). This required that he build a *general* theory of a *monetary* economy.

Keynes argued that economics must model reality and that the key to model building is to use one's intuition and knowledge of the real world to identify the key characteristics from which one deduces the other crucial characteristics which it is essential to include. On this basis he discarded some of the hard core assumptions of neoclassical theory: Say's law, money merely as a medium of exchange, certainty, perfect knowledge, equilibrium in the labour market, the convergence of the economy to full employment, that adjustments to disequilibrium are stabilizing. Instead, he recognized the importance of modelling the economy in real time, and the importance of money, as both a measure and a store of value. Keynes argued that the model must explain both real and monetary phenomena of the system as a whole in conditions of 'shifting equilibrium'. Present-day Keynesians who object to the way Keynes's theory has been integrated into neoclassical economics are trying to develop alternative SRPs. Post-Keynesians like Minsky (1982, 1975) and Davidson (1978) claim that the neoclassical/Keynesian synthesis ignores the most important part of Keynes's argument and method, and that neoclassical models treat the economy as a barter economy, abstracting from the monetary aspects of the economy. Neo-Keynesians/neo-Ricardians, such as Garegnani (1978, in Eatwell and Milgate, 1983) are working on long-run macro models organized around the dependence of the level of output and employment on income distribution. These writers provide separate explanations of the forces determining relative prices, distribution and output (Eatwell and Milgate, 1983; Eichner and Kregel, 1975).

Marx's SRP developed out of the nineteenth century classical interest in the impact of class divisions and class income on capitalist growth, and on the long-run viability of the system. Marx took for granted the transitory nature of capitalism. He considered it the penultimate stage of historical development towards a truly human society in which people could experience their species' essence. His research programme was very broad: to elucidate the 'law of value' which regulates the origin, existence, development and death of capitalism. Marx objected to the classical economists' preoccupation with the study of exchange which masked the exploitative nature of the system by ignoring relations of production. Marx's analysis starts with the basic historical fact of capitalist commodity production – value production – production for exchange and profit. Identifying commodities as *values* (abstract, homogeneous labour), his theory describes the operation of the *law of value*, a macro theory of the production and circulation of capital – and of capital accumulation as a process of class struggle. Present-day Marxists are engaged in a series of problemshifts based on their critiques of Marx and on the need to study modern capitalism. Although mainstream economists have rejected the labour theory of value as the basis for price theory, Sraffa (1960) revitalized the classical SRP by developing a general equilibrium theory of price determination based on supply/production conditions rather than on individual consumer/factor owner choice.

The unacceptability of the Marxian SRP for the school curriculum is obvious from a casual look at my summary of its hard core content in Table 1.

Table 1 Focus and hard core of three scientific research programmes in economics: neoclassical/Keynesian synthesis, Keynes and Marx

Content	Neoclassical/Keynesian synthesis	Keynes	Marx
Scope and focus	Analysis of exchange: optimal resource allocation, optimal choices; macro models developed from micro foundations	The macro *monetary* economy: determinants of aggregate employment and output, the causes of unemployment and the influence of money on real aggregates	The law of value which regulates capitalist development and demise: through a critique of classical political economy (bourgeois theory)
Society	A system of exchanges between individuals, required because of scarcity and specialization	Society as a whole is not necessarily a sum of its parts; the performance of the social whole affects the ability of individuals to pursue the good; in class society, distribution of the benefits may not be related to contribution	Capitalism is a way of life dominated by capitalist class relations, capitalist control of production and exploitation of workers; it is a transitory stage of history; its development and transformation is propelled by class conflict
Human motives and behaviour	Motivated by pecuniary self-interest, individuals behave as constrained maximizers, reacting rationally to make the best choice to *given* conditions	Emphasizes psychological propensities and decisions based on the logic of partial belief, because decisions are based on incomplete information under conditions of uncertainty; e.g. investment based on 'animal spirits'	Based on class position and forms of class conflict; working class consciousness develops as a rational response to exploitation, to experiencing the contradiction between one's life activity and choices and one's species' (creative) powers
Characteristics of the economy	A competitive money market system which nevertheless operates like a barter system: given tastes and technology; perfect certainty, knowledge and resource mobility; factor and product substitution. Say's law holds	An industrial, capitalist, *money* economy operating in real time: it is inadmissible to abstract from time, money, uncertainty, to model the economy as a barter system; spending is based on psychological propensities and income distribution; rejects Say's law	A system of capitalist commodity production: value (capital) is created in production by workers but realized and accumulated through exchange by capitalists; thus theory must analyse *both* the production and circulation of capital as a whole and the effect of changing forms of class conflict
The operation of the economy	A general equilibrium system of self-regulating markets which tends to full employment and to an equitable distribution of income based on endowments and tastes for leisure versus work	No necessary convergence to full employment; adjustments to disequilibrium may be destabilizing; the labour market is not usually in equilibrium; a tendency for long-run stagnation	The law of value asserts itself only as a blinding average: capital accumulation, continual revolution in technology, a reserve army of the unemployed, business cycles, concentration and centralization, development of world capitalism

Unfortunately for economic education, a good deal of insight into the functioning of capitalism has been generated by this programme. However, not even the post- and neo-Keynesian views can be found in high school texts; nor is the Austrian view represented. In fact, most of the text presentations discussed in the next section resemble neoclassical economics *before* Keynes more than the neoclassical/Keynesian synthesis.

Analysis of high school texts in economics

Major influences on content

In recent years there have been two major influences on textbook content: curriculum development and teacher training by the Joint Council on Economic Education, reflecting the economic education priorities of the economics profession and national business leadership (to a smaller extent, leadership in the labour movement); and state mandates, reflecting interests in economic education of local business and lay groups.

The Joint Council Master Curriculum Framework   The Joint Council on Economic Education (JCEE) has played a crucial role both in promoting economics in the school curriculum and in determining its content. A major instrument for guiding K-12 economics content has been the *Master Curriculum Guide in Economics: A Framework for Teaching the Basic Concepts*. The Framework, first published in 1977, was revised in 1984, but remains substantially the same in basic content (Hansen, 1977; Saunders, 1984). Table 2 gives the Framework as presented in 1977 and Fig. 1 presents these concepts as a schematic model of the nature of economic organization of society and economic decision making. Table 2 shows the 1977 Framework outline because it is the version which was available at the time the texts reviewed in this paper were written. In fact, in the new version, except for some reorganization, there is very little change in the list of concepts.

The general education goal promoted by the JCEE Master Curriculum is to increase economic literacy, the ability of students to make reasoned judgements based on informed reaction to the news media and to national events, capabilities which the authors consider prerequisites for responsible

Table 2   JCEE Master Curriculum Framework

A   The basic economic problem
1   *Economic wants
2   *Productive resources
3   *Scarcity and choices
4   *Opportunity costs and trade-offs
5   Marginalism and equilibrium

B   Economic systems

6   Nature and types of economic systems

7   *Economic incentives

8   *Specialization, comparative advantage, and the division of labour

9   Voluntary exchange

10   *Interdependence

11   Government intervention and regulation

C   Microeconomics: resource allocation and income distribution

12   *Markets, supply and demand

13   *The price mechanism

14   Competition and market structure

15   'Market failures': information costs, resource immobility, externalities, etc.

16   Income distribution and government redistribution

D   Macroeconomics: economic stability and growth

17   *Aggregate supply and productive capacity

18   *Aggregate demand: unemployment and inflation

19   Real and money income; price level changes

20   Money and monetary policy

21   Fiscal policy: taxes, expenditures, and transfers

22   Economic growth

23   *Savings, investment, and productivity

E   International economics

24   Absolute/comparative advantage, trade barriers, exchange rates

F   Economic institutions

G   Concepts for evaluating economic actions and policies

Economic goals: freedom, economic efficiency, equity, security, price stability, full employment, and growth

H   Measurement concepts

rates, averages, real vs. nominal, index numbers, tables and graphs

---

*Major concepts.

Source: After *A Framework for Teaching Economics: Basic Concepts,* Joint Council on Economic Education, 1977

citizenship, and crucial to effective operation of our social system and to the well-being of the individual.

The 1977 Framework makes it clear that the document represents the views of the academic profession:

> This statement summarizes the structure and substance of economics as commonly understood by economists. It also lists and describes those economic concepts we believe are most useful in achieving the larger objectives of educating high school graduates to be responsible citizens and effective decision-makers throughout their lives. (p. 1)

Fig. 1   A schematic framework of economics

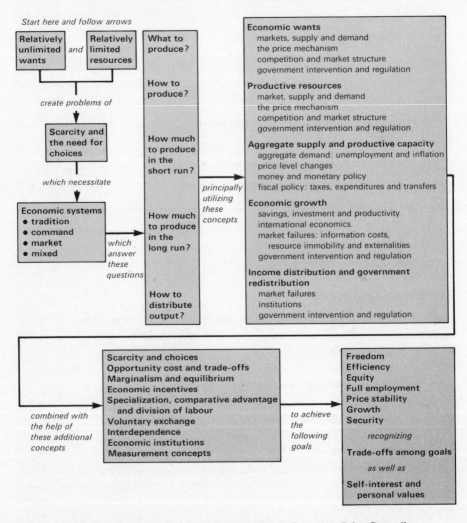

Source: From *A Framework for Teaching the Basic Concepts,* Joint Council on Economic Education, 1977, pp. 28–9

The authors of the 1984 Framework define economics as

> . . . the study of how the goods and services we want get produced, and how they are distributed among us. This part we call *economic analysis*. Economics is also the study of how we can make the system of production and distribution work better. This part we call *economic policy*. Economic analysis is the necessary foundation for sound economic policy. Another, slightly different definition of economics, favored by many economists, is this: *Economics is the study of how our scarce productive resources are used to satisfy human wants.* (p. 3)

The authors state that the Framework is a mechanism through which the economics profession seeks to influence the public, remarking,

> 'Professional economists continue their efforts to apply existing knowledge, to extend their knowledge, and to communicate the knowledge to students, teachers, the citizenry, and key decision-makers. We see this report as an extension of these activities' (1977, p. 3).

The authors voice the mainstream view of the limits of economists' understanding of the world, that while economic policy based on accepted theory can prevent recurrence of a 1930s depression, it is not yet able to control unemployment and inflation; and that economists need to learn more about making government activities effective. Interestingly, for the latter problem the 1984 report substitutes the profession's disagreement about the *extent* of the governmental role in the economy (p. 4). The authors also give the mainstream explanation of the basis for theoretical and policy disagreements among economists. According to this view, they are the result of the complexity of the economic phenomena under study, of measurement difficulties, and of unanticipated effects of economic activity, *not* of fundamental differences in hard core belief. Furthermore, the authors attribute much of the confusion in discussions of economic problems to 'a failure to distinguish between analysis (what *is* happening) and value judgements (what *ought to be* happening); a distinction between positive and normative economics which they obviously want teachers and students to learn. They create the impression that economic analysis is value-free and actually *does* explain what *is* happening in the real world. The authors expect students to learn to make normative judgements based on 'the' scientific analysis provided through economic education.

Nevertheless, the 1984 Framework authors recognize growing discontent in economics and fundamental differences among economists:

> As this is being written, the discipline of economics is alive with controversy and discontent: there are several 'schools' of economics: there are calls for making economic analysis more realistic by explicitly introducing more aspects of political science, sociology, psychology, law, and the like into the discipline; there exists dissatisfaction with how much economists have contributed to improving the economy's performance. (p. 5)

It is significant, however, that the Framework does not reflect to teachers the nature of debates in economics or the fact that these disagreements stem from different views about 'the economic problem' and about the nature of capitalism.

The 1984 revised Framework differs from the earlier version in four respects:

1 It represents a further refinement in the definition of concepts and a reordering of them into major categories.

2 It increases the emphasis on a 'reasoned approach to economic decision making' by introducing a 'decision grid' procedure for teaching students to choose between alternatives by analysing all the alternative choices on the basis of all the important criteria.

3 It places more emphasis on teaching students measurement methods thereby showing the relevance of economics to achieving mathematical and social studies skills development goals.

4 It does not use the Fig. 1 presentation of the Framework as a conceptual structure.

The Framework is a highly refined statement of the basic conceptual and theoretical framework of the neoclassical/Keynesian synthesis. It does not distinguish, however, between concepts in the hard core and scientific theory. The policy questions included are restricted to mainstream views and controversies – government intervention to combat market failures, monetary and fiscal policy alternatives to maintain stability and promote growth, government deficits, international trade restrictions and exchange rate fluctuations. For instance, in the 1984 edition the authors introduce the rational expectations thesis and its policy implications, but do not discuss post-Keynesian or neo-Ricardian belief in the interaction of growth and income distribution which justifies planning and incomes policies. As the centre of the profession drifts to the right, so we see the same drift in the Framework between 1977 and 1984.

The Framework is very similar to the ECON 12 structure of the discipline reported as early as 1967 and published in the *Economics in Society* programme (EIS) in 1974 (Wiggins and Sperling, 1967; and Helburn *et alia*, 1974). It is heartening to see much of the work from EIS reproduced in this document. However, since there is no attribution to the earlier curriculum project, it is not clear whether the similarity demonstrates the diffusion of EIS, reinvention of the wheel, or simultaneous discovery. More significant is the difference between the JCEE Framework and the EIS approach, indicating a move away from presenting economics as a science and teaching students scientific skills and values, and a move towards presenting a consensual lens. This shows up in the following characteristics of the JCEE Framework:

1 It does not invite students to explore the meaning of basic concepts to promote student insight into the process of learning about the world as a process of individual inquiry.

2 The 1984 Framework no longer presents the concepts as a structure or model which means that it does not seem to encourage teachers to think in this way, so they, in turn, will not encourage student understanding of economics as *structured* knowledge, structured by the concepts employed.

3 It does not emphasize model building as a process of abstraction which students can and should learn to use; rather, it reinforces the notion, rampant in economics, that models are mathematical and are created by experts.

4 It does not promote scientific values and attitudes: an understanding of the tentativeness of knowledge and an appreciation of the importance of controversy, that new understanding comes from observed discrepancies between theory and empirical observation, that scientific theory is necessarily based on underlying beliefs about the nature of the subject to be studied scientifically.

The state mandates   About half the states in the US (24) currently mandate economics instruction of some kind. The mandates reflect a rising interest in economic issues, interest group lobbying for economics education, and the increasing importance of accountability in education (Brennan and Banaszak, 1982). The mandates specify the required number of units of instruction (usually less than one unit), grade placement, competency requirements (in eight states), and content focus. Twelve states mandate a free enterprise focus, ten a general economics education focus, and eight a consumer education focus. Table 3 shows the economics concepts most frequently found in thirteen of the state frameworks, ranking the concepts according to the frequency of use.

The list includes all 12 of the minimum concepts specified by the JCEE Framework and several more. This list indicates that the mandates focus on the economic activities of production, consumption, distribution and exchange; the organization of economic institutions and sectors such as business, labour, banking, and government; teaching the basics of the 'free enterprise system'; and teaching differences between capitalism and communism.

Use of discipline structure in high school economics texts

To find out how the mandates and the JCEE Framework get translated into texts, I analysed the following nine texts published since 1980, including four texts which I have been told are among the best sellers.

1 Brown, K. and Warner, A. (consulting editors) 1982 *Economics of our Free Enterprise System* McGraw Hill

2 Clayton, G. and Brown, J. E. 1983 *Economic Principles and Practices* Charles E. Merrill

3 Hodgetts, R. M. and Smart, T. L. 1982 *Essentials of Economics and Free Enterprise* Addison Wesley

Table 3   Economic concepts most frequently found in thirteen* selected state
Frameworks, competency statements and courses of study

Economic concept	Frequency
Supply and demand	13
Basics of free enterprise system	13
Scarcity	12
Government regulation	12
Inflation	11
Taxes	11
Economic growth	11
Government spending	11
Production	11
Tradition, command and market systems	10
Investment	9
Specialization	9
Role of price	9
Consumer decision-making	9
Organization of business	8
Savings	8
International trade	8
Labour organizations	8
Economic stability	8
Competition	7
Profit motive	7
Interdependence	7
Interrelationship between resources	7
Role of money	7
Exchange transactions	7
Income distribution	7
Monetary policy	7
Fiscal policy	7
Consumption	6
Price determination	6
Capitalism versus communism	6

*States represented: Arizona, California, Florida, Georgia, Louisiana, Maryland, Mississippi, Missouri, North Carolina, South Carolina, South Dakota, Texas and Utah

Source: From Brennan and Banaszak, *A Study of State Mandates and Competencies for Economic Education,* 1982, p. 13 CDEE, University of the Pacific

4   Mings, T. 1983 *The Study of Economics: Principles, Concepts and Applications* Dushkin Publication Company

5   Sampson, R. J. and Marienhoff, I. 1983 *The American Economy: Analysis, Issues, Principles* Houghton Mifflin

6   Smith, R. F., Watts, M. and Hogan, V. 1981 *Free Enterprise – The American Economics System* Laidlaw Brothers

7   Wilson, J. H. and Clark, J. R. 1984 *Economics: The Science of Cost, Benefit and Choice* South-Western

8   Wolken, L. and Glocker, J. 1982 *Invitation to Economics* Scott, Forsman

9   Wyllie, E. and Warmke, R. 1980 *Free Enterprise in the US* South-Western

Table 4 summarizes my evaluation of the relative importance of the JCEE Framework versus the state mandated curriculum focus, and the use of both the substantive and methodological structure of the discipline. Table 5 shows the percentage of total pages given to concepts in the JCEE Framework, mandated content, and to content outside the JCEE Framework and the mandates.

From my analysis of these texts I conclude the following:

1   The information provided in Tables 4 and 5 shows that the JCEE Framework and state mandates are major determinants of the structure and content of these texts. In my view, all but four of the texts are clearly organized around the basic structure provided by the JCEE. Even Brown/ Warner, Hodgetts/Smart, Smith/Watts/Hogan, and Wyllie/Warmke, which are not *organized* specifically around the Framework, nevertheless base their books on the standard definition of economics, the goal of economic literacy, and they teach most of the concepts included in the Framework. That these books are 'mandate-inspired', designed around one or more of the state requirements, is indicated by the free enterprise rhetoric, lower reading levels, and the page percentages devoted to institutions, personal economics, free enterprise economics and communism versus capitalism. The three most 'academic' books – Mings, Sampson/Marienhoff and Wilson/Clark – follow the spirit of the JCEE Framework and completely cover even its more difficult material. These three books show very little impact of the mandates, and one wonders if they are finding a market. Two books, among the best executed of the group – Wolken/Glocker and Clayton/Brown – while organized to satisfy the mandates, nevertheless emphasize the JCEE Framework. Significantly, they are also best sellers.

2   All nine texts organize content around the basic JCEE definition of economics and of the economic problem. All nine texts use all 12 basic JCEE Framework concepts, and most of the other recommended concepts. Thus, this analysis corroborates the hypothesis that US high school

Table 4   Use of discipline structure approach

	Brown and Warner	Clayton and Brown	Hodgetts and Smart
Use of substantive structure			
JCEE Framework	*	**	*
Mandated curriculum	**	*	***
Use of methodological structure			
Models	*	*	—
Empirical data	—	**	**
How to use the method			
Scientific method	—	—	—
Model building	—	—	—
Measurement	—	—	—
Reasoned decisions	—	**	—

*** The only focus.   ** Relatively strong focus.   * Some attention given.

Table 5   Content priorities: percentages of pages devoted to major topics

	Brown and Warner	Clayton and Brown	Hodgetts and Smart
JCEE Framework			
Basic concepts	16	12	6
Micro: resource allocation and income distribution	11	19	10
Macro: stability and growth	3	36	21
International	9	4	5
Economic institutions	34	17	29
Mandated content			
Personal/consumer economics	22	2	21
Capitalism vs. communism	—	5	4
Nature of private enterprise	6	—	6
Other content			
Third World	—	3	—
Comparative systems	—	—	—
US policy problems	—	3	—

Mings	Sampson and Marienhoff	Smith, Watts and Hogan	Wolken and Glocker	Wilson and Clark	Wyllie and Warmke
***	***	*	**	***	*
—	—	**	*	—	**
**	**	*	**	*	—
**	**	*	**	*	—
—	**	—	—	—	—
—	—	—	—	—	—
*	**	—	**	*	—
*	**	—	—	**	—

Mings	Sampson and Marienhoff	Smith, Watts and Hogan	Wolken and Glocker	Wilson and Clark	Wyllie and Warmke
10	13	11	5	19	9
37	20	18	27	29	8
34	17	19	33	36	23
7	4	6	5	3	5
—	17	13	5	4	18
—	20	13	11	—	40
—	—	6	—	—	3
—	—	7	5	—	—
5	4	—	4	—	—
6	4	6	5	—	—
—	—	—	—	9	—

texts use the mainstream discipline conceptual structure. However, in the four books influenced mainly by the state mandates, it sometimes required considerable searching to find the JCEE approved concepts. These books appear to pay lip service to the JCEE Framework. However, interestingly enough, to some extent they only pay lip service to the free enterprise orientation, and provide fairly standard, if highly simplified, viewpoints of the subject. Only a couple of the books are distressingly propagandistic and, significantly, in these books the more complex concepts from the JCEE Framework were mentioned in passing or not at all. Table 5 shows that the books influenced more by the economics profession tend to show a larger percentage of pages devoted to micro and macro economics; they tend to ignore or limit the specifically mandated content of free enterprise, consumer education, and communist/capitalist economics; they include content such as Third World economies or US policy problems; they incorporate the study of communist society into a comparative systems section.

3 Despite some very effective teaching of some aspects of economic methodology, in general the books do *not* emphasize the methodological structure of the discipline. Most texts use the diagram of the law of supply and demand and the production possibilities curve; they present summary statistical data in tables and graphs. Several of the books discuss economics as a science and describe the scientific method. However, they do not emphasize model building and theory construction as a process of abstraction which can take many forms. Except for requiring students to learn the models presented, they do not teach students about model construction or theory building or give them practice using them. They imply that models are mainly mathematical and are constructed by the experts, something to be learned by students. Two of the books – Clayton/Brown and Sampson/ Marienhoff – provide a broader range of illustrations of models such as flowcharts, providing insight, by way of illustration, into how students themselves might engage in model building. However, as far as I could determine, even these books do not invite students to build their own models.

Most of the books make substantial use of statistical data presentations and they teach students most of the measurement concepts suggested by the JCEE. Furthermore, they sometimes teach students to interpret data, construct index numbers, work out interest rates and rates of return, etc. Primarily, the objective seems to be economic literacy – how to understand the business section of the newspaper, *not* to introduce students to scientific thinking and procedure. Wolken/Glocker do a serious and superb job of intermixing short activities which teach measurement skills in a lively and effective way bordering on programmed instruction. To my mind they use a procedure which considerably improves on that used in EIS.

4 Given the JCEE Framework emphasis on the reasoned approach to decision making, there is not as much emphasis as I expected on develop-

ing students' decision-making skills. Although all the books emphasize opportunity costs early in their presentation, and they consider economics the social science related to decision making, they *do not* train students in taking decisions. The two exceptions to this are the Clayton/Brown and Sampson/Marienhoff books. Even the Wilson/Clark book, which uses the words 'cost', 'benefit' and 'choice' in its title, is so didactic in its teaching strategy that the authors do not emphasize student practice in decision making.

5 In most of the books there is an interesting disparity in the treatment of macro and micro theory. Although macro theory *per se* is almost nonexistent in all but the three more academically-oriented books, most of the books provide a rather detailed development of the law of supply and demand. They introduce some aspects of consumer demand theory such as income and substitution effect of a change in price, demand and supply elasticities, the law of diminishing returns, supply and demand curves and the diagrammatic presentation of price determination and changes in prices. All this theory serves an important purpose, to demonstrate market equilibrium and the adjustment of supply to demand. All books present income distribution mainly as a subject in microeconomics. They mention or imply that income is earned by factor owners for their contribution to production, but only a few books – Mings, Wilson/Clark – present the neoclassical theory of wage determination. One book presents a utility theory of value (Wyllie/Warmke).

6 Although most books mention industry structure and market failures, only the three academically-oriented books give serious treatment to the subject. Even they are not as thorough as the JCEE Framework presentation of market failures. Wolken/Glocker devote a chapter to competition in American markets which is a thorough treatment of market structure, but they give only six pages to government intervention, and from the point of view of government *functions* rather than from the point of view of *market failures*. The other books devote only one to seven pages to the topic of market structure, limited mainly to mere definitions, with no mention of market failures.

7 The macro economy is treated at some length in all the books; however, my percentage estimates are misleading because I included treatment of money, banking and the Federal Reserve as part of macro when this subject was usually an institutional description of the banking sector of the economy. Except for Mings and Wilson/Clark, there is no real macro theory presented. Most books discuss macro problems through a description of business cycles and an enumeration of definitions. The policy discussions are very superficial in most books, although several books mention the monetarist/Keynesian debate, and supply-side economics. Mings, Hodgetts/Smart, Sampson/Marienhoff and Wilson/Clark mention a fuller range of policy alternatives. Only Mings, Sampson/Marienhoff and Wilson/Clark give a serious treatment to monetary and fiscal policy. Most

of the books limit their discussion of monetary and fiscal policy to a few pages of definitions and a brief description of the monetarist/fiscalist policy controversy.

8   Overwhelmingly, the books provide a consensual lens and an officially defined interpretation of reality – entirely within the accepted neoclassical tradition. If anything, the bias is towards strict neoclassical economics with little Keynesian synthesis except in the three more academically-oriented texts. The differences between the books are mostly in terms of quality and depth of coverage of the paradigm. There is no multiplicity of perspectives. The only indication of different perspectives comes in the short biographical inserts in the few books which include heterodox thinkers like Veblen, Boulding, and Galbraith. Otherwise, there is no recognition of different schools of thought with different perspectives about the nature of economics or of capitalist economies. Stated differences in policy controversies are invariably viewed as differences in interpretation of facts or differences in values. There is no recognition of the concept of class conflict. The books refer to sources of authority in short biographies of well-known economists, sometimes of successful businessmen and businesswomen or government officials.

9   The most shocking evidence on indoctrination comes, of course, in the treatment of communism versus capitalism, a subject mandated to be taught in some states. However, I was not prepared for the extent of myth-making and ignorance displayed by the authors. It was not only the mandate-oriented books which were appalling. Most books called Sweden and Great Britain 'socialist' countries. Although they defined socialism in terms of ownership of the means of production coupled with democratic forms of government, *no* text identified the percentage of industry owned privately in Sweden and Great Britain, statistics which would clear up the problem of definition pretty quickly. In discussing the Russian revolution, most books described or implied a blood-bath perpetrated by the Bolsheviks; *none* of the texts mentioned the concept of counter-revolution and the relationship between violence and counter-revolution, a notion which is extremely important today, with US involvement in counter-revolutionary activity in Central America.

Treatment of Marx's ideas was mostly wrong or oversimplified. One example should suffice: the Sampson/Marienhoff presentation, the best of the lot, nevertheless gives a purely economic–determinist view of Marx and states erroneously, 'for the capitalist law of supply and demand, Marx substitutes the labor theory of value' (p. 405). This statement is quite incorrect; Marx recognized the interaction of supply and demand in determining market prices but, along with classical economists, assumed constant returns to scale and therefore that demand has no effect on long-run equilibrium price. I could go on and on with examples of misinformation and misinterpretation of Marx's economics, and do not think it unfair to conclude that the sections on Marx and communism/socialism in most of these texts could not possibly have been researched.

10 Except for two or three books – Wolken/Glocker, Sampson/Marienhoff, possibly Mings – the books are mainly didactic presentations with little real emphasis on active student involvement in learning. Most learning objectives, which are often stated in the texts, are related to low-order cognitive skills. Only one book – Sampson/Marienhoff – seriously deals with controversy and provides adequate material on which to build inquiry activities. The Wolken/Glocker book is beautifully designed to develop social studies skills and uses some inquiry techniques for this purpose, but the book does not really show a commitment to involving students in controversy. Mings uses provocative readings to interest students, but does not really engage them in activities involving policy controversy.

11 To conclude, none of the books consider as problematic the basic concepts and social vision of mainstream economics. Except for the occasional brief biography of Keynes or Galbraith, the only alternative school of thought which is mentioned is Marxism, which is usually introduced as a foil, not as a serious alternative world view. Overwhelmingly, students in the US are learning basic concepts from the neoclassical paradigm as a catechism; to a lesser extent, they are learning to use these concepts to understand the profession's view of basic economic policy controversy. To a still lesser extent, the texts introduce students to the mechanism of trade-off or marginalist thinking. In general, the JCEE Framework and the diffusion of its content in the curriculum via textbooks is a real tribute to the profession's 'maturity' and 'normality' in Katouzian's sense of the word. Except for the more openly propagandistic influence of the state mandates, the profession, through the JCEE, has been able to control the marketplace of ideas about economics in our 'free market society'.

Summary and recommendations

With a couple of outstanding exceptions, most of these books present pretty dull stuff, particularly for able students. For streetwise kids, the content of the books intended for them, for the average student, probably contradicts their life experience. Conformity to expectations of authority is not the way they intend to make their way, and these books may possibly reinforce rebellion against school and authorities. If they do reinforce conformity among the docile students, which might be their major *purpose*, possibly they are quite successful. For capable and curious students, future leaders, the only texts which are appropriate are the three academically-oriented ones; but even these mostly lack the basic ingredients which Popkewitz says are necessary. They do not introduce students to economics as science, into the process of inquiry and knowledge creation, to the tentativeness of knowledge, to the ideological basis of all science and the political underpinnings of social science, to the diversity of opinion and ferment in economics today. Most important, they do not give students experience in model building, analysis, and evaluation of controversy in order to extend their abstract reasoning powers and their moral judgement.

What can be done?

It turns out that those of us who read Schwab were thinking of single structures and we accepted the discipline paradigm as essentially unproblematic background knowledge. Only later have I realized that there are multiple structures based on different views of the viability of capitalism. Professional economic educators may be in the same situation I was in 20 years ago, or they may be unyielding in their view of one correct social vision. Probably they are a bit of both, mediated by a strong dose of practicality. Textbook writers may have a mission to improve economics education, but they must meet the test of the market. Clearly state mandates want students to become good consumers, to trust and believe in free enterprise and business leadership, and they have *ordered* the schools to teach to these objectives.

If I knew then what I know now I would proceed differently. I would not try to reform economic education through textbook writing, but through teacher education. I would want to impress upon future and existing teachers that economics is based on a belief system, that one basis for diversity is in the alternative views of how the economy really operates, that scientific activity flourishes by trying to pick between alternative SRPs through critical analysis and empirical falsification. I would introduce my students to some of the diversity and let them explore the different implications of different SRPs for public policy. I do this in my university teaching, and I am aware of the problems. Introducing economics in this way makes the subject more abstract. But it can be done and it engenders student interest. Given the selectivity in the English system, from a strictly pedagogical point of view, it should be more possible than in the US.

I am not optimistic, not only because of the effectiveness of the economic profession in its control of education, but also because of traditional teaching practices which emphasize the importance of didactics for maintaining classroom discipline. Nevertheless, to make change in the right direction, each of us in our various roles can make some difference:

1 Textbook writers can explore how far they can go to brighten up texts with real controversy without losing their market.

2 Teacher educators have an obligation to teach alternative SRPs and to interest teachers in exploring them. In England this means pushing this content into the A level examinations.

3 Those training potential leaders need to incorporate political economy into the curriculum to open up the alternatives to gifted students.

4 The profession needs to encourage more cross-fertilization between SRPs and to legitimize debate on fundamental issues.

5 The bottom line is that teachers in the schools are responsible for their own intellectual development to be in a position to pass on their knowledge and enthusiasm for learning and questioning to their students.

References

Blaug, M. 1980 *The Methodology of Economics: or How Economists Explain* Cambridge University Press

Brennan, D. C. and Banaszak, R. A. 1982 *A Study of State Mandates and Competencies for Economic Education* Center for the Development of Economic Education, Stockton, California

Brown, K. and Warner, A. (consulting eds.) 1982 *Economics of our Free Enterprise System* McGraw Hill, New York

Bruner, J. S. 1960 *The Process of Education* Harvard University Press, Cambridge, Massachusetts

Clayton, G. and Brown, J. E. 1983 *Economic Principles and Practices* Charles E. Merrill, Columbus, Ohio

Davidson, P. 1978 *Money and the Real World* Macmillan

Eatwell, J. and Milgate, M. 1983 *Keynes's Economics and the Theory of Value and Distribution* Oxford University Press

Eichner, A. S. and Kregel, J. A. 1975 'An essay on post-Keynesian theory: a new paradigm in economics' *Journal of Economic Literature* **13**(4) pp. 1293–314

Hansen, W. L., Bach, G. L., Calderwood, J. and Saunders, P. 1977 *Master Curriculum Guide in Economics for the Nation's Schools, Part I – A Framework for Teaching Economics: Basic Concepts* Joint Council on Economic Education, New York

Helburn, S. W., Sperling, J., Evans, R. and Davis, J. 1974 *Economics in Society: Strategy and Methods* Addison Wesley, Menlo Park, New Jersey

Hodgetts, R. M. and Smart, T. L. 1982 *Essentials of Economics and Free Enterprise* Addison Wesley, Menlo Park, New Jersey

Kahn, R. 1978 'Some aspects of the development of Keynes's thought' *Journal of Economic Literature* **16** (June), pp. 545–59

Katouzian, H. 1980 *Ideology and Method in Economics* New York University Press, New York and London

Kuhn, T. S. 1970 *The Structure of Scientific Revolutions* 2nd enlarged edn., University of Chicago Press, Chicago

Kuttner, R. 1985 'The poverty of economics' *The Atlantic Monthly* (February) pp. 74–84

Lakatos, I. 1970 'Criticism and the growth of knowledge' in I. Lakatos and A. Musgrave (eds.) *Criticism and the Growth of Knowledge* Cambridge University Press

Mings, T. 1983 *The Study of Economics: Principles, Concepts and Applications* Dushkin Publication Company, Guilford, Connecticut

Minsky, H. P. 1975 *John Maynard Keynes* Columbia University Press, New York

Minsky, H. P. 1982 'The financial instability hypothesis: capitalist processes and the behavior of the economy' in C. Kindleberger and J. Laffarque (eds.) *Financial Crisis: Theory and History* Cambridge University Press

National Task Force on Economic Education 1961 *Economic Education in the Schools: Report of the National Task Force* Committee for Economic Development, New York

Popkewitz, T. S. 1977 'The latent values of the discipline-centered curriculum' *Theory and Research in Social Education* **V**(1) pp. 41–60

Popper, K. 1963 *Conjectures and Refutations: The Growth of Scientific Knowledge* Routledge and Kegan Paul

Robinson, J. 1975 'A personal view' in M. Keynes (ed.) *Essays of John Maynard Keynes,* Cambridge University Press

Sampson, R. J. and Marienhoff, I. 1983 *The American Economy: Analysis, Issues, Principles* Houghton Mifflin, Boston

Saunders, P., Bach, G. L., Calderwood, J. and Hansen, W. L. 1984 *Master Curriculum Guide in Economics: A Framework for Teaching the Basic Concepts* 2nd edn., Joint Council on Economic Education, New York

Schwab, J. J. 1962 'The concept of the structure of a discipline' *The Educational Record* (July) pp. 197–205

Schwab, J. J. 1964 'Structure of the disciplines: meanings and significances' in G. W. Ford and L. Pugno (eds.) *The Structure of Knowledge and the Curriculum* Rand McNally, Chicago

Smith, R. F., Watts, M. and Hogan, V. 1981 *Free Enterprise – The American Economics System* Laidlaw Brothers, River Forest, Illinois

Sraffa, P. 1960 *Production of Commodities by Means of Commodities: Prelude to a Critique of Economic Theory* Cambridge University Press

Wiggins, S. and Sperling, J. 1968 *To Design and Evaluate a Twelfth Grade Course in Principles of Economics, Final Report* (ED 028093) ERIC Document Reproduction Services, Bethesda, Maryland

Wilson, J. H. and Clark, J. R. 1984 *Economics: The Science of Cost, Benefit and Choice* South-Western, Cincinnati, Ohio

Wolken, L. and Glocker, J. 1982 *Invitation to Economics* Scott, Forsman, Glenview, Illinois

Wyllie, E. and Warmke, R. 1980 *Free Enterprise in the U.S.* South-Western, Glenview, Illinois

Is economic science scientific – or is it better than that?

Graham Dawson

Head of Economics, Birkenhead School

The argument of this paper is that economics incorporates, while transcending, the methods of the physical sciences. Positive economics manifests objectivity in the investigation of what is. Normative economics evinces rationality in the justification of what ought to be.

Introduction

Two problems confront the advocate of economics as a science: the meaning problem and the value problem. The meaning problem can be stated as follows: science aims at objectivity through abstraction from subjective points of view, yet economics investigates actions which have a subjective meaning for the agent. The value problem can also be stated briefly: scientific theories can be tested against experience, but in economics what counts as passing or failing the test of experience depends on the values of the economist.

I shall argue that economics constitutes objective knowledge and incorporates, while transcending, scientific procedures. My solution of the meaning problem is that economics abstracts from subjective points of view in so far as it investigates the consequences, intended or unintended, foreseen or unforeseen, of actions. My solution of the value problem is that economics is not a purely positive discipline but makes normative claims, which are amenable to rational justification. Thus, economics employs scientific procedures to explain the effects of actions and then explores a relatively uncharted area of human knowledge, namely, reasoned argument about questions of value. In going beyond what is, to reconnoitre what ought to be, economics offers an understanding of matters about which science must be silent. Far from being an inferior imitation of scientific inquiry, economics is a more perfect manifestation of human rationality.

The structure of this paper reflects the doctrine of perspectivism propounded by Lukes (1982). He advances two arguments in support of his claim that scientific methods are of limited applicability in the study of human action. The first is that 'the interpreter's perspective cannot be divorced from the account he gives; that there can be no perspective-neutral interpretation and explanation' (p. 302). This position he terms 'strong perspectivism', but it will be discussed in this paper as the value problem. The second argument is that 'interpretation and explanation must make reference to actors' perspectives' (p. 302). This position he terms 'weak perspectivism', but it will be discussed here as the meaning problem. The change in terminology reflects my belief that there are two problems for the advocate of economics as a science, not two aspects of a single problem, varying only in severity.

The meaning problem

The meaning problem arises because scientists aim at objectivity by abstracting from subjective points of view, whereas students of social behaviour must define the phenomena they seek to understand in terms of the meaning they have for the people whose intentions are behind them. Accordingly, science and economics appear to belong to different forms of knowledge (Hirst, 1974): science to the empirical form, economics to knowledge of other minds. Economists face a dilemma: either they use the methods of science and treat human actions as mere events without meaning, in which case they must abandon any claim to be practising a *human* or *social* science; or they seek to elicit the subjective meanings behind the observable actions of economic agents, in which case they will be obliged to renounce any claim to be practising a human or social *science*. Economics, it seems, cannot be both scientific and an investigation of human action.

The hermeneutic tradition in the study of human behaviour can be traced back to Weber:

> The external courses of religious behaviour are so diverse that an understanding of this behaviour can only be achieved from the viewpoint of the subjective experiences, ideas, and purposes of the individuals concerned – in short, from the viewpoint of the religious behaviour's 'meaning'. (1963, p. 1)

The implications of this view for the study of human behaviour in general were expounded in a notable work by Winch (1958). Whereas natural scientists are free to investigate phenomena which they have defined in accordance with 'their own' criteria, students of human behaviour must confine themselves to the criteria used by the people whose actions they are trying to explain.

> 'Understanding' . . . is grasping the *point* or *meaning* of what is being done or said. This is a notion far removed from the world of statistics and causal laws. (1958, p. 115)

More recently, Lukes (1982) has argued that the Galilean style of reasoning and the Cartesian conception of knowledge are inapplicable to social and economic explanation. Science, so understood, aims at 'objectivity, involving increasing abstraction from particular, internal and subjective points of view' (p. 299). According to Lukes, however, 'some areas of social enquiry are inherently perspectival' (p. 301), by which he means that the description and explanation of at least some social phenomena cannot be detached from their surrounding beliefs, attitudes, assumptions and moral and political judgements.

An imaginary example may help to clarify the significance of the meaning problem. Suppose that an observer wants to explain why I have resumed church attendance after an interval of some years. He asks me and I reply that I believe regular church-going to be a necessary condition for the salvation of my soul or that I find it a uniquely satisfying expression of my love of God. In other words, I give a religious reason. The observer then discovers that my boss's beautiful daughter started attending the same church shortly before I did; or that my mother-in-law visits my wife every Sunday morning; or that my rich grandfather, from whose will I hope in the not too distant future to benefit, has recently become a 'born again' Christian. In other words, he discovers a possible ulterior motive by framing an inductive generalization about a man's behaviour in connection with beautiful women in a position to advance his career, mothers-in-law or wealthy relatives near to death.

The new explanation will be perfectly intelligible to me and I may even admit that an ulterior motive does indeed influence my behaviour. Even if I refuse to accept it, this may merely reflect my resentment at being found out or my shame at the realization that I have been deceiving myself. In any case, the point is that even where the goal of inquiry is the discovery of the intention behind the public behaviour, the methods of science, observation and inductive reasoning have a part to play. The fact that actions have a subjective meaning does not entail the inapplicability of scientific procedures. For such methods may be instrumental in increasing agents' understanding of their own motives.

The significance of this outcome for economics can now be elucidated. Actions of interest to the economist are sometimes described in terms which attribute to agents intentions of which they may be unaware and which they may be unwilling to own. Trade union leaders who describe their own behaviour as protecting the jobs or living standards of their members might see it presented in the media as jeopardizing the economic recovery, trying to overturn the democratically elected government or carrying out the Politburo's orders. Similarly, government ministers who see themselves as fighting inflation might be described as using unemployment to punish the working class, increasing the inequalities in society or rewarding their cronies in the City. Actions which might be described in these ways are certainly among the phenomena requiring explanation by a theory of wage inflation.

Two theories of wage inflation will be outlined here (see Smith, 1982). A monetarist theory of the sort advocated by Milton Friedman begins by supposing that the government adopts an expansionary fiscal and monetary stance, perhaps in response to the representations of a pressure group or in an effort to win votes with an election budget. The expansionary policy causes excess demand, which leads to wage inflation as employers try to attract scarce labour to increase output. Since prices are set as a mark-up over costs, price inflation emerges, giving rise to expectations of further price rises. A feedback effect on wages ensues and a wage–price spiral is set in motion. An alternative theory of wage inflation is offered by mainstream UK Keynesianism. The first impetus is given by social forces. Trade union militancy as an expression of class conflict or over a specific issue, such as relativities or a desire to maintain disposable income after income tax increases, directly causes wage inflation. Price inflation follows through the familiar mark-up process. As workers and firms alike price themselves out of markets, unemployment rises. This leads the government to introduce an expansionary fiscal and monetary policy in an attempt to halt the rise in unemployment.

Obviously, the main difference between the two theories is that one sees an expansionary fiscal and monetary stance as the cause of inflation, while the other regards such a policy as its consequence. In order to decide between the rival accounts, it is to the methods of science that the economist must turn. There is a role here for the variable-correlators of that 'good ol' time science'. The question which arises is how the explanation of wage inflation differs from the understanding of church attendance in such a way that scientific techniques play the dominant part in the former but only a supporting role in the latter.

There seem to be three significant differences between explaining wage inflation and understanding church attendance. First, there is the relative simplicity of observed behaviour in the case of religious worship. The act of worship is either an end in itself, as an expression of the believer's love of God, or a means to an end only once removed, as when church attendance is seen as a condition of salvation. The ulterior motive, if present, merely substitutes one immediate end for another. By contrast, the phenomena to be explained in the case of wage inflation consist of a fairly complex chain of causes and effects. Second, there were no unintended or unanticipated consequences set in train by attending church (so long as we exclude the irksome attentions of a social scientist investigating one's behaviour). However, both theories of wage inflation include unexpected effects. The monetarist does not assume that the government intended to initiate a wage–price spiral and the theory is meant to be true even of periods when the balance of economic opinion would not have enabled it to anticipate such an outcome. Similarly, the Keynesian does not have to assume that trade union negotiators, seeking to safeguard their members' living standards, intend to cause unemployment or even that they foresee it. Third, the intentions of the agent are relatively unproblematic, or, to put it another way, the subjective meanings their actions have are relatively uncomplicated. For the most part, economic agents are assumed to be trying to further their own interests as they perceive them.

There are two reasons for the comparative unimportance of agents' intentions in economics. First, in so far as economic acts may have remote and either unintended or unforeseen consequences, economists are faced with a choice about defining them. The profession chooses to define actions by their effects rather than by the intentions behind them. Since the object of economics is to study the allocation of scarce resources to the production of alternative goods and services, this is clearly a reasonable decision. For if we wish to explain and, where appropriate, improve the allocation of resources, we need to know how they are in fact allocated. We need to know what the world is like, not what it would have been like if only everything had gone well. And so we define actions according to their effects. For instance, if a government claims to be pursuing a tough monetary policy, we do not meekly take their word for it. We look for signs of monetary austerity. Should every measure of money supply be well outside its target range, real interest rates low and the pound sterling under pressure on the foreign markets, we may agree in overruling the government's self-description. What justifies the action-description 'pursuing a tough monetary policy' is not a matter of subjective meaning but of objective fact. And this springs from the economist's characteristic interest in actions which are initiated by simple or transparent intentions but have remote consequences which may be unintended or unforeseen.

The second reason for the relative unimportance of intentions in economic analysis concerns the intentions themselves. How intentions should be brought into economics is best investigated by considering developments in macroeconomics since Keynes. It is clear that economists of all the major schools of thought allow a role for the intentions of economic agents. In doing so they go beyond the mere correlation of variables which record observations of public behaviour. Economists postulate unobservables, as they must if they are to be in a position to present their discipline as scientific. For the physical sciences routinely posit unobservables to explain what is observed. And so the monetarist theory of wage inflation assigns a vital role to expectations, while Keynes notoriously relies on the amorphous notion of business confidence to explain investment – or explain why it is inexplicable. But there is nevertheless a wide divergence between monetarist and Keynesian treatments of intentions.

Keynesian economics, or at least that interpretation of it which Coddington has called 'hydraulic Keynesianism' (1983, pp. 12–17, 102–5, 110–13 and 116), regards economic agents, with the apparent exception of businessmen, as not really *agents* at all. Instead they are a diaphanous medium through which government policy might be transmitted with no risk of resistance or refraction. Workers are the victims of money illusion, happy to take it for granted that every 10 per cent wage increase means a 10 per cent improvement in the standard of living. No thought is given to what might be happening to prices. Monetarism, or rather rational expectations theory, holds that people will make the best use of the information available to them. Workers will, for instance, realize that an increase in real wages during a period of inflation at 10 per cent requires a rise in money wages in excess of that figure. Consequently, government efforts to reduce unemployment at the cost of no more than 10 per cent inflation will be thwarted: a stable rate of inflation is rendered impossible by the way in which people react to government policy. Economic agents are seen to be exactly that: independent sources of action, interacting with government rather than endlessly duped by it. The moral to be drawn is that the effect a government policy has may depend upon how people respond to it. And that may in turn depend upon what they perceive the intention behind the policy to be, on how its social meaning is understood. The events of 1979–80 in the UK can reasonably be interpreted as evidence for the view that if a government pursues a tight monetary policy but is not widely believed to be doing so, then unemployment will be much higher than it would have been had the strict money supply control been anticipated. It is clearly disastrous for economists to regard people as though they had no intentions other than those whose presence makes for the convenient implementation of government policy.

Unfortunately, one school of thought has accommodated intentions in a way which is just as calamitous as the hydraulic Keynesian neglect of them. Austrian subjectivism allows little or no room for the variable-correlators. That at any rate is how one commentator interprets Hayek's methodological individualism:

> Economic explanation must always be about the action of *individuals;* and it is an error to suppose that the relationships between economic aggregates display any regularity which is of scientific interest. (Barry, 1984, p. 59)

If this is meant to diminish the utility of probabilistic laws or generalizations which make no predictions about the actions of any particular individual, it is certainly wide of the mark. It is obviously true that statistical laws or trends in economics do not enable us to say of any particular person that he or she is going to do this or that. But this in no way reduces their usefulness. For example, the prediction that an increase of 1p in the tax on a packet of twenty cigarettes would raise an extra £35 million in revenue may provide helpful guidance to the Chancellor even though it does not tell him anything about any individual.

The nature of statistical inference shows how intentions can be incorporated into economic analysis. The occurrence of intentions other than those which must be ascribed to any agent performing a certain class of action can be dealt with in the same way as irrational choices are shown to be consistent with the rationality assumption of classical economics. Suppose that the action in question is that of accepting a wage settlement, and we assume that a rational agent will take a view about the future rate of inflation in deciding a satisfactory figure. The intention ascribed to a typical agent in these circumstances will be to achieve a target increase in real wages. Some agents may have very different intentions, such as those referred to earlier in discussing action-descriptions: they may hope to bring down the government, demonstrate their 'industrial muscle' or express their loyalty to a perceived ideal of working class solidarity. The existence of deviant intentions does not destroy the possibility of prediction any more than impulse buying or the effects of advertising undermine the rationality assumption of classical economic analysis. For irrational intentions are by definition randomly distributed. Therefore, given a sufficiently large sample, intentions to pursue wage settlements in excess of the target will be cancelled out by intentions to accept something less (out of a sense of duty to patients or pupils, for instance). The outcome is therefore *as if* each agent made the best use of available information in formulating a target rise in real wages (see Minford and Peel, 1983 and Dawson, 1980).

The solution to the meaning problem is, then, that economics investigates the effects of actions, intentions entering the analysis in so far as their perception influences the effects an action has. Thus, B's perception of A's intentions might determine how B responds to A's action. Some branches of the human sciences, such as sociology, focus mainly on the meaning an action has for the agent performing it. Even here there is a limited role for scientific procedures. The priority given by economists to the investigation of the effects of actions allows scientific techniques greater scope. And so economic knowledge approximates more closely to empirical knowledge than to knowledge of other minds.

The value problem

The value problem is that it is impossible in economics to devise an empirical test for a theory which does not depend on the values of the economist. Lukes claims that 'the interpreter's perspective cannot be divorced from the account he gives' (1982, p. 302). And Montefiore maintains that the Marxist and the liberal will be unable even to agree on how to describe a social phenomenon, such as a strike:

> . . . where one description assumes the absence and the other the existence of some fundamental conflict of interests, the choice of terms may willy-nilly commit one to an at least indirect support of or opposition to one side or the other. (1966, p. 191)

The value problem can be traced back to Hume: 'Reason is, and ought only to be, the slave of the passions, and can never pretend to any other office than to serve and obey them' (1966, p. 125). Reason tells us what actually is the case, but the passions determine what ought to be. In a famous passage, Hume argues that it is logically impossible to deduce an 'ought' from an 'is': it 'seems altogether inconceivable, how this new relation can be a deduction from others, which are entirely different from it' (1966, p. 178). The prospects for a policy science appear bleak, for it seems to be an attempt to establish connections between areas having nothing at all in common. Science, as the province of reason, investigates what is, whereas policy, trying to discover what ought to be done, has been exiled to the barren shores of passion.

Logical positivism, as the inheritor of the Humean legacy, forced economics to confront the value problem. Science alone produced theories which could be empirically verified and accordingly constituted knowledge. Sentences expressing value judgements were held to be meaningless. A popular response was to palm economics off as a purely positive science, whose function it was to discover appropriate means to ends decided upon else-where. And where would that be? The assumption was that all value judgements were as arbitrary as subjective tastes or preferences. It is futile to try by rational argument to persuade someone who likes strawberries to like peaches instead. All that the economist could do was to accept such preferences as part of his raw data and offer advice on how to allocate resources so as to maximize strawberry production. In the public sphere, the 'elsewhere' was, of course, the government; but its decisions carried no rational authority, for it was merely the source of power. Economic reason, it seemed, served, and ought only to serve, political passion.

Positive economics is therefore an attempt to come to terms with scepti-cism, in this case scepticism about moral knowledge. This 'historic compro-mise', whereby economics preserves its status as a policy science only by reducing policy to technical questions about means to irrationally chosen ends, must, it will now be contended, be rejected. For it concedes the central point at issue, which is that there is no place for reason in the determination of ends, that there can be no rational argument over what ought to be.

The strategy for repudiating moral scepticism is to draw attention to the unrealistic demands it makes. This is a standard reply to the sceptic and one which is exemplified by Coddington's position on certainty. The sceptic argues that we can never achieve certainty about anything, and so, since knowledge requires that we be certain, it, too, is forever beyond our reach. As Coddington points out, we do not start from certainty but from ignorance: approximations to the truth, provisionally accepted as knowledge until they are falsified, are to be welcomed as steps away from ignorance, not dismissed as backslidings from certainty. Coddington is, as it were, inviting us to see intellectual activity, not as an attempt to regain the epistemological paradise from which we have been expelled, but rather as an effort to construct the edifice of knowledge in the epistemological desert into which we are born. 'The price of copper twenty years hence is a thoroughly uncertain thing,' he remarks. But, rather than bewail this, we should, he urges, recognize how far behind we have left complete *un*certainty: 'for the belief . . . that the price of copper will, in 2002, be greater at 1982 prices than 10 cents per ton, and less than \$1 billion per ton, is not at all uncertain' (1983, p. 52).

The moral sceptic similarly assumes that, in the absence of certainty about values, there can be no moral knowledge at all, no scope for reason in the determination of values. We are sunk in moral ignorance, with as many conflicting values as there are individuals. A maelstrom of irreconcilable subjective tastes is claimed to be the counterpart of a chaos of unjustifiable opinions concerning matters of fact. Is discourse about values really like that? Is deadlock over values a besetting difficulty in economics?

Three points will be made in reply to these questions: (1) that there is more agreement over values than is frequently assumed; (2) that, when value conflict does occur, it stimulates rather than obstructs research in economics; and (3) that economists are particularly well placed to understand how reason can play a part in resolving some value conflicts.

1   Utilitarianism provides the moral basis of much economics. The principle of utility states that an action is right in so far as it tends to promote the general happiness. The happiness of an individual can be thought of as consisting in part of satisfaction or utility provided by the goods and services he or she consumes. Economics regards consumers as utility-maximizers and holds that, under certain conditions, a perfectly competitive market will maximize social welfare, that is, the aggregate of individual utilities. Cost–benefit analysis is simply an attempt to operationalize the Benthamite felicific calculus. And so economics is part of the utilitarian programme for making morality as rational, indeed as scientific, as possible. Granted the initial commitment to the principle of utility, the question whether an action ought to be done, or an institution exist, becomes an empirical one. It becomes a matter of estimating the consequences for human good and harm of alternative courses of action, in order to ascertain which will bring about the greatest balance of pleasure over pain, happiness over misery, utility over disutility.

It is easy to underestimate the scope in economics for empirical inquiry within a shared framework of utilitarian values. One example will have to be enough to illustrate the general point. Coddington claims that 'what distinguishes Keynesian policies is that they take a utilitarian view of the public finances' (1983, p. 1). Instead of relying on an internal criterion of good housekeeping, seeing a balanced budget as intrinsically good, Keynesians assess the consequences of the budget, balanced or not, for the whole economy. And Coddington concludes that this 'utilitarian perspective on the public finances may be contrasted with the idea that there may be precepts of 'sound finance' or financial 'propriety', 'rectitude', 'responsibility' and so on' (pp. 2–3).

However, he seems to have mistaken the popular presentation of monetarist policies for the sole economic argument in their favour. For monetarism has been defended on grounds which are implicitly utilitarian. If it is believed that random shocks make it impossible to predict the precise course of the economy, and that government intervention through budget manipulation will only add to the uncertainties, then it is reasonable to conclude that a fixed policy of balanced budgets will tend to promote the general welfare. Thus, Parkin and Bade maintain that the inability of *any* economic theory satisfactorily to explain the Great Depression of 1929 to 1934 'does not bode well for the Keynesian policy recommendation, which, in order that it may improve matters, must be based upon the presumption that we know rather a lot about the way in which the economy behaves' (1982, p. 525).

It may reasonably be concluded that a utilitarian perspective is not uniquely Keynesian. We are not faced with an irresolvable clash of paradigms, with deadlock between those who see fiscal and monetary rectitude as an end in itself and those who are willing to tolerate budget deficits and monetary laxity for their beneficial effects on the economy. The issue of deficit finance versus sound money, pump-priming versus good housekeeping, is in principle amenable to resolution by empirical investigation. Do we or do we not know enough to get fine-tuning right most of the time? Is repeated government intervention or an unwavering 'hands-off' approach the policy which will promote 'the greatest happiness of the greatest number'? These are empirical rather than ethical questions, albeit difficult ones to answer.

2 Nevertheless, it would be ridiculous to deny that economists sometimes disagree over values. Indeed, they face the value problem in its sharpest form: economic theories cannot be tested against experience, because what counts as a test depends upon the economist's perspective, in particular his or her values.

It is true that values influence economists' policy recommendations. This is perfectly proper, for that is, after all, what values are for: they guide action. But it does not follow, and is not true, that values decide the outcome of empirical tests, thereby rendering them futile. Values influence the choice of a criterion for evaluating the performance of a policy, practice or institution. Whether or not a particular policy, practice or institution measures up to that criterion, whether or not it passes the test, is, however, a straightforwardly empirical matter. Deciding to judge something in terms of a certain standard and reporting the fact that it measures, or fails to measure, up to that standard are logically distinct. Popper has distinguished standards from facts with great clarity: 'through the decision to accept a proposal . . . we create the corresponding standard; yet through the decision to accept a proposition we do *not* create the corresponding fact' (1966, p. 384). To adopt an example from Mackie, it is a factual question how well a particular sheepdog has performed in trials, but, if one wants to keep the dog only as a pet, the result of the trials can reasonably be disregarded in selecting the animal. As Mackie puts it, 'given any sufficiently determinate standards, it will be an objective issue, a matter of truth or falsehood, how well any particular specimen measures up to those standards' (1977, p. 26).

This distinction between creating standards and recognizing facts can be applied to a major economic controversy to illustrate the importance of value judgements in economics. The merits of the free market economy is such a controversy. Two questions can be distinguished: first, whether market economies have a better growth record than centrally planned ones; and second, whether they have other advantages or disadvantages which might outweigh the result of an investigation into comparative growth records.

It is clear that the first question can be analysed in terms of the dichotomy between facts and standards. We choose economic growth as the criterion of success and then attempt to answer the purely empirical question as to whether market economies outgrow planned economies. There are obvious pitfalls in such an investigation: for instance, there are no absolutely pure types and many major economies are more or less evenly divided between private and public sectors. Nevertheless, it is in principle possible to isolate the effects of culture, stage of economic development, political stability, immigration and so on in order to ascertain whether, *ceteris paribus,* a policy of leaving everything but narrowly defined public goods to the market would maximize growth. Suppose that the inquiry concluded that market economies are more likely to promote growth than centrally planned ones. We would still not know enough to advise a population whether to leave the economy to run itself or plan everything that moves. Yet it would be unnecessarily fastidious if, having pointed out the way to high economic growth, we left everyone else to decide if that is where they wanted to go.

Progress in economics will be advanced by a robust attitude towards values. The choice of growth as the criterion for judging the performance of an economy is entailed by the utilitarian foundations of conventional economics. Growth is taken to be an indicator of social welfare or aggregate utility. But, even within the same utilitarian framework, other purely economic criteria present themselves. Unemployment and inflation are obvious examples. We are still limited to one ultimate value, utility: it is simply that it has been seen to be a complex condition. For one's estimate of one's future utility will be affected by the probability of suffering hyper-inflation or unemployment. And so an awareness of the complexity of utility will stimulate research into the incidence of unemployment and inflation as well as growth. Empirical inquiry settles the land mapped out by value analysis.

The aggregate level of utility, material well-being, is by no means the only value known to economists. A familiar objection to taking national income per head as a criterion of living standards is that it neglects the distribution of income. A more radical critique has been put forward by Mishan, who maintains that two premises underlying judgements of social welfare are unjustifiable, the premises being

> first, that a more equal distribution of the nation's output of economic goods constitutes an improvement in social welfare, and second, that an increase in goods per capita and the availability of new goods likewise constitute an improvement in welfare. (1983, p. 38)

In each case the expression of a 'new' value stimulates empirical investigation. A commitment to equality makes the distribution of income a worthy subject of research. Scepticism about the value of material progress may prompt inquiry into the adverse effects of economic growth on the quality of life and the environment. I have argued elsewhere that the method of acquisition, as well as the consumption, of goods and services is a source of utility or disutility (Dawson, 1984a and 1984b). To the liberal, acquiring goods by market transactions yields utility through the exercise of freedom and independence; to the collectivist, a spirit of fellowship might be fostered by the provision of state-financed goods and services free at the point of consumption. Empirical inquiry into how goods and services are acquired is likely to be undertaken only if human dignity or respect for persons are among the values prevailing in society. The more pluralistic a society's value system is, the more comprehensive and discriminating is its empirical research into its economy likely to be. It is a commonplace notion that the human sciences cannot be entirely value-free because values determine the choice of subjects for investigation. The less familiar thought offered here is that this aspect of the human sciences is a strength rather than a weakness.

3   The reason that this fact about the human sciences is sometimes regarded with suspicion is that values are commonly assumed to be the province of the passions. That values are instead a proper subject for rational argument is the third answer to the questions raised by moral scepticism. The main contention is that we do as a matter of evident fact revise judgements of value in the light of experience. Moreover, some of the tricks of the economist's trade can help to elucidate the rationality of this activity of revision.

In talking of libertarians and egalitarians, of patriots and pacifists, and so on, we sometimes find ourselves speaking as if we believed that every individual holds only one value or at least is committed to one supreme value. This is one of those assumptions which have only to be stated to be seen to be false. For each of us has a hierarchy or constellation of values, each of which is given a relative weight. Indeed, it is the mark of the fanatic to cleave to one value regardless of the damage thereby done to other values. To speak of our value systems is a step in the right direction, although it probably ascribes formality to what is for most of us an improvised adjustment of partially conflicting rules of thumb. Even so, our attitude to values exemplifies a phenomenon not unknown to economists, namely, the trade-off. And this is what enables reason to enter into the making of judgements of value. For it will be of interest to us to know the terms of the trade-off between, say, equality and economic growth. Someone might advocate complete equality of incomes on the assumption that it could be achieved with only a marginal deterioration of the rate of economic growth. If, however, there were empirical evidence which suggested that the cost of equality would eventually be a uniform income equivalent to two-thirds of the current official poverty line, the would-be egalitarian would be likely to revise his or her opinion. Similar examples involving liberty and community or fellowship, autonomy and compassion, material progress and the environment or any other pair of rival values can easily be imagined. What appear to be cases of deadlock over values may turn out to be the product of assumptions about the terms of the relevant trade-offs made in ignorance of the facts.

Indifference analysis can be used to give more formal expression to these inklings of the role of reason in ethics. Its scope appears to be twofold: to clarify the logic of the situation and to provide the necessary empirical data. The moral agent can be regarded as a rational utility-maximizer, utility consisting of the manifestation of values in social and economic life, in customs and institutions. Suppose that one such agent is trying to resolve a conflict between moral principles: is the good society one which maximizes the average standard of living regardless of income distribution or one which enforces complete equality of income regardless of the standard of living everyone shares? The moral sceptic maintains that the agent's passions will incline him one way or the other. Depending on his subjective preferences, he will obtain the utility from a rich inegalitarian society, a poor egalitarian one or any of a range of societies combining living standards and income distribution in varying proportions. In terms of economic analysis, the moral agent is on the indifference curve U_1U_1 in the figure. Precisely where he is on U_1U_1 is, of course, indeterminate. This is the truth in moral scepticism, but it is far from being the whole truth.

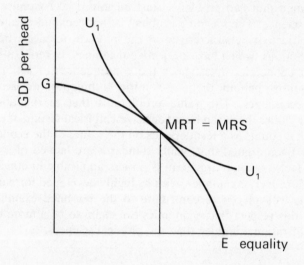

Figure 3   Consumer equilibrium and moral choice: the moral agent chooses rationally between GDP per head and equality; he gives each sufficient weight so that MRT = MRS.

The moral sceptic overlooks the fact that not all combinations of national income per head and income distribution are possible. What is needed is a production possibility frontier (PPF) for values (GE in the figure). The slope of the PPF is the marginal rate of transformation of equality into GDP per head (MRT); it expresses the opportunity cost of equalizing the distribution of income. The moral agent will be in equilibrium when MRT = MRS (the marginal rate of substitution of equality for GDP per head shown by U_1U_1). Thus, indifference theory gives formal expression to familiar aspects of the growth versus equality debate. For instance, in a society which already has a relatively equal distribution of income, only the fanatical egalitarian will be willing to bear the high opportunity cost in lower average living standards (or a reduced growth rate) of achieving complete equality, shown by the steep slope of the PPF as it approaches the *x*-axis. Conversely, in an extremely inegalitarian society with a very high average GDP, few would contest some measure of income redistribution, for the shallow gradient of the PPF near the *y*-axis indicates the low opportunity cost in forgone growth of greater equality. This is as far as abstract analysis can go. Empirical research is now required to plot the indifference curves and value production possibility frontiers for real-world societies, a task which is perfectly feasible in principle but of daunting magnitude and complexity in practice.

Conclusion

It has been argued that two problems must be solved if economics is to be presented as a science. The meaning problem is that economics cannot hope to attain the objectivity characteristic of the physical sciences, because it studies human actions, which have subjective meanings. In reply, it has been contended that economics investigates the consequences of actions rather than the intentions behind them. Scientific techniques are accordingly applicable in economics. The value problem is that in the absence of agreement over values there can be no decisive empirical testing of economic theories, for what counts as a test depends on the values of the economist. In response it has been argued that, while standards are indeed of a different category from facts, rational argument is no less applicable in ethics than in the sciences. Moreover, economics, with its highly developed formal analysis of trade-offs, is well placed to contribute to the reasoned examination of values. It is in this respect that economics can claim to be a more complete manifestation of rational inquiry than the physical sciences.

References

Barry, N. 1984 'The Austrian challenge to orthodoxy' *Economic Affairs* **4**(3) (April – June)

Coddington, A. 1983 *Keynesian Economics: The Search for First Principles* Allen and Unwin

Dawson, G. J. A. 1980 'The objectivity of economics' *Economics* **16**(1) (Spring)

Dawson, G. J. A. 1984a 'Less state, more welfare' *Economic Affairs* **4**(2) (January)

Dawson, G. J. A. 1984b 'Freedom, state and tradition' *The Salisbury Review* **2**(4) (July)

Hirst, P. H. 1974 *Knowledge and the Curriculum,* Routledge and Kegan Paul

Hume, D. 1966 *A Treatise on Human Nature* vol. 2, Dent

Lukes, S. 1982 'Relativism in its place', in M. Hollis and S. Lukes (eds.) *Rationality and Relativism* Blackwell

Mackie, J. L. 1977 *Ethics: Inventing Right and Wrong* Penguin

Minford, A. P. L. and Peel, D. 1983 *Rational Expectations and the New Macroeconomics* Martin Robertson

Mishan, E. 1983 'Not by economics alone' *The Salisbury Review* 1(4) (Summer)

Montefiore, A. C. 1966 'Fact, value and ideology', in B. A. O. Williams and A. C. Montefiore (eds.) *British Analytical Philosophy* Routledge and Kegan Paul

Parkin, M. and Bade, R. 1983 *Modern Macroeconomics* Philip Alan

Popper, K. R. 1966 *The Open Society and its Enemies* vol. 2, Routledge and Kegan Paul

Smith, G. 1982 'Wage inflation: a survey' in M. J. Artis, C. Green, D. Leslie and G. Smith (eds.) *Demand Management, Supply Constraints and Inflation* Manchester University Press

Weber, M. 1963 *The Sociology of Religion* Beacon

Winch, P. 1958 *The Idea of a Social Science* Routledge and Kegan Paul

The evolution of economic education thought as revealed through a history of the *Master Curriculum Guide in Economics: Framework for Teaching the Basic Concepts*, revised 1984

John M. Sumansky

Program Director, Joint Council on Economic Education, New York

This paper discusses the origin and evolution of economic education ideas contained in the *Master Curriculum Guide in Economics: Framework for Teaching the Basic Concepts*. Specific attention is focused on the contribution of economists to (1) identify a core set of economic concepts which made the task of teaching economics at the pre-college level manageable, (2) establish a place of importance for reasoned decision making, employing the tools of economics, in dealing with personal and social economic problems, and (3) develop a case for economic understanding based on the desirability of having an economically enlightened citizenry. The paper concludes with an outline of the future potential contribution of economists to ideas that are likely to influence the next edition of the Framework.

Introduction

One of the more remarkable features of the economic education movement in the US is that it continues to be driven by the discipline of economics; fuelled by the educational imperative rather than by some system-serving, apologetic effort to indoctrinate. This is not to say that unwholesome elements are not present in economic education in the US. Various special interest groups including business, labour, and private citizens sponsor various 'brands' of 'economic education' which suspiciously mirror the ideologies of the sponsors. Fortunately, such programmes do not attract much attention either in or out of the nation's schools. The single largest economic education programme – espousing education in economics rather than indoctrination – is that represented and led by the Joint Council on Economic Education (JCEE).

The dogged pursuit of education in economics by the JCEE and others affiliated to it, fending off the allure of easy dollars to sell this or that ideology, has resulted in a programme of economic education which blends, in symbiotic harmony, scholarly features with programme delivery. It *matters* what and how economics is taught at least as much as does delivering programmes and services to those who teach and learn. While it might be interesting and informative to describe in detail the evolution of the delivery system represented by the JCEE and its national network of affiliated state council and university centres, this paper focuses instead on the *evolution* of *thought* on several crucial economic education elements; including the objectives of the economic education movement, the targeting of programme efforts and the definition of the discipline in terms consistent with the intellectual characteristics of student learners.

The JCEE's bent towards education in economics has made it easy for the economics profession to have great influence on major programme thrusts. Nowhere is the influence of economists or evolution of thought on economic education better manifested than in the JCEE's publication entitled *Master Curriculum Guide in Economics: Framework for Teaching the Basic Concepts* (1984). Tracing the evolution of the Framework from its earliest predecessors enables us to see the direct influence and contribution of the economist to the more pragmatic programme delivery aspects of economic education.

This paper begins with the passage of the Employment Act of 1946 and surveys three documents which are the direct predecessors of the recently revised Framework (1984). The paper ends with a statement of potential future contributions by economists to the economic education programme.

Setting the mission for economic education

The passage of the Employment Act of 1946 was a great watershed in US economic life. This act empowered Congress to 'coordinate and utilize all its plans, functions, and resources for the purpose of creating and maintaining . . . maximum employment, production and purchasing power' (Employment Act of 1946, US Congress). The Act also created the President's Council of Economic Advisors, the first chairman of which was Edwin Nourse, who also served as Vice Chairman of the JCEE in its earliest days. Dr Nourse was an economist of considerable stature, and the impact of his views on the need for economic education were to be felt through to the present day. In a sense, this paper follows the progression of ideas he set in motion.

For example, in 1953 (four years after the incorporation of the JCEE) Nourse set out ideas which would persist throughout the history of the formal economic education programme. He wrote:

> the student should find in his school a place where his spontaneously formulated questions about economic matters will be put in a meaningful context, perhaps restated or broken down so as to help him discover for himself the path along which he will need to proceed if he is to get more useful answers to other and more intricate economic problems as he goes along life's path. [Furthermore], it is necessary . . . that some way be found through which the teacher can connect

the real and spontaneous questions of the student with the organized knowledge about the economic process which has been developed by the economics profession. Stated from the other side, if formal economics is to achieve usefulness by influencing behavior of workers, citizens, and businessmen, it must find simplified ways of organizing its data analysis; it must state its generalizations in terms that are meaningful to the practical problems of economic life as met by people whose training in economics does not go beyond high school. They are the group who will, in the last analysis determine how well or ill our economy actually works. (1953, pp. 297–8)

Nourse wrote this passage before the full ramifications of the Employment Act were realized. Twenty years later he observed a new reality which came to be known as the 'citizenship argument' for economic education. As a direct result of the Employment Act, he observed that the

role of the federal government in the economic life of its people had undergone substantial expansion. This freer use of the people's government to energize and stabilize the people's economic life unleashed new productive power and . . . exposes the people to new social and political dangers. Whatever problems continue to persist in our economy will need the thoughtful and enlightened considerations of citizens who have had economics courses in high school and college. Economic education of students provides the tools of analysis and reasoning which they must have in order to be counted upon to help solve the problems that will persist in their adult lives. (1966, p. 235)

Nourse's writings clearly implied several things about economics and economic education:

1 Economics is a life skill.

2 Economics has value not only as knowledge for its own sake, but also because of what it can contribute to the lives of people.

3 Economics should be, indeed, must be taught to those who do not go on to college.

4 Teachers must be helped to teach economics to students.

5 Economics must be simplified and made meaningful to life.

6 Economic reasoning is important.

7 Economic knowledge can contribute to an enlightened citizenry.

These were powerful ideas and they captured the essence of what was to become the single most influential programme in US economic education, that represented by the efforts of the JCEE.

Nourse was not alone in expressing the need for pre-college economics instruction. For example, in a 1961 article in the *American Economic Review*, G. L. Bach wrote, 'over the past few years, it has become increasingly obvious to the leaders in the profession that we could not indefinitely continue our hands-off policy toward economic education in the high schools'.

Such sentiments caused the American Economic Association, then presided over by President Theodore W. Schultz, to accept the challenge of the Committee on Economic Development to appoint a National Task Force on Economic Education. It was with this appointment that the feelings of the profession were translated into ideas that would result in actions designed to make a lasting impact on economic understanding.

The National Task Force Report

The Task Force, which comprised five leading economists and two leading educators,* was asked to 'describe the minimum understanding of economics essential for good citizenship and attainable by high school students, with the goal of providing helpful guidelines for high school teachers, administrators, and school boards' (National Task Force Report, 1961, p. 4).

The Task Force, in effect, embarked on the onerous task of outlining what aspects of the economics discipline *should* be taught at the pre-college level. They would need to specify the economic knowledge base consistent with economic literacy of the kind needed for *responsible* citizenship and *effective* participation in the economy.

Nourse's point of view was dominant in the Task Force's Report. The authors were in agreement that knowledge of *basic* economics was important, but so too were the thought processes that enabled one to *use* effectively that knowledge in various aspects of one's life as citizen, employee, business leader or consumer.

Nourse's focus on 'tools of analysis' is also to be found in the Task Force Report, and the term *concepts* is used to describe a 'kit of tools' which can be made available to students. While the Task Force reported that many economics concepts were complex, they pointed out that 'some of the most valuable and powerful ones are simple and easily accessible without extensive formal training in economics. These are the ones that should be emphasized in the high schools' (p. 17).

This statement suggested that the Task Force was going to set out the core of fundamental ideas in economics; the building blocks upon which more complex ideas could be built and which could be accumulated to result in more sophisticated comprehension of economic phenomena. The idea that economics could be simplified and in the process made more accessible to pre-college students was also consistent with Nourse's belief. It is also significant to note that economists began the work.

*George L. Bach, Chairman, Dean of the Graduate School of Industrial Administration, Carnegie Institute of Technology; Arno Bellack, Professor of Education, Columbia University; Lester Chandler, Chairman, Department of Economics, Princeton University; M. L. Frankel, Director, Joint Council on Economic Education; Robert A. Gordon, Chairman, Department of Economics, University of California, Berkeley; Ben Lewis, Chairman, Department of Economics, Oberlin College; Paul Samuelson, Professor of Economics, Massachusetts Institute of Technology; and Floyd Bond, Dean, School of Business, University of Michigan.

In somewhat broader terms, the Task Force took a fairly strong position on the importance of pre-college economics instruction. Economics *needed* to be taught to high school students because economic understanding would contribute to all aspects of their future lives. The Task Force was unanimous on this point also. The argument for pre-college economics instruction took on the flavour of an argument for the public provision of a 'merit good'. The Task Force had stated what was clearly a value judgement – students *ought* to know more economics because it was good for them and good for society, and it should not be left to the market to provide it.

The Task Force Report was a major accomplishment. Economics had been restated in more fundamental terms and presented as a guide to what students should know about economics by the time they left school. But it was incomplete. No guidance was offered as to how these knowledge levels were to be developed by high school students. In the words of the Task Force,

> [our] purpose [is] to suggest the institutions, facts, and analysis that are essential for a reasonable understanding of the modern economic system, *not* to suggest how the material should be presented in the high schools. We do not expect that all students in all schools will have the opportunity (and some will not have the ability) to absorb all that is suggested. *Each school and teacher will have to decide what should be taught, in what courses, and in what ways.* (pp. 22–3; my emphasis)

This statement is quite extraordinary given that the Task Force on the one hand concluded that teachers were very poorly equipped to teach economics, and then on the other thrust on to teachers the difficult task of deciding what economics ought to be taught and where and how to teach it! Nonetheless, by narrowing the scope of the discipline and providing a brief analysis of its basic building blocks, the Task Force made the task of pre-college instruction in economics at least appear to be manageable.

It was clear that Nourse had a great influence on the development of several key ideas – perhaps all that persist today. That influence can be seen in the Task Force's view that economic education should begin in the secondary school, that economics needed to be simplified and it was the economics profession which had the responsibility for doing so, that economics must be shown to have relevance to daily life, and that the need for economic education grew as the effects of the Employment Act of 1946, in Nourse's words, exposed people to 'new social and political dangers'. Finally, the Task Force Report furthered the idea of a 'disciplinary core', based on 'concepts' as its fundamental building blocks.

In retrospect, the Task Force Report contributed three main ideas: economics could be reduced to a relatively small number of ideas; the economist had a continuing responsibility to help the teacher; and knowing how to 'think through' economic problems was as important as knowing the analytical tools.

These ideas were nurtured and developed and later were either deepened and/or transformed as review of successive documents will reveal.

Teachers' Guides to DEEP – the Framework's predecessor

The late 1950s and early 1960s ushered in the JCEE's pilot testing of the schools-oriented Developmental Economic Education Program (DEEP). One major point of view held by the DEEP effort was that with proper help and guidance, local school systems could develop model curricula which could then be used by other school systems. However, experience with this effort showed that transferring model curricula simply would not work, given local control of local curriculum decision making (JCEE, 1969). One school system was not likely to adopt wholesale an entire curriculum developed at another location. Therefore, shortly after the release of the Task Force Report, the JCEE proceeded to develop a teacher-oriented document based on the National Task Force Report designed to support the fledgling DEEP. The Guides were intended to inform the curriculum rather than to define it. This document was actually two documents: *Teachers' Guide to Developmental Economic Education Program: Part I, Economic Ideas and Concepts* and *Part II, Suggestions for Grade Placement and Development of Economic Ideas and Concepts* (1964).

The intention of Part I of the Teachers' Guide was to develop further the economic concepts dealt with in the Task Force Report 'so that teachers might more easily rely upon it to enhance *their own* understanding of economics' (p. iii; my emphasis). Part I was to be an economics primer for teachers and it discusses more than 135 economic concepts in 46 pages, and it does so with great aplomb.

However, this Guide differs strikingly from its immediate predecessor in several respects:

1 The notion of economic concepts is emphasized. Unlike the Task Force Report, which dwelt at length on various 'problems' and 'topics', a concerted effort is made to identify key *ideas* that underlie sophisticated economic phenomena.

2 Part I does not lay any claim whatever to being a curriculum document. Rather, its stated objective is to help improve teachers' economic understanding. The second goal, to aid curriculum groups, was left for a second volume (Part II). (This pattern, economics in one volume, curriculum in another, is one that persisted over the years.)

3 Noticeably absent from Part I is a discussion of 'rational decision making', even though it held a fairly prominent place in the Task Force Report.

The Teachers' Guides to DEEP were major documents which today are known to but a few in economic education. This is unfortunate, especially since the two guides taken together represented a major advance in thinking about economic education. Not only could economics be reduced to core ideas, but these could be broken down still further and taught to students of all ages. While Part I did not go nearly far enough in reducing the number of key ideas (recall that more than 135 ideas are listed in the table of contents), it did succeed in separating concepts from their problem context.

The Teachers' Guides to DEEP were quite well received in the nation's schools. They represented a transition phase between the Task Force Report and the present-day version of the Framework, which has come to have a life of its own, separate from that of the curriculum applications guides. In retrospect, these two volumes were very good pieces of work. Yet curiously enough, when one reads the next two editions of the Framework, no mention is made of them. In fact, in the early 1970s, when the JCEE embarked on its Master Curriculum Guide project, the Framework pays recognition to the Task Force Report rather than to the two Teachers' Guides to DEEP.

The first Framework (1977)

The JCEE's Master Curriculum project was an effort to produce a series of guides to economics in the curriculum appropriate to different grade levels. The Master Curriculum project would refine Part I of the DEEP Guides and expand Part II into multiple volumes. The anchor volume of the series, entitled *A Framework for Teaching Economics: Basic Concepts* (JCEE, 1977) was begun in 1973 under the direction of S. Stowell Symmes of the JCEE. The writing committee was chaired by W. Lee Hansen, University of Wisconsin, and included G. L. Bach, a member of the 1960 Task Force; James Calderwood, a contributor to the first Task Force Report; and Phillip Saunders, Professor of Economics at Indiana University.

Even though the similarities between the Task Force Report, the DEEP Guides and the Framework are unmistakable and understandable, the Framework represented a major contribution to economic education. It clearly surpassed the Task Force Report and the DEEP Guides in several respects.

The Framework contained a clear separation of economic concepts from topics and issues. The idea that the substance and power of economics could be captured in a limited and manageable number of concepts was made pre-eminent. The list in Table 1 contrasts greatly with the 135 concepts discussed in the Guides. The Framework (1977) reduced the discipline of economics to 24 key ideas, fundamental to developing more sophisticated, mature economic thinking.

The Framework developed more fully the idea of rational (reasoned) decision making presented in the Task Force Report. The Task Force Report identified four stages of a rational choice model: define the problem, identify goals, choose from among alternatives, and analyse consequences (pp. 14–15). In the Framework, the idea is explicitly presented as a six-step model, containing the following steps: define the problem, identify goals, look for alternatives, identify requisite concepts, analyse consequences of each alternative, evaluate which alternative is best (p. 6).

The Framework authors offered this model as a way of helping students 'to organize their thinking as they address economic issues and questions' (p. 6). By contrast, the Task Force Report did nothing to show teachers and curriculum advisors *how* the model could be applied.

Table 1 List of concepts as presented in the 1977 Framework

The basic economic problem

1 Economic wants
2 Productive resources
3 Scarcity and choices
4 Opportunity costs and trade-offs
5 Marginalism and equilibrium

Economic systems

6 Nature and types of economic systems
7 Economic incentives
8 Specialization, comparative advantage and the division of labour
9 Voluntary exchange
10 Interdependence
11 Government intervention and regulation

Microeconomics: resource allocation and income distribution

12 Markets, supply and demand
13 The price mechanism
14 Competition and market structure
15 'Market failures': information costs, resource immobility, externalities, etc.
16 Income distribution and government redistribution

Macroeconomics: economic stability and growth

17 Aggregate supply and productive capacity
18 Aggregate demand: unemployment and inflation
19 Price level changes
20 Money and monetary policy
21 Fiscal policy: taxes, expenditures and transfers
22 Economic growth
23 Savings, investment and productivity

The world economy

24 International economics (uses the concepts above)

Source: From *Framework for Teaching Economics: Basic Concepts,* Joint Council on Economic Education, 1977, p. 9

Table 2   The reasoned approach and its use in the 1977 Framework

The model:	Application of model to	
six–step reasoned approach (p. 6)	case of scarce oil (p. 36)	case of airport congestion (p. 38)
1 Define problem 2 Identify goals 3 List alternatives 4 Identify relevant concepts 5 Analyse the consequences 6 Evaluate the alternatives	1 Basic facts 2 Consequences of oil rise 3 Two alternatives and analysis of their effects 4 Evaluating the alternative 5 Conclusion	1 Define problem 2 Specify goals 3 Analyse 4 Use results to evaluate options 5 Decide

Source: Data from *Framework for Teaching Economics: Basic Concepts,* Joint Council on Economic Education, 1977, pp. 6, 36, 38

In spite of the Framework's fine effort to illustrate how a reasoned approach could be used to develop an understanding of the issues of coffee prices and airport congestion, the reasoned approach did not appear explicitly and was not applied consistently enough to make a real impression on the user of the Framework. For example, Table 2 compares the six-step reasoned approach appearing on p. 6, with the approaches employed to discuss issues near the end of the Framework (pp. 36–51).

While each case as presented does employ an example of a 'reasoned approach', a clear and consistent use of the model developed earlier could have had much more impact had it been applied faithfully. The reasoned approach is not highlighted enough in the case discussion, thereby giving readers the impression that it is unimportant.

The final similarity between the Task Force Report and the Framework, and perhaps the most unfortunate one, is that the Framework avoids the question of how teachers were to translate the economic knowledge so well defined in the Framework into classroom practice. Note the tone of the following statements which appear in the Framework:

> . . . nothing prevents teachers who understand and want to incorporate other [than the most basic] concepts from doing so . . . all of [the] concepts should be introduced into the K–12 curriculum at some point. *We leave it to the curriculum resource groups to indicate the sequencing and grade placement of the various concepts.* (p. 7; my emphasis)

This is an unfortunate statement because the Framework's stated purpose on p. 1, is that 'this guide is primarily for curriculum resource groups whose task is to spell out the grade placement and most appropriate methods for teaching those concepts in grades K–12'.

My own view is that the statement of purpose was in error. As with Part I of the DEEP Teachers' Guide, the Framework was intended to be an economics primer for teachers. This intent is made clear later in the Framework's statement of purpose. The authors write that the Framework is an 'attempt to build on the Task Force Report to specify the essential structure and content of economics that should be learned'.

From 1977 until 1984, the impact of the Framework has been significant, but not without controversy. For example, because the Framework defined economics as that branch of the social sciences which deals with how people use productive resources to satisfy their wants, one critic, Boyer (1978), took the view that the presence of this definition was a clear sign that the JCEE *favoured* this 'kind' of economics. He regarded other similar definitions as clear evidence that the JCEE was pandering to special interest groups, especially business interests.

Boyer writes that the Framework is a good example of using the 'disciplines and structure of knowledge concept of education which takes the conventional academic principles of economics as the basis for education and excludes the realities of the economic decisions that are being made in the "outside" world' (1978, p. 31). To Boyer this is a clear signal that the Framework does not wish to come to grips with the 'evil' of the profit motive, and instead of alerting students to its evils, encourages value judgements which accept the existing system. 'This kind of economic education is faithful to the dominant ideology of the American business community, the government, and the majority of academic economists', he writes (p. 31).

If Boyer's criticisms of the Framework were true, then big business should have been especially pleased at the 'profit motive' section in the Framework. However, in the confidential reviews of the Framework sent to the JCEE, several major US corporations in fact took umbrage at the treatment of several economic concepts. One held strongly that greater emphasis should have been given to profits and their 'importance in determining efficiency'. Another major US corporation writes,

> the concept of 'profit' is inadequate as discussed on pages 13 and 34. There is no description of the use of profit for such things as shareholders' dividends and what this does to provide capital to preserve the financial health of the business. Those still under the delusion that profits are surplus money that are pocketed or wasted by executives will find very little to refute this.

Other specific examples could be cited, but nearly all corporations who critiqued the Framework felt that it did not treat profits as favourably as they would have liked.

Academic and business critics were not the only groups to take exception to things they found in the Framework. Organized labour was among them. One major US trade union wrote a strongly worded letter to the JCEE stating that they found a 'most serious problem' with the way the Framework handled the topics of full employment and economic systems, not to mention international trade. The unions were most concerned that full employment was listed as an economic goal, rather than as a social goal. They write, 'the full employment goal should be stated in human terms as that of making sure jobs are available for people who are willing and able to work'. The Framework, through its mistreatment of these topics, 'misled the reader'.

While it would be both interesting and informative to continue to list specific objections to the Framework, suffice it to say that the JCEE's spirits were buoyed with each additional piece of criticism. Criticisms from the left and right suggested that it was in the middle. Perhaps the Framework had charted the correct path.

In spite of the fact that the 1977 Framework represented a major contribution of economists to economic education by narrowing the scope of the discipline, teachers reading it could not help but feel uneasy with the idea that they were more or less left to their own devices to translate the ideas into classroom practice. The intellectual distance between the Framework and the Strategies Guides* for teaching concepts at various grade levels (which were to follow), was simply too great.

What the Framework did contribute was a clear statement of the decision-making model. The impact of this idea was to be seen in many other curriculum materials appearing in economic education developed after the Framework. In effect, the 'reasoning model' had been raised to equality with the analytical tools.

As the years since publication of the original Framework progressed and more and more Strategies Guides developed, pressures began to mount to revise the Framework. The pressures came from several sources. One was certainly from economics itself. The discipline had been through some upheaval in the late 1970s and early 1980s. Statements about economics and even some concept definitions presented in the Framework were thought to be a bit too self-serving. Two examples of such statements are: 'although economists now believe they now have the knowledge and tools to prevent, for example, massive economic depressions . . .', and 'few could deny the need for economizing through government action . . .' (p. 3).

A second source of pressure came from economic educators. Much greater reliance was coming to be placed on the Strategies Guides and many called for a Framework which more closely related to them. Besides, they argued, we have more than a half a decade's experience with the Strategies Guides and Framework, experience which ought to be called upon and used to strengthen the Framework.

Third, in the early 1980s, research on learning and instruction as it related to economic education began to establish itself as a major source of nourishment to economic education. More researchers were beginning to look at how economic knowledge was accumulated – especially among younger students. In 1982 a national symposium on learning theory and economic education was held in the US†. Learning theory research became a permanent feature of the national economic education effort, providing new insights into developing a Framework that presented the best thinking of what

*Published by the JCEE as Part II of the *Master Curriculum Guide in Economics* (see References).

†*National Symposium on Learning Theory and Economic Education* conducted by the Joint Council on Economic Education, sponsored by the Calvin K. Kazanjian Economics Foundation, Chicago, Illinois, May 1982.

concepts are, and how students of varying ages learn them. If the Framework was to be strengthened as a teacher/curriculum resource tool, it was clear that learning/instruction theory issues were going to have to be addressed.

In anticipation of revising the 1977 Framework, a leading US education scholar, Dr Merlin Wittrock, was commissioned to review the 1977 Framework and discover from what and how it was written, what 'learning theory' if any was being subscribed to and if it was compatible with present education knowledge.

The study by Dr Wittrock concluded that the Framework was a classic example of cognitive learning theory. The Framework did not treat concept learning as learning for its own sake, but rather because concept knowledge contributed to understanding. Two particular statements found in the Framework typified the Framework's cognitive learning theory bent: 'economic concepts are most important in promoting economic understanding among our students' (JCEE, 1977, p. 6), and 'the essence of economic understanding lies in being able to make sense out of an unfolding array of economic issues coming to our attention' (JCEE, 1977, p. 4).

What Wittrock found in his review of the 1977 Framework was a subscription to cognitive learning theory which emphasized the learning of facts and concepts ordered in a systematic and logical way designed to enhance understanding (Wittrock, 1982). Secure in the knowledge that a sound 'learning theory' was present in the 1977 Framework, work began on its revision.

Master Curriculum Guide in Economics: Framework for Teaching the Basic Concepts (JCEE, 1984)

Twenty-three years had passed since the publication of the National Task Force Report and seven had gone by since the publication of the 1977 Framework when the revised edition of the Framework (1984) was released. The evolution of thought on economic education is perhaps best underscored by focusing on changed emphasis, additions and/or deletions found in the 1984 Framework.

The role of the Framework is unchanged   Clearly, the 1977 Framework had assumed a central role in the development of economic education curriculum materials both within the JCEE's publication programme and by private publishers. Numerous private, commercial texts appeared on the market with explicit indicators of having been directly influenced by the Framework. Thus it was not the intent of the 1984 Framework to tamper with success. The 1984 Framework, like its predecessor, defines and describes the 'concepts that . . . are most useful in achieving a larger educational objective – that of enabling students, by the time they leave secondary school, to understand enough economics to make reasoned judgements about economic questions' (JCEE, 1984, p. 1).

The 1984 Framework as a curriculum document The 1984 Framework continues to identify curriculum groups as its target audience. But unlike its predecessors, the 1984 Framework makes several important attempts to help curriculum people and to link the Framework document directly to the Strategies Guides. Absent from the 1984 document is the statement found in the 1977 document to the effect that 'we leave it to the curriculum resource groups to indicate the sequencing and grade placement of the various concepts' (JCEE, 1977, p. 7). In place of this statement, several major sections were added to help teachers and resource people.

On p. 10, an introductory statement on the nature of economic concepts is presented which clearly reflects the influence of individuals interested in learning/instructional theory. This statement is the first attempt in the Framework to suggest that all concepts are not equal in terms of their complexity and ability to be learned by students of different ages.

The 1984 Framework goes further along these lines and deals extensively with the issue of the grade placement of concepts. Section VI (pp. 67–71) is a marked departure from previous documents in that a laudable effort is made to suggest the ways and means of translating discrete pieces of economic knowledge (concepts) into classroom practice and activity. This section deals not only with the curriculum context of economic instruction, but also with the very nature of economic concepts.

A concerted attempt is made to link concepts to a sound cognitive theory of instruction involving active learners and their life experiences.

The Framework reflects the state of economic knowledge In the 1977 Framework, the statement on the state of economic understanding was overwhelmingly an optimistic one. In 1984, a new paragraph appears which reads:

> As this is being written, the discipline of economics is alive with controversy and discontent: there are calls for making economic analysis more realistic by explicitly introducing more aspects of political science, sociology, psychology, law and the like into the discipline; there exists dissatisfaction with how much economists have contributed to improving the economy's performance. (JCEE, 1984, p. 5)

The decision-making model Over the years since the National Task Force Report, the decision-making model has grown in relative clarity and importance. Although quite well developed, though inadequately applied in the 1977 document, the heightened prominence of the decision-making model in the 1984 Framework is noticeable not so much in terms of its exposition in the early sections, but rather in its explicit application in Section VI, 'Applying economic understanding to specific issues' (pp. 58–66). In this section, unlike the 1977 version, a five-step decision-making grid is applied faithfully and most effectively to two cases. *Use* of the 'reasoned approach' in the 1984 Framework succeeds in doing what Nourse had suggested over 30 years ago, merging the analytical tools with an economic reasoning process. In the 1984 Framework they are presented together as partners and made explicit.

Measurement concepts and methods   During the late 1970s and early 1980s in the US, much public alarm was generated about inadequate mathematics skills of students, and many teacher-reviewers of the 1977 Framework were critical because they felt the 1977 document gave only passing coverage to the measurement concepts and methods employed in describing, explaining, measuring and assessing economic phenomena. Whereas the 1977 Framework spent but one page describing seven important measurement concepts, the 1984 Framework devotes six and a half pages to illustrating and defining the use of important measurement tools like tables, graphs, charts, ratios, percentages, index numbers and averages.

The evolution of thought – a restrospective

In retrospect, what started out as a project to define minimum knowledge levels for high school graduates to attain, ended up by identifying the core ideas of economics. Certainly the two are not inconsistent with one another. Indeed, it can be argued that, given the very restrictive realities of education at pre-college levels, the identification of core ideas has made it much easier to decide what of economics is most important to teach. There is little doubt that the early work by Nourse which placed the burden of simplifying the discipline on the economist was taken up by the profession and developed into the central theme of economic education – the concepts are the tools one needs to be economically literate.

But beyond that theme, the notion of a 'way of thinking' grew in relative importance and emphasis. Even though it disappeared for a short while in the DEEP Teachers' Guides, the 'reasoning or problem-solving model' has now been raised to a stature almost equal in importance to the concepts themselves.

The somewhat more subtle idea, that economic understanding was crucial to good citizenship, continues to reappear throughout the literature in economic education. Nourse argued quite convincingly that because government was given broad powers over the use of common resources, democracy and common sense demanded that citizens be able to interpret government policies and that votes be cast wisely. Unlike some other early ideas in economic education, the citizenship argument persists mostly on its emotional appeal. The operational significance of the citizenship argument remains undefined. It remains unclear exactly how economic knowledge gets translated into better behaviour of private citizens, if at all.

The next edition of the Framework

At the risk of overstating the significance of the Framework, I suggest that the concepts presented in the 1984 document are akin to having identified what physicists in the 1950s believed to be the smallest particles of matter – the atom with protons, neutrons, and electrons. Their research technologies prevented them from knowing that even finer decompositions of the atom were but a few years away. Up, down and charmed quarks would soon become part of everyday language.

Such is the case with economics and its concepts. Research programmes and technologies are pushing the discipline toward a search for the 'quarks of economics'. The search will be spearheaded by economists who will decompose concepts even further and thereby expand greatly the prospect of teaching only the most elemental ideas to young students. These are sure to make a significant impact on future editions of the Framework.

Also on the very near horizon is a move by several US scholars to establish economic education as a discipline in its own right, complete with its own unique set of ideas, philosophies and methodologies. The extent to which they succeed will determine the future course of the Framework.

Significant new research programmes are under way in which 'expert' and 'novice' thinking in economics is being explored. The definition of how experts and novices differ in approaches to solving economic problems would be most revealing and is likely to have great influence on the next Framework.

The increased use of the computer both as instructional and research tool is opening up vistas not yet imagined. The prospects for defining optimal sequences for acquiring economic knowledge are greatly expanded through computer-based research projects.

Finally, the continuing efforts to establish new relevance for the discipline of economics, perhaps increasingly in a multi-disciplinary context, will most assuredly lead to changes in the way in which economic knowledge is described and explained in future Frameworks. As in the past, future Frameworks will mirror the best thought of economists, which in turn will reflect on the programme and practice of economic education.

References

Bach, G. L. 1961 'Economics in the high schools: the responsibility of the profession' *American Economic Review* **51**(2) p. 582

Boyer, W. H. 1978 'Economic miseducation' *Educational Perspectives* **17**(2)

Joint Council on Economic Education 1964 *Teachers' Guide to Developmental Economic Education Program, Part I – Economic Ideas and Concepts; Part II – Suggestions for Grade Placement and Development of Economic Ideas and Concepts*

Joint Council on Economic Education 1969 *DEEP 1969 – Perspectives on a Five Year Experiment in Curriculum Change*

Joint Council on Economic Education 1977 *Master Curriculum Guide in Economics for the Nation's Schools, Part I – A Framework for Teaching Economics: Basic Concepts*

Joint Council on Economic Education 1984 *Master Curriculum Guide in Economics: Framework for Teaching the Basic Concepts*

Joint Council on Economic Education (various years) *Master Curriculum Guide in Economics, Part II – Strategies for Teaching the Basic Concepts, K–3, 4–6, 7–9, Social Studies, World History*, etc.

National Task Force on Economic Education 1961 *Economic Education in the Schools: Report of the National Task Force* Committee for Economic Development, New York

Nourse, E. 1953 'Persistent problems of the American economy' *Social Education* **17** (November)

Nourse, E. 1966 'Current aspects of our persistent economic problems' *Social Education* **30**(4) (April)

Wittrock, M. 1982, unpublished letter to the Joint Council on Economic Education, October 8

Towards a new paradigm for the teaching of economics

Ron Wilkes

Lecturer in Education, University of Queensland, Australia

The results of 'practical curriculum theorizing' in the development of a
new paradigm for the teaching of economics are presented. This
paradigm is based on a three-dimensional model of a mixed economy,
derived from the system of national accounts, and provides
simultaneously a new structure for both the content and the pedagogy of
economics education in secondary schools.

Introduction

When Sir Richard Stone won the Nobel Memorial Prize in Economic Science
in 1984, the challenge presented to educators in the field of economics
contained a mixture of elements, both familiar and unusual. The familiar lies
in the broad question that must be asked repeatedly in relation to the highest
achievements in any discipline, namely: to what extent and in what forms
should these ideas be incorporated in the teaching of the subject at various
levels? The unusual aspect of Sir Richard Stone's award is that the work for
which it was given (the development of the system of national accounts) is far
from new, having originated during the Second World War and having
become a seemingly self-evident way of perceiving the structure of national
economies and of measuring aggregate economic performance. The formal
recognition of fundamentals that have long been taken for granted might
appear to present no challenge at all to educators. However, in this paper it
will be argued that the well established system of national accounts provides a
basis for the development of a new paradigm for economics education.

The paradigm to be presented is the result of a particular mode of
theoretical research, which has been called practical curriculum theorizing
(Gough, 1984), and which can be traced to the writings of John Dewey and
other progressive educators (Schubert *et alia*, 1984). The main characteristics
of this type of theorizing, as described by Schwab (1969) and subsequently
expanded upon by others such as Reid (1978, 1981), are that it is exploratory,
eclectic, tolerant of ambiguity, open-ended, pragmatic in relating knowledge
to policy and action, and open to dialogue. According to Reid (1981),

practical curriculum theorizing, from what he terms the deliberative perspective, contains assumptions broadly allied to those of classical liberalism, including 'a belief in the possibility of improvement through working with present institutions, and in the efficacy of consensual approaches to the identification and solution of problems'.

Several problems in the teaching of economics in Australian secondary schools were the starting point for the theorizing whose results are reported in this paper. Attempts to resolve these problems have given rise to a proposed paradigm for economics education that differs from present practice both in its pedagogical form and in the following aspects of content. First, it is focused primarily on the economy; second, its sequencing of content is unorthodox; and third, it contains provision for the development of a range of learning outcomes not confined to the cognitive domain. Each of these points will be considered before proceeding to a description of the paradigm.

The economy as prime focus – a problem of priorities

When I began to teach economics in high schools at the beginning of the 1960s, the opening chapter of what was then the only suitable textbook (Nankervis, 1961) was entitled 'The national income' and dealt with aggregates derived from the system of national accounts. The other textbook from which I taught (Drohan and Day, 1964) was organized around a series of circular flow diagrams which had the effect of establishing and subsequently reinforcing a model of the economy as the context for learning. In the preface to his book, Nankervis justified the approach via national economic aggregates in the following terms: 'It is more *realistic* and *intelligible* than is an introduction through abstract laws and principles and is more *interesting* than would be a long preamble concerning the historical background' (my emphasis). In my opinion this sort of clear-headed wisdom has been lost, at least in Australia, under the influence of the movement that has treated economics as a set of scientific principles capable of application to all forms of human behaviour, under conditions of choice (e.g. Mundell, 1968; McKenzie and Tullock, 1975; North and Miller, 1978). Among the many topics tackled through this approach are the economics of crime, the economics of sexual behaviour and the economics of euphoria. As an exercise in territorial expansion the movement was interesting, but for secondary school economics it has served little purpose, tending to trivialize both the topics treated from an economic perspective and the economic concepts employed in the analysis.

When committees of economists and educators have deliberated on the aims and scope of economics education in schools they have always given high priority to an understanding of how the national economy works (National Task Force on Economic Education, 1961; Report of a Joint Committee of the Royal Economic Society, The Association of University Teachers of Economics and The Economics Association, 1973; Hansen *et alia*, 1977). This consensus is sufficient justification for treating the national economy as an important topic for curriculum innovation. However, I would go further than this consensus position. After 25 years in the field, I am firmly of the opinion that, in terms of subject matter, the economy is much more important than anything else and that our curricula should be designed to reflect this priority. This view is summed up in a slogan that has emerged from a debate about school economics in one Australian state. 'Economy, not economics' is the catch-phrase of those who believe that the economy is not just an important topic but the most (or even the only) important topic.

The problem of content sequence

It is a commonplace remark that in economics everything is related to everything else. This notion is applicable both at a theoretical level within the various paradigms of the discipline and at a functional level in terms of the workings of a national economy, or even the world economy. As Galbraith has observed, 'economic and political life is a matrix in which each part interconnects with the others and all move together' (Galbraith and Salinger, 1978).

This characteristic of the subject has been widely recognized in writings about its place in the school curriculum, including reference to economics as a seamless web of reasoning (California State Department of Education, 1961), as a cohesive perspective (Calderwood *et alia,* 1970) and as a field in which there is danger of students placing topics in separate mental pigeon holes (Assistant Masters Association, 1971). The interrelatedness of economic ideas and the holistic nature of the subject stand out as considerations of fundamental importance for curriculum development.

Any working system may be viewed as consisting of three levels: its elements or component parts, the relationships that link those elements and the organizational principles pertaining to the operation of the entire system. In teaching about the economy as a working system, one major danger is of excessive fragmentation; of failure to achieve adequate integration within and across these levels. This problem of compartmentalization of knowledge is exacerbated by the extended linear sequences that are typically involved in instruction, whether of intermittent time allocation or of the conventional topic-by-topic style of progression adopted in textbooks. We cannot teach about the economy as a totality and so we teach it bit by bit, which puts us on the path to overemphasis of parts to the neglect of the whole. One solution to this problem is a whole–part–whole pattern of alternation, an approach employed in some textbooks and one used in classrooms by skilful teachers. The concept of advance organizer (Ausubel, 1968) constitutes a well estab-lished basis for this type of approach, but no set of theoretical propositions can definitively resolve such practical questions as the exact nature of the pattern of alternation between whole and part, the scale on which particular attempts are made to deal with the interrelatedness of things and the overall balance between the larger picture and the smaller elements that go to make it up.

At a later stage, this paper deals with an approach to teaching about the economy in which both substantively and procedurally, i.e. in terms of a direct connection between content and method, the whole is always visible, not merely as a backdrop but as a structural feature of the economics classroom and its activities. This is achieved through a three-dimensional explanatory model of an economy.

The problem of the range of learning outcomes

Commentators on secondary education in Australia have often noted its narrow, academic character (e.g. Connell *et alia,* 1975; Kirby, 1984), generally in the course of discussion of Australia's relatively low rates of participation in full-time education beyond the years of compulsory schooling. Several research studies have found strong evidence that community expectations of schools extend well beyond the traditional area of fostering achievement in the cognitive domain (e.g. Collins and Hughes, 1979; Campbell and Robinson, 1979). Piper (1977) found that in the field of social education, specific items of learning from the traditionally dominant area of knowledge and understanding of facts, explanations and theories were rated as substantially less important than items such as

learning how to communicate with others

learning how to relate to others

learning how to co-operate with others

learning how to make considered choices

developing a sense of personal identity

developing a sense of personal worth

developing a sense of personal integrity

knowing where and how to obtain information when it is needed

learning how to interpret information and argument

learning how to make considered value judgements

In a research study of my own (Wilkes, 1979), Piper's model of learning about society was applied specifically to economics education. The general pattern of results obtained by Piper was replicated in each of the groups surveyed, i.e. members of the business community, recent school leavers, teachers of economics and teachers of commercial subjects. In questions dealing with what should be the content of economics education for all secondary school students, each of the items listed above was given higher priority by teachers than any of the 20 major topics taught in school economics courses.

One kind of response to the call for schools to adopt a wider conception of learning is to put the difficult items, such as those listed above, in the 'too hard basket', particularly in relation to problems of evaluating student performance. Alternatively, such items have sometimes been dismissed on the grounds of an alleged 'motherhood' character, by which is meant that they are unlikely to be opposed by anyone, but at the same time are easily rejected by those unable, or unwilling, to take on the duties of conceiving, delivering and nurturing. In my view, these responses are an evasion of responsibility.

Under prevailing conditions of continuing high youth unemployment in all developed nations, combined with widespread restructuring of national economies, there are particular responsibilities on economics educators to strengthen the educational aspect of their field in an effort to achieve two goals, each of which has been substantially increased in importance by the social stresses of the times.

First, the need for the young to understand how their nation's economy operates, both in itself and in relation to the world economy, is of the utmost importance. Through such understanding they will realize that the economy is not some malevolent machine that arbitrarily imposes severe penalties on powerless individuals, but simply one arena of a tough, competitive world in which a particular kind of rationality operates. As a matter of both individual and societal need, this sort of basic economic understanding should be seen as the right of all. Universal economic literacy demonstrated in terms of specified performance standards and acquired under conditions of mastery learning is what economics *educators* should be pursuing, in the cognitive domain. Steps in this direction are outlined in the next section of this paper.

A second and closely related challenge to widen and strengthen the education side of the field lies in the affective domain. I see value in exploring the possibility of promoting positive attitudes towards the economy and towards oneself as an individual actor within it. In the economic sphere there is a strong tendency for beliefs about the future to operate as self-fulfilling prophecies. For the sake of problematical but important societal processes, economics education could be used in an attempt to replace the all-too-prevalent mood of economic fatalism with one of optimism, suitably tempered by realism. By providing for non-traditional patterns of classroom organization in which learning could be stimulating, satisfying, co-operative and free of the threat of failure, the general model of economics education whose description follows has potential to facilitate the development of a variety of worthwhile affective objectives.

A proposed model for teaching an understanding of the economy

Simplified systems of national accounts have a lengthy history in Australian secondary school economics, but, in general, they have been taught only as a particular kind of introduction to macroeconomic issues towards the end of a two-year course. This paper contains a proposal for their use as a central activity over an extended time period either at an early stage in an economics course or as a modular unit in some other kind of course. The simplified accounts used by Downing (1964) and by Williams and Stevenson (1975) are the basis for the specific suggestions in this paper. These accounts constitute a highly condensed, but still fairly intricate, means of classifying and summarizing the flow of economic activity. As such, they are a formalized content structure, but they also provide a basis for structuring pedagogy through the physical arrangement of the classroom as well as learning activities.

Imagine setting up a model of the economy based on the national accounts. This can be achieved effectively in a classroom in which a central table is surrounded by five other tables. On the central table is a box whose function is to symbolize the process of production in a mixed economy. Four of the other tables represent sectors of the economy – households, corporate trading enterprises (including public enterprises), government, and overseas – while the fifth represents the process of capital formation as expressed in the National Capital Account. The items of aggregate expenditure (consumption by households, consumption by government, private and public enterprise investment in the Capital Account, public works investment, also in the Capital Account, and exports minus imports* from the overseas sector) are shown as labels on pieces of string coming from their respective tables and entering the top of the central box. From the bottom of this box the items of aggregate income generated by production are shown by further labelled pieces of string going to the tables corresponding to the appropriate sectors. These forms of income are wages and salaries, and profits of unincorporated enterprises, which go to households, profits of corporate trading enterprises, and indirect taxes. Presented in this way, these items from the Production Account serve as a three-dimensional model of the basic economic activity contained in the identity of aggregate expenditure, production and income.

Given the linkages described above, each of the five peripheral tables will be linked by at least one item (in the form of a labelled piece of string) to production, in the central position. From a content perspective, these five tables represent parts of the economy, but from a pedagogical point of view they constitute work stations in the classroom, in what amounts to a deliberately decentralized learning environment. Once students are allocated to these work stations the basis exists for an assortment of classroom activities in which the focus alternates between part and whole, but the whole is always a visible context for learning through the three-dimensional model. Thus, structures derived from those of the highest standing in the discipline serve to structure both content and method in the economics classroom.

Of course, the workings of an economy are far from fully articulated in what has been described so far. To complete the picture of dealings between

*In preliminary trials, imports have been shown running in parallel with exports, but with a different colour string. As an extension of this colour coding of imports it would be possible to wind string or a lighter thread of the same colour around the line for each of the items of both consumption and investment expenditure to indicate that they contain an import component.

sectors and to show the relationship of saving and investment that is implicit in the Capital Account, and whose locus in the model is the work station for capital formation, would require time and careful attention. In preliminary trials, inter-sector transfers, comprised of taxation, social welfare, dividends and sector savings that flow to finance investment through the work station for capital formation, have been added to the model using a different colour for both the pieces of string and the labels so as to distinguish transfer items from those that relate directly to production. An equally important area for gradual development would be the exploration of the nature of the somewhat mysterious box whose function is to symbolize the process of production. Unpacking and demystifying the box would be a strong theme on which the teacher could play, with variations that could be large in number and wide in scope. For example, productivity in production, labour force participation and changes in manufacturing industry are some of the topics that could be tackled at various levels of sophistication and in various ways. Group activities at the work stations would serve various purposes. In terms of understanding the model of the economy, one type of activity would be to undertake detailed investigations pertaining to the sectors, the results of which would be reported to the whole class in plenary sessions. This would involve students in developing skills of finding, processing and presenting information. There is scope for use of microcomputers in these activities, not as an adjunct to orthodox teaching methods, but as an integral part of the planned learning strategies.

In the kind of learning environment envisaged, self-development and development of social skills would also be facilitated. These areas would need to be specified and communicated to students so as to make them conscious of the teacher's intentions. A range of evaluation techniques would need to be used to gauge progress in these fields.

As an alternative to having students work on teacher-supplied tasks, it would be possible to have each group formulate questions to ask of other groups. This process of generating questions would help to prevent students from concentrating too much on their particular sector to the neglect of other parts of the whole picture. There is also scope for such inter-group questions to be generated and answered spontaneously in plenary sessions, thereby adding a dimension to the skill development area. Rotation of groups could be employed to give students experience of all sectors.

In plenary sessions, either under teacher direction or in conjunction with group or individual work, a number of activities could be undertaken to complete the study of the economy. It is important to note that each of these activities could be undertaken at various levels of complexity and difficulty, making the overall approach suitable for lower ability senior secondary students at one end of the continuum and mainstream academic students at the other, in the 15–16 years age group. The brief description of activities that follows is geared mainly to the needs and capabilities of lower ability students.

1 Economic indicators The conventional indicators of the state of an economy could be introduced, either singly or as a group. Most of these indicators can be related directly to production and thus are analogous to making measurements of the state of health of the activity inside the central box in the model. For example, in examining the rate of unemployment the question becomes one of the extent to which the process of production is taking up available labour. In the case of inflation the question is, 'How stable are the prices of the goods and services that pass to consumers through production?' Similar treatment could be given to other well-known indicators such as retail trade, new motor vehicles, new dwellings and private investment. Financial indicators such as interest rates and bank deposits might be presented as measures of the state of the financial sector and given a physical location at the table for capital formation. In the same manner, exchange rate movements and foreign trade performance are measures relating to and located in the overseas sector.

2 Feeling the pulse of the economy The existence of a physical model with linkages that represent quantifiable flows of activity offers scope for taking students through the ups and downs of national economic performance. From their various vantage points at the work stations and in contact with some of the lines symbolizing flows, students would be able to 'feel' and report on prevailing conditions as the model of the economy is taken, for example, through a hypothetical boom period followed by a slump. Similarly, the class could work through a period of sustained economic growth or declining international competitiveness, looking directly in each case at the symbols of the economic flows through which such things are experienced. Any kind of impact on the economy could be considered in this 'abstracted operational' setting, in a manner not necessarily confined to the essentially positivistic and quantitative economic considerations that the model is designed to explicate. Matters of a structural kind such as the relative size of government and private sectors or factor shares of aggregate income could also be brought clearly into focus in the context of this classroom model of the economy.

3 Driving forces in an economy Once the parts of an economy and their relation to one another become clear to students, questions could be posed on what makes the system work. This leads into basic features of a market economy as well as to questions on the role of government in a mixed economy. The motives, intentions and actions of decision makers in the economy, both individual and group, would need to be examined. As well as leading into the whole field of economic decision making, this opens up the area of inter-group conflict in economic and related political spheres.

4 Co-ordination in an economy Another important focus of attention in relation to the whole system is the question of the means by which the economy is able to achieve its degree of smoothness of operation. In other words, what are the means of co-ordination of economic activity? This question would be answered in terms of the nature and functions of the price mechanism, together with instances of government intervention in particular situations.

5 Controversial issues Because the whole is always visible, and is often the focus of teaching and learning, any controversial issue or any current news item that involves the economy could be introduced at any time without being irrelevant. The structures of learning would be such as to provide a stable and permanent context in which anything economic has obvious relevance.

6 Economic values and goals What are the important economic values and goals in our society and how well are they being achieved? The model provides a suitable setting for considering such questions. Helburn and Davis (1982, p. 7) suggest that the relevant values and goals are freedom, justice, progress, stability, security and efficiency. Consideration of the questions posed above could occur at various levels of sophistication and could be tackled in a variety of ways. However, regardless of the approach adopted, it would be necessary to consider the normative side of the issues raised in considering such values and goals.

A few observations need to be made on the differences between the model described above and circular flow representations of the economy, whether in the form of diagrams or of physical models with liquid flows. The most obvious point is that the proposed three-dimensional model is integral to the physical arrangement of the classroom and to the related teaching and learning activities. Apart from this pedagogical difference there are three distinctive features of the work-station model in terms of its economics. First, the macroeconomic equation

$$E = O = Y$$

is a central point in it. Second, it is an expandable model in the sense that the items included from the national accounts could be either increased beyond those mentioned in this simplified treatment or kept to a workable minimum in order to focus on what is judged to be relevant at the time. Finally, the process of production is visibly at the heart of the model.

Evaluation of student performance

No discussion of a paradigm for teaching would be complete without considering evaluation, but since the overall proposal is a rough sketch rather than a blueprint, the treatment of this area is necessarily impressionistic and deals with only a few major points.

As mentioned previously, the general model presented in this paper is meant to be adaptable to a variety of settings. In mainstream courses, in which teachers are constrained by the requirements of a grading system, it could be expected that norm-referenced evaluation of student performance would continue to be the dominant pattern. If, on the other hand, teachers were free from such constraints, then the way would be clear for a greater degree of diversification of both learning experiences and their evaluation.

This could lead to the use of a comprehensive set of techniques such as tests, checklists, attitude inventories, direct observation and both self- and peer-evaluation by students. In such a setting, evaluation of student performance could make use of criterion-referenced approaches and could adopt profiles and descriptive feedback along the lines advocated by Rowntree (1977).

Two additional features of the proposed paradigm would make it desirable to depart from conventional patterns of achievement testing. First, the use of group and individual tasks at the various work stations would mean that students engage in a number of different sets of learning activities and this would reduce the common ground, in terms of content covered, on which to base norm-referenced testing. Second, to the extent that there is a common core of cognitive learning, stemming from the goal of imparting to all students an understanding of how the economy works, a model of mastery learning and testing as presented by Bloom (1976) would be preferable. In an ideal classroom, microcomputers would be used to facilitate the operation of the mastery learning model.

Even from this brief discussion, it is clear that this proposed new paradigm for the teaching of economics would require a radical reconstruction of evaluation practices so as to bring them into line with the diversity and emphasis of the teaching and learning.

Economics and the economy

An economic literacy of the kind whose scope and mode of development has been described would be a worthy part of the general education of all secondary school students. Indeed, I would argue that nothing more from the discipline is needed as a contribution to effective citizenship. In the particular case of those students who wish to proceed further with the study of economics, I can think of no better foundation than an understanding of how a mixed economy works.

As long ago as 1964, Schwab wrote that

> a pluralism of substantive structures and of bodies of knowledge is characteristic of the social sciences generally and of many humane studies. There is more than one body of economic knowledge. . . . If we dogmatically select one of several bodies of theory in a given field and dogmatically teach this as the truth about its subject matter, we shall create division and failure of communication among our citizens.

If Schwab's observation about economics was true in 1964, how much more so would it be today? And how shall we decide which brand of economics to teach, or how to present competing brands to students in a manner that is both intelligible and intellectually honest? Helburn and Davis (1982, pp. 28–43) examine four competing paradigms of economics, each of which seeks to explain the operation of a developed economy in the non-communist world. Such major issues as the beliefs, assumptions, goals and policy measures of each of these paradigms should be examined and would be enhanced as areas of study by an understanding of the economy as a working system acquired through the approach described earlier in this paper. Such a sequence would serve the purpose of genuine pluralism.

I believe that we would have better economics in our economics education if we began with a structured study of how an economy works. The structures of national accounts are not the only ones available for this purpose but their particular appeal lies in their potential for structuring both pedagogy and subject matter. For too long economics education has had more rigour in its economics than in its education. Content has dominated and method has been the fleeting afterthought; the area of minor concern in which there are always options. If we take our educational responsibilities seriously, this situation must change. To correct the imbalance we need more rigour on the education side. Not just the rigour associated with attempts to be scientific in specific tasks, but in conceptualizing, planning and executing pedagogy, in all its dimensions and on the largest possible scale.

As a research exercise, such a task is, in the first instance, theoretical rather than empirical. Perhaps a final statement on this distinction should be left to the highly distinguished economist, Stone, whose work gave rise to the practical curriculum theorizing reported in this paper:

> The past has seen many a battle of giants over the respective merits of the theoretical and empirical approaches to economic problems. There are signs that this false dichotomy is becoming recognized more and more widely for what it is. Only recently 'measurement without theory' has been condemned in high places and if theory without measurement has not come in explicitly for similar treatment the shift of interest as evidenced in the literature leaves the unexpressed views little in doubt. These remarks . . . are intended to combat the notion that either theory by itself or empiricism by itself has exclusive charge of the key to useful knowledge. . . . The great need is to get the specialists in different aspects of a given field to work together, show a reasonable understanding of and respect for one another's disciplines and advance to problems which none could tackle on his own. (Stone, 1951)

Only one thing needs to be added. Although economics education is an area of both theoretical and empirical research, it is, above all, a field that is practical. In such a setting, the ultimate value of any kind of research will depend directly on its utility to practitioners.

References

Assistant Masters Association 1971 *The Teaching of Economics in Secondary Schools* Cambridge University Press, p. 77

Ausubel, D. P. 1968 *Educational Psychology: A Cognitive View* Holt Rinehart and Winston, New York

Bloom, B. S. 1976 *Human Characteristics and School Learning* McGraw-Hill, New York

Calderwood, J. D., Lawrence, J. D. and Maher, J. E. 1970 *Economics in the Curriculum* Wiley, New York

California State Department of Education 1961 *Report of the State Central Committee on Social Studies to the California State Curriculum Commission* Sacramento, p. 26

Campbell, W. J. and Robinson, N. M. 1979 *What Australian Society Expects of its Schools, Teachers and Teaching* Department of Education, University of Queensland

Collins, C. W. and Hughes, P. W. 1979 'Expectations of secondary schools: a study of the views of students, teachers and parents' in B. R. Williams (ed.) *Education, Training and Employment: Report of the Committee of Inquiry into Education and Training* vol. 2, Australian Government Publishing Service, Canberra

Connell, W. F., Stroobant, R. E., Sinclair, K. E., Connell, R. W. and Rogers, K. W. 1975 *12 to 20: Studies of City Youth* Hicks Smith, Sydney

Downing, R. I. 1964 *National Income and Social Accounts* Melbourne University Press, Melbourne

Drohan, N. T. and Day, J. H. 1964 *Australian Economic Framework* Cassell, Melbourne

Galbraith, J. K. and Salinger, N. 1978 *Almost Everyone's Guide to Economics* Houghton Mifflin, Boston, p. 140

Gough, N. 1984 'Practical curriculum theorizing' *Curriculum Perspectives* **4**(1) pp. 65–9

Hansen, W. L., Bach, G. L., Calderwood, J. D. and Saunders, P. 1977 *Master Curriculum Guide in Economics for the Nation's Schools, Part 1 – A Framework for Teaching Economics: Basic Concepts* Joint Council on Economic Education, New York, pp. 27–8

Helburn, S. W. and Davis, J. E. 1982 *Preparing to Teach Economics: Approaches and Resources* Social Science Education Consortium, Boulder, Colorado

Kirby, M. 1984 'Fumbling with the key' *Education News* **18**(11) pp. 24–7

McKenzie, R. B. and Tullock, G. 1975 *The New World of Economics* Irwin, Illinois

Mundell, R. A. 1968 *Man and Economics* McGraw-Hill, New York

Nankervis, F. T. 1961 *Descriptive Economics* Longman, Melbourne

National Task Force on Economic Education 1961 *Economic Education in the Schools: Report of the National Task Force* Committee for Economic Development, New York

North, D. C. and Miller, R. L. 1978 *The Economics of Public Issues* Harper and Row, New York

Piper, K. 1977 *Essential Learning About Society* Australian Council for Educational Research, Melbourne

Reid, W. A. 1978 *Thinking About the Curriculum* Routledge and Kegan Paul

Reid, W. A. 1981 'The deliberative approach to the study of the curriculum and its relation to critical pluralism' in M. Lawn and L. Barton (eds.) *Rethinking Curriculum Studies* Croom Helm, p. 167

Report of a Joint Committee of The Royal Economic Society, The Association of University Teachers of Economics and The Economics Association 1973 *The Teaching of Economics in Schools* Macmillan, p. 11

Rowntree, D. 1977 *Assessing Students* Harper and Row

Schwab, J. J. 1964 'Structure of the disciplines: meanings and significances' in A. W. Ford and L. Pugno (eds.) *The Structure of Knowledge and the Curriculum* Rand McNally, Chicago, p. 29

Schwab, J. J. 1969 'The practical: a language for curriculum' *School Review* **78**(V) pp. 1–24

Schubert, W. H., Wills, G. H. and Short, E. C. 1984 'Curriculum theorizing: an emergent form of curriculum studies in the United States' *Curriculum Perspectives* **4**(1) pp. 69–74

Stone, R. 1951 *The Role of Measurement in Economics* Cambridge University Press, p. 82

Wilkes, R. 1979 *Economic Education in the Secondary Curriculum – An Evaluation* Australian Chamber of Commerce, Canberra

Williams, M. and Stevenson, K. 1975 *Australia: A Mixed Economy* Longman, Melbourne

Response *William Baird*

Two of the papers (Sumansky, Wilkes) consider the nature of economic knowledge in the context of a single paradigm. Dawson, in his discussion of the meaning and the value problems, appears to adopt a single paradigm when treating the latter and might be said to have looked for a single paradigm for the former. Helburn investigates several paradigms, each with its associated Scientific Research Programme (SRP), in an attempt to show how the tentativeness of knowledge might be brought to the attention of students.

The nature of developmental problems varies within the set of papers. Helburn and Sumansky report in terms of a framework of externally developed guidance when outlining the nature of economics as it is presented to students. Dawson says little about this, perhaps because the material of the paper is at an earlier stage of development. Wilkes outlines the barest skeleton upon which teachers are free to build up the flesh in a holistic treatment of the discipline.

The main theme of Dawson's paper is that knowledge of the discipline can best be advanced by separation of the meaning problem from the value problem. This view is worthy of discussion despite the fact that the illustrations from economics do not appear to correspond closely with the points made. One suspects that, if there were no Keynesian/monetarist controversy, the meaning problem would have been treated in terms of a single macroeconomic paradigm – one which contained an adequate treatment of expectations. Treatment of the value problem is coherent if and only if it is assumed that there exists a unique, well-behaved utilitarian social welfare function – the paradigm implicit to this part of the paper. It would therefore appear that, if the separate treatment of these two problems advances knowledge, the search must be for two paradigms. Once these have been agreed and developed, there would need to be adequate and equal provision of materials for each. One remains unhappy that the form of the paradigm used in the context of the value problem rules out game theory, mixed strategies and the possibility of irreconcilable conflicts of interest.

Helburn seeks to demonstrate the aspects of the discipline which might be used to make students aware of the tentativeness of knowledge, but the rigorous treatment of the argument tends to obscure a fundamental question. The question is, How many of the several hard core bases need to be brought to the attention of students in order to achieve the desired objective? And, as a follow-up, How are these to be presented? If they are presented in paradigm form, possibly in the context of comparative economics, Will the objective be lost because students will treat these as more dogma? One suspects that the objective may be achieved only if the bases for alternative SRPs are developed in the context of the students' own economy. Here, as with Dawson, lies an area requiring equal provision of materials. The fundamental difference between the two papers is that Helburn would require this development in both the meaning and the value divisions.

On the problems which arise in operating within an externally determined framework, Helburn indicates the frustrations of working to a narrowly defined paradigm. The suggestions for improvements to the situation are detailed and fit into the argument deployed in this note.

Sumansky's paper gives an invaluable insight into the development and evolution of an external framework, which is to be used both by teachers who have a background in economics and those who have no experience in the subject. It is unlikely that the use of a single paradigm was adopted to meet the needs of the non-economists, but it may be that the evolution and refinement – with all the increasing detail – was, in part, conditioned by their needs. The effect would appear to have been a tightening up of the paradigm, leading to an increased tendency for students to learn the catechism, rather than begin to appreciate the tentativeness of knowledge. One fresh point which comes to light is that development of the subject is not dependent on resources alone, it also depends on the quality of the teaching stock.

Quality of the teaching stock and the nature and extent of resources available are of prime importance when one seeks to evaluate the claims made in Wilkes' paper. There is no doubt that a holistic approach would be an improvement on compartmentalized presentation of the recognized content of an economics course. Wilkes writes in terms of a single paradigm, but this point transcends the constraint in the paper. Given the dominant SRP in the profession, there should be little difficulty in providing the teacher with the appropriate (simplified) information required to develop the model. The ability to sandwich relevant microeconomic concepts as the model develops, so that an integrated whole is created, depends on the quality of the teaching stock. (Some sandwiches are better with the filling removed!)

On movement out of the cognitive domain, particularly in the direction of inculcating (self-fulfilling) beliefs about the future, one has serious reservations. For there to be any real prospect of success, the implication must be that the whole is to be presented in terms of the prevailing orthodoxy. It would appear that this paper offers a 'new' paradigm which will only be able to achieve its objectives if the socially acceptable paradigm is built on to the skeletal outline. One must ask the question, Is this 'new' paradigm a paradigm? Or does the paper merely present a novel way of treating that paradigm for which most information exists in the students' economy?

This leads to a more general question: If a loosely structured framework is provided by an external source, will this not have the inevitable consequence that a narrow, one-paradigm approach will be adopted, since information will tend to reinforce the socially acceptable?

To conclude, if one wishes to display economics in all its scientific glory to students, the main drift of the arguments in the papers would appear to be that:

1 an external source should determine the paradigms to be used

2 the same source should develop materials relevant to each of the paradigms, in terms of the students' own economy

3 a holistic treatment should be adopted

4 the tentativeness of knowledge should be displayed

5 the teaching stock should be appropriately trained.

Response *Robert Wilson*

The paper presented by Wilkes is directed towards three fundamental questions: what should we teach, who should we teach it to, and how should student progress be assessed? The ideas presented and the issues raised in this one paper alone provide sufficient material for a series of three-day conferences.

Wilkes considers his proposed three-dimensional model to be a significant improvement on the standard circular flow representations of the economy which appear in most economics textbooks. From the verbal description given of the classroom model of an economy, it is hard to regard it as three-dimensional: the vertical plane appears to be an artefact, achieved by allowing aggregate expenditure items and aggregate income items to enter the top and bottom of a box rather than via its sides. This device does not appear to have any significance in terms of what might be inferred from it about the operation of an economy. If production is to be the core of the model, then a genuine vertical component can be introduced by depicting primary, secondary and tertiary production as a three-tiered block. As described, it is hard to see the model in visual terms as more instructive and self-explanatory than a well-produced and properly colour-coded chart.

Wilkes sees the placing of production 'visibly at the heart of the model' as an unambiguous virtue. Given the overriding aim of bringing pupils to an understanding of how an economic system works by highlighting driving forces within an economy, other possible models come to mind. The centre core could well be government; the peripheral tables/work centres might then be production, consumption, saving, investment, exporting and importing. Such a model could be used to support the contention that in a modern economy (and particularly in the modern, mixed, industrial economy which Wilkes is considering) the major driving force is government, through the influence that governments exert on the activities which constitute the work stations. Regrettably, this revised model still gives a poor representation of 'driving' in that it is static. If a model is to be a permanent feature of a classroom, why not mechanize it and replace string and sticky tape with belts and pulleys; with government in the form of a (small) electric motor? Is this not an area in which computer graphics have a part to play?

Wilkes' adoption of activity-centres with pupils assigned different tasks is to be welcomed. It is not immediately obvious how the work stations suggested by Wilkes permit groups to commence activity at each of them simultaneously right from the outset of a course. It is hard to see, for example, how a group will make much headway with regard to capital formation until they have come to an understanding of the work being undertaken at the households table. An alternative approach to group activity is to assign each group an activity related to a common theme rather than five disparate ones. For example, one group might be trying to discover why firms seek to gain control of rival firms whilst another group investigates the way in which firms raise finance – two separate aspects of production. It will be interesting to see where Wilkes' trail eventually leads him.

The measurement of attitudes to economics issues: some problems

David J. Whitehead

Senior Lecturer in Education (Economics), University of London Institute of Education

This chapter describes one aspect of a research project conducted between 1980 and 1984. In 1980–81, an Economics Attitude Scale was devised and piloted. The final version was administered as a pre- and post-test to a random sample of school students in 1981 and 1983. Factor analysis of the pre-test responses to the attitude scale revealed that its factorial structure was complicated, and generated the hypothesis that attitudes to economic issues might not be unidimensional along a radical/conservative continuum. This hypothesis was supported by analysis of the post-test responses, which revealed that the underlying structure of the scale had changed. This raised doubts about the validity of earlier researchers' attempts to measure attitude changes simply by summating scores on a scale, without investigating any possible change in its factorial structure.

Introduction

The measurement of attitude change is deeply problematic. Attitudes are often embedded in the individual's personality, having been formed in early childhood. They may be firmly established by the time a child reaches secondary school (Piper, 1976). What appears to be attitude change may merely represent adjustment or accommodation to what is expected of pupils by their teachers.

Attitudes tend to cluster together, rather than existing as independent entities. Any particular attitude has complex and subtle connections with other attitudes on a variety of different issues. Changes in attitudes are likely to occur very slowly, if at all, and such changes may be difficult to detect, harder still to measure.

Despite this general stability in attitudes, on an individual basis they may be liable to fluctuate somewhat unpredictably. Some people may always know exactly where they stand on a given issue; others may tend to waver or be ambivalent. Such changes present very difficult problems in interpreting responses to attitude measures, especially with respect to the complex task of trying to measure *changes* in attitudes.

Attitudes are not purely affective. They are a tangled skein of cognitive and affective elements, which vary over time between individuals and from one attitude to another. In attempting to measure attitudes and attitude change, there is always the danger of confusing differences or changes in the mixture of cognitive and affective elements in the attitude with differences or changes in the attitude itself. Not only is it questionable whether any individual attitude measure represents a true measure: any perceived change in attitude that has been measured may be a genuine measure of change, or it may simply be an effect of the unreliability of the instrument. One aspect of this unreliability is the tendency of respondents to give the answers they feel are expected of them, rather than those which represent their real attitudes.

Another problem related to the validity of attitude measures is that with most scales that are practical for classroom use, only *verbal* attitudes may be measured, and verbal attitudes may have a very low correlation with actual behaviour (not that behaviour necessarily reflects 'real attitudes' any more than verbal expression of them does).

Perhaps one reason why so little progress has been made in the development of knowledge concerning attitudes has been the extreme complexity of both the conceptual and measurement aspects briefly outlined above. It is important that these reservations are borne in mind when considering the implications of the research reported in this chapter.

The main impression to be derived from earlier research into the affective domain in economics education is the extreme complexity of measuring attitude change in economics students. At least three different kinds of attitude change have been measured: attitudes towards the subject itself; movement of attitudes towards those held by professional economists ('economic sophistication'); and liberal–radical/conservative attitudes.

Many of the studies are unsatisfactory in their research design. Frequently, non-random samples are selected, no control groups are set up, and results cannot be generalized. The typical experiment involves the 'treatment' of a one-semester economics principles course, but rarely is any information provided about the content or objectives of such a course. It must be doubted whether substantial attitude change could be observable after such a short period of time. Moreover, no attempts are made to assess whether any measured attitude changes persist over time, for example over the six months following the end of the economics course. The impression is frequently gained that researchers are interested in other variables than attitudes, and that the attitude instrument is added to spice the experiment, without too much effort or ingenuity being devoted to its development. It is difficult to avoid the conclusion that after 20 years of research in this field, it is not possible to make any authoritative pronouncement about the various hypotheses concerning attitudes of economics students tested in the reported studies.

Most studies of attitude change in economics students have assumed that the scale which was developed and employed measured only one underlying dimension which explained the correlations between the items constituting the scale. Whether this is in fact the case is seldom put to the test by factor analysis of the items. If such studies employ a scale which is assumed to be unidimensional, though factor analysis would suggest multidimensionality, then this casts serious doubt on the scale's validity and on the interpretation of differences in scores. In other words, the researcher would be assuming, for example, that differences in scale scores are due to the degree of presence of liberalism/conservatism, when factor analysis would have led him to infer that several attitudes underlay the scale, and that such simplistic interpretations were inadmissible. Also, the reported reliability indices assume unidimensionality.

A more rigorous procedure to adopt with any attitude scale would be to find a factor analytic model that best predicted the observed correlation matrix (Kim and Mueller, 1978). If more than one significant factor emerges, this may raise the suspicion that the attitudes that the scale is attempting to assess are not unidimensional. It is commonly assumed that economic attitudes and their expression are polarized (Kerlinger, 1980). It is accepted that economic radicals and economic conservatives exist, and that each extreme group has a set of appropriate attitudes. But it is generally assumed, according to Kerlinger, that whatever the radical believes is opposed by the conservative and his beliefs and vice versa. If this were the case, then one might postulate one general factor of attitudes with radical views on economic issues at one end of the continuum and conservative views on economic issues at the other (and similarly with people, groups, items and scales). While it is generally recognized by social scientists that many attitudes are multidimensional, the 'bipolarity assumption' often applies to economic issues. In other words, with economic issues it is assumed that opposed ideas will be found with respect to each issue. Such opposed ideas would be manifested by positive and negative correlations between responses to radical and conservative attitude statements and by positive and negative factor loadings. However, Kerlinger disputed this bipolarity assumption. He postulated that there are a number of first-order social attitude factors, that each of these factors is basically liberal (L) or conservative (C) (the terms liberal and conservative are used in the American context), but not both, with only L or C items on it, and that second-order factor analysis of the correlations among the factors will yield an orthogonal two-factor structure, one second-order factor having L factors and the other C factors (Kerlinger, 1967).

Subsequent analysis of covariance structure tests of the implications of the two-factor hypothesis and the one-factor bipolarity hypothesis resulted in more support for the former than for the latter (Kerlinger, 1980). But Kerlinger stressed that this did not mean that the bipolar model was never applicable to social attitudes, merely that it was misguided to assume that they were always bipolar. Another reservation is that bipolar attitude structure may exist under certain sampling conditions, for example, if the sample has a large proportion of extreme respondents from the radical and conservative wings.

Factor analysis of a scale

The importance of Kerlinger's work is to emphasize to attitude scale constructors the possibility that the attitudes being measured by their scale may not be unidimensional. This possibility was investigated with an attitude scale developed in 1981–82 as an instrument for measuring the change in A level economics students' attitudes to statements on economic issues (see Appendix). The responses to a pre-test administered to 1006 students were factor analysed. The experimental group consisted of 523 students who were beginning an A level economics course in 1981, and the control group comprised 483 students of A level subjects other than economics.

Factor analysis was used to investigate whether the set of 18 items which constituted the Attitude Scale could be considered to be indicators of one or more than one latent variable. Examination of the correlation matrix might reveal positive relationships among the 18 items, but closer analysis might indicate that relationships between the items within some subsets were present, whilst no relationships between subsets were evident. A factor analytic approach might then be used to discover whether these observed correlations could be explained by a small number of factors. For example, instead of a unidimensional radical/conservative continuum, one might find additional factors which differentiated between economic issues and political/social issues.

The assumption of unidimensionality underlay the initial development of the scale. Almost none of the earlier research had even addressed itself to this problem; unidimensionality was normally taken for granted. (One exception is Laracuente, in Dawson, 1980.) If it had been anticipated that possibly more than one underlying factor contributed to the responses to the scale, factor analysis might then have been used as an exploratory device, to ascertain the minimum number of latent variables that could account for the observed covariation, and as a means of exploring the data. It might have even proved possible to construct a unidimensional scale (a factor scale) if the pilot scales had been factor analysed.

Nevertheless, the use of factor analysis in this case was in one sense exploratory, even though it was applied after the final scale had been constructed. It might be regarded as having performed the function of testing the hypothesis of unidimensionality. If the factor analysis were to indicate that more than one factor existed, this would not render the scale nugatory, but would necessitate a more sophisticated subsequent analysis of the results of the pre- and post-tests, since multidimensionality would introduce many complex problems of interpretation.

Factor analysis of the pre-test results from September 1981 indicated that doubts about the unidimensionality of the Attitude Scale were justified. This implied that it would not be possible to make a direct comparison of pre- and post-test scores on the scale in order to measure attitude change. Moreover, it might be the case that the underlying attitude dimensions changed over the period of the study, so that factor 1 at the post-test stage might not consist of exactly the same cluster of items as it did at the pre-test. Such complications would make interpretation of the results extremely hazardous.

The next phase in the examination of the scale was to factor analyse the pre-test responses. The purpose of analysing the 1006 respondents' scores on individual scale items was to ascertain whether the scale exhibited uni-dimensionality, or whether it contained within it a number of separate attitude dimensions.

The data matrix consisted of the responses of the 1006 subjects to the 18 items of the Attitude Scale. A correlation matrix was obtained using the SPSS FACTOR program (Nie *et alia,* 1975); it indicated that a number of the inter-item correlations were low. Thus the initial doubt concerning a unifying concept running through the items was confirmed. The most unsatisfactory item from this aspect was item 15, which did not correlate with any other item. The item was: 'High tax rates have removed the incentive to work hard'. Presumably responses to this statement were not strongly related to any of the underlying factors measuring various attitude dimensions, though the item's face validity with respect to a conservative economic viewpoint would seem to be quite high. Next, the varimax rotated factor loadings were examined, using 0.30 as the cut-off point for assessing the contribution of a factor to an item. (The only comparable research used a cut-off point of 0.25 (Mann and Fusfield, 1970).) Four initial factors were extracted, with an eigenvalue greater than 1.

This comprehensive factor analysis of the scale demonstrated that the hypothesis of unidimensionality with respect to the 18 items seemed unten-able. Certainly one principal factor could be distinguished, but the subsidiary factors seemed to be significant. The revelation of separate factors appeared to indicate different attitude dimensions, so that total scale scores could not support the weight of interpretation originally intended. Analysis of the pre-test data and of changes between pre-test and post-test data would have to be in terms of an individual factor, comprising a particular cluster of items.

Having appeared to have established multidimensionality (in the scale, but not necessarily in economic attitudes) it was decided to explore further the specificity and interpretation of the items by use of quartimax rotation. Quartimax rotation aims to reduce the complexity of a variable to the minimum, that is, to rotate the initial factors in such a way that a variable loads highly on one factor but almost zero on all others. It is important to note that since quartimax emphasizes simplification of the rows of the factor matrix, the first rotated factor tends to be a general factor (many variables tend to load highly on it) while subsequent factors tend to be subclusters of variables.

It was decided to rotate all 18 variables of the scale. Table 1 provides the quartimax rotated factor matrix, and Table 2 the eigenvalues of the factors extracted together with the percentage variation explained by each.

From Table 1 it may be seen that most items loaded on factor 1. The only items which did not load at least 0.3 on factor 1 were variables 5 and 15. These both loaded on to factor 2. A number of items loaded significantly on more

Table 1   Quartimax rotated factor matrix after rotation with Kaiser normalization

	Factor 1	Factor 2	Factor 3	Factor 4
ISC1	0.40841	0.49217	-0.21279	-0.12926
ISC2	0.33635	0.44846	-0.14756	-0.02468
ISC3	0.42579	-0.09374	0.04215	0.06451
ISC4	0.48051	0.14938	-0.12911	-0.12045
ISC5	0.18222	0.39586	0.13520	0.01785
ISC6	0.40597	-0.03069	-0.04854	-0.02328
ISC7	0.41021	-0.06437	-0.05141	0.09918
ISC8	0.57785	0.27116	-0.02169	-0.18675
ISC9	0.45254	0.02682	0.05797	-0.05048
ISC10	0.46587	0.13015	0.01359	0.16220
ISC11	0.51548	0.06022	0.15952	0.00371
ISC12	0.33339	0.07094	0.05593	0.37806
ISC13	0.38826	0.19424	0.50429	0.01703
ISC14	0.37503	0.15433	-0.18666	0.21472
ISC15	0.03411	0.32240	0.06968	0.11098
ISC16	0.35053	-0.12094	0.06842	-0.01292
ISC17	0.37310	0.12106	-0.10526	0.27770
ISC18	0.40890	0.05465	0.21084	-0.17907

Table 2   Eigenvalues of factors extracted

Factor	Eigenvalue	Percentage of variation*	Cumulative percentage
1	3.24927	68.2	68.2
2	0.65691	13.8	82.0
3	0.48404	10.2	92.2
4	0.37348	7.8	100.0

*Percentage of explained variation for a four-factor solution.

than one factor, namely variables 1, 2, 12, 13. These complex items were eliminated. Given that variables 12 and 13 were the only items loading on factors 3 and 4, it was decided to run another factor analysis for a two-factor solution. This analysis employed varimax rotation with a two-factor solution on variables 3–11 and 14–18.

The varimax rotated factor matrix (two-factor solution) and eigenvalues for the factors extracted are presented in Tables 3 and 4. Of the 14 variables

Table 3   Varimax rotated factor matrix after rotation with Kaiser normalization: items 3–11, 14–18

	Factor 1	Factor 2
ISC3	0.46697	−0.03098
ISC4	0.40065	0.32325
ISC5	0.10505	0.34171
ISC6	0.40038	0.08035
ISC7	0.39749	0.06849
ISC8	0.48262	0.38085
ISC9	0.42589	0.16736
ISC10	0.42470	0.20597
ISC11	0.47565	0.20290
ISC14	0.31689	0.22576
ISC15	−0.04587	0.32219
ISC16	0.39281	−0.05687
ISC17	0.31197	0.23204
ISC18	0.35260	0.19574

Table 4   Eigenvalues of factors extracted: items 3–11, 14–18

Factor	Eigenvalue	Percentage of total variation	Cumulative percentage
1	3.18842	22.8	22.8
2	1.18389	8.5	31.2
3	1.09406	7.8	39.0
4	0.96614	6.9	45.9
5	0.90651	6.5	52.4
6	0.86157	6.2	58.6
7	0.84144	6.0	64.6
8	0.81248	5.8	70.4
9	0.76439	5.5	75.8
10	0.74579	5.3	81.2
11	0.69504	5.0	86.1
12	0.69049	4.9	91.1
13	0.66682	4.8	95.8
14	0.58297	4.2	100.0

retained in the analysis, only two (5 and 15) loaded only on factor 2. All the other items loaded more than 0.3 on to factor 1.

Some reservations may be expressed about the factor analytic approach adopted. If the students taking the pre-test Attitude Scale did not have a mature, consistent set of attitudes towards economic issues, with respect to the conservative/radical dimension, then it might be that the factor analysis and reliability tests provided too critical a picture of the scale. This possibility would have been avoided if the scale had been trialled and validated not on beginning students of economics but on those completing their course.

Moreover, factor analysis of the scale items does not provide unambiguous evidence of the theoretical dimensionality underlying the attitude statements. The observed bifactorial structure might be a function of a single theoretical dimension which has been contaminated by a method artifact (such as response set), rather than indicative of two separate, substantive dimensions (Carmines and Zeller, 1979). Thus in principle, the factor analysis leaves the theoretical structure of economic attitudes indeterminate.

In order to investigate the unidimensionality of the scale in the light of the post-test data, the responses to the scale items given in May 1983 were factor analysed. The data matrices consisted of six groups: the whole sample at the pre-test stage, divided into experimental (A) and control (B) groups; the attrited sample of pre-test cases who also took the post-tests, again divided into experimental (C) and control (D) groups, and the groups which remained at the post-test stage (identical in composition to C and D). Correlation matrices were obtained through the SPSS FACTOR program. Next, the varimax rotated factor loadings were examined, using 0.30 as the cut-off point for assessing the contribution of a factor to an item. Table 5 gives the number of factors extracted for each group together with the percentages of variation explained by each factor.

Next, the first factor extracted for each group was analysed, to investigate which items loaded on it in each case. The results are presented in Table 6.

Items which loaded on both pre- and post-test experimental cases for whom complete information was available were 1, 4, 9, 10 and 11. Those which loaded similarly for the control group were 3, 6, 8, 9, 10, 14 and 16.

Next, an analysis was made of which items loaded on factor 2, to investigate the stability of the second factor extracted. The results are presented in Table 7.

It is possible for the experimental condition to exert an influence on the scale at various levels. The normal level investigated is changes in scores between pre- and post-tests attributable to the 'treatment'. But at a higher level, it may be that the teaching of economics changes the underlying factorial structure of the attitude statements in the test. If that were so, one would expect to obtain a different factorial structure for the experimental group than for the control group at the post-test stage.

In face validity terms, it could be argued that all 18 items permit responses from 'radical' to 'conservative'. So deviations from consistency as indicated by failure of an item to load on factor 1 may simply illustrate an individual's

Table 5　Factor loadings for the Attitude Scale

Cohort		Group size	Number of factors extracted	Percentage of total variation explained					
				F1	F2	F3	F4	F5	F6
A	⎤ pre	1006	5	21	8	7	6	6	
B	⎦	1006	5	23	8	7	6	6	
C	⎤ attrited	712	6	21	7	7	6	6	6
D	⎦ sample	712	5	24	8	7	6	6	
E	⎤ post	712	4	30	7	6	6		
F	⎦	712	3	34	8	6			

Table 6   Items loading on factor 1 for six groups

Items	A	B	C	D	E	F
1	0.55		0.36		0.54	0.46
2	0.63				0.58	
3		0.44		0.49		0.54
4			0.56		0.56	0.52
5	0.39					
6		0.45	0.32	0.52		0.44
7			0.39			0.55
8	0.43	0.40		0.44	0.53	0.63
9		0.42	0.39	0.42	0.52	0.70
10		0.37	0.34	0.41	0.30	0.54
11		0.31	0.32		0.32	0.54
12						0.37
13		0.31		0.31		
14				0.36		0.51
15						
16		0.43		0.35		0.40
17			0.47			0.39
18						0.30

Table 7   Items loading on factor 2

Group	Items loading 0.3 or more
A	3, 7, 8, 9, 11, 16
B	1, 2, 8
C	1, 2, 5, 8
D	1, 4, 8
E	2, 10, 12, 14, 17
F	1, 2, 5, 13, 14, 15, 17

lack of theoretical consistency in responding. This does not imply a criticism of individual respondents. Indeed, it may be that the study of economics develops a more complex appreciation of the issues and a reduced inclination to express polarized sentiments. Such a hypothesis receives support from Table 6, column F, which indicates that 14 items loaded on factor 1 for the control group at the post-test stage, whilst only seven loaded for the experimental group (column E). Support for the hypothesis that the teaching of economics changes the factorial structure of the scale is given by comparing columns C and E of Table 6. Whilst five items loaded on factor 1 for the experimental group, at both pre- and post-test stages (1, 4, 9, 10, 11), another five items loaded only at one stage (2, 6, 7, 8, 17). Items 6, 7 and 17 loaded only at the pre-test stage, items 2 and 8 only at the post-test stage. Particularly interesting is the inclusion of items 2 and 8 at the post-test stage. Both are concerned with the ownership of industry, and it may be that the teaching of economics sensitized students to the kind of analysis needed to make judgements about this sort of issue, whereas at the pre-test stage, they had no consistent viewpoint.

For the control group, no fewer than eight items loaded at one stage but not at the other, seven of the eight loading only at the post-test stage (13 pre; 1, 4, 7, 11, 12, 17, 18 post). It might be hypothesized that lack of exposure to economic analysis did not disturb a normal maturational trend towards consistent responses to statements on economic issues. In other words, such non-economics students might tend to respond to the statements from a more polarized political standpoint, whilst the economics students would tend to see much greater complexities and be much more hesitant in lumping together what they now conceive as disparate issues.

While the scale does seem to contain a general factor, it must be admitted that in aggregate, not many items contribute to it. From Table 6, it can be seen that nine of the 18 items feature twice or less from each group (2, 5, 7, 12, 13, 14, 15, 17, 18). Taking just the groups for whom complete data are available (C, D, E, F), the following items load 0.30 or more on factor 1 in at least three of the four columns: 1, 4, 6, 8, 9, 10, 11. It could be maintained that at least these items constitute a general factor. It also appears that considerable differences exist between the complete pre-test sample and those who remained at the post-test stage. For the experimental group, only one item loaded at the pre-test for both groups (A and C): item 1. However, for the control group, seven items loaded for both groups (B and D): 3, 6, 8, 9, 10, 13, 16.

To develop a theoretical explanation of the instability of the factorial structure over time is difficult. Nevertheless, it would be avoiding the issue to proceed through the usual stages of analysis unquestioningly (as was done in most of the earlier studies) on the assumption that the same factorial structure holds at both pre- and post-test stages. Almost all the empirical studies take as meaningful the comparison between group means with respect to the continuum implied in the underlying structure (such as radical/conservative attitudes to economics issues). But the experimental condition may actually be influencing the way in which attitudes are grouped and structured.

One indication of this possibility is that the number of factors extracted is reduced at the post-test stage. Inspection of Table 5 shows that for the experimental group, six factors are extracted at the pre-test stage, and four at the post-test; for the control group, five is reduced to three. Again, for groups C and D, 21 per cent and 24 per cent respectively of the variation in Attitude Scale scores is explained by the general factor 1, whilst for E and F (at the post-test stage), 30 per cent and 34 per cent are the respective figures. In all cases, the general first factor is predominant, and there is very little to choose between the subsidiary factors, on all of which items load between 6 and 8 per cent. Table 7 indicates that the second factor extracted for each group did not exhibit stability. Only two items, 1 and 2, appeared to load at all frequently on this factor. The small percentages of variation explained by each of the minor factors indicated that they might be discarded in subsequent analysis. While the detailed analysis of the factorial structure of the Attitude Scale may be viewed as excessively critical, it is important in that it establishes not only that the measurement of attitude change is extremely complex, but that it might for all practical purposes prove impossible. Though infrequently discussed, such issues should not be obscured or glossed over. It may be that the teaching of economics attempts to change students' perspective – or at least this may be an unintended but systematic outcome. In other words, the teaching may not simply move students along a continuum of knowledge and/or attitudes, but may alter the substructure of their understanding and attitudes. Ideas which they previously grouped together they may now separate, and similarities which they had originally ignored may now be apparent to them.

Whichever way the above statistics are interpreted, it appears that the basis of comparison is problematic. The first general factor is not common and stable between pre- and post-test for experimental and control groups. Indeed, only two items (9 and 10) load in all four cases.

Conclusion

It must be stressed again that it is not necessarily permissible to argue from the multidimensionality of the scale to the multidimensionality of attitudes in the student population. It is the characteristics of the instrument that have been analysed: though changes between pre- and post-test do imply some complexity in attitude structure.

As stated above, Kerlinger considered that a bipolar attitude structure might be more likely to be revealed for example if the sample had a large proportion of extreme respondents from the radical and conservative wings. It is unlikely that the samples used in this study corresponded to that description. In the rare cases where it was known to the researcher that a respondent was for example a militant conservative or radical, highly consistent responses of 1 s or 5 s on the Likert scale were displayed.

If the new methodological dimension of factor analysis had not been introduced for the examination of the scale, the finding that its use was problematic would not have been made. Further, if the study of changes in achievement is fraught with conceptual and practical difficulties, *a fortiori* the study of attitude change is highly complex, not least because any instrument is sampling a general attitude by means of only a very few items. The problems encountered in this research project ought to cause commentators to eschew the rash expression of generalizations about the effects of the study of economics on students' attitudes to economics issues.

Appendix: Economics Attitude Scale

1 Private enterprise is the most efficient economic system

2 Nationalization of more industries is likely to lead to inefficiency, bureaucracy and stagnation

3 It is up to the government to make sure that everyone has a secure job and a good standard of living

4 Capitalism is immoral because it exploits the worker by failing to give him full value for his productive labour

5 The individual should be free of government influence, free to make money and spend it as he/she likes

6 Poverty would be almost completely abolished if we made certain basic changes in our social and economic system

7 The tax system in the UK today is unfair to the poor

8 Our most important industries ought to be owned and/or controlled by society as a whole, for the good of all the people, rather than by private business seeking profits

9 Each person has a right to demand an equal share of the assets of the economy

10 Trade unions have a beneficial influence on the economy

11 Private property is too unequally distributed in Britain

12 People should be encouraged to seek work by reducing unemployment benefits

13 If someone earns a lot of money, he or she should be taxed more heavily than an average income earner

14 The level of unemployment is admittedly high, but is necessary to solve our economic problems   1 ☐ 2 ☐ 3 ☐ 4 ☐ 5 ☐

15 High tax rates have removed the incentive to work hard   1 ☐ 2 ☐ 3 ☐ 4 ☐ 5 ☐

16 Jobs should be taken to where the unemployed are, rather than expecting the unemployed to move   1 ☐ 2 ☐ 3 ☐ 4 ☐ 5 ☐

17 Cutting public expenditure is essential if the economy is to return to prosperity   1 ☐ 2 ☐ 3 ☐ 4 ☐ 5 ☐

18 Income from owning shares and property should be more heavily taxed than income from working   1 ☐ 2 ☐ 3 ☐ 4 ☐ 5 ☐

Please check that you have responded to every statement.
Thank you very much for your co-operation.

References

Carmines, E. G. and Zeller, R. A. 1979 *Reliability and Validity Assessment* Sage University Paper 17, p. 67

Dawson, G. G. 1980 *Attitudes and Opinions on Economic Issues* Empire State College Center for Business and Economic Education, Research Report No. 2, p. 81

Kerlinger, F. N. 1967 'Social attitudes and their criterial referents: a structural theory' *Psychological Review* 7 pp. 110–22

Kerlinger, F. N. 1980 'Analysis of covariance structure tests of a criterial referents theory of attitudes' *Multivariate Behavioural Research* 15 pp. 403–22

Kim, J. and Mueller, C. W. 1978 *Introduction to Factor Analysis* Sage University Paper 13

Mann, W. R. and Fusfield, D. R. 1970 'Attitude sophistication and effective teaching in economics' *Journal of Economic Education* 1 pp. 111–29

Nie, N. H., Hall, C. H., Jenkins, J. G., Steinbrenner, K. and Bent, D. H. 1975 *Statistical Package for the Social Sciences* 2nd edn., McGraw-Hill

Piper, K. 1976 *Evaluation in the Social Sciences* Australian Council for Educational Research, Canberra, p. 72

The effect of instruction in basic microeconomics on interventionist/non-interventionist attitudes

William A. Luker
Professor of Economic Education and Dean of the School of Community Service, North Texas State University, Denton, Texas

William D. Witter
Assistant Professor of Economic Education and Director of the Centre for Economic Education, North Texas State University, Denton, Texas

Walton H. Sharp
Assistant Professor of Labor and Industrial Relations and Director of Labor Studies, North Texas State University, Denton, Texas

This paper is an examination of the effect of instruction in basic microeconomics on attitudes of pupils towards *laissez faire* as an organizing principle of modern economic life.

Introduction

This study examines the effect of an introductory course in microeconomics on student attitudes toward *laissez faire* as an organizing principle of modern economic life. The work is an extension of previous research conducted by Dawson (1966), Luker (1972), Luker and Proctor (1981), Rothman and Scott (1973) and Thompson (1973). The paper's general hypothesis is that instruction in basic microeconomics produces a bias in favour of *laissez faire* as an organizing principle of modern economic life. To test this general assertion, two operational sub-hypotheses were developed:

1 Other things held constant, students who have completed a basic course in microeconomics will be significantly less interventionist (more committed to *laissez faire*) than students completing comparable-level courses in macroeconomics, political science, and sociology.

2 Other things held constant, students enrolled in a basic course in micro-economics, from pre- to post-measurements, will be significantly less

interventionist than students completing a comparable-level course in macroeconomics, sociology, and political science.*

Significance of the study

The significance of the study is that the hypothesized effect is not a necessary function of the subject matter of microeconomics. It is the contention of the authors of this paper that the positive principles of the discipline can be used to pursue allocative ends other than those produced by free enterprise markets, for example, democratic socialism. This view is shared by a large number of economists, such as Lange and Taylor (1938) and Lerner (1944). Thus, the work centres on the pedagogical imperative that the task of instruction in economics is to show how economic principles can be used to assure rational and efficient resource allocation whatever a society's ends, rather than to propagandize in favour of *laissez faire* markets.

Description of methods

This study was a quasi-experiment using students at North Texas State University.

The sample

The sample consisted of all students (1599) enrolled in all classes of Introductory Microeconomics (18 classes), 10 classes of Introductory Sociology, 10 classes of Introductory Political Science, and 7 classes of Introductory Macroeconomics at North Texas State University in the autumn semester of 1984. Approximately 30 per cent of the economics courses were taught by full-time, permanent members of the university's economics faculty. The remainder of the classes were taught by adjunct professors (about 20 per cent) recruited from the professional and business communities of the Dallas/Fort Worth area (for example, from the regional bank of the Federal Reserve System), and graduate students (about 50 per cent) working towards a master's degree. The economics courses made no use of more complex mathematics (calculus, matrix algebra), relying totally on graphical, arithmetic, simple algebraic, or heuristic explanations.

Neither of the two economics courses, micro/macro, were prerequisites for each other. About 60 per cent of the macro students had taken college-level introductory micro. No more than 10 per cent of the micro students had taken macro. Less than 1 per cent were taking the two courses concurrently.

---

* The second operational sub-hypothesis is directional, testing the nature and significance of change (if any) from the pre- to the post-measurement. The statistical technique used was an analysis of covariance change (Cohen and Cohen, 1983).

The textbooks used in the micro and macro courses were respectively *The Micro Economy Today* (Schiller, 1983) and *The Macro Economy Today* (Schiller, 1983). The course instructors adhered to a common syllabus fashioned around the textbooks. A process review of the instruction indicated a close adherence to the syllabuses. However, while all courses covered the same material, the relative weighting and time spent on each of the topics varied over the full range of skills, interests, experience, values and attitudes of the instructors. Even though the instructor attitude towards intervention and non-intervention was included as a covariate, no effort was made to measure, control, or link the effect of these other variables on post-measurement attitudes. The *ceteris paribus* assumption was that topic weighting (emphasis, time, techniques of instruction, student cognitive styles, increases in student economic understanding) would cancel or wash, thereby leaving the generalized effect of the course.

The major topics covered in the micro classes were as follows:

1 the process of choice and the economic problem

2 the market economy

3 establishing prices

4 changes in supply and demand

5 production and costs

6 competition

7 monopoly, oligopoly, and monopolistic competition

8 functional income distribution

9 the unresolved problems of the market

The major topics covered in the macro course were:

1 measuring aggregate economic activity

2 consumption and saving

3 aggregate demand

4 the investment multiplier

5 money and the banking system

6 the central bank

7 the maintenance of full employment and economic growth

8 the maintenance of price stability

9 international economics

The experimental design

The quasi-experimental design was a modification of Design 10 by Campbell and Stanley (1971). This design uses intact experimental and control groups as opposed to the random creation of groups in classical experiments. The design relies heavily on adequate model specification, reliable covariates and regression partialling for protection against threats to internal validity. The use of convenient intact groups restricts generalizability which must then be achieved by replication. The students in the sample were tested to determine the degree of their interventionist/non-interventionist attitudes at the beginning and at the end of the semester. The interventionist/non-interventionist attitudes of the instructor were also tested at the beginning of the semester. A student questionnaire was administered at the beginning of the semester to obtain covariate data on student gender, year of study, ethnic group, prior study of economics and principal subject studied.

Research variables

The dependent variables were the post-test interventionist/non-interventionist class means on seven scales: aggregate interventionist/non-interventionist (AIN); interventionist/non-interventionist attitude toward income distribution and living standards (IIS); interventionist/non-interventionist attitudes toward externalities (IE); interventionist/non-interventionist attitudes toward singular personal issues (IP); interventionist/non-interventionist attitudes toward problems of the ageing (IOA); general interventionist attitudes (GI); and a general *laissez faire* commitment (GLF). All seven of the interventionist/non-interventionist scales were defined by a researcher-developed, 23-item, five-point Likert scale, a copy of which is included as Appendix A. The statements focus on the individual's propensity to favour or oppose intervention in free markets. The items used in the scale are relatively free of economic analytical content and, therefore, are not simple surrogates for economic understanding. The 23 statements were divided between interventionist (12) and non-interventionist (11) attitudes. This method was used to minimize the respondent's tendency to assume that all items reflected the same orientation towards intervention or non-intervention and respond accordingly.

Another reason for this method of construction was to provide an opportunity for the respondent to agree with some items while disagreeing with others. Thus an individual tending towards non-intervention might agree with 11 items and disagree with 12. Such an individual would then have both positively- and negatively-related scores on items reflecting similar content, depending on the direction or orientation of the item towards intervention or non-intervention.

The 23-item scale was factor analysed using a varimax orthogonal rotation (principal factor analysis), the results of which are summarized in Appendix B. The six sub-scales described earlier were derived from this factor analysis. The reliability of the seven scales was estimated using Cronbach's alpha

(1951), and are respectively: AIN = 0.76, IIS = 0.60, IE = 0.48, IOA = 0.64, IP = 0.64, GI = 0.45, and GLF = 0.54. The AIN scale was an aggregate of all 23 statements on the interventionist/non-interventionist questionnaire. The IIS sub-scale was constructed from factor 1, the IE sub-scale from factor 2, the IP sub-scale from factor 3, the IOA sub-scale from factor 4, the GI sub-scale from factor 6, and the GLF sub-scale from a sample combination of factors 5 and 7. Rather than treating factors 5 and 7 separately, they were combined into a GLF scale because this combination seemed intuitively more satisfying.

The covariate independent variables were gender, instructor attitudes, pre-test student attitudes, previous courses in economics, major subject studied, student race/ethnic group, student academic classification, student retention rate, and instructor status (full-time or adjunct/teaching fellow). The retention rate was measured by calculating the percentage of students who completed the course. The rate was calculated by dividing the number of students completing the course by the number registered at the beginning. The class means and proportions (instead of individual student scores) were used throughout as the basic analytical data point, thereby reducing the analytical sample size from 1599 to 45.

The control group variables were classes in sociology, political science and macroeconomics. These variables were dummy coded and analysed in that mode. The quasi-experimental variable, microeconomics, was designated as the reference group.

Analytical procedures

The data were analysed using multiple linear regression and an analysis of covariate change (Cohen and Cohen, 1983). The intervention scales were reverse-scored so that a high score was non-interventionist, and a low score was interventionist. The sub-scale scores, which were orthogonal to each other, were regressed against the aggregate, and the residuals were used in the analysis.

The findings

The following is a discussion of the multiple regression analysis of the dependent variable AIN on the independent variables.

The variable macroeconomics and two interaction variables (macro and business; macro and no economics) were statistically significant. The essence of this finding was that, everything else being equal, the macro groups were more interventionist on the average than the micro groups on the post-test AIN measure. This main effect was conditioned by the two interactions which showed that the interventionist effect of the macro course was inhibited by both the presence of increased percentages of business majors in the macro course, as well as increased percentages of students with no courses in economics in their backgrounds. That is, in any given macroeconomics class, as the percentage of students majoring in business administration increased, the interventionist effect of the macro course was diminished. The same is true of the condition where the percentage of students with no economics in their backgrounds increased. In other words, the interventionist effect of macroeconomics is diminished when there are larger numbers of students majoring in business administration and students with no economics in their backgrounds. The obverse of this generalization is also true: the lower the percentage of business majors and the higher the percentage of students with a micro background, the greater the interventionist effect of the macro course.

The change in the mean scores from the pre- to the post-test shows that the micro groups did not change significantly, while the macro groups became significantly more interventionist. The partial correlation coefficient (PR) for the macro main effect was -0.44479. The partial coefficient for the macro, business interaction was 0.43808 and for the macro, no economics interaction, 0.37605. The multiple coefficient of determination was 0.64695. Other significant main effects were instructor attitude (PR = -0.57219) and retention rate (PR = 0.41689).

The regression analysis of the dependent variable IIS on the independent variables showed that, with respect to the study's basic hypothesis, there were no significant relationships.

The analysis of the dependent variable IE on the independent variables indicated that, with respect to the study's basic hypothesis, no significant relationships were found.

The analysis of the dependent variable IP on the independent variables showed that the two main effect variables, macro economics and political science, were statistically significant. Two interaction variables (macro and business, and political science and business) were also significant. The significant main effect variables indicated that the macro and political science groups were, on the average, more interventionist than the micro groups. These main effect findings were conditioned by statistically significant interactions indicating that the interventionist effect in both macro and political science courses diminished as the proportion of business students increased.

The partial correlation coefficients for the macro and political science main effects were respectively -0.37316 and -0.34349. The partial coefficient for the macro, business interaction was 0.37544.

A covariate analysis of regression change for the micro, macro, and political science variables on the variable IP indicated that the macro and political science groups became significantly more interventionist, while the micro group did not change significantly. The multiple coefficient of determination was 0.64060. Other significant variables were freshman (PR = 0.36465) and business major (PR = 0.39518).

The analysis of the dependent variable IOA on the independent variables showed that the variables, macro economics and sociology, were significantly more interventionist on the post-test than the variable, microeconomics.

A covariate analysis of regression change for the macro, micro and sociology groups showed that the macro and sociology groups became significantly more interventionist, while the micro groups did not change significantly.

The partial correlation coefficients for the macro and sociology main effects were respectively -0.31382 and -0.37509. The multiple coefficient of determination was 0.57865.

The analysis of the dependent variable GI on the independent variables showed that, with respect to the basic hypothesis, no significant relationships were found.

The analysis of the dependent variable GLF on the independent variables showed that the macro groups were significantly more interventionist than the micros.

These main effect findings were also conditioned by a statistically significant interaction showing that the interventionist effect of the macro course was diminished as the population of the business majors in the class increased.

An analysis of regression change for the macro and micro groups showed that the micro groups became significantly less interventionist from the pre- to the post-test. The macro groups did not change significantly.

The partial correlation coefficient for the macro/micro comparison was -0.38060. The multiple coefficient of determination was 0.43058.

Concluding remarks

The basic hypothesis, as it related to the aggregate interventionist/non-interventionist scale (AIN), was not corroborated. The hypothesized causal effect of microeconomics on non-interventionist attitudes was not sustained. While the micro course did not appear to change student attitudes, the macro, political science, and sociology courses did seem to encourage an interventionist bias in areas which were not intrinsic to the course content. This finding is consistent with Luker (1972), but partly contradicts Luker and Proctor (1981).

The above conclusion does not hold across the sub-scales; however, in addition to the AIN scale, it held for only two sub-scales:

1 issues relating to personal intervention (IP)

2 issues relating to old age (IOA)

With reference to general *laissez faire* issues (GLF), the microeconomics course produced the hypothesized effect which is partly consistent with Luker and Proctor (1981).

These main effects, plus the interactions reported in the findings, open the door to some interesting speculative inferences. The findings seem to indicate that the micro course, which in the main is populated by students with little or no formal training in economics, has a non-interventionist effect through a limited range of concepts. However, a careful look at the macro main effects and their interactions strongly suggests that when knowledge gained in the micro course interacts with the macro experience, the result is a strong interventionist attitudinal change. Thus, while the micro course alone might produce a non-interventionist attitudinal shift on some narrow range of issues, the combined interactive effect of micro and macro courses produces a relatively strong interventionist attitudinal shift. Therefore, on the basis of the evidence, the general hypothesis must be rejected.

Beyond that rejection, however, the issues centre, in some measure, on whether such an effect is generalizable. Indeed, there are at least three reasons why generalization might not be warranted:

1 Perhaps the effect might be unique in that the sample is limited to North Texas State University.

2 The interventionist/non-interventionist scale constructed especially for this study needs substantial reworking to improve the reliability and validity of its aggregate and sub-scale measures. (Three of the sub-scales had reliability coefficients less than 0.60.)

3 The *ceteris paribus* assumptions are problematic. As described earlier, the pedagogical techniques of the instructors, differential content valences, and student increases in economic understanding were not measured, controlled or linked to post-measurement interventionist/non-interventionist attitudes.

The authors of this paper believe that, to some degree, North Texas State University is not unique. Further, they believe the interventionist/non-interventionist instrument to be modestly valid and reliable and that the *ceteris paribus* assumptions hold over a wide range of instructors, students and institutions. However, additional research must be conducted before clear pedagogical implications can be identified. The additional possibilities for further research centre on the following areas:

1 The work must be replicated in other institutional environments.

2 The measuring instrument must be refined in terms of its validity and reliability.

3 Instructor pedagogical techniques and topic valences must be linked to the post-measurement outcomes.

4 Specific measured changes in student understanding in economics must be linked to post-measurement outcomes.

If, after replication and refinements along lines mentioned above, the general effect holds, what pedagogical implications are suggested? The answer depends partly upon the goals and values of economic educators. Certainly, if increased intervention in areas not directly related to the subject matter is an unintended by-product of instruction, changes both in pedagogical techniques and in subject matter selection, sequencing, and/or weighting – or interactions of the two – are in order. On the other hand, if a general increase in intervention is perceived as desirable, some economics educators will breathe sighs of relief.

Appendix A: The interventionist/non-interventionist scale

N/I*	Abbreviation	Statement
N***	GUNS	It is a violation of people's rights to demand that they register their guns
I**	DANGER	Consumers should be protected against dangerous products
N***	MINWAGE	There should be a law against a minimum wage
I**	PUBLED	Society benefits from free public education for all children
N***	SEATBELT	No one should be required to wear a seat belt
I**	PARKS	Admittance to public parks should be free to all citizens
I**	POORED	Federal grants should be provided for the education of poor children
I**	HELMETS	Everyone who rides a motorcycle or moped should be required to wear a crash helmet
I**	LIVSTAN	Everyone should be provided with sufficient income to maintain a decent standard of living
I**	JOBS	Government has an obligation to provide jobs for all persons seeking work
N***	LIBRARY	Libraries should provide user fees to cover all maintenance and operating costs
N***	ENVIRON	The problem of pollution in America has been overstated by environmental groups
N***	POVERTY	Poverty will always exist, with or without government programs
I**	ELDERLY	An adequate standard of living for the elderly should be guaranteed after retirement

(continued)

I**	MEDCARE	All people should have adequate medical care regardless of income
N***	GOLD	The government would solve many problems if it went back to the gold standard
N***	UNEMPL	Too much time and money are spent on unemployment. If people want to work, they should find a job
I**	DECENT	Every American has a right to a decent level of income
N***	LAISSEZ	If the American economy is left alone its problems will be solved
I**	DEPRESS	Everything must be done to prevent a depression like the one in the 1930s
N***	BUMS	The only people who are hungry are lazy bums
N***	LIABL	A company should not be held liable for the product it sells
I**	PETS	Owners of dogs and cats should be required by law to have their animals inoculated regularly

*For analytical purposes the I questions were reverse scored so that an aggregate high score is a non-interventionist attitude and a low score is interventionist.

**Questions in which a high score indicated a positive attitude towards interventionism.

***Questions in which a high score indicated a positive attitude towards non-interventionism.

Appendix B: A summary of the factor analysis of the interventionist/non-interventionist scale

The interventionist/non-interventionist test was factor analysed using a varimax orthogonal rotation. Table 1 is a summary of the eigenvalues, percentage of common variance, and the cumulative percentage of common variance of each factor.

The communality estimates for all questions were averaged (mean = 0.29)* and used as the criterion for factor acceptance.

Table 2 is a summary of the factor loadings for the varimax orthogonally rotated factor solutions for seven factors. Only factor loadings larger than 0.25 are shown.

*This criterion for factor acceptance is based upon a modification of the latent root criterion. While many factor analysts use only the criterion of an eigenvalue of 1, the use of the principal factor analysis (as opposed to principal components) permits a downward adjustment of the criterion. In common factor analysis either the estimate of the common variance of the set of variables or the average of the communality estimates for all variables may be used (Hair *et alia*, 1979).

Table 1   Factor eigenvalues

Factor	Eigenvalue	Percentage of common variance*	Cumulative percentage of common variance
1	3.59046	45.7	45.7
2	1.36189	17.3	63.0
3	0.91779	11.7	74.7
4	0.76620	9.7	87.4
5**	0.39723	5.1	89.5
6	0.30444	3.9	93.4
7**	0.28668	3.6	97.0
8***	0.24009	3.0	100.0

Trace = 7.86400

*The percentage of total variance attributable to common variance is 30.2.

**Factors 5 and 7 were combined to produce the GLF sub-scale.

***Factor 8 was dropped from the analysis because it did not meet the factor inclusion criterion of 0.29.

Table 2   Rotated factor loadings

Factor 1*		Factor 2		Factor 3	
Statement	Loading	Statement	Loading	Statement	Loading
JOBS	0.58227	PARKS	0.44823	ELDERLY	0.65433
UNEMPL	−0.54460	POORED	0.41703	MEDCARE	0.51962
LIVSTAN	0.53288	PUBLED	0.40940		
POVERTY	−0.45045	DANGER	0.36233		

Factor 4*		Factor 5**		Factor 6	
Statement	Loading	Statement	Loading	Statement	Loading
HELMETS	0.70313	GUNS	0.43847	DECENT	0.42321
SEATBELT	−0.60513	ENVIRON	0.40090	DEPRESS	0.37740
		MINWAGE	0.33401	PETS	0.33462
		LIABL	0.26873		

Factor 7**	
Statement	Loading
GOLD	0.36064
LAISSEZ	0.35770
BUMS	0.29586

*Factor 1 and factor 4 both have at least one statement with a negative factor loading. The reason for these negative signs has to do with the way the statements were constructed. That is, in factor 1 UNEMPL and POVERTY are worded in such a way that agreement is non-interventionist, while JOBS and LIVSTAN are worded so that agreement is interventionist.

(continued)

The factor analysis was developed before the statements were reverse scored thus those questions with a high score on non-interventionism would necessarily load with a sign that was opposite to those questions in which a high score was interventionist.

**Factors 5 and 7 were combined to produce sub-score 7, general *laissez faire*.

The 0.30 criterion for the significance of factor loadings is commonly accepted. If, however, the sample size is very large, as was the case here ($n = 1599$), some downward readjustment of this criterion is permissible. One statement with a factor loading less than 0.30 was retained because the authors found its retention intuitively satisfying (Hair *et alia*, 1979).

The signs of the loadings and the groupings tend to confirm the interventionist/non-interventionist sets.

References

Campbell, D. and Stanley, J. 1971 *Experimental and Quasi-Experimental Analysis* Rand McNally, Chicago, pp. 45–50

Cronbach, L. 1951 'Coefficient alpha and the internal structure of tests' *Psychometrika* **16** pp. 197–336

Cohen, J. and Cohen, P. 1983 *Applied Multiple Regression/Correlation Analysis* 2nd edn., Lawrence-Erlbaum, Hillsdale, New Jersey, pp. 417–22

Dawson, G. 1966 'Changing students' attitudes' *Improving College and University Teaching* **1** pp. 200–3

Hair, J., Anderson, R., Tatham, R. and Grablowsky, B. 1979 *Multivariate Data Analysis* Petroleum, Tulsa, Oklahoma, pp. 231–7

Lange, O. and Taylor, F. 1938 *On the Economic Theory of Socialism* University of Minnesota

Lerner, A. 1944 *The Economics of Control: Principles of Welfare Economics* Macmillan

Luker, W. 1972 'The relationship between economic knowledge and certain elements of the affective domain' in A. Welch (ed.) *Research Papers in Economic Education* Joint Council on Economic Education, New York, pp. 10–15

Luker, W. and Proctor, W. 1981 'The effect of an introductory course in microeconomics on the political orientation of students' *Journal of Economic Education* **12** pp. 54–7

Rothman, M. and Scott, J. 1973 'Political opinions and the TUCE' *Journal of Economic Education* **2** pp. 116–24

Schiller, B. 1983 *The Micro Economy Today* Random House, New York

Schiller, B. 1983 *The Macro Economy Today* Random House, New York

Thompson, F. A. 1973 'The interaction of cognition and affect: the issue of trade' *Journal of Economic Education* **4** pp. 111–15

Response   *Michael Watts*

Measuring economic attitudes is a notoriously difficult task. It is even more difficult to explain changes in these attitudes. Frankly, little progress has been made in these areas over the past two decades in economics education research. Most studies still begin by developing an attitude instrument that is unique to that particular study, or at least to one of the authors of the study. Sample sizes are typically small and taken from one site – normally the host institution of the author(s). The likelihood for replication using the same instruments approaches zero. In short, the researcher who studies economic attitudes still has licence to begin with a nearly blank tablet, and what references there are are likely to be earlier studies which posed similar questions without developing conclusive answers or definitive procedures to address the questions.

Several recent studies do represent significant progress in the face of these general shortcomings, however. Two studies published in the *American Economic Review* looked for consensus positions on current economic issues among large samples of economists from several nations (Frey *et alia*, 1984; Kearl *et alia*, 1979). Another developed indexes of student attitudes towards the study of economics and attitude sophistication, defined as agreement with consensus positions of economists and economics educators (Walstad and Soper, 1983). Progress *is* being made, but the progress is slow and decidedly not steady.

How do the two studies presented here (Whitehead and Luker *et alia*) fit into this general picture? Whitehead's paper is a clearly focused and well executed attempt to document findings that are important but perhaps not really surprising. Positions on individual policy issues such as those covered in the survey used in this study are almost certainly influenced by a complex set of forces. Earlier studies have been able to explain far less of the variance in such attitude measures than in cognitive measures. Reflecting this, the issues involved in these measures often transcend the popular labels applied by the press and researchers. For example, many 'liberal' economists (such as Lester Thurow) have written on disincentive effects of income and payroll taxes, so it was not surprising to see the problems with this item in Whitehead's scale. Attempts to develop an index of conservative/liberal positions by adding together responses on a series of statements face even more pitfalls. One weakness of this paper is that we are not given descriptive or reliability statistics on the overall scale.

What is best about the study, though, is the questions it explicitly raises concerning the underlying structure of responses to attitude scales and, implicitly, when it may and may not be appropriate to develop overall attitude indexes by adding together responses on individual questions or policy statements. What seems to be indicated is that such responses should be summed only if an objective criterion for doing so can be established. The criterion might be, as suggested here, internal evidence of unidimensionality in responses to the scale. Or a criterion external to the scale may be appropriate, such as the consensus positions of economists or attitudes towards the discipline as used in the Walstad and Soper study. It will, of course, be more difficult to justify the use of a liberal/conservative index, but perhaps not impossible. Discriminant analysis has been used, for example, to separate Republicans and Democrats or, historically, Radical and non-Radical factions in the British parliament, based on voting or other response patterns involving issues similar to those listed here. If researchers can develop and validate instruments that accurately classify respondents into such categories, results from analysis of the variance and change on responses to these instruments should be far more generalizable than anything now available from studies which use the liberal/conservative labels.

Turning to the paper by Luker *et alia*, it is difficult to be so positive. The authors themselves discuss several important limitations to the study concerning weak reliability measures of their survey instruments, a limited sample, and lack of controls for a number of key variables. While this list of limitations is important, it is by no means complete. The paper suffers from *ad hoc* theoretical and statistical procedures throughout, beginning with the statement of the central hypothesis and extending literally through the last sentence. Specifically, the hypothesis is that the microeconomics class 'produces a bias in favour of *laissez faire*', but we are never told if this bias is expected because of 'bias' in the textbooks used in the course, or among the instructors, or from the current structure of the discipline itself. The last sentence offers the conclusion that 'if a general increase in intervention is perceived as desirable, some economics educators will breathe sighs of relief.' There is nothing in the paper apart from brief references to Lange, Lerner and 'society's ends' (unspecified) to indicate what kind of intervention the authors have in mind, however, so at present one is led to take the concluding sentence as a rather vague expression of their own bias.

Earlier in the paper a number of variables and interactive terms are introduced with no discussion of their expected impact on the attitude measures, and in some cases it is not at all clear why a variable was included or why certain interactive terms were created. It is not indicated, for example, whether the 'macro and no economics' term which 'inhibited' interventionist responses was, *de facto*, a way of noting students who had not completed a microeconomics course, and if so, why this effect is or is not contrary to expectations. Reviewing the attitude instrument used in the study also reveals several items which seem ambiguous at best in terms of identifying interventionist attitudes. For example, many conservative non-interventionists favour grants (vouchers) for the education of poor children, or might consider a law prohibiting minimum wages as itself a form of undesirable intervention.

With respect to statistical procedures, the major problem in the paper is the use of partial correlation coefficients to 'test' significance – a worse than dubious procedure. Nowhere are there statistics provided, whether comparing means or regression coefficients. The overall significance of including the interactive terms should be, but is not, tested by using joint-*F* tests. We are told that class means are used as dependent variables instead of individual student scores, but not why. Factor analysis is the chosen procedure to create several sub-scales, except in one case where two scales are combined because this seems 'intuitively more satisfying'.

In short, this paper suffers from many of the problems that have resulted in the very limited progress in the study of economic attitudes over the past two decades. That results largely because there are many complex problems to be addressed in this area. Still, better ways to meet these problems are available, and more seem to be developing.

References

Frey, B. S., Pommerehne, W. W., Schneider, F. and Gilbert, G. 1984 'Consensus and dissension among economists: an empirical inquiry' *American Economic Review* **74** pp. 986–94

Kearl, J. R., Pope, C. L., Whiting, G. C. and Wimmer, L. T. 1979 'A confusion of economists?' *American Economic Review* **69** pp. 28–37

Walstad, W. B. and Soper, J. C. 1983 'On measuring economic attitudes' *Journal of Economic Education* **14** pp. 4–17

Response   *Lindsey Collings*

The papers by Whitehead and Luker *et alia* both describe attitude surveys used with groups of economics students. Whitehead studied groups of A level students in 1981 and 1983 while Luker *et alia* compared students studying microeconomics, macroeconomics, politics and sociology before and after one-semester courses in 1984 at university in Texas.

Whitehead's research started at a time when it was thought to be simple to construct a scale to measure changes in economic attitudes, in this case along a radical/conservative continuum. Only after the questionnaire had been administered in 1981, for the pre-test, was factor analysis carried out, and it then became clear that a very complex set of factors underlay the apparently straightforward questions. Whitehead believes that the changes he found in responses between 1981 and 1983 could be explained either by changes in the students' attitudes or in the underlying factors. It is difficult to draw conclusions when the origin of the changes is not clear.

Luker *et alia* took a narrower field of economic policy, attitudes to intervention, and, starting his research later, was aware of the possible complexity of factors involved. Luker was able to use factor analysis when drawing up his questionnaire and the benefits of doing this are very clear. Seven underlying factors emerged and he was able to use these to develop seven sub-scales, e.g. interventionist/non-interventionist attitudes towards income distribution, and, similarly, attitudes to intervention over the problems of ageing. Because of this approach, the results are considerably clearer and therefore of more value. He found that students studying only micro courses did not experience a shift towards non-interventionist attitudes on the sub-scale concerned with general *laissez-faire* attitudes. A similar use of the factors found by Whitehead to develop sub-scales would have made it possible for a much clearer picture to emerge from his work.

It would be interesting to see future work in this field where scales were drawn up for British students along the lines followed by Luker *et alia*. Narrow areas of policy would need to be chosen with factor analysis carried out at the design stage. Particularly careful piloting and refinement of the questions would be needed to ensure that the results could be analysed clearly. It is assumed that the factor analysis itself is adequate to ensure that the questionnaire can be developed into a fully useful measure. There could be a danger that the resulting questions would be in such a simplified form that it would be easy for the respondents to feel that they could predict the desired answer and give the answer that they felt was wanted. For this reason it might be an advantage to use questions on policies which did not have a specific UK context; some of those in the Luker questionnaire, for example, while having clear relevance to a particular kind of intervention, would not readily fall into any UK policy area, e.g. that owners of dogs and cats should be required by law to have their animals inoculated regularly.

Even though Whitehead found it difficult to explain the changes he found, it could still be significant if his research were repeated and the same outcome resulted. A predictable result is of value – we can predict what would happen to matter near a black hole without being able to comprehend fully the process involved. Nevertheless, it would be impossible to explain any different results which occurred with other student groups and for that reason a questionnaire designed with the use of factor analysis would be necessary.

A different way of studying attitude changes might be to use computer simulations. The students' behaviour in response to economic problems could be examined (and analysed by computer). Such behaviour would be a better guide to changing attitudes than verbal responses.

Studies of attitude change could be very valuable, especially if longitudinal studies were carried out. They could illuminate possibilities of teacher bias, the effects of changing emphases in the syllabus (such as more emphasis on monetarism), changing fashions in the media treatment of economic issues and changes in economic attitudes among non-specialists as a result of economic literacy projects.

After seeing the difficulties that Whitehead experienced, it would be easy to take the view that the study of changing attitudes is too complex to be worthwhile. Fortunately, Luker *et alia* have shown a way forward. Although both studies are essentially snapshots of only one group, wider and longer term studies would be very valuable.

At the moment, attitudes towards economic policies are a vital concern. Economic attitudes are political attitudes. Economic advisers change with each government depending on their approach to economic policies. Teachers should seize the nettle of studying the way their courses may be changing the attitudes of future citizens. Further, if all prospective economics students are little Keynesians or little monetarists this implies that the efficacy of these approaches is proved. If the aim is rather to train students to have open enquiring minds, few preconceptions and an appreciation of the need to test policies, then an examination of attitude change in this direction would also be desirable.

Response *David Butler*

Interest in the effect of courses in economics on student attitudes has recently been heightened in the UK by pronouncements on the importance of economic understanding in the core curriculum. While both these papers (Whitehead and Luker *et alia*) relate to post-compulsory education they do start to pose the types of questions which will need very careful consideration in any formulation of economics courses for younger students. At the very least, they point out the very complex nature of attitudinal changes and the problems involved in any attempts to measure them.

Whitehead's paper, which is part of a larger research project, examines the actual research methods used in conducting an analysis of attitude measurement and change. His criticisms of the methods employed in earlier research lead him to believe that 'after 20 years of research in this field, it is not possible to make any authoritative pronouncement about the various hypotheses concerning attitudes of economics students . . .' His own research applies factor analysis to an attitude scale, and the results lead him to the conclusion that doubt must be cast on the unidimensionality of responses along a radical/conservative continuum. This inevitably raises more questions about attitudinal changes than it answers but leads us farther down the methodological path than before. The work provides an important framework with which to attempt to start analysing some of the variables that might influence attitudes such as the economic and political standpoint of the teacher, the ability of the students and particular peer group 'norms'.

Whitehead suggests that the evidence points to the control group of non-economists exhibiting more polarized attitudes than the group taking the course in A level economics. An interesting question raised by this is the influence of the precise nature of the course content. There is little real variation in the UK between the syllabuses of the various examination boards so we might well have to look outside traditional A level courses in any attempt to analyse this influence.

Luker *et alia* tackle some of these questions in their study of students at North Texas State University. Using factor analysis employing varimax orthogonal rotation, they tested the general hypothesis that students taking a microeconomics course would exhibit more *laissez-faire* attitudes than either non-economists or students who had taken a macroeconomics course. They identified and examined a number of covariate independent variables such as gender, student retention rate, teacher attitudes and the subject in which the student was majoring. They rejected the general hypothesis but considered that 'while the micro course alone might produce a non-interventionist attitudinal shift on some narrow range of issues, the combined interactive effect of micro and macro courses produces a relatively strong interventionist attitudinal shift.'

They themselves suggest that the research needs to be replicated in other institutional environments as well as checking on the reliability of the *ceteris paribus* assumptions. Equally important would seem to be the need to test the general findings against a variation of microeconomic syllabuses.

Clearly more work needs to be carried out in this very important area and extended to an examination of the effect of economics courses on younger students. These papers are very valuable in raising teacher awareness of the whole question of attitudes and the direction of attitudinal change brought about by the teaching of economics.

Teaching economics in the primary school: content and methods

Anna Maria Ajello
*Department of Psychology of Developmental and Socialization
Processes, University of Rome 'La Sapienza'*

Anna Silvia Bombi
*Department of Psychology of Development and Socialization,
University of Padua*

Cristina Zucchermaglio
*Department of Psychology of Developmental and Socialization
Processes, University of Rome 'La Sapienza'*

This paper presents an economic curriculum for primary schools, which
has been used experimentally in five classes in Rome for three years
(with pupils from 8 to 10 years old). Reasons for content selection and
teaching methods are given. Finally some thoughts are shared about how
children of this age acquire economic knowledge.

Introduction

In this paper we describe a socioeconomic curriculum for primary schools
with which we have been experimenting between 1982 and 1985 in five classes
in schools in Rome.

We wanted to begin this research project for many reasons. In Italy, new
curricula for state primary schools are about to be released, for children aged
6–11. In these curricula, a section devoted to the acquisition of economics
ideas in the area of social studies has been included for the first time. Up till
now, such ideas have been included only in a limited way in school activities,
through reading exercises or as knowledge from history or human geography
which are never thoroughly taught.

Such concepts were treated more systematically only by teachers interested
in educational innovation, particularly through environmental studies. It is
therefore clear that there is an urgent need to devise and experiment with
curricula for teaching ideas which have previously been excluded from our
scholastic tradition.

The inclusion of social studies in primary school curricula constitutes a positive innovation. For the first time, the importance of giving younger students some key ideas about their social environment has been recognized. This is an essential task in general education which cannot be entirely postponed to secondary school, given its scope and complexity. A thorough knowledge of present social phenomena should facilitate the study of history and human geography, allowing pupils to compare their direct experiences with those of pupils distant in time and space.

We believe that it is useful to begin early the basic study of social phenomena, considering the different social sciences as neither identical nor opposed perspectives from which it is possible to examine human reality. Every social science constitutes, from this point of view, a language whose basis can be acquired more systematically if the area which it refers to is identified early.

On a theoretical level, the acquisition of socioeconomic ideas is a relevant goal both from a psychological and a developmental point of view: in both fields however the data so far available are relatively scarce. Educational research has, in fact, concentrated on the acquisition of basic skills such as reading and writing, or on more traditional disciplines such as mathematics or, in a more limited way, history.

In the field of developmental psychology, the growth of social knowledge has long been considered as identical to development of moral reasoning (Rest, 1983); to this traditionally dominant area, other areas of study, such as the comprehension of various aspects of politics, have emerged only relatively recently (Shantz, 1983).

As far as the development of economic ideas is concerned, a large descriptive study, written by one of us (Berti and Bombi, 1981), has revealed a series of ideas on work, money, production and trade that become closer to adult understanding between the ages of 4 and 14. For example, children develop ideas on buying and selling and on prices. Initially, payment for goods in stores is seen as a type of ritual, as is the 'change', whose function as compensation between the goods' value and the money paid is not understood.

Many children explain this usage as an act of kindness by the shopkeeper or as the need for the buyer not to remain without money. Subsequently, children understand the use of money in shops but continue to have incorrect ideas about profits: they in fact believe that shopkeepers can still make a profit by selling goods at the same or at lower prices than they paid for them. This conviction, which is supported by mathematical mistakes, is based on some 'pre-economics' misconceptions about the nature of prices: some children believe that the price is an invariable characteristic of the product and thus the shopkeeper (if he is 'honest') cannot change it; others believe that the price reflects the shopkeeper's labour, but the children have taken into account only one production phase. With this line of reasoning, goods cost more in the factory, where 'people work harder to make them', and less in the store, where 'all the shopkeeper has to do is wait for customers'.

Finally, children around 10–11 years old understand that the price increases between the various transactions.

Many considerations emerge from such data, the most important being that the presence of structured, ordered conceptions at different age levels attest to the children's efforts to understand (and their interest in) certain phenomena, even if they have not received systematic teaching.

In the absence of such teaching, the growing complexity of children's ideas can be considered an expression of their growing cognitive abilities and of the consequent possibility of connecting the scattered information they grasp from direct observation, adult conversation and the mass media.

This does not mean that appropriate teaching would not be useful. The spontaneous ideas found in these research projects and in other studies on children (Furth, 1980; Jahoda, 1979, 1983; Strauss, 1954; Tan and Stacey, 1981) appear more developed with growth, but – and this constitutes the second point which is useful to consider – these ideas do not go beyond a fairly ingenuous and general common sense. The various perspectives from which social phenomena can be considered (moral, sociological, psychological, political, economic and historical) are at times mixed and confused and at times too specialized, almost as if, for example, there are facts that pertain exclusively to morality, others that pertain exclusively to politics, etc.

The explanations of smaller children reflect adult common sense, especially in the confusion between different explanatory levels. In particular, psychological and moral ideas tend to be used to analyse typically economic questions: differences in prices, goods' prices as only payment for labour, etc.

During the elementary school years, this confusion (or, in Piagetian words, 'syncretism') is partly overcome, but – since adult common sense is the only point of reference – the children do not go beyond a pre-economics level of sophistication and they do not have any kind of awareness of the existence of an economic model and much less of a plurality of models.

From this point of view, the data of developmental research suggest the need for 'economic literacy' which would provide a basis similar to that provided by the primary school in mathematics and language.

Naturally the problem of appropriate pedagogy arises: a project whose goal is to teach socioeconomic ideas must take into account the cognitive limits of elementary school children.

It is not possible simply to provide an explanatory model of socioeconomic phenomena, to confront the data that pupils find in everyday life. However, direct experience, in its complexity and richness, does constitute data which any teaching method must take into account.

The economics perspective

The key concept of the proposed three-year curriculum is the 'economic system based on the division of labour and trade'. From this it follows that salaries must be higher than production costs, so that the producers can buy the goods that they need. But this concept is too general and abstract to be directly taught to children of primary school age. Instead, we prefer to use the idea of 'chain of production' which is also less abstract and permits us to stress that the prices of goods increase from production to consumption; the prices of goods themselves include a percentage of the paid work in each phase of the process.

With such a concept it is possible to concentrate on macroeconomic phenomena, such as work, industrial and agricultural production, distribution and transportation of goods, and different kinds of sale (markets, supermarkets, department stores). These aspects are not necessarily theoretical, but they constitute a necessary step for the construction of a theoretical base: we prefer an economic systems approach rather than the traditional approach based on 'needs', 'demand' and 'supply'.

In other words, although it is true that in primary school it is not possible to teach economics by explicit reference to its theoretical models, it is also true that the choice of some topics rather than others reflects a general theoretical conception of the discipline.

The three-year curriculum

The social economics course runs for three years, and is divided into three sections – the primary, secondary and tertiary sectors:

1 Work and profit in shops and industry (third grade, 8 years old)

2 Agricultural activity and distribution of primary products (fourth grade, 9 years old)

3 The department store and its services (fifth grade, 10 years old)

A complete syllabus for each year is given in the Appendix.

The third grade

In the first year, the course begins with the recognition of parents' work and proceeds to the concept of work as continuous, remunerated activity. The classification of jobs by different criteria and the distinction between employers and the self-employed permit students to understand that self-employed workers must obtain means to continue working. Moreover, the reference to industry makes children aware that the prices of goods must necessarily increase in the various productive phases, because the goods produced include a percentage of paid work.

Emphasizing this point, the idea of price has been underlined as only due to the labourer's work; in order to stress the necessary increase in the goods' value during the productive process. We have excluded many other aspects which children must deal with in their everyday life, such as sales, discounts, variation of prices in different types of shops, and so on. This is because the role of daily experiences in the child's acquisition of knowledge is frequently, indeed more frequently than realized, a source of confusion rather than a source of significant knowledge (see also Thomas, 1984). For example, children frequently consider discounts a real decrease in price compared with what the shopkeeper paid to the factory and they therefore do not see them as a marginal, but as a regular phenomenon. For the same reason, a visit to a factory is suggested, but only to consider the different phases of production, avoiding allusion to other aspects (machines, division of labour, authority roles, working environment and so on).

We think that it is important that pupils learn about social reality by environmental studies, so that they may make sense of it. But it is also important to select carefully those aspects that are shown to the pupils, so as to prevent this reality from appearing confusing (Ajello, Bombi and Ponte-corvo, 1984).

The fourth grade

In the second year attention is centred on the production and distribution of agricultural products. Primary activities are in fact unknown to children who live in cities. Nowadays, the few ideas they possess are characterized by strong value judgements (or prejudices) which reveal substantial misunder-standing. The farmer is seen as an unsophisticated, poor man who is inferior to the city dweller. At other times, rural life is seen as free, unconstricting and peaceful. From the opposite view, industrial society is seen as either entirely positive or entirely negative.

During this year, primary activity is described as it is experienced in modern society, namely availability of agricultural produce during the whole year; distribution and diffusion of such produce; the industrial processing of some products to prevent their fast deterioration. The reference to deteriora-tion of agricultural produce allows us to deal with price variability (for example, the fact that prices change during the course of the morning). So a second key concept is provided in this course: that of 'general rules and exceptions to these rules'. Price, for example, is a general rule, with some exceptions which explain variation. Thus pupils begin to understand the idea of equilibrium between costs and profits, which is fundamental to economics.

The fifth grade

In the third year, attention is focused on the functioning of the department store as a particular service in modern society (a service which is included in a network of other services, primarily transport).

This theme is not completely new, because some of these aspects have already been dealt with (in considering the destination of both industrial and agricultural products). Nonetheless, from an economic point of view, the study of this theme with children allows us to focus on an unsolved question: 'How is it that selling more of a product permits one to sell at a lower price?' This question requires explanation of a fundamental aspect of industrial society. It also exemplifies a characteristic of social phenomena – that of having more than one explanation. Children have to understand that department stores can sell at lower prices for a number of reasons: they pay less to the factory for their own products, they skip a step in the chain of distribution, they save on transportation expenses, they centralize the organization of administrative services, and high management costs can be distributed over a large number of products. Furthermore, it has been possible in this course, especially with reference to this last aspect, to have children quantifying the importance of such factors, by getting them to work on the data. This enables them to test such hypotheses for themselves.

Several general educational observations are appropriate:

1 Pupils work by performing tasks   It is our conviction that pupils learn more when they are actively involved in *doing* rather than passively listening.

2 Consideration of pupils' initial knowledge   Everyday knowledge has a fundamental role in the acquisition of further knowledge. If one wants to increase student learning efficiently, then new concepts must be related and integrated with prior understanding, primarily by considering the type and characteristics of current knowledge of themes which one wants to deal with in school.

3 Classroom discussion   This is the most characteristic aspect of the course from an educational point of view, and we have taken into account that different types of discussion may have different objectives (Ajello and Zucchermaglio, 1985). As other researchers have shown (Barnes, 1976), when the teacher directs the discussion in a certain way, it is possible to grasp from what the children say the type of connections they establish: the cognitive obstacles, the particular mental representation, the connections which they establish between phenomena (different from those established by adults, of course), etc. Furthermore, the cognitive performances which the pupils display when they discuss are significantly superior to those displayed in other school activities. For these reasons, a fundamental role in the course is given to discussion.

But from previous investigations (Pontecorvo, Costiglia and Zucchermaglio, 1985; Pontecorvo and Zucchermaglio, 1984; Pontecorvo and Ajello, 1984), we know that the efficient conduct of discussion does not just depend on the teacher's natural ability. It depends not only on disciplinary competence but also on the teacher's capacity to listen to what pupils have to say and on his or her general cognitive flexibility. It also depends on the social climate of the classroom and the children's experience of this way of working in the class.

For these reasons, we ran preparatory training courses (10 sessions of four hours each) for teachers before the beginning of each three-year course, and we paid particular attention to the development of their ability to conduct discussion (Ajello and Bombi, 1985).

Discussion and conclusions

To test the effectiveness of this course, various kinds of data were collected. Class discussions were tape recorded and fully transcribed in order to analyse their content and compare their quality in the successive phases of the experiment. In addition to this kind of analysis, dealing with the whole class, various individual experiments were done, the most important of which consisted of a series of wide-ranging, semi-structured interviews carried out every year with each pupil before and after the course. Moreover, during the last year of the experiment, written materials and drawings about course topics (i.e. department store organization) were collected from each child.

So far, only the interviews carried out with third- and fourth-year classes have been analysed (Ajello, Bombi, Pontecorvo and Zucchermaglio, 1984, 1985). The comparison between the level of answers given before and after the experiment reveals significant progress on the whole between the two interviews. The amount of progress, however, varies depending on the topic dealt with in the interviews. These differences raise several problems in interpreting the results; in this paper we will present only a few comments about the most relevant topics of the course.

The environment and its educational use

Among the more problematical concepts for children are some of those concerning factories and industrial production, in particular the role of 'the boss' and pricing.

When we devised the course for 8–10 year olds, we were aware of these difficulties. All the developmental studies on children's economic ideas, since the early work of Danziger (1958), show this, and some researchers have explained it by referring to how little experience children have of factories. Hence we included in the course a carefully arranged visit to a factory, so as to direct children's attention *only* to specific aspects, to avoid an overloading of simultaneous information. This selective observation proved to be difficult to realize, probably because of the interconnection of situations and roles, i.e. the 'boss' can be the owner of the factory or simply a manager; he or she might also have been directly involved with the construction of the factory; he or she may or may not have other managers who give orders directly to the workers. In these conditions, it is necessary to help the children to identify the crucial aspects of the process and to separate them from the marginal ones. But this can only be done from a disciplinary perspective. Far from being in itself a help, the environment can only be used as a learning resource on the basis of abstractions. The teacher can assist the children in this process by choosing only some truly representative aspects on which to focus their attention and by avoiding stressing other aspects.

The chain of distribution and its direction

Another difficulty that children encountered was in reconstructing the chain of distribution of goods. The concept of goods distribution is a complex one, because the child must co-ordinate several pieces of information by means of an active process of reconstruction. This process is particularly problematical for several reasons: the concept of a 'chain' is itself based on a particular theoretical perspective, which allows us to detect, among the thousands of facts available, those relevant to distribution. A picture of the chain of distribution must be constructed with the children to allow them to select the relevant data and understand them.

Another problem concerns the beginning of the chain, from which the children are asked to reconstruct the transportation of the goods. This reconstruction is quite easy (at least in the main phases of the chain) if the factory is taken as the starting point. If, on the other hand, we start from the availability of goods in the shops, it is more difficult to go back to the factory. For the child the chain is not a sum of separate events but a whole structure that can be better grasped from a particular perspective, one which follows the real sequence of events through time. In this respect, children might adopt a 'narrative model' which is very familiar to them because of the experience of listening to stories and listening to descriptions of real events at home or in the classroom. Alternatively, the children may be helped in arriving at the *shop* (which is very familiar) by the question, 'Where do factory products go?' And so the idea of the existence of the factory (less familiar) is recalled by the question itself. The opposite happens when the question is, 'Where do the shop goods come from?', centring the attention on the more familiar element of the chain and leaving aside the less familiar ones.

Large-scale selling in department stores

During the first two phases of the course with third and fourth graders, children could not explain the fact that some shops (particularly the large ones) sell goods at lower prices than others. A rather common kind of explanation was based on the temporal dimension of the economic process. For instance, children claimed that a shopkeeper who sells a lot of goods in the same day realizes a huge profit, forgetting that he or she must have spent a lot to buy all those goods. Other children countered this with the fact that expenses can occur day by day, thinking that the shopkeeper's profit shouldn't necessarily be higher than the costs. Children seem to be incapable of considering the economic process in abstract terms out of the temporal context in which the relevant events (buying, selling, paying, earning) occur.

In the last part of the course, with fifth graders, the difference between prices was explained on the basis of the different *management costs*. Children were told that in a large shop like a department store, such costs, even if they are higher, are divided into small percentages charged on the retail prices of numerous goods.

The use of a technical term, together with the necessary explanations, seems to have been particularly useful in this case. A preliminary inspection of the data (still to be elaborated) revealed, in fact, that a large majority of the children acquired the new linguistic terms and used them properly, not only referring to the shops but also to other appropriate situations (i.e. to factory pricing).

Following Vygotsky's (1984) perspective about 'systematic concepts', we think that children can use scientific concepts – properly explained – at a higher cognitive level than everyday ideas, because the former are not loaded with the myriad of meanings which are associated with the latter. Accurate terminology not only increases children's linguistic ability, but seems also to strengthen reasoning in a specific learning context.

Disciplinary and pre-disciplinary approach

We are conducting a qualitative analysis of children's 'errors', examining the difference between the experimental group and a control group, in which children were not given the course units. The mistaken answers given by the control group are different from the mistaken answers given by the ex-perimental group. The first, in fact, very often gave 'non-disciplinary' explanations, which refer to phenomena completely extraneous to the considered economic field: i.e. to explain why some shopkeepers sell at a lower price than others, children from the control group claimed that those shopkeepers are 'more honest' or 'more benevolent' towards their clients. Children participating in our experiment, however, even when they did not give the completely correct answers, maintained their reasoning in a 'quasi-economic' perspective, very rarely using concepts pertaining to other social domains (moral, psychological, etc.).

This seems to us another reason to start early in teaching economics, although in the primary school, children's acquisition will be limited in some cases to the pre-disciplinary concepts. The gradual differentiation between the fields of various social sciences is in itself the first relevant target for educational development.

Acknowledgements

This study is part of a larger research project entitled 'Discourse and reasoning in the classroom: identifying the constants and the variables in different fields of knowledge and with different methods of intervention and surveying' (director Professor Clotilde Pontecorvo), financially supported by the Italian National Council of Research (CTB 8400481).

We are very grateful to Clotilde Pontecorvo for the numerous helpful suggestions she gave us while carrying out the studies described in this paper.

We are very grateful to David Whitehead too, for careful reading of our first draft.

Appendix: Syllabus for the three-year curriculum

Syllabus for third grade (8 years old)

Work and profit

UNIT 1   *Parents' and grandparents' jobs*
Activity carried out in small groups – classification of jobs in different ways.
Teaching objectives: to clarify that jobs are different and can be classified in different ways; they are similar in their means of payment; there is a distinction between self-employment and being employed by someone else.

UNIT 2   *Analysis of two examples of self-employment*
Discussion in the classroom about three problems:
(1) who pays?, (2) for what work?, (3) what is the wage used for?
Teaching objectives: to understand what one receives a wage for; what expenses have to be met from wages.

UNIT 3   *Pricing in shops*
3.1 Discussion in the classroom to prepare the questions to ask two self-employed workers.
Teaching objectives: to write an outline of an interview about what the interviewed workers do, what they need for their work, whom they buy from, how they decide the price of goods, what the consumer pays them for.
3.2 Interview in the classroom with two self-employed workers.
Teaching objectives: to discuss some common characteristics of two self-employed people; to clarify that prices are set with specific criteria and that these criteria depend on different aspects; to find out where the goods they sell come from.
3.3 Discussion to stress the given information.
Teaching objective: to consolidate the received information by clarifying it.

UNIT 4   *Productive cycle and pricing in industry*
4.1 Classroom discussion to prepare questions to ask in the factory.
Teaching objectives: to direct the attention of the children to some specific aspects of work in industry: (1) the different phases from the start to the end of production; (2) the production cycle considered as the sum of different tasks.
4.2 Visit to a factory and acquisition of necessary information.
Teaching objectives: to clarify the reasons for the different prices of raw materials and the final product.
4.3 Concluding discussion.
Teaching objectives: to stress and to clarify the received information;

to understand the reason for the increase in price of the goods in the factory from the beginning to the end of production.

UNIT 5   *Increase in prices*
Simulation game for groups of children: pupils have to find as many phases as possible to make a product; in fact for every phase, they can increase the price by a percentage. The group who finds the highest price wins the game.
Teaching objective: through the game, the children must consolidate the idea that the price increases during the phases of production.

Syllabus for fourth grade (9 years old)

The distribution of agricultural produce

UNIT 1   *Food*
Classroom discussion: what do we eat?
Teaching objective: to activate the children's ideas about agricultural produce.

UNIT 2   *Agricultural products*
The teacher shows some agricultural products, e.g. bread, oranges, tomatoes, eggs, jam, green peas. He or she then leads a discussion of two guiding questions: (1) where do we buy them?; (2) where does the production of each product start?
Teaching objectives: to single out the plan of production; to stress the beginning and the end of the production chain of agricultural produce.

UNIT 3   *Farming*
3.1   Colour slides about wheat and its production.
Teaching objective: to stress the different phases of production, with the different types of machinery.
3.2   To put in order 12 pictures about wheat production with some comments: activity in pairs.
Teaching objective: to consolidate the characteristics of farming.
3.3   Concluding discussion about three questions: (1) what other things are produced in the country?; (2) what does the farmer do about the crops?; (3) if you were a farmer, what would you take into account for pricing?
Teaching objectives: to identify the passage of agricultural produce to another economic agent; to understand the criteria for pricing from the farmer's point of view.

UNIT 4   *Intermediate activity*
Team game, based on transportation and the factory, transportation and selling: children have to put 12 pictures about the productive

cycle of jam into the right order. Classroom discussion: (1) what is the right order?; (2) why?
Teaching objective: to extend the linkage of the chain from production to consumption.

UNIT 5   *The wholesale market*
Individual activity: reading and answering questions about an extract.
Teaching objectives: to identify two characteristics: (1) reserved selling*; (2) wholesale selling.

UNIT 6   *The different commercial outlets for agricultural produce: shops, markets, department stores*
Extracts from different price-lists in different shops and at different times (individual activity). Concluding discussion to identify the reasons for the different prices; to distinguish the general rule from marginal aspects in the variation in agricultural product prices.
Teaching objectives: to recognize the variation in prices; to identify the variation as a movement around a basic price; to understand the necessity for balance between costs and revenue.

Syllabus for fifth grade (10 years old)

The department store and its services

UNIT 1   *The department store*
Individual activity:
1.1 'Draw a department store'.
1.2 'Write a letter to another child who lives in the country and explain what a department store is and how it works'.
Teaching objectives: to activate children's ideas through different media; to diagnose those ideas.

UNIT 2   *To give the right name to different commercial outlets*
Individual activity to link pictures and names. Concluding discussion to consolidate the terminology.
Teaching objective: to clarify the different words which signify commercial outlets.

UNIT 3   *Jobs in department stores*
3.1 Group activity to draw a big picture with all the jobs of a department store.
3.2 Concluding discussion to decide which group has found the most jobs; to distinguish internal or external jobs in the department store.
Teaching objective: to consider the department store as a service in the centre of other services.

* Reserved selling: in Italian wholesale markets, only the shopkeepers can buy goods.

UNIT 4   *The costs of management of the department store*
Reading of an extract about these costs and answering questions (individual activity).
Teaching objective: to identify the difference between the shop and department store.

UNIT 5   *A visit to a department store*
4.1   Preparation of some questions to ask the public-relations officer in the department store.
4.2   Visit and interview.
4.3   Concluding discussion.
Teaching objective: to centre on the problem of selling more at a lower price.

UNIT 6   *Delivery and selling of goods in the department store*
Slides on this question discussed by the teacher. The same pictures for each child to put into the right order.
Concluding discussion.
Teaching objectives: to distinguish the two different phases of delivery and selling in the department store; to distinguish between the two moments (separate in time).

UNIT 7   *Mathematical exercise*
Pricing in the department store and in the shop (individual activity).
Teaching objective: to understand pricing in the department store from a quantitative point of view.

UNIT 8   *Meeting between the children from the six classes (two by two) who participated in the experiment.*
Teaching objective: to generalize what they have learned about the department store.

UNIT 9   *The department store*
Individual activity: 'Now you are more competent, plan and draw again the department store and write a new letter to the same child to explain how the department store works' (see Unit 1.2).
Teaching objective: to clarify the increase of knowledge about the curriculum content.

References

Ajello, A. M. and Bombi, A. S. 1985 *Formare gli Insegnanti alla Sperimentazione: Una Proposta per i Contenuti Sociali* (in press)

Ajello, A. M., Bombi, A. S. and Pontecorvo, C. 1984 'Una proposta di scienze sociale nella scuola elementare: l'apprendimento delle nozioni di lavoro e guadagno' in M. Groppo (ed.) *Psicologia dell'Educazione* vol. 1, Unicopoli, Milan

Ajello, A. M., Bombi, A. S., Pontecorvo, C. and Zucchermaglio, C. 1984 'How to teach economy in the primary school: the concepts of work and profit' paper presented to the 5th European Conference on Economics Education, Manchester, September 3–8

Ajello, A. M., Bombi, A. S., Pontecorvo, C. and Zucchermaglio, C. 1985 'How to teach economy in the primary school: the role of familiarity' unpublished manuscript

Ajello, A. M. and Zucchermaglio, C. 1985 'Come pensa l'insegnante che il bambino impari nelle discussioni in classe' *Orientamenti Pedagogici* 1

Barnes, D. 1976 *From Communication to Curriculum* Penguin

Berti, A. L. and Bombi, A. S. 1981 *Il Mondo Economico nel Bambino* La Nuova Italia, Florence

Danziger, K. 1958 'Children's earliest conceptions of economic relations' (Australia) *Journal of Social Psychology,* **47** pp. 231–40

Furth, H. 1980 *The World of Grown-ups* Elsevier, New York

Jahoda, G. 1979 'The construction of economic reality by some Glaswegian children' *European Journal of Social Psychology* **9** pp. 115–27

Jahoda, G. 1983 'European "Pay" in the development of an economic concept: a study in Zimbabwe' *British Journal of Developmental Psychology* **1** pp. 113–20

Pontecorvo, C., Costiglia, D. and Zucchermaglio, C. 1983 'Discorso e ragionamento scientifico nelle discussioni in classe' *Scuola e Città* **10**

Pontecorvo, C. and Zucchermaglio, C. 1984 'L'interazione tra processi e contenuti di conoscenza: le discussioni in classe' in M. Groppo (ed.) *Psicologia dell'Educazione* vol. 1, Unicopli, Milan

Pontecorvo, C. and Ajello, A. M. 1984 'Insegnanti e processi di conoscenza: il ruolo dell'insegnante nelle discussioni in classe' *Studi di Psicologia dell'Educazione* **2**

Rest, J. R. 1983 'Morality' in P. H. Mussen (ed.) *Handbook of Child Psychology, Vol. 3: Cognitive Development* Wiley, New York

Shantz, C. V. 1983 'Social cognition' in P. H. Mussen (ed.) *Handbook of Child Pschology, Vol. 3: Cognitive Development* Wiley, New York

Strauss, A. 1954 'The development of conception of rules in children' *Child Development* **25** pp. 193–208

Tan, H. and Stacey, B. 1981 'The understanding of socio-economic concepts in Malaysian Chinese school children' *Child Study Journal* **11**(1)

Thomas, L. 1984 *Investigation of economic understanding among pupils aged 12–16: context and purpose* paper presented to the 5th European Conference on Economics Education, Manchester, September 3–8

Vygotsky, L. S. 1934; English translation 1962 *Thought and Language* MIT Press, Chicago

Children's use of cost–benefit analysis: developmental or non-existent?

Marilyn Kourilsky

Professor and Director of Teacher Education, University of California at Los Angeles

Edna Graff

Princeton School District, Cincinnati, Ohio

The main purpose of the study was to ascertain whether the use of cost–benefit analysis by children tends to be age related, a function of instructional mediation, both, or neither. The subjects included 220 first, second, third, and fourth graders ranging in age from 6 to 9 years old. Of these, 114 subjects were assigned to the treatment group. All subjects lived in a predominantly white neighbourhood and attended one of two neighbouring schools. Each subject was individually interviewed; responses were tape recorded and later scored by two trained judges who were specialists in economics.

The major results indicated that children as they get older seem to have both a better understanding of cost–benefit analysis and a tendency to invoke such reasoning in everyday decision making. Also participation in an instructional programme, Mini-Society, appears to produce both a greater understanding of and proclivity to utilize cost–benefit analysis.

Introduction

That economic literacy is an important goal has been recognized in the US and throughout the world (Kourilsky, 1985). Stigler (1970) stated, 'I would argue that economics belongs in everyone's education once we have learned how to teach it' (p. 81). To date, 27 states have mandated the teaching of economics in some form in secondary, or in some cases, elementary schools. The question remains, do we know how to teach it?

Even kindergarten children can learn economic decision making and analytic concepts, provided that standards of appropriate concentration and focus are met (Kourilsky, 1977; Robinson, 1963). The same was found true for children in subsequent grades (Luker, 1981; Walstad, 1980; Ritt, 1969; Jefferds, 1966). However, to what extent are they able to master principles of economics? When are they developmentally ready to be introduced to specific economic concepts? Finally, can we make a case that because economics *can* be learned at a particular grade level, it necessarily *should* be taught? To answer the above questions we need greater communication and perhaps a professional liaison between two disciplines – economics and psychology. For example, it is a widely held belief among developmental psychologists that youngsters both at the pre-operational and concrete stages (Piaget, 1952) are unable to master and apply such economic concepts as cost–benefit analysis. It is alleged that the pre-adolescent has little sense of the costs to some that follow from the benefits to others (Adelson, 1975). Some economists, on the other hand, have empirically demonstrated that young children do not find the concept of cost–benefit analysis beyond their grasp if 'proper' instructional techniques are employed* (Luker, 1981; Walstad, 1980; Kourilsky, 1977; Fogel, 1976; Ryan and Carlson, 1973). A case could be made for teaching a particular economic concept at a designated grade if either (1) the individual would be personally benefited by enabling him or her to *transfer* (from a test-situation) the concept to personal decision making and/or (2) society would be benefited by enhancing the individual's ability to vote rationally or otherwise contribute usefully to social decision making (Kourilsky, 1983).

The economist would benefit greatly from approaching the question of what to teach and when to intervene by knowledge and application of developmental psychology, whereas the developmental psychologist would benefit from information on what kind of teaching results in outcomes previously believed to be developmentally inappropriate for youngsters.

This study addresses the three following questions in the above areas of interest:

1 Is economic cognition (the understanding of cost–benefit analysis) greater for those children exposed to instructional intervention – the Mini-Society – than among those who receive 'regular' social studies instruction?

2 Is the proclivity to use economic reasoning in daily decision making, both with respect to monetary decisions and time-allocation decisions, greater for children exposed to the treatment – the Mini-Society – than for those who were not exposed to the treatment?

3 Are understanding of cost–benefit analysis and/or the proclivity to use economic reasoning in daily decision making age related?

The ranking of economic decisions

Economic reasoning can be conceptualized in terms of a cost–benefit decision-making hierarchy that integrates scarcity, alternatives, and opportunity cost (Kourilsky and Murray, 1981). At level 1 of the hierarchy, the student will have *identified scarcity* as a relevant decision-making issue and

---

*Cost–benefit analysis: a process of making a decision by evaluating different options in terms of benefits forgone versus benefits anticipated.

will have explicitly or tacitly specified scarce resources. For example, in deciding whether to buy a German shepherd puppy, level 1 thinking is reflected in such statements as 'Dogs cost a lot of money', 'I'm not a millionaire', 'Who is going to walk and bathe the dog?'

At level 2, specific *alternative uses* for the identified resources are acknowledged, i.e. particular benefits or opportunities are recognized. The following statements are examples of level 2 thinking: 'The money to buy the German shepherd puppy could be used to buy a bike, a pair of skis, a Lhasa Apso dog, two weeks at sports camp, and lots of other things.'

At level 3, the individual is able to identify those alternative uses (for resources) that are realistically within his or her consideration set and then rank them in terms of the *anticipated benefits* of each. The following represents level 3 reasoning: 'I would really rather spend two weeks at sports camp this summer than buy a dog. I don't think the fun of having a dog is worth giving up the time away from my homework to walk it each day. I'm having a hard enough time getting a C in arithmetic now; besides, I'm pitcher on the Little League baseball team, and we practise on Saturdays. I'd hate not being able to play baseball on Saturday, but that's the only time I'd have to wash the dog. Maybe I'll buy a dog next year.'*

The use of economic reasoning in decision making is not necessarily the only or the 'best' paradigm for problem solving. However, previous research has shown that individuals and families utilizing economic reasoning in their daily decision making gain increased satisfaction (Kourilsky and Murray, 1981).

Methodology

Participants

The participants included 220 first, second, third, and fourth graders ranging in age from 6 to 9 years old (53 first graders, 59 second graders, 55 third graders, and 53 fourth graders). Of these, 114 participants were assigned to the treatment group and 106 to the control group. All participants lived in an upper middle class predominantly white neighbourhood and attended one of two neighbouring schools. These schools were selected because

1 all youngsters participate in the treatment – the Mini-Society – only once in *either* the first, second, third, or fourth grade, and

2 one social studies teacher implements a Mini-Society class and a 'regular' social studies class at each of the four grade levels.

Student assignment to Mini-Society classes is on a random basis.

---

*Note that at level 2 students can explicitly identify competing 'opportunities' but do not explicitly 'weigh' the alternatives.

The treatment: the Mini-Society

Mini-Society is an economics-oriented/experience-based programme in social studies designed for elementary school pupils (Kourilsky, 1983, 1974). The system is based on three principles, which suggest that learning is enhanced when it involves

1 active as opposed to passive participation,

2 real as opposed to vicarious experiences, and

3 actual decision making in which the learners bear the consequences of their decisions.

In Mini-Society, students create their own microcosmic version of an adult economy. In the creation and development of their classroom society, students necessarily experience and then resolve various economic and social problems like those encountered by any society. However, experiencing dilemmas is only one of two interwoven components of the system; the second, the formal debriefing of concepts and ideas derived from the experience, is as essential as the experience itself.

The system is generated when the teacher activates scarcity situations that are inherently motivating (e.g. 'not enough felt-tip pens, classroom chairs, or spaces on a field trip, to go around'). Scarcity is the universal problem that provides the impetus for the formation of any economy. Having experienced scarcity, children are assembled into a debriefing group where the teacher helps them focus on the dilemma and derive possible resolutions to their problem. The children's resolutions are often similar to those utilized in adult economies.

At least 82 per cent of the children eventually attempt a price mechanism to allocate the scarce resources. They design and print currency with which they bid for the scarce resources and determine who may purchase them. The debriefing group continues to serve as a 'town meeting' where students resolve other problems and make various societal decisions.

As the Mini-Society continues, children find various ways of earning money to provide the desired purchasing power. Some become entrepreneurs, selling goods such as wallets, or services such as needlework lessons. Others choose to become salaried workers, either in the society's private sector, or in civil-service positions identified and demanded by the society's membership.

As the daily business and societal activities continue to expand, Mini-Society citizens are faced with a number of predictable dilemmas which their teachers are specifically trained to debrief. In formal debriefing sessions, the children's actual experiences become the foci of inquiry lessons on relevant concepts ranging from distribution of wealth and charity versus compensation to economic shortages and sunk costs.

As students experience social, political and economic problems, explore various resolutions and their implications, and implement as well as bear the consequences of their resolutions, they are operating in a society which to them *is* the real world.

Tests

To test the students' *economic cognition* a 'true–false, justify your answer' questionnaire was read to each subject on an individual basis. Their responses were tape recorded. Each of the five questions was aimed at levels of cognition beyond recall, including both simple and complex application questions. Scores ranged from 0 to 10 points with each response worth 2 points. This economic cognition instrument developed by M. Kourilsky and J. F. Barron in 1965 has an alpha coefficient (Cronbach) of 0.882, indicating a high degree of internal consistency.

Each answer was scored separately by two trained judges (not the experimenter), both specialists in economics, who were unaware of whether the subjects were treatment or non-treatment. Using the Pearson product–moment correlation, the interscorer consistency of the two judges was established at 0.946.

A sample question and example of scoring is as follows:

Paying $500 for a package of M & M candies would be paying a very high price.

Examples of possible responses and scores are as follows:

0 = 'Yes' or 'No', with no additional, or with incorrect information forthcoming after prompting.

1 = 'Yes – it costs me a lot. Five hundred dollars is a lot of money.' The response shows some *knowledge of opportunity cost*.

2 = 'Yes – it costs me a lot. I could get the best bike in the world for that much money, and that's worth more than a package of candy.' *A reason is given*; the alternative forgone is explicated.

The economic test was administered in an interview to control for differences in subjects' reading ability, to diminish the possible threat of a test-like situation, and to allow young subjects the leeway to express complex ideas without being constrained by their limited writing abilities.

Skill in *economic reasoning with respect to monetary decisions* was determined by the subjects' response in the following situation:

Ten items, each approximately one dollar in value and high demand items for this age group, were displayed for the subject to examine. The subject was then told that he or she could have the opportunity to 'earn' one item from the selection of Snoopy pencils, Eraser-Mate pens, candy, bubble-gum, a kite, book, etc. In order to earn the item, the subject was given the following directions:

'You must tell me everything you are thinking as you are making the decision as to the item you want to have for your own. Be sure you describe how you are making your choice. Tell me why you choose the one item you may have for your own. Remember to think *out loud*. Remember to tell me everything you are thinking. Remember to tell me why you choose the one item you would like to have for your own.'

The responses were tape recorded and later scored separately by the above-mentioned judges (economists) at the highest level of economic reasoning exhibited. They were unaware of whether the subjects were in the treatment or non-treatment group. Examples of possible responses and scores are as follows:

0 =   No recognition of economic reasoning – 'I want the candy. I like it.'

1 =   Recognition of the existence of scarce resources – 'I can't have everything – I want the pencils.'

2 =   Ability to identify specific alternative uses for scarce resources – 'I want the pencils, but then I can't have the candy, the jacks, the kite and the book.'

3 =   Ability to identify those alternative uses that are realistically within one's consideration set and rank them in terms of anticipated benefits – 'I really want the pencils which means I can't have the jacks which I could not only play by myself, but could play with my friends. I will give up the pencils and take the jacks.'

Skill in *economic reasoning with respect to time allocation* was determined by the subjects' response to the following situation:

Because of the current energy crisis, President Reagan has determined that, after one week, there will be no television for a long time. To get you used to the coming crisis, your parents have stipulated that you may only watch one hour of television a week. You may watch the one hour any day or any time you choose. What would be the programme(s) you would choose to watch and why?

Again the responses were tape recorded and later scored by the above-mentioned judges as a 0, 1, 2 or 3, based on the highest level of economic reasoning exhibited. Examples of possible responses and scores are as follows:

0 =   No recognition or use of economic reasoning – 'The Dukes of Hazzard.'

1 =   Recognition of the existence of scarce resources – '"The Dukes of Hazzard", because it lasts for an hour, and I only have one more hour.'

2 =   Ability to identify alternative uses for scarce resources – 'I could watch "The Incredible Hulk" or "The Dukes of Hazzard" or "Trapper John". Boy, I have a lot of choices.'

3 =   Ability to identify those alternative uses that are realistically within one's consideration set, and rank them in terms of anticipated benefits – 'I could watch "Little House on the Prairie", which I like; I also like "The Incredible Hulk"; but, I think I would choose "The Dukes of Hazzard" because I like it more. There is a lot of action, and a lot of car chases, and I really like cars.'

The interscorer consistency between the two judges had been piloted, using the Pearson product–moment correlation coefficient, and the following results were obtained: economic reasoning/monetary 0.91; and economic reasoning/time allocation 0.84.

Procedure

Treatment subjects participated in 10 weeks of Mini-Society (three times a week for 50 minutes per session) in the second semester (February – June) of the academic year while non-treatment students concomitantly participated in the schools' 'regular social studies programme' (three times a week for 50 minutes per session). In the last two weeks of May, all of the students, both the treatment and non-treatment groups, were tested on

1 their understanding of cost–benefit analysis (economic cognition)

2 their use of economic reasoning (cost–benefit analysis) in personal decision making with respect to monetary decisions

3 their use of economic reasoning (cost–benefit analysis) in personal decision making with respect to time-allocation decisions

Each subject was individually interviewed by one of two trained interviewers away from the classroom environment.* The student's responses were tape recorded to ascertain the student's level of economic cognition.

The subjects were first asked the five cognition questions. Then they were shown the 10 items and allowed to earn one of these by 'thinking out loud'. Last, they were given the time-allocation dilemma and asked to respond.

The tapes were then evaluated individually by two scorers – not the interviewers. The data was statistically analysed with the primary goal of ascertaining determinants of economic cognition and reasoning. A post-test-only control group was utilized. Subjects in this type of design are randomly assigned to two or more groups. The groups then receive their respective treatments and a post-test. Because the post-test-only control group design involves random assignment and a control group, this design constitutes a true experiment and serves to control for all sources of internal invalidity except mortality (Shavelson, 1981; Gay, 1981; Campbell and Stanley, 1963). To compare the means of the different groups a three-way analysis of variance was used (sex by grade by treatment).

Results

With regard to study question 1, the effect of treatment on economic cognition, it appears that instructional intervention – the Mini-Society – is an important determinant of economic cognition at each grade level. Table 1 and the figure present the means both by grade and treatment.

Thus it appears that children exposed to instructional intervention – the Mini-Society – significantly out-perform non-treatment students with respect

* Three independent scorers were utilized to analyse the interview consistency in 20 interviews (10 each) conducted by the two interviewers. They were unable to detect any differences in the interview technique of the interviewers, with the boys and girls, or with treatment and non-treatment subjects.

Table 1   Economic cognition score means by grade and treatment

	Grade 1	Grade 2	Grade 3	Grade 4
Control group	0.41 ($n = 27$)	0.69 ($n = 32$)	0.73 ($n = 26$)	0.90 ($n = 21$)
Treatment group	1.50 ($n = 26$)	2.26 ($n = 27$)	2.65 ($n = 29$)	3.75 ($n = 32$)

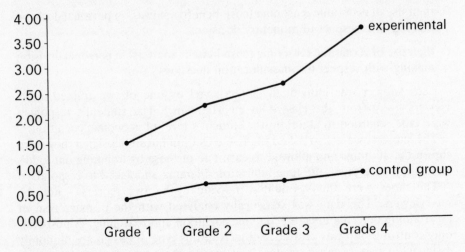

Graphical representation of the results of Table 1

to demonstrating their knowledge of cost–benefit analysis. In fact, the analysis of variance reveals a significance level of <0.01 (F_1, 204, = 98.61).

In study question 2, we were interested in ascertaining whether the proclivity to use economic reasoning (cost–benefit analysis) in everyday decision making was related to treatment. With respect to monetary decisions

Table 2   Monetary decision score means by grade, treatment and sex

Grade		Experimental condition		Sex	
Grade 1	1.00 ($n = 53$)	Control group	1.01 ($n = 106$)	Male	1.10 ($n = 106$)
Grade 2	1.10 ($n = 59$)	Treatment group	1.48 ($n = 114$)	Female	1.40 ($n = 114$)
Grade 3	1.33 ($n = 55$)				
Grade 4	1.62 ($n = 53$)				

it was found (see Table 2) that treatment was a significant factor ($p<0.01$) in economic decision making (F_1, 204, = 8.02).

Similar results were obtained for decisions pertaining to time allocation (F_1, 204, = 8.02). Thus participation in the Mini-Society does appear to result in transfer of economic reasoning to everyday decision making, both with respect to monetary and time-allocation decisions.

We examined in study question 3 whether the understanding of cost–benefit analysis and the transfer of such reasoning to everyday decision making was age related. It appears that age is a potent factor in determining economic cognition (F_3, 204, = 10.56) as well as economic reasoning with respect to monetary decisions (F_3, 204, = 4.21). However with respect to time-allocation decisions the findings are inconclusive. Specifically with respect to time allocation, the interaction of grade, treatment and sex is significant (F_3, 204, = 3.49) and at the control group level there is an interaction between grade and sex (F_3, 98, = 3.20) which indicates that girls do better at certain grade levels than boys and vice versa (Table 3).

Table 3   Time allocation score means by grade, treatment and sex

	Grade 1	Grade 2	Grade 3	Grade 4
Male (control)	0.69	0.39	0.36	0.77
	($n = 13$)	($n = 18$)	($n = 14$)	($n = 13$)
Female (control)	0.14	0.86	0.92	0.62
	($n = 14$)	($n = 14$)	($n = 12$)	($n = 8$)
Male (treatment)	0.25	0.92	0.85	1.00
	($n = 8$)	($n = 13$)	($n = 13$)	($n = 14$)
Female (treatment)	1.00	0.78	1.00	1.33
	($n = 18$)	($n = 14$)	($n = 16$)	($n = 18$)

In summary, the analysis of variance reveals that in terms of economic cognition the tests for the three specific main effects were significant. As they get older students seem to have a better understanding of cost–benefit analysis (F_3, 204, = 4.21), and overall, girls score higher than boys (F_1, 204, = 4.62). Also the treatment produces a significant effect.

In everyday decision making with respect to personal monetary decisions, the interaction of grade and treatment and sex is significant. Also, as they get older students appear to have a greater proclivity to utilize cost–benefit analysis, and girls tend to outscore boys.

Discussion

With regard to study question 1, the effect of instructional intervention on economic cognition, it was not surprising to find that treatment was an important factor. Almost all previous research has indicated that instructional intervention does result in acquisition of economic concepts. It is however interesting to note that the previous studies also indicate a lack of transference and retention and conclude that the typical instructional intervention leads to a mastery of economic concepts only at the recall level rather than at higher levels of cognition (Craig and O'Neill, 1973; Saunders, 1970 and 1980; Harbury and Szreter, 1970; Sulkin and Pranis, 1969; Moyer and Paden, 1968; Dawson and Bernstein, 1967; Clayton, 1964). However, in this study a verbal test was administered which utilized questions that were all beyond the recall level of the cognitive domain (Bloom, 1956).

Thus the difference between treatment and non-treatment subjects may suggest that the particular intervention, Mini-Society (or similar type of mediation), gives students an advantage in mastering concepts beyond the memory level. This advantage (which may or may not be attributed to the Mini-Society itself) may explain why these 6–9 year old children could both apply and even transfer these concepts to everyday life decisions (study question 2), whereas children of the same age in other economic education studies could in most cases only regurgitate the economic content.

However, it appears that with respect to 6, 7, 8 and 9 year olds the ability to transfer economic reasoning to *monetary* decisions is greater that to *time-allocation* decisions. In fact, treatment is much less important as a determinant of economic reasoning with respect to time allocation than it appears to be with regard to money or even economic cognition itself. In terms of time allocation, even with instructional intervention, most students at best were reasoning at level 1 of the hierarchy. It is possible that in verbalizing about time decisions, subjects failed to make their analysis explicit; however it seems no more probable that this would be the case with respect to time decisions than with respect to monetary decisions.

More likely, children fail to perceive a time budgetary constraint analogous to the money budgetary constraint. The budget constraint on money is probably more salient and visible than the constraint on time. However, by the fourth grade children were using higher levels of economic reasoning with respect to time-allocation decisions than college students (Kourilsky and Kehret-Ward, 1983). Such a finding, if replicated, has curricular implications for economists. Given that economic reasoning is an important objective, it may be unwise to wait until college to introduce students to the discipline of economics. Also, in most courses, illustrations of economic principles are almost always in terms of goods, services, or money. We should also utilize examples that include time as a valuable resource. Perhaps eventually it would not take up to the time of mortality for people to realize that 'time may be worth more than money'.

Our last study question asked whether the understanding and transfer of cost–benefit analysis are age related. The results clearly indicate that the age of the student is an important factor, especially with regard to economic cognition and economic reasoning (monetary). It is both easy and seductive to interpret these findings to mean that both economic cognition and transfer of such cognition are developmental in the Piagetian sense. (Cognitive development, based upon a Piagetian model, results in cumulative changes in information processing and response. These changes are set in general age-related categories, which provide a range within the developmental hierarchy. The four basic stages are: sensorimotor, 0–2; pre-operational, 2–7; concrete operations, 7–11; and formal operations, 11–15.)

However, our results simply suggest as a provocative hypothesis that the economic reasoning hierarchy is not only a descriptive and perhaps a normative hierarchy but also a developmental hierarchy. Youngsters at the concrete operations stage are definitely improving their ability both to manifest and invoke knowledge of cost–benefit analysis. At this point it would be premature to conclude that such a finding indicates more than 'as children get older they get smarter'. However, there is a definite pattern that suggests that the invoking of cost–benefit analysis indeed may be a developmental process. Future research might focus more closely on this issue and determine specific cumulative stages occurring developmentally.

An unanticipated outcome of the study was the pattern of gender-related differences at specific age levels. In general, girls appear to outperform boys in terms of economic cognition and reasoning. Both previous research (Ferber *et alia,* 1983) and our observations suggest that whereas these differences may be statistically significant, they are not necessarily substantively meaningful. Since interview procedures were utilized, it is possible that the girls' inherent verbal fluency tended to allow them to outperform boys. On the other hand, it is also possible that, if exposed to economics early enough, girls may have an advantage over boys in their propensity to understand and apply such concepts.

In sum, we now know that children have definite potential ability to use cost–benefit analysis, which can be accelerated by instructional intervention. The remaining question is whether such reasoning is developmental.

Acknowledgements

This research has been made possible by a grant from the Charles Stewart Mott Foundation. Many thanks to Lory Furse and Ellen Ortiz for their lively conversation and useful suggestions pertaining to the interviewing of the children.

References

Adelson, J. 1975 'The development of ideology in adolescence' in S. Dragastin and G. Edler (eds.) *Adolescence in the Life Cycle* Hemisphere, Washington, D.C.

Bloom, B. G. (ed.) 1956 *Taxonomy of Educational Objectives: Cognitive Domain* David McKay, New York

Campbell, D. T. and Stanley, J. C. 1963 *Experimental and Quasi-Experimental Designs for Research* Rand McNally, Chicago

Clayton, R. E. 1964 'Performance in economics at school and university' *Vestes* 7 pp. 120–27

Craig, E. and O'Neill, J. B. 1973 'The predictability of economic relationships' *Journal of Economic Education* 5 pp. 92–4

Dawson, G. G. and Bernstein, I. 1967 *The Effectiveness of Economics Courses in High Schools and Colleges* New York University Center for Economic Education, New York

Ferber, M. A., Birnbaum, B. G. and Green, C. A. 1983 'Gender differences in economic knowledge: a reevaluation of the evidence' *Journal of Economic Education* 14 pp. 24–37

Fogel, L. R. 1976 *An Evaluation of the 'Adventure: Economics' Series Through Statistical Measurement of Learning Achievement in the Intermediate School* Dissertation Abstracts International

Gay, L. R. 1981 *Educational Research: Competencies for Analysis and Application* Charles E. Merrill, Columbus, Ohio

Harbury, C. D. and Szreter, C. D. 1970 'The value of prior experience of economics for university schools' *Journal of Economic Education* 2 pp. 56–62

Jefferds, W. J. 1966 'A comparison of two methods of teaching economics in grade one' unpublished Ed.D. dissertation, University of California, Berkeley

Kourilsky, M. L. 1974 *Beyond Simulation: The Mini-Society Approach to Instruction in Economics and Other Social Sciences* Educational Resource Associates, Los Angeles

Kourilsky, M. L. 1977 'The Kinder-economy: a case study of kindergarten pupils' acquisition of economic concepts' *Elementary School Journal* 77 (3) pp. 182–91

Kourilsky, M. L. 1985 'Economics: educational programs' in T. Husén and T. N. Postlethwaite (eds.) *International Encyclopedia of Education* Pergamon Press, New York

Kourilsky, M. and Kehret-Ward, T. 1983 'Determinants of economic reasoning in monetary and time-allocation decisions' *Journal of Economic Education* 14 pp. 23–31

Kourilsky, M. and Murray, T. 1981 'The use of economic reasoning to increase satisfaction with family decision making' *Journal of Consumer Research* 8 pp. 183–8

Luker, W. A. 1981 'An evaluation of DEEP: does it really work?' unpublished paper, North Texas State University

Moyer, E. and Paden, D. 1968 'On the efficiency of the high school economics course' *American Economic Review* 58 pp. 870–77

Piaget, J. 1952 *The Origins of Intelligence in Children* Norton, New York

Ritt, S. I. 1969 'An experimental study of the capacity of fourth and fifth grade children to understand selected economic concepts' in H. A. Sulkin and C. R. Friedman (eds.) *Research in Elementary School Economics* Occasional Papers No. 30, Industrial Relations Center, University of Chicago

Robinson, H. F. 1963 *Learning Economic Concepts in Kindergarten* Dissertation Abstracts International

Ryan, F. L. and Carlson, M. 1973 'The relative effectiveness of discovery and expository strategies in teaching toward economic concepts with first grade students' *Journal of Educational Research* **66** pp. 446–50

Saunders, P. 1970 'Does high school economics help?' *Journal of Economic Education* **2** pp. 39–55

Saunders, P. 1980 'The lasting effects of introductory economics courses' *Journal of Economic Education* **12** pp. 1–14

Shavelson, R. J. 1981 *Statistical Reasoning for the Behavioral Sciences,* Allyn and Bacon, Boston

Stigler, G. J. 1970 'The case, if any, for economic education', *Journal of Economic Education* **1** pp. 77–84

Sulkin, H. A. and Pranis, R. W. 1969 'Effect of elementary school economics program on children of lower economic status' in H. A. Sulkin and C. R. Friedman (eds.) *Research in Elementary School Economics* Occasional Papers No. 30, Industrial Relations Center, University of Chicago

Walstad, W. B. 1980 'The impact of trade-offs and teacher training on economic understanding and attitudes' *Journal of Economic Education* **12** pp. 41–8

A three-level model in economics education

Alphons L. A. Moret
Robert N. J. van Oosten
Dutch National Institute for Curriculum Development

Instead of describing the process of learning the language of a discipline such as the science of economics as gradually growing from concrete to abstract, we may distinguish three levels: a 'Ground level', a 'Descriptive level' and a 'Theoretical level'.

We think that the transitions from one level to another are rather radical. In our view many teaching processes start at too high a level; the Ground level is often neglected and the Descriptive and Theoretical levels are not recognized. The results of such teaching are frequently a kind of apparent economic knowledge. Such knowledge often lacks applicability. The process of 'raising the level' may be described best in a 'conversation-model' of economics education.

Introduction

Many writers on economics education implicitly start from the idea that conceptualization gradually develops from concrete to abstract. Their articles tend to reject the terminology for concrete economic phenomena used by non-specialists and show a high respect for 'the' scientific language of economics.

We shall argue that a three-level model is a better instrument for the analysis of economics education than the concrete–abstract approach.

History of the idea

The idea of a three- (or four- or five-) level model is relatively new. In 1957 Pierre Marie van Hiele and his wife Dina van Hiele-Geldof wrote joint dissertations proposing a model for the development of geometric thought (van Hiele, 1957; van Hiele-Geldof, 1957). Their model, which evolved from their experiences in secondary schools in the Netherlands and their studies with Professor Freudenthal (University of Utrecht), posits the existence of discrete levels of thought and phases of instruction which help students to develop from one level to another. These ideas were generated by van Hiele and were picked up for further research in the Soviet Union and, later, in the US. Wirszup (1976) mentioned the results of the Soviet experiments as 'the most radical change in Russian mathematics education in nearly a century'.

A general description of the model

We call the level at which pupils generally start secondary education the *Ground level* (G). Pupils are not *tabulae rasae,* they do have some notion of what economics is about. For example, if you show them a list of current economic terms together with terms from other sciences, they are quite able to make distinctions between them. They do have some experience with economics – they buy or exchange things, they know that one has to work in order to manage in life, they recognize a banknote – but these are all vague notions. Van Hiele took the example of a rhombus, which is a figure recognized by nearly all pupils. If you show them ordinary rhombuses of various sizes and colours and ask them, 'Are these all rhombuses?', they will answer 'yes'. But if you show them ordinary rhombuses and a square and ask the same question, they are confused. Most pupils say 'no', some say 'yes'; but they cannot convince each other. We call this situation 'need for language' – a fertile situation which we are aiming at. The need for language motivates students to proceed to a higher level. (Part of this paper is devoted to a discussion of the question as to how to structure this process.)

At the Ground level people speak everyday language: *parents* earn *wages,* not *income; things* are *made* in *factories*, instead of *goods* being *produced* by *industry*. A distinguishing mark of everyday language is its rich character. Words like 'earn', 'poor', 'worker' and 'save' may have varying meanings depending on the context. In everyday language you may say, after tidying up the shed, 'This was a *productive* afternoon', at the same time lamenting, 'What a pile of rubbish a family *produces* in a year'. Everyone will understand you but your words do not fit into a consistent network of scientific economic language. Roest (one of the pioneers of the three-level model) made the following distinction: 'In everyday language, the word is still alive. The word has a varying meaning which can only be understood from its context. Everyday language is creative; existing words may generate new meanings. In the world of science, however, many words are used as terms with a fossilized meaning, in a way "frozen".'

This world of 'frozen' terms is called the second level, the *Descriptive level* (D), which consists of key words related to one another. A concept is defined with the help of other concepts (in economics, for example, production, consumption, capital goods, employment and so on); we speak of *networks of concepts* (see network diagrams, Figs. 1 and 2). A network at the Descriptive level must be consistent (we call this 'discipline D'), but one should keep in mind right from the beginning that the networks are 'constructs' (we call this 'freedom D').

It is of fundamental importance for pupils to realize that at the Descriptive level many criteria for the ordering of phenomena exist, each of which will lead to a different description of (economic) phenomena. Such realization cannot be achieved until sufficient attention is paid to the freedom to select an ordering criterion for the Descriptive level. Once a pupil (or a group of pupils or class) has chosen a certain ordering criterion or certain ordering criteria, the pupil is bound to his or her choice of description (reasoning and arguing) and to the consistent application of such ordering criteria (unless, of course, the unsuitability of the choice has become evident). Thus, within the freedom of choosing ordering criteria (freedom D), this choice/selection is obligatory (discipline D). Let us illustrate this with an example. If you ask, 'Is your cooker at home a capital or a consumption good?', the answer must depend on the network of concepts chosen. We give two examples in Figs. 1 and 2.

It is evident that the cooker is a capital good in network A but a consumption good in network B. Consequently, if you next ask, 'Are you producing something when cooking on your cooker at home?', the answer must be consistent: you are producing something if the cooker is a capital good (network A), but you are not producing something if it is a consumption good (network B).

It is surprising that this network-character has been neglected in many economics textbooks.

The Descriptive level is a frame of reference. At this level there is room for argument. In a discussion, one may convince others by arguments from

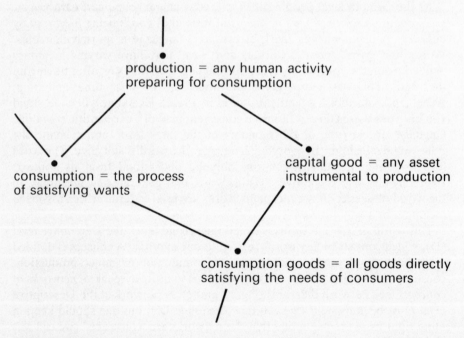

production = any human activity preparing for consumption

consumption = the process of satisfying wants

capital good = any asset instrumental to production

consumption goods = all goods directly satisfying the needs of consumers

Figure 1   Part of network A

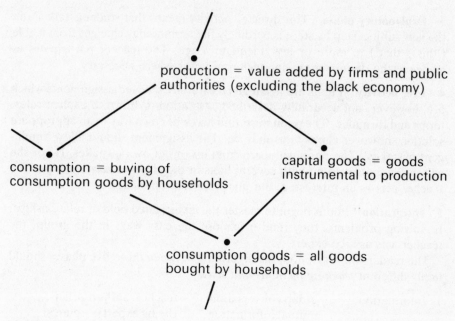

Figure 2   Part of network B

networks based on agreement. It can be asserted that the Descriptive level is reached when people, being aware both of freedom D and of discipline D, unhesitatingly and consistently use the terminology of a network of concepts on which they agree.

Before saying something about the third level, we shall answer a crucial question: In what way can we help pupils to pass from the Ground level to the Descriptive level?

Many classroom experiments (analysing verbatim reports) have led curriculum developers to make a distinction between the following five phases.

1 Information   The teacher starts a discussion in the class, asking questions aimed at putting old words in a new context. However, pupils will get to know this new context only roughly and intuitively. Accordingly, pupils obtain information about the new context which they will be working on during subsequent lessons. In the meantime the teacher obtains information about the group: are these words sufficiently clear and will the new subject have an impact on them (reciprocal information)?

2 Restricted activity   Pupils are given carefully chosen (accurately defined) assignments. These tasks enable them to tackle new items before they have acquired the appropriate vocabulary. The teacher is involved with the group when he or she hands out the assignments, gives directions, checks whether the tasks are executed appropriately and encourages when necessary.

3 Explanatory phase This directed activity means that students talk about the new subject step by step; accordingly the terminology changes from feeble ('this', 'that') to more or less adequate usage. The teacher participates as leader of the discussion, giving technical terms where necessary.

4 Free activity Pupils are again given carefully selected assignments which are, however, not accurately described. Attention is drawn to explicit rules, terms and formulae. The pupil must find his or her own way to an appropriate solution, however clumsy this may be. The assignment should allow 'intelligent mistakes'. The pupil will learn from his or her own mistakes. He or she will become acquainted with several links in the chain of relationships. The teacher acts as an interested, but uncommitted, on-looker.

5 Integration Pupils begin to master the investigated field of relationships. In solving problems, they tend to choose the easy way. In the group, the teacher acts as a co-expert.

The reader will notice that distinguishing between these five phases should imply different *teaching methods and styles:*

1 Information	group conversation; mutual information	teacher: authoritarian (being expert); pupils: docile
2 Restricted activity	practical assignments, individually or in small groups	
3 Explanatory phase	group discussion; introduction of scientific jargon	teacher: democratic; pupils: active participation
4 Free activity	practical assignments, individually or in small groups	teacher: *'laissez faire'*; pupils: restricted to the subject, self-activating
5 Integration	useful contribution to later group or individual work	

A possible objection to this scheme of work is that it is absurd to expect a teacher to switch from an authoritarian to a democratic attitude or vice versa. Nevertheless, we think such a switch a necessary tool which, however, should not be conceived as authoritarian and democratic lessons alternating. This brings us to a more complicated approach to the five phases mentioned above. The scheme is only a model, constructed to design and analyse lessons. Real lessons may show more than one, or even all five phases during the process of passing to a higher level.

Consider, for example, the situation in which pupils are simultaneously working on consumption assignments from phase 4 (free activity), on production assignments from phase 2 (restricted activity) and on fixed cost assignments from phase 1 (information). This means, in this case, that a teacher, being aware of these different phases, should assume alternating authoritarian and democratic attitudes. Why should this be considered strange? Does not a good teacher always blend these attitudes according to circumstances? The only difference is that now he or she has a model to justify this behaviour.

We shall now discuss the third level. Let us recall the question about the cooker, which might invite discussion about networks A and B. Which one is 'better'? Why should we label the cooker as a consumption or capital good? Note that the discussion is now not about economic phenomena as such: we speak about 'frozen' terminology. We ask questions about the motives for choosing a certain network of concepts; about which consequences spring from which network. In network A we may recognize the viewpoint of a welfare economist, in network B that of an economist advising the government on economic policies.

If the discussion turns to these kinds of questions, then we are dealing with the third level, otherwise called the *Theoretical level* (T).

The use of the three-level model in describing teachers' dissatisfaction with economics education

The evaluation of pre-university economics education with the aid of this three-level model may be considered in the light of a well-known phenomenon which disturbs some economics educators. At a certain stage many pupils may come up with a host of definitions and solve standard problems and they may gain sufficient marks in examinations, but these pupils still fail to apply their knowledge (for instance, in analysing a newspaper article or in arguing about public policies).

Many teachers will recognize this. Many educators take the view that schooling involves too much drilling and dictation of notes. Concepts, theories and models taught in this way are too prescriptive in character. Let us illustrate this with a case every economist will recognize. We start with the well-known two-sector Keynesian model:

$$Y = C + I \tag{1}$$

$$C = cY + C_{au} \qquad \text{where} \quad 0<c<1 \quad \text{and} \quad C_{au}>0 \tag{2}$$

$$I = I_{au} \qquad \text{where} \quad I_{au}>0 \tag{3}$$

$$(au = autonomous)$$

In this model, I stands for net investment. So replacement investment (assumed to reflect capital depreciation) is deducted from gross investment. After extensive explanation in which careful attention is paid to the restricting hypotheses of this 'simple' model, a pupil comes up with the following question:

> Households receive disposable income from firms. So firms retain funds for depreciation. Households buy consumption goods from firms. But if, as a consumer, you buy something, an amount for depreciation is included in the firm's selling price. So these enterprises then receive the depreciation twice. How is that? Is this model an employers' trick to make some illegal money? Is this not a fund out of which the government might create new jobs?

Is this a stupid question? On the contrary, we think not. What then was wrong with the way the concept was taught? Is the flaw to be found in the model or in the textbook? Did the teacher give bad explanations or did he himself not quite understand the model? Or, alternatively, was the teacher a victim of his own learning at university?

With the aid of the three-level model, the phenomenon may be described as follows. These pupils have not passed (through the five phases described above) from the Ground level (G) to the Descriptive level (D). They have been engaged by their teacher and textbook on the Descriptive level straight away and, what is more, with only one network of concepts. These concepts are mostly not presented to them as forming a network but as reflecting 'the' scientific language. Because the first step from G to D has been omitted, the language D is foreign to them; they learn it by heart like foreign words (and often with the same reluctance). Moreover, they do not realize that the same words (like 'consumption', 'production') may have different meanings in daily life and in economic jargon. If they use an economic definition, they are neither aware of freedom in the choice of a network (freedom D) nor of the disciplinary character of the network (discipline D). In addition, it is evident that they are not aware of the background and consequences of networks of concepts, because they have not reached the third level (T).

Let us express this differently. Many pupils only have 'formal' knowledge as opposed to 'legitimate'. We speak about legitimate knowledge (often reduced to formulae, schemes, models) if one has a rich abundance of concrete examples in mind and if one uses concepts like consumption or production

1   conscious of the nature of the relationship between these concepts

2   conscious of alternatives, belonging to other networks of concepts

3   conscious of the background and consequences of the choice of the network used

If this awareness is absent, we speak of 'formal' knowledge. Frequently, education (even at university level) results in many teachers acquiring a host of 'formal' knowledge (just as the authors did).

Some illustrations

In our project 'Economics 13–16', we started a discussion about the above-mentioned phenomenon among groups of teachers according to the following procedure. We asked them to fill the following list in quickly:

Examples	Production?	
	Yes	No
1 a doctor prescribing medicine		
2 the manufacture of colour TVs by Philips		
3 repairing your car in your leisure time		
4 assisting at in-service training of teachers		
5 selling of goods by a department store		
6 studying for a profession		
7 the work of a domestic servant		
8 refining oil		
9 keeping hens on a poultry farm		
10 a teacher giving lessons to his neighbour's son in exchange for mowing his lawn		

(Notice that the left hand column is formulated in terms of the Ground level, whereas in the right hand column the term 'production' refers to the Descriptive level.)

After the teachers had filled in this list, a discussion took place about the criteria used to identify an activity as production. We definitely recommend this procedure, which may be followed in the classroom as well. If it is a group just beginning the study of economics, the discussion is typical of the stage of Ground level to Descriptive level (G→D).

Pupils are not able to convince each other, thus bringing about a *need for terminology*. They come to see the necessity for agreement and they will understand that different types of agreement are possible. When teachers are discussing the list, the stage D→T comes to the fore. Their conversation centres on the nature of the definitions: why should one define production this way or another? It appears that not everyone is aware of a network of concepts.

Another example of a lesson activity may help to illustrate this point. It refers to the beginning of the stage G→D. We give the assignment to 13 year olds, to whom it appeals considerably.

What's going on at home?
1 Circle in pencil from the list [Fig. 3] any word which you think indicates activities that have something to do with working.

2 Circle in blue the words which you think refer to leisure.

Fig. 3   What's going on at home?

In the teachers' guide (Moret and van Oosten, 1984/85, part II, p. 31), we gave the following explanation of this pupil assignment:

Forming concepts

In economics, people's pursuit of prosperity and the problems of choice with which they are confronted in this pursuit is a central issue. In addition to the concept of prosperity, concepts such as income, production, consumption and labour play an important part in gaining insight into this pursuit of prosperity. So teachers should attempt to make pupils completely conversant with the meaning of these ideas and the views on which the various meanings of these ideas are based. This effort can be moulded into concrete form by linking them, in the first instance, with the meaning that pupils attach to these ideas in their colloquial speech. Or, if pupils do not yet use these concepts themselves (as for instance with 'prosperity' or 'producing') they might be linked with other ideas which contain clear elements of the economic concepts (as happiness → prosperity and working → producing). The above requires that central ideas, such as income or production, when they are introduced, are linked with the pupils' own experiences. A number of assignments can be set which are all within the context of 'production', without having previously given a definition of the term. For this would lead to formalism and superficial knowledge. Indeed, to prevent this, pupils' experiences are taken as the starting point, then these experiences are built upon, either by other pupils' experiences or by the teacher (through suitable assignments or through the teacher's own contribution). Only if these experiences have become sufficiently wide and the ground has been prepared should economic ideas be formally presented to bring some order to their experiences. In other words, experiences and problems should be provided which require, as it were, sorting out by means of concepts. Too often we see the reverse: pupils are given concepts, words without real content, because the experiences that would enable them to order such ideas are lacking, and they do not feel a need for such ideas.

By giving the pupils the opportunity to arrive at their own descriptions that can be compared with the descriptions of others, arguments may start playing an important part in the process of acquiring technical language. Moreover, we shall gain a better insight into discrepancies between the language of the pupils' world and the language of economics. It becomes possible to gain some understanding of how our pupils acquire knowledge and insight so that we may develop a more conscious, more specific control of the learning process.

Later in the course materials, the concept of 'work' is made more explicit by fitting it into the networks A and B mentioned earlier. From a welfare economist's point of view, we defined 'work' in network A as any human activity directly or indirectly preparing for consumption; working is then identical to producing, the 'informal sector' included. From a government economist's point of view, we defined 'work' in network B as a kind of job that pays a wage (excluding the black economy); work means human activities in firms and public authorities. In other words, human activities in the formal sector only.

In network A one may say that much work is done by unemployed people and housewives at home; in network B this is impossible by definition.

Two pupils' answers   We will finish our illustrations with excerpts from two pupils' answers, showing the passage from G→D in relation to the concept 'work'. This is somewhat difficult because its character and style vanishes in translation; nevertheless we will try.

After a passage from a book about families and labour in the Middle Ages, the following question was asked: 'Families of serfs and peasants were an economic unit for production and consumption. If you compare that with families today in the Netherlands, do you think that this still holds true? Give your opinion in approximately ten sentences and support your arguments by examples.'

Two answers will do for an illustration (second-year lower-stream pupils, around 13 years old). (In the Dutch original, the pupils made spelling and other mistakes.)

> 1   No, in former days they made everything themselves, for example the women made butter and cheese from milk and baked bread themselves. And they used to spin cloth out of flax and wool. Nowadays one does not do so much together. Often only the men work. And the women need not work as hard as in former days. And to get more money the women sometimes go and work somewhere, so they still have time for that.

> 2   No, in former days, clothes, butter, cheese etc. were self-made. Today one goes to the shop for them. In former days, the whole family worked to earn their living. Now father does that. And mother works at home. The children go to school and need not work like children used to. Grandad and Grandma don't work either. They have a pension or live in an old people's home.

Note that in both extracts, 'work' is not yet used consistently as a term of the Descriptive level; the words have not yet been 'frozen'. Work has the ambiguous meaning of activities you are paid for ('a job') and the state of being active in a useful way. The use of language is very unsophisticated (both linguistically and in terms of economics), but much of value is being said.

The ideas developed in this paper are based (as far as economics education is concerned) on material developed over years of experimenting by de Miranda (1985). Some implications are also derived from our experiences in the project 'Economics 13–16' between 1978 and 1984. A brief description of this project is provided in the Appendix in order to clarify the context.

Some implications of the use of the three-level model

Possible consequences of the three-level model for pupils' motivation derived from the 'Economics 13–16' project   The project was concerned with the age group 13–16 and the lower streams of general education. Educationalists used to think that economics was far too difficult a subject for this group. In many countries, there is no economics education for this age group. Since many pupils leave school before or at the age of 16, this results in a population most of whom have not been introduced, at school, to a field which has great influence on their lives. Developers of the economics curriculum for this age group often introduce topics which are thought to be easily tackled: a watered-down extract from an economics textbook, consisting of terms and concepts considered to be not too difficult and stripped of all intricate relationships. Pupils generally think such lessons to be dull, and colleagues, parents etc. find them of little importance.

In the 'Economics 13–16' project we tried, having been inspired by the three-level model, to concentrate the whole curriculum on the stage Ground level to Descriptive level, with a few forays towards the Theoretical level. This implied, as was shown above, starting with pupils' experiences in pupils' language and trying to pass to the Descriptive level with its freedom and discipline. While working on this (we made teaching–learning materials for three years in collaboration with practising teachers) we discovered how deep-rooted the neglect of the stage G→D is. There is a widespread practice among teachers and writers of textbooks to start at the Descriptive level. Starting from pupils' language and experiences is often castigated as childish, but we discovered that many people who began with this point of view were eventually 'converted' as a result of working with the experimental teaching–learning materials. They noticed that pupils became interested in the subject matter, because it related to them personally. This deserves special attention now that a so-called 'new type' of pupil has come to the fore. Much has already been written about this new type of pupil. One tends to say, 'These pupils cannot sit still any more', or, 'They are less and less willing to work automatically on the authority of the one who is in charge, the teacher', or, 'They have so many other things which they find more important and which they enjoy, like television, radio, their hi-fi equipment and the discothèque'.

So here we deal with the motivation problem. Pupils should be motivated by learning activities as well. This motivation may be achieved by starting the course with *their* experiences and interests, and by dealing with subjects that are practically useful for the future as well as for the present. By starting from the Ground level in this way, pupils were more inclined to talk to each other about these lessons and their parents were more interested as well. In a period when pupils' interest in school work was in general decline, the economics lessons gave rise to fewer complaints. Although, as in any educational situation, various factors have influenced the results, the following conclusion can be drawn: recognizing the Ground level to Descriptive level stage is important for arousing pupils' motivation.

Another implication: better half a stage than 'formal' knowledge Stressing the procedure of gradually progressing from the Ground level takes up so much time that the Descriptive level is not always reached. We have discovered this phenomenon in the lower stream of general education.

Our experience of the 'Economics 13–16' project (which includes four years of final examinations) convinced us that it is much better to accept this than to neglect the G→D stage, drilling pupils with knowledge which as we stated above can be little better than 'formal'. Such superficial knowledge is of little use, not being functional, whereas pupils who have completed half a stage between the Ground and Descriptive levels have been given a taste, even if it is only a small taste, of real knowledge. The completion of half a stage gives pupils the opportunity for further development (e.g. in further education or in the adult world) and since a firm link with their own experiences is being forged, what they have learnt will be functional and not so quickly forgotten.

Some thoughts about the character of the three-level model

1   A discussion model of education   Discussion plays an essential role in the three-level model. In fact, all five phases (information, etc.) in the process of rising to a higher level are activated through various types of discussion.

Discussion, here, is not merely a method of teaching; it is based on a fundamental view of how man has developed science. Scientific language is considered to result from the search for means of communication among scientists. 'Searching' implies the possibility of going the wrong way. Pupils must develop the freedom to search, in the process of which they will become acquainted with the sensation of learning by their own mistakes and enjoying the fruits of their creative thinking. Of course, we do not defend 'sloppy language'; discipline is desirable not only in the way discussion is conducted but also in the use of language, but only so far as pupils' freedom has led them to a conscious choice of a network of concepts. In reality, several stages in the course of passing to a higher level will occur together (see above) and discussion often shows the following two elements: a disciplinary fixation on fossilized terms and a creative searching for new ones.

2   A problem-stating model   A problem-solving approach has been widely accepted in education. Knowledge must be functional. But the fact that problems should be formulated before one attempts to solve them has often been neglected. In structuring the curriculum from the three-level model described above, pupils are given more opportunities to develop a problem-formulating attitude. In our society, where change is the rule, such an approach is of great value. Often, vaguely recognized problems have been formulated too late and/or in too imprecise a way.

3   An induction model   The three-level model may place the old controversy about deduction–induction in a new light. It is evident that induction plays an important role in the model, especially in the stage G→D. Real experience is the starting-point. While a specific network of concepts is chosen, deduction may play an important role too, but only if the legitimate character of knowledge (cf. above) is considered.

4   No concrete–abstract model   At first sight one might conceive the Ground level as concrete and the other levels as abstract. But the three-level model starts from another point of view.

The Ground level consists not only of concrete, perceptible economic phenomena but also of abstractions which are, however, not explicit. For instance, in pupils' language, words like 'commerce' or 'work' are already abstractions. In addition the Ground level includes many ideas about unseen or remote matters (such as local government proceedings or the way of life in Brazil), ideas which more or less match 'reality'. At this level relationships may also be involved. A pupil may be convinced that tax reductions are favourable for shopkeepers. Probably this image in pupils' minds is one of the most important elements of the Ground level: opinions which are based not on rational arguments but, for example, on what has been learnt in family life.

The Descriptive level on the other hand is typically a frame of references built up from consistent networks of concepts that describe economic phenomena. These concepts are abstractions. At this level, independent of the network chosen, consumption is never, for example, someone who is chewing gum.

This also holds good for the Theoretical level. However, it has a different frame of reference: no economic phenomena are being described; one is talking about the framework of the Descriptive level.

5   An emancipation model   The teacher's role in the three-level model is fundamentally democratic, although during some phases it is characterized as being authoritarian (cf. above). Pupils are accepted as equal partners eventually. They are stimulated to take initiatives, to think creatively and to be critical about other people's statements and writings. Moreover, in the process of reaching the Theoretical level they learn to think critically about the background and consequences of existing terminology. Consequently the three-level model achieves emancipatory objectives.

6   The relative importance of the three-level model   In education, models ought to be evaluated first against the background of discontent amongst educators. If a model appears to be a good instrument to describe and analyse this discontent then this is all to the good. If it has, in addition, a perspective for improving classroom activities it may be labelled 'fertile'. The three-level model satisfies these two criteria more than any other model we know. It has, in our view, yet to be superseded.

In conclusion, we indicate some specific areas for further research and development.

Areas for further research and development

The development of a curriculum based on the above conceptual framework will be an enormous enterprise for years to come. It can only be done by conscientiously analysing verbatim reports of lessons, pupils' assignments and feedback, re-analysing etc. However, experiments carried out up till now do indicate that the work is worthwhile. In the Netherlands a start has been made by a group under the supervision of de Miranda. But most of the work still has to be done.

Two other types of research are important:

1 analysis of mistakes by economics students and examination of these mistakes in relation to the students' pre-university education, keeping the three-level model in mind

2 investigation of how far pupils who have received economics education for some years have retained their understanding, trying to measure how far the school, family, peer group, etc. have influenced the results (the interesting research carried out by Kokosowski (1973, 1978) in France may be an appropriate starting point)

Finally, we would like to draw attention to two quite different issues:

1 How may the scientific structure of economics be analysed from the viewpoint of this three-level model?

2 How may pupils' language at the Ground level be analysed? What kind of economic ideas do they have, and what language do they use to express them? The French research by Albertini and Vergès (1977) contributes greatly to our understanding of this question.

Appendix: The 'Economics 13–16' project

The project was carried out by the Dutch National Institute for Curriculum Development (SLO). The authors were the central team of the project group.

Main objective On behalf of the Minister of Education the SLO has developed a curriculum and examination programme for Economics for the 'MAVO' (the MAVO is the lowest stream of general secondary education for the 12–16 age range). The curriculum refers to the second, third and fourth years of the MAVO. In the second year the subject is compulsory for two hours a week and in both the third and fourth years it is optional for four hours a week. Examinations take place at the end of the fourth year.

Additional objectives In order to achieve our main objective, the development of the economics curriculum, the project was concerned with the development of a complete set of teaching–learning materials (including extensive teachers' guides) together with the development of teaching principles and methods and the analysis of pupils' learning processes.

Strategy of curriculum development and dissemination The development of the curriculum was paralleled by the development of teaching–learning materials as part of a cyclic process, based mostly on classroom practice.

Many schools participated in the process of developing curriculum materials (about 350 schools were involved during the last stage). Besides schools, a number of institutes were actively involved, including the Association of Economics Teachers (VECON), the Central Institute for Test

Development (CITO), the National Pedagogical Centres (LPC) for diagnostic tests and dissemination, the Teacher Training Centres (NLO) for in-service training, the Advisory Committee for Curriculum Development (ACLO-ER) and the National Inspectors.

Periodically, as part of the cyclic process of development, conferences were organized in order to discuss the curriculum products. In this way, and by working in close co-operation with these institutions, the final version of the curriculum was based on general approval.

The strategy incorporated the idea that both the development of the curriculum and its dissemination should, as far as possible, be a concurrent rather than a consecutive process.

Timing The project started in 1978 and continued until the end of 1984. In 1982 all MAVO schools (1200) started work based on the course. At the start of 1985 the SLO presented a definitive, revised version of the curriculum to the Minister of Education.

General view of the approach and content The course aims to enable pupils to function in their present and future roles as consumers, workers and citizens. A selection of course topics, based on an analysis of life situations in the context of these present and future roles, was made, also taking into account pupils' own interests and learning abilities in addition to the fundamental structure, basic concepts and principles of the economics discipline.

The course is a blend of the following aspects (in order of importance):

1 personal economics

2 economics issues

3 economics concepts

4 business economics (including organization of commerce and industry)

5 comparative economic systems

Consumer education is an important part of the curriculum.

The approach in the experimental course material was active, pupil-oriented, with pupils' own interests and experiences as the main starting point.

References

Albertini, J. M. and Vergès, P. 1977 'Les formations à l'économie des adultes et adolescents' *Les Cahiers Français*, Paris **179**

Fuys, D., Geddess, D. and Tischler, R. (eds.) 1984 *English Translation of Selected Writings of Dina van Hiele-Geldof and Pierre M. van Hiele* Brooklyn College of City University of New York, School of Education, New York

Haan, J. de and Miranda, J. de 1979–1984 *Leerplanontwikkeling voor het vak*

Organisatie (Curriculum development for the subject organisation) Reports 1–5, Katholieke Hogeschool, Tilburg, Netherlands

Hiele, P. M. van 1957 *De Problematiek van het Inzicht, Gedemonstreerd aan het Inzicht van Schoolkinderen in Meetkundeleerstof* (The problem of insight illustrated by schoolchildren's insight into the subject matter of geometry) with English summary, Dissertation, University of Utrecht, Netherlands

Hiele, P. M. van (ed.) 1985 *Structure and Insight* Academic Press, New York

Hiele-Geldof, D. van 1957 *De Didaktiek van de Meetkunde in de Eerste Klas van het VHMO* (The teaching-learning principles of geometry in the lowest class of the secondary school) with English summary, Dissertation, University of Utrecht, Netherlands

Hoffer, A. 1983 'Van Hiele-based research' in R. Lesh and M. Landau (eds.) *Acquisition of Mathematics Concepts and Processes* Academic Press, New York

Horbach, P., Leeuwen, R. van, Maris, W., Miranda, J. de and Zuiderwijk, P. 1975 *Vernieuwing Economie-onderwijs: Didactisch Verslag van een Project aan de Juridische en Sociale Faculteiten te Tilburg* (Innovation in economics education: report concerning teaching learning principles of a project at the Law and Social Sciences Departments, Tilburg) Katholieke Hogeschool, Tilburg, Netherlands

Kokosowski, A. 1973 *Formation Économique et Pédagogie des Sciences Sociales* Tema (Thesis, University of Paris, 1972)

Kokosowski, A. 1978 *Enseigner les Sciences Économiques et Sociales* PUF l'éducateur, Presses Universitaires de France

Miranda, J. de 1985 'About the possibility of an empirical general didactics' in P. M. van Hiele, (ed.) 1985 *Structure and Insight* Academic Press, New York

Moret, A. L. A. and Oosten, R. N. J. van 1984/85 *An elaborated Illustration of the Economics 13–16 Project of the SLO (Parts I–V)* Stichting voor de Leerplanontwikkeling, Enschede, Netherlands

Roest, J. F. 1973 *UIT-WEI-dingen* Werkgroep Empirische Inleiding, p. R 1968–4

Senk, S. L. 1984 'Research and curriculum development based on the van Hiele model of geometric thought' paper prepared for the Working Group on geometry etc. at the Fifth International Congress on Mathematical Education, Adelaide, Australia, August

Voorde, H. ten 1977 *Verwoorden en Verstaan* Dissertation, University of Amsterdam [English summary also in *European Journal of Science Education* I pp. 469–70]

Wirszup, I. (trans.) and Hoffer, A. (ed.) 1968 *Problems in the Formation of Geometric Ideas in Primary-Grade School Children* Prosveshchenie Publishing House, Moscow

Wirszup, I. 1976 'Breakthroughs in the psychology of learning and teaching geometry' in J. L. Martin and D. A. Bradford (eds.) *Space and Geometry* ERIC SMEAC, Columbus, Ohio

Response   *Keith Wood*

The message of the papers by Kourilsky and Moret and van Oosten is that teachers should encourage pupils at an early age to consider the language of economics in ways which are appropriate to their development. This is unexceptionable. There is sound advice offered, too. Pupils should be actively involved in learning; vicarious experiences should be avoided because of their unreality; and pains should be taken to organize discussion in which pupils can talk about economic phenomena in the context of their own experiences.

On this last point, a salutary reminder emerges that teachers are unlikely to be effective organizers of discussion without taking definite steps to develop this skill. Educators at all levels should take note. Replication of the procedure of Moret and van Oosten for the discussion of production would provide further insights into the importance of organizing such discussion. The authors' observation that pupils perceive a need for terminology when they fail to convince each other in discussion is exemplary.

There is, however, something disturbing in the suggestion of Moret and van Oosten that, at the Descriptive level of their three-level model, a pupil's question may have more than one answer if it is not simultaneously possible for the pupil to explore why a choice of answer is available (at the Theoretical level). Pupils may be less than content with a discipline which nurtures what may otherwise appear as ambiguity at the Descriptive level. With reference to the cooker example cited in the paper, would it be more satisfactory to ask under what circumstances a cooker may be classified as (a) capital good, (b) consumer good? This question focuses on the need to reach agreement.

It seems possible that network B relating to this example may not emerge from the Ground level without the Theoretical level intervening. Network B appears to be a sub-set of network A resulting from the problem of the valuation of production which is not sold in the market. Network B is in a sense artificial. In both networks, the definitions of a capital good are similar. Could pupils be encouraged to confront these ambiguities if they arise in their discussion and, in so doing, move towards the creation of links between the networks? Economists' viewpoints might be distinguished not by the network which they employ but by the values and emphasis which they place on certain parameters within the structure thus created. If not, how many networks are there?

Kourilsky's finding that, possibly due to their greater verbal fluency, in general girls appear to outperform boys in the age range 6–9 years in terms of economic cognition and reasoning is very interesting. Evidence from public examinations in the UK and Hong Kong shows that girls' performance in economics is lower than that of boys at the secondary fifth-form level (age 16) for reasons which are not clear. Kourilsky tentatively suggests that exposure to economics at an earlier age may provide girls with an advantage over boys in their propensity to understand and apply economic concepts. If this is so, the introduction of economics at the primary level of schooling may act to neutralize whatever negative factors combine to give economics as a school subject its male bias. This collection of papers provides many valuable suggestions for ways of introducing economics to younger pupils.

Response   *Richard Dunnill*

Moret and van Oosten's paper describes their progress made in improving the provision and teaching of economics to lower stream 13–16 year olds in the Netherlands. Their work seems to be based upon three questions familiar to economics educators:

1 How can we deal with the disaffection of many (lower stream) students in the mid 1980s?

2 How can we teach concepts and skills that are transferable to everyday life?

3 How can such students be helped to get inside the discipline of economics?

The paper proposes a theoretical model as a means of answering these questions, and gives examples of how the model has worked in the classroom.

The authors suggest that answers to all these questions lie in the use of a language-based interactive model of teaching and learning. The theoretical model rejects traditional concrete–abstract approaches, arguing instead for a three-level view of learning: Ground level, Descriptive level, Theoretical level. This is based on the idea that language is the key to real learning. If students' own economic language is used as a starting point (Ground level), then, via increasingly unstructured activities and discussion, students will gradually be able to place economics concepts within the context of a framework of such concepts (the Descriptive level). A discussion about the reasons behind the choice of a particular concept network would then expose the value judgements present and allow the use of such thinking in everyday life (leading to the Theoretical level).

This appears to raise a number of questions:

1 Is the three-level model very different from an expanded version of the concrete–abstract view?

2 Can the authors' view of economics as best learned through concept networks be justified?

3 Are the authors suggesting that this model allows all 13–16 year olds access to the Theoretical level, or will only a few progress that far?

The practical illustrations in the paper begin with two sorting activities.

These are similar to a technique also being developed in co-operation with some London schools. They are used to facilitate the classifying and structuring of concepts and as an enjoyable means of generating students' interest, developing thinking and building up co-operation and organization. They also provide an uncomplicated method of assessment. The third illustration is of a type of data-response exercise. Two students' answers are provided. These appear to leave wide open the questions of interpretation and assessment. How do the authors know that their students are thinking in the required manner?

The paper sees the three-level model as providing an answer to teachers' dissatisfaction with traditional economics education. I certainly share that dissatisfaction, and support the authors' demand for legitimate knowledge of use in everyday life as opposed to traditional formal learning designed to pass examinations and little else! But is the authors' answer convincing? The authors present four ways in which they feel their work is innovative – it is *discussion based*; it involves students in *problem stating as well as problem solving*; it is *inductive* from the students' own experience; and it *emancipates* the students and the teacher in being more democratic. These ideas are certainly interesting and are echoed in the curriculum development with which I am involved.

An excerpt from the teachers' guide used in the paper gives a clear view of the application of these four ideas:

> . . . experiences and problems should be provided which require . . . sorting out by means of concepts.

The curriculum project involved, 'Economics 13–16', is also interesting in providing younger students with two hours of economics per week, with older students having the option of four hours per week, with a course based upon the theory explained in the paper. A number of questions do, however, need to be asked regarding the development of these ideas.

Under the scheme as outlined above, students may well be able to master concepts in the context of concept networks, but how do the authors know that students will be able to employ the right concept in the right situation in everyday life? The emphasis in the paper on a conceptual basis to learning can be accepted, but it does seem to ignore skills other than those directly linked to language and academic achievement. Attitudes and values are not really mentioned at all. Are not these essential elements of an economics education? The fact that 'Economics 13–16' concentrates on lower stream students and emphasizes Ground and Descriptive level activities is another source of concern. Is this innovative approach not suitable for all 13–16 year olds? The whole question of streaming is also worth investigating from a general educational perspective as well as from that of economics educators.

In conclusion, I would fully support the view of the authors that language is a vital ingredient in a new radical economics curriculum; that the ideas of activity-based discussions, and problem-stating and problem-solving activities are to be commended; and that the idea of induction and of emancipating both teachers and students is to be welcomed. To have achieved a project such as 'Economics 13–16' is a feat in itself. However, I would urge the team involved to examine again the three questions posed at the start of this paper.

Our disaffected students will certainly respond positively to the new approach, but will teachers need help or re-training? (We must beware of the Hawthorne effect clouding our judgement.)

I remain to be convinced that real transferable economics is being taught but I look forward to being proved wrong! Finally, is the authors' view of economics as concepts in networks really economics? Even if it is, how do they know when a student is thinking in such a manner? How can we assess economics thinking? Also, given that only lower stream students are involved, I am left wanting to know the authors' views about economics courses for all students.

Response   *Paul Clarke*

When economics education for the 5–16 age group is discussed, the assumption is often made that conceptualization develops from a concrete to an abstract level. Moret and van Oosten argue that an initial emphasis on concrete experience in practice means the younger student is given 'topics which are thought to be easily tackled; a watered-down extract consisting of terms and concepts stripped of all intricate relations.'

In contrast, Moret and van Oosten argue that students' own 'Ground-level' experience consists not only of economic phenomena but also of a more abstract understanding of relationships between economic phenomena. Too often, teachers start at a 'Descriptive' level where 'students are given concepts, words without real content, because the experiences that would enable them to order such ideas are lacking, and they do not feel a need for such ideas.'

More attention should be given to that stage where students develop their Ground level to a Descriptive level – where they begin to link together economic phenomena using networks. The criteria for these networks should be of the students' own choice, but once established, they have to be consistently applied. Discussion about the reasons for choosing certain criteria and their consequences when applied would represent a third stage, a 'Theoretical' level.

Moret and van Oosten argue that this three-level model offers a better insight into discrepancies between the language of the students' world and the language of economics.

Experiential learning is a key characteristic of the model and teachers may find themselves involved in a variety of different, possibly unfamiliar roles as students are encouraged to pass from one level to another using group discussion, and group or individual assignments. Discussion plays an essential role in that it activates all five of the recommended phases in the process of raising students' understanding to a higher level. The value of students' own Ground-level experience is borne out in the two papers on primary school economics education (Ajello *et alia* and Kourilsky). Ajello *et alia* recognize some spontaneous development in students' ideas from 4 to 14 years of age but suggest that without intervention, their economic understanding is confined to a general common-sense level, and the criteria used to link economic phenomena reflect a confusion of economic, social and moral ideas.

Their three-year programme for 8–10 year olds helps students to investigate their interdependent and highly-specialized economic system, simplified as a 'chain of production'. The programme highlights the importance of students' initial knowledge, activity-based learning and classroom discussion. They expect their students to be able to move towards a 'Descriptive' level; for example, in their second year of study, variation in the price of agricultural products is used to introduce a 'key concept' of general rules and exceptions to these rules.

However, there are restrictions placed on the students' freedom to choose the criteria by which they link together economic phenomena. The authors argue that the role of daily experience in a student's acquisition of knowledge is often a source of confusion, and so, on a factory visit, students' attention is directed to the different phases of production rather than to machinery, division of labour, authority roles etc.

Some links were clearly more difficult for students to make than others. Start and finish points in a chain of production were difficult to identify because students viewed the chain not as a sum of separate parts but a whole structure. They also seemed to find the process of pricing difficult in the abstract, out of the temporal context in which the relevant events occur. However, the authors feel with some confidence that their students were more inclined to use economic or quasi-economic reasoning to explain economic events as a result of their course than those in a control group.

Kourilsky's paper describes interviews with 6–9 year olds who had experienced a 'Mini-Society' programme and were then asked to demonstrate their economic understanding by applying cost–benefit analysis to a variety of problems. It is perhaps no surprise, given previous research, to find that a teaching programme can result in the acquisition of some economics, but to find 6–9 year olds able to answer questions that go beyond memory recall to higher levels of cognition is significant. The interviews suggested also that students' ability to apply cost–benefit analysis to monetary decisions was greater than to decisions involving time allocation. This may, of course, reflect the students' greater awareness of the budget constraint on money than any constraint on time.

Overall the paper suggests age to be an important factor in regard to economics understanding and, more tentatively, that the ability to use economic reasoning may be a developmental process.

These three papers combined make an important case for economics education at the primary level and draw particular attention to the economics experiences brought to the classroom by even very young students. They suggest that student responses may tell us much about developmental stages in economics understanding. The processes suggested for raising students' level of understanding have far-reaching implications for the role of the teacher in the classroom and might best be described by Moret and van Oosten's term as a 'conversation-model' of economics education.

The role of student choice in economic learning models

John F. Chizmar

Professor of Economics and Acting Associate Provost, Illinois State University

Prior research on economic learning models has generally assumed that student human capital variables and time combine to produce learning. Focusing on the economics course in question, these studies usually assume that time is exogenous. However, because students exercise choice in the manner in which they allocate their time to their economics course, all other courses and leisure, time is not exogenous. This study expands the literature on economic learning models by viewing the learning process as a problem in time allocation for the student.

Introduction

How often have we as researchers in economics education felt compelled to conclude our studies with a caveat suggesting that changes in student achievement may not be the sole or even dominant benefit of a different teaching approach? (Wetzel, 1977) If we assume that students are rational decision-makers with various goals, then they must be viewed as maximizing their satisfaction by making decisions concerning the allocation of their time – one of their few choice variables – among various activities. Achievement, then, must be viewed as a function of a student's ability *and* of the amount of time the student allocates to the subject in question. Consequently, a student can utilize an improved teaching technique in one course to capture more achievement in that course, more achievement in other courses, more leisure time, or a combination of the three. Pondering the absence of economics in economics education, McKenzie (1977, p. 9) has concluded, '. . . by not considering student choice, we may have simply failed to make our studies sufficiently general and have failed to view the learning process as a problem in time allocation for the student. The student may transfer the efficiency benefits acquired in one course to his study of other subjects and to other noneducational activities.'

By concentrating the analysis and data collection myopically on the course in question, economics educators have missed an opportunity to expand the analysis to reflect the full range of student choices. Such data are insufficient to distinguish sharply between valid and invalid hypotheses concerning the learning process. Following Mayer (1980) who admonished the economics profession to 'devote more time to data collection', this paper reports on a research design which generates the data necessary to investigate the learning process as a problem in time allocation for the student.

By using a simple maximizing model of the learning process as a problem in time allocation for the student, developed by Allison (1977), time devoted to the study of economics is shown to be an important determinant of economics achievement. In addition, the model is used to begin to trace the gains in efficiency introduced into the learning process by a pedagogic innovation (computer assisted learning) across the many activities in which students typically engage.

Model

It is assumed that the student is a utility maximizer endowed with a set of abilities and tastes. The student is forced to make time-allocation decisions in light of a teaching technology defined by the quality of the student's instructor and the pedagogy employed by the instructor. Basically, the student has control over only one input – time. Assume that time is allocated along a single dimension and that time so allocated produces a vector of grades and consumption benefits in some fixed proportion. Time is allocated among three activities: economics, all other courses and all other activities. As explained by Allison (1977, p. 9):

> Utility is a function of the direct utility of the three time allocations and of the expected grade to be received in economics and other courses. For an individual student:

$$U_i = f_i \left(\text{TIME}_{\text{economics(EC)}}, \text{TIME}_{\text{all other courses(AOC)}}, \right. \tag{1}$$
$$\left. \text{TIME}_{\text{all other activities(AOA)}}, \text{EXPGR}_{\text{EC}}, \text{EXPGR}_{\text{AOC}} \right)$$

$$\text{TIME}_{\text{EC}} + \text{TIME}_{\text{AOC}} + \text{TIME}_{\text{AOA}} = 24 \text{ hours/day}$$

$$\text{EXPGR}_{\text{EC}} = g_i(\text{TIME}_{\text{EC}})$$

$$\text{EXPGR}_{\text{AOC}} = g_i(\text{TIME}_{\text{AOC}})$$

> where EXPGR is the anticipated grade, TIME is student time, and U_i is the utility received by the ith student. The marginal conditions are as follows:

$$\frac{\delta U_i}{\delta \text{EXPGR}_{\text{EC}}} \times \frac{\delta \text{EXPGR}_{\text{EC}}}{\delta \text{TIME}_{\text{EC}}} = \frac{\delta U_i}{\delta \text{TIME}_{\text{AOA}}} \times \frac{\delta U_i}{\delta \text{TIME}_{\text{EC}}} \tag{2}$$

$$\frac{\delta U_i}{\delta \text{EXPGR}_{\text{AOC}}} \times \frac{\delta \text{EXPGR}_{\text{AOC}}}{\delta \text{TIME}_{\text{AOC}}} = \frac{\delta U_i}{\delta \text{TIME}_{\text{AOA}}} \times \frac{\delta U_i}{\delta \text{TIME}_{\text{AOC}}}$$

Time is allocated to economics and to all other courses until the expected utility of the increased grade derived from the final hour of study equals the disutility of the study itself. In particular, then, students with a taste for study are expected to study more and students with a taste for other activities are expected to study less. Those with a taste for high grades would study more as will students who believe themselves to be more efficient at the margin in studying.

These theoretical expectations yield a set of behaviour equations for the *i*th student which can be written as:

$$TIME_{EC} = f([Ts], EXPGR_{EC}, TIME_{AOC})$$ (3)

$$TIME_{AOC} = f([Ts], EXPGR_{AOC}, TIME_{EC})$$ (4)

where [Ts] is a vector of student tastes and interests.* In addition, teacher and pedagogical inputs are assumed to enter directly.

Achievement is assumed to then be indexed on ability and effort controlling for teacher and pedagogical inputs. In particular, the achievement function becomes

$$ACH_{EC} = f([ABIL], TIME_{EC}, [TEACH], [PED])$$ (5)

where

ACH_{EC} = index of student achievement in economics

[ABIL] = vector of student abilities

[TEACH] = vector of teacher characteristic

[PED] = vector of educational inputs other than instructor

Equations (3)–(5) represent one solution to modelling the learning process as a problem in time allocation for the student. Potentially, such a model can begin to trace the gains in efficiency introduced into the learning process by a change in educational methods across the many activities in which students typically engage.

This potential can, perhaps, be more easily seen with an example. Suppose the researcher is interested in investigating the impact of computer assisted learning (CAL) on the student's economics achievement. Traditionally, researchers have investigated this question solely within the context of the course in question. The consensus of such investigations appears to be that CAL either has no impact or, if it has an impact, the impact is negative. In either case, given the positive costs associated with CAL, it is concluded that CAL should not be utilized. Suppose, however, that the introduction of CAL in the economics course makes it possible for the student to attain a given

---

*Allison (1977, p. 10) operationalized her model to a single effort equation focusing on the economics course in question.

achievement in economics with less time input.* For example, the student could substitute CAL for class attendance or simply use study time more efficiently with CAL. In this circumstance, the student (given achievement in economics) can produce higher achievement in other courses or consume more leisure. These latter benefits, when compared with the costs of CAL, could yield a favourable assessment of the effectiveness of CAL.

Estimating the model

The first step in estimating the model described implicitly in equations (3)–(5) is to choose the model's explicit functional form. For the sake of simplicity it is assumed that each equation in the system is linear. Thus, equations (3)–(5) are written explicitly as follows:

$$TIME_{EC} = \beta_0 + \beta_1 [Ts] + \beta_2 EXPGR_{EC} + \beta_3 TIME_{AOC} \quad (6)$$
$$+ \beta_4 [TEACH] + \beta_5 [PED] + \varepsilon_1$$

$$TIME_{AOC} = \alpha_0 + \alpha_1 [Ts] + \alpha_2 EXPGR_{AOC} + \alpha_3 TIME_{EC} \quad (7)$$
$$+ \alpha_4 [TEACH] + \alpha_5 [PED] + \varepsilon_2$$

$$ACH_{EC} = \delta_0 + \delta_1 [ABIL] + \delta_3 TIME_{EC} + \delta_4 [TEACH] \quad (8)$$
$$+ \delta_5 [PED] + \varepsilon_3$$

Equations (6) and (7) explicitly recognize the simultaneous nature of the student's time-allocation decisions. Having specified that $TIME_{EC}$ and $TIME_{AOC}$ are simultaneously determined, ordinary least squares (OLS) will yield biased and inconsistent estimates of the coefficients of equations (6) and (7). Consistent parameter estimates can be obtained using two stage least squares (2SLS).

Equations (6) and (8) suggest a recursive relationship between time allocated to economics ($TIME_{EC}$) and achievement in economics (ACH_{EC}). ACH_{EC} depends upon $TIME_{EC}$ in equation (8) but there is no feedback of ACH_{EC} to $TIME_{EC}$ in equation (6). Under the further assumption that ε_1 and ε_3 are independent it follows that $E(\varepsilon_3/TIME_{EC}) = 0$ (the so-called orthogonality assumption) and equations (6) and (8) are recursive. Under these assumptions, OLS estimation of equation (8) will yield parameter estimates that are unbiased and consistent. If ε_1 and ε_3 are not independent, i.e. if $E(\varepsilon_1\varepsilon_3) \neq 0$, then $E(\varepsilon_3/TIME_{EC}) \neq 0$ and OLS is an inappropriate estimation technique. Hausman (1978) has derived an asymptotic t-test of the orthogonality assumption. Chizmar and Spencer (1980) have described the test within an economics education context.

The second step in estimating the model of the learning process as a problem in time allocation for the student requires that data be collected on

---

*This possibility has been suggested by a number of researchers. See, for example, Chizmar *et alia* (1977).

operational equivalents for each of the variables described in equations (6)–(8), not only for the economics course but also for a common set of other courses (and leisure). This task is confounded by the fact that students take many different courses and many different schedules. The traditional technique of focusing data collection only on the economics course in question will not work. Even if the analysis were focused on an economics course enrolling hundreds of students, one would expect to find only a small number of students whose schedule of other courses completely coincided. Thus, the researcher is faced with a 'degrees of freedom' problem, i.e. an insufficient number of observations in the cells of the research design representing common other courses.

In the Fall semesters of 1980 and 1981 a research design calculated to increase the number of students taking a common schedule of courses was implemented at Illinois State University. Two common schedules, an honours student track and a non-honours student track, of the same five popular introductory courses – Principles of Economics 1, Finite Mathematics for Business and Social Sciences, Fundamentals of Speech Communication, American Government and Politics, and Language and Composition 1 – were blocked out. Each student who elected one of these schedules had the same five instructors at the same times during the week.

Data collection was concentrated in a 27-day period which constituted the third quarter of the macro principles of economics course.* At the beginning of the period a pre-test of economics achievement and a pre-questionnaire designed to measure students' taste for work and attitudes towards each of their five courses and instructors were administered.† During the period under investigation students were required to keep a daily log of their time-allocation decisions. More specifically, they were asked to report the number of minutes per day allocated to study in each of their courses, the number of minutes per day allocated to a part-time job (if any), and whether they attended any scheduled classes that day. At the end of the period a post-test of economics achievement and a post-questionnaire concerning students' tastes for work and attitudes towards their courses and instructors were administered. This already rich data set was augmented with information taken from each student's admissions file. The resulting data set contained some 840 variables on 81 students.

Table 1 provides a detailed description of the operational equivalents chosen to represent the variables contained in equations (6)–(8) including mean and range values.‡ $TIME_{EC}$ and $TIME_{AOC}$ measure the amount of time

---

*Polachek *et alia* (1978) suggested focusing on a period of less than a full semester as a way of minimizing measurement error.

†The pre- and post-questionnaires closely resemble those devised by Allison (1977, Appendix A).

‡As pointed out by Allison (1977, p. 15), a potential errors-in-variables problem exists. Many of the variables chosen as operational equivalents do not neatly correspond to a given true (or latent) variable. One possible solution would be to estimate the model using LISREL.

Table 1   Descriptions, means, and ranges of variables

Variable symbol	Mean	Minimum value	Maximum value	Description
$TIME_{EC}$	1011.32	410.00	1965.00	Total minutes allocated to economics; sum of class time and study time
$EXPGR_{EC}$	3.09	1.00	4.00	Expected grade in economics: 4 = A, 0 = F
MALE	0.55	0.00	1.00	Dummy variable: 1 indicates male
HIGRDS	1.41	1.00	5.00	Importance of high grades: 1 = of great importance, 5 = of no importance
IMPORT	2.95	1.00	5.00	Student response to question, 'I feel there are more important things to do than study': 1 = not at all, 5 = a great deal
POLACT	3.27	1.00	5.00	Importance of political activity: 1 = of great importance, 5 = of no importance
LOVEREL	2.03	1.00	5.00	Importance of love relationships: 1 = of great importance, 5 = of no importance
RELIG	2.55	1.00	5.00	Importance of religious commitment: 1 = of great importance, 5 = of no importance
$INSTR_{EC}$	1.48	1.00	5.00	Student rating of the economics professor: 1 = excellent, 5 = poor
$COUR_{EC}$	1.73	1.00	5.00	Student response to question, 'What is your overall impression of the economics course in comparison with other courses taken at ISU?': 1 = outstanding, 5 = poor
CAL	0.48	0.00	1.00	Dummy variable: 1 indicates used computer assisted learning
$TIME_{AOC}$	5377.95	2085.00	12385.00	Total minutes allocated to all other courses; sum of class time and study time

(continued)

Variable	Mean	Min	Max	Description
WORK	0.33	0.00	1.00	Dummy variable: 1 indicates held a job
$EXPGR_{AOC}$	3.06	1.00	4.00	Average expected grade in all other courses: 4 = A, 0 = F
$INSTR_{AOC}$	2.62	1.50	4.25	Average student rating of the professors in all other courses: 1 = excellent, 5 = poor
$COUR_{AOC}$	2.69	1.50	4.50	Average student response to question, 'What is your overall impression of each of your courses (other than economics) in comparison with other courses taken at ISU?': 1 = outstanding, 5 = poor
PRTEST	14.37	7.00	24.00	Student performance on the economics assessment exam given as a pre-test
POST	25.00	16.00	33.00	Student performance on the economics assessment exam given as a post-test
ACT	24.61	3.00	32.00	Student ACT score, comprehensive
$PREPAR_{EC}$	1.11	1.00	2.00	Student rating of the preparation of the economics instructor: 1 = well prepared, 5 = unprepared
HONOR	0.48	0.00	1.00	Dummy variable: 1 indicates honours student
HSECON	0.31	0.00	1.00	Dummy variable: 1 indicates had a high school economics course

(in minutes) that students allocated over the 27-day period of the experiment to class and study in economics and all other courses, respectively. The vector [Ts] is represented by the variables MALE, WORK, HIGRDS, IMPORT, POLACT, LOVEREL, and RELIG. MALE is considered a proxy for taste for school work (MacDowell *et alia*, 1977) as is the variable WORK. The other proxy variables for [Ts] are more direct Likert scale measures of the student's taste for study, high grades, and other dimensions of interest taken from the post-questionnaire. $EXPGR_{EC}$ and $EXPGR_{AOC}$ are calculated from the student's responses to a question on the pre-questionnaire concerning their anticipated grade in economics and all other courses. $INSTR_{EC}$, $INSTR_{AOC}$, $COUR_{EC}$, and $COUR_{AOC}$ reflect pedagogical inputs and are Likert scale measures of the student's evaluation of his or her instructors and courses, respectively, taken from the post-questionnaire.

CAL is a pedagogical input which measures whether the student used computer assisted learning. An experimental group of approximately 48 per cent of the students in the study was given the additional assignment of running a six-equation computer simulation model of the macroeconomy developed by Treyz (1971). Each student in the experimental group was given a handout which explained the simulation's underlying economic model and contained instructions explaining how to access the computer simulation. The simulation model *per se* was not discussed in class, although the economic concepts it presented were discussed. Students in the experimental group were invited to seek help from the instructor if necessary.

The computer simulation model placed students in an active learning mode. Pedagogically, it presented the macroeconomy as a black box. Students discovered how the black box worked by changing the inputs that go into the box and observing changes in outputs from the box. During a computer session, the simulation required students to respond interactively to a series of questions and set forth an additional series of questions which students were asked to answer as a homework assignment. Students in the experimental group were required to submit a printout with all questions completed as a graded assignment.

ACH_{EC} is represented by POST, the student's score on the economics assessment given as a post-test. The vector [ABIL] is represented by the variables ACT and HONORS. The vector [TEACH] is represented by the variables $INSTR_{EC}$ and $PREPAR_{EC}$. $PREPAR_{EC}$, the only variable not already discussed, is a Likert scale variable taken from the post-questionnaire. The vector [PED] is represented by $COUR_{EC}$ and CAL. The variables PRTEST and HSECON were added to control for the stock of economics knowledge the student has upon entering the experiment.

The model envisages that the student, upon arriving at the mid-way point in the semester, decides how to allocate his or her time to economics, all other courses, work, and leisure during the next quarter of the semester so as to attain the desired vector of anticipated grades. Once these decisions have been made, the actual time allocated to economics determines, in part, achievement in economics during the period. CAL is – to use a metaphor – the stone thrown into the water. The model allows the researcher to observe the effect of CAL not only on time allocation and achievement in the economics course but also the ripple effects of CAL on time-allocation decisions in all other courses.

Results

OLS estimates of coefficients of equations (6)–(8) are presented in Table 2. (For purposes of comparison, 2SLS estimates of the coefficients of equations (6) and (7) are presented in Table 3.) Because of missing values the number of observations was reduced from 81 to 75.

The results presented in Table 2 suggest a number of propositions about the student time-allocation process. The first is the importance of the role of tastes in the student time-allocation decision. In equation (6), HIGRDS has the expected sign and is statistically significant. Its coefficient suggests that a one unit change in the Likert scaled HIGRDS variable (e.g. a change in the priority of high grades from 'of some importance' to 'of great importance') is accompanied by a 123-minute increase in time devoted to economics over the period in question. This result is similar to that obtained by Allison (1977, p. 21). The coefficient of IMPORT also has the expected sign and, with a *p*-value of 0.08, is significant at the 10 per cent level. The other taste variables in equation (6) are insignificant at standard levels of significance.

In equation (7), the taste variables POLACT and LOVEREL have the expected sign and are statistically significant at the 10 per cent level. Their coefficients suggest that as more importance is attached to political activity and love relationships, respectively, less time is allocated to study and class for all other courses. Unfortunately, the coefficient of HIGRDS in equation (7) has the wrong sign and is statistically significant. (This perverse result might be due to multicollinearity between $EXPGR_{EC}$ and HIGRDS. The simple correlation between $EXPGR_{EC}$ and HIGRDS is -0.37. Although absolutely its value is not large, relatively it is among the highest intercorrelations extant among the regressors.)

Table 2　OLS estimates of equations (6)–(8)

Model: Equation (6)	SSE	3027506	*F* ratio	9.19
	DFE	62	Prob $> F$	0.0001
Dep var: $TIME_{EC}$	MSE	48830.74	*R*-square	0.64

Variable	Parameter estimate	Standard error	*T* ratio	Prob $> \lvert T \rvert$
INTERCEPT	880.44	222.57	3.96	0.00
$EXPGR_{EC}$	−25.04	45.05	−0.56	0.58
MALE	−73.94	59.86	−1.24	0.22
HIGRDS	−123.12	48.34	−2.55	0.01
IMPORT	−45.41	25.32	−1.79	0.08
POLACT	−17.17	29.35	−0.59	0.56
LOVEREL	−18.13	31.36	−0.58	0.56
RELIG	20.44	21.39	0.96	0.34
$INSTR_{EC}$	−27.15	51.63	−0.53	0.60
$COUR_{EC}$	41.88	59.57	0.70	0.48
CAL	291.65	56.50	5.16	0.00
$TIME_{AOC}$	0.08	0.01	5.31	0.00
WORK	29.79	63.71	0.47	0.64

Model: Equation (7)   SSE   152144968   *F* ratio   5.85
                      DFE   62   Prob > *F*   0.0001
Dep var: TIME$_{AOC}$ MSE   2453951   *R*-square   0.53

Variable	Parameter estimate	Standard error	*T* ratio	Prob > |*T*|
INTERCEPT	−5169.75	2435.71	−2.12	0.04
EXPGR$_{AOC}$	1118.51	456.49	2.45	0.02
MALE	−259.26	440.33	−0.59	0.56
HIGRDS	875.66	376.77	2.32	0.02
IMPORT	176.27	179.88	0.98	0.33
POLACT	404.51	190.48	2.12	0.04
LOVEREL	383.12	214.85	1.78	0.08
RELIG	−69.19	157.47	−0.44	0.66
INSTR$_{AOC}$	18.03	547.21	0.03	0.97
COUR$_{AOC}$	−280.38	424.60	−0.66	0.51
CAL	−714.56	524.61	−1.36	0.18
TIME$_{EC}$	4.42	0.73	6.04	0.00
WORK	502.32	450.21	1.11	0.27

Model: Equation (8)   SSE   630.09   *F* ratio   3.39
                      DFE   64   Prob > *F*   0.0013
Dep var: POST   MSE   9.84   *R*-square   0.35

Variable	Parameter estimate	Standard error	*T* ratio	Prob > |*T*|
INTERCEPT	8.75	3.82	2.29	0.02
PRTEST	0.22	0.10	2.10	0.04
ACT	0.31	0.13	2.48	0.02
MALE	2.17	0.78	2.76	0.01
TIME$_{EC}$	0.004	0.001	2.93	0.00
INSTR$_{EC}$	0.45	0.77	0.58	0.56
PREPAR$_{EC}$	−0.98	1.42	−0.69	0.49
CAL	−0.05	0.92	−0.05	0.96
COUR$_{EC}$	0.33	0.77	0.42	0.67
HONORS	−0.42	1.05	−0.40	0.69
HSECON	0.18	0.81	0.22	0.82

The anticipated grade in economics ($EXPGR_{EC}$) is an insignificant determinant of $TIME_{EC}$ in equation (6); however, the anticipated grade in all other courses ($EXPGR_{AOC}$) appears to be a significant and positive determinant of $TIME_{AOC}$ in equation (7). The latter result implies that a one-unit change in $EXPGR_{AOC}$ (e.g. from a 'B' to an 'A') increases $TIME_{AOC}$ by 1118 minutes over the period in question. Allison (1977, p. 21) found that higher recent or current grades in economics reduced effort in the economics course.

The results presented in Table 2 also suggest that students who allocate more time to economics are likely to allocate more time to all other courses and vice versa. The coefficient of $TIME_{AOC}$ in equation (6) and the coefficient of $TIME_{EC}$ in equation (7) are both positive and significant. The results further suggest that holding a part-time job does not seem to affect the time allocated to economics or to all other courses. The coefficient of WORK is insignificant in both equations.

The final proposition about the student time-allocation process concerns the effect of CAL on the student's time allocation in the economics and all other courses. CAL appears to be a positive and highly significant determinant of $TIME_{EC}$. Students in the experimental group spent an average of 292 minutes more on economics during the period under investigation, other things constant, than students in the control group. Further, there is some weak evidence that students in the experimental group allocated less time to their other courses. The OLS estimate of the coefficient of CAL has a value of -714; however, with a p-value of 0.18, it is not significant at standard levels of significance.

The OLS estimates of the parameters of equation (8) suggest a number of propositions about the learning process as a problem in student time allocation.* The first is that ability and time allocated to economics do appear to matter. The coefficients of ACT and $TIME_{EC}$ are both positive and highly significant. The coefficient of $TIME_{EC}$ implies that a 250-minute increase in the time allocated to economics increases performance on the economics assessment by one point, other things constant. To put this result in context, 250 minutes amounts to a 4.16-hour increase in time allocated to economics over the 27-day period of the experiment or 9.3 minutes per day.

From the marginal products of ACT and $TIME_{EC}$ the marginal rate of substitution of $TIME_{EC}$ for ACT can be calculated, i.e. $MP_{ACT}/MP_{TIME_{EC}} \simeq$ 74.5. This result indicates that, over the joint domain of the function, less able students can compensate for deficiences in ability (as measured by ACT) with extra effort. It implies that an increase of 298 minutes (approximately 5 hours) over the period is necessary to offset a four-point ACT disadvantage and keep achievement constant. Thus, approximately a one-standard-

---

*The asymptotic t-test of the orthogonality assumption suggested by Hausman (1978) here has a value of 0.49 with a p-value of 0.62. This result suggests that OLS yields unbiased and consistent estimates of the parameters of equation (8).

deviation decrease in ACT can be offset by a one-standard-deviation increase in $TIME_{EC}$.[*]

Consistent with the result found by many other researchers, the coefficient of MALE is positive and highly significant. Its coefficient implies that males perform, on average, 2.17 points higher than females on the economics assessment, other things constant. If anything, the mystery of this result is heightened by the results reported in Table 2. In addition to the direct effect of MALE on economics achievement there is also an indirect effect. The indirect influence of MALE on achievement can be calculated by multiplying the coefficient of $TIME_{EC}$ from equation (8) by the coefficient of MALE from equation (6). Because the estimate of the coefficient of MALE in equation (6) indicates that males tend to allocate less time to economics, the indirect effect, i.e. $0.004 \times (-73.94) = -0.30$, is negative. However, the indirect effect is not large enough to offset the direct effect. Thus, it appears that the oft-found superior economics performance of males is *not* due to increased time allocated to economics on the part of males.

Table 3   2SLS estimate of equations (6) and (7)

Model: Equation (6)	SSE	4348244	F ratio	4.76
	DFE	62	Prob > F	0.0001
Dep var: $TIME_{EC}$	MSE	70132.97	R-square	0.48

Second stage statistics

Variable	Parameter estimate	Standard error	T ratio	Prob > $|T|$
INTERCEPT	896.88	267.47	3.35	0.00
$EXPGR_{EC}$	26.27	82.20	0.32	0.75
MALE	−176.76	143.41	−1.23	0.22
HIGRDS	−116.81	58.42	−2.00	0.05
IMPORT	−50.07	30.86	−1.62	0.11
POLACT	3.91	43.43	0.09	0.93
LOVEREL	7.34	48.57	0.15	0.88
RELIG	25.84	26.46	0.98	0.33
$INSTR_{EC}$	−54.96	70.40	−0.78	0.44
$COUR_{EC}$	124.98	123.17	1.01	0.31
CAL	353.28	100.63	3.51	0.00
$PRED.TIME_{AOC}$	0.002	0.09	0.02	0.99
WORK	106.10	119.69	0.87	0.39

[*]ACT and $TIME_{EC}$ have standard deviations of 4.13 and 337.22, respectively.

Model: Equation (7) SSE 196214706 *F* ratio 2.66
                     DFE   62 Prob > *F* 0.0061
Dep var: TIME$_{AOC}$ MSE 3164753 *R*-square 0.34
Second stage statistics

Variable	Parameter estimate	Standard error	*T* ratio	Prob > |*T*|
INTERCEPT	−9285.39	4866.23	−1.91	0.06
EXPGR$_{AOC}$	1295.81	546.34	2.37	0.02
MALE	381.06	798.79	0.48	0.64
HIGRDS	1296.03	591.86	2.19	0.03
IMPORT	284.79	229.94	1.24	0.22
POLACT	322.22	230.65	1.40	0.17
LOVEREL	327.35	249.95	1.31	0.20
RELIG	−144.80	193.36	−0.75	0.46
INSTR$_{AOC}$	102.11	626.78	0.16	0.87
COUR$_{AOC}$	−201.80	488.21	−0.41	0.68
CAL	−1906.79	1303.85	−1.46	0.15
TIME$_{EC}$	7.52	3.13	2.40	0.02
WORK	169.09	605.38	0.28	0.78

Turning to the question of the impact of computer assisted instruction on economics achievement, the coefficient of CAL in equation (8) is insignificant. This result indicates the probable absence of any direct influence of CAL on economics achievement. However, there is evidence of an *indirect* influence operating through the coefficient of TIME$_{EC}$. An estimate of the indirect effect of CAL on POST can be calculated by multiplying the coefficient of TIME$_{EC}$ from equation (8) by the coefficient of CAL from equation (6), i.e. $0.004 \times 292 = 1.226$. This suggests that CAL increased POST scores by an average of 1.226 points over the period of the experiment.

The results in Table 3 generally agree with those in Table 2. However, R^2s for the 2SLS results are generally lower than those for OLS. The 2SLS estimates are inconclusive about whether TIME$_{EC}$ and TIME$_{AOC}$ are simultaneously determined. The predicted value of TIME$_{AOC}$ is insignificant in the TIME$_{EC}$ equation; however, the predicted value of TIME$_{EC}$ is positive and highly significant in the TIME$_{AOC}$ equation.* The former result suggests the possibility that some sort of recursive relationship exists between TIME$_{EC}$ and TIME$_{AOC}$; the latter result implies that the more time the student devotes to economics, the more time that student devotes to all other courses.

---

*In light of the results reported in Table 2, this result is puzzling. Perhaps the first-stage estimate of the predicted value of TIME$_{EC}$ introduces multicollinearity into the estimates of the second stage.

Conclusions

It is well known that a given data set can be consistent with various model specifications. Ultimately, through the interaction of theory and empirical evidence, the learning model will become refined. This paper moves a small step in that direction. By viewing the learning process as a problem in student allocation of time, a behaviour model yielding a set of refutable hypotheses is generated (McKenzie, 1977, p. 9). The results of this paper are consistent with a simple maximizing model of the learning process as a problem in time allocation for the student. The results indicate that students who have a taste for study and high grades do indeed allocate more time to studying – both in economics and all other courses. Holding a part-time job appears to have no effect on the time students allocate to college work. However, achievement in economics does appear to depend in part on the amount of time allocated to economics. In particular, those who allocate more time to economics attain a higher achievement.

The results of this paper with respect to the pedagogic issue shed light on the process by which computer assisted learning affects economics achievement. The evidence reported here suggests that there is no *direct* influence of CAL on economics achievement. This result is consistent with that reported by other researchers. However, there does appear to be an indirect influence of CAL on economic cognition operating through $TIME_{EC}$.

If future research further substantiates these conclusions, there are profound implications for the development of curricular materials and classroom conduct. Activities which enhance the time students allocate to a given subject enhance achievement. This result, while not unexpected, reinforces what each instructor seems doomed to have to rediscover on his own in the practical laboratory called the classroom.

References

Allison, E. 1977 'Educational production function for an introductory economics course' Discussion Paper no. 545, Harvard Institute of Economic Research

Chizmar, J. F., Hiebert, L. D. and McCarney, B. J. 1977 'Assessing the impact of an instructional innovation on achievement differentials: the case of computer-assisted instruction' *Journal of Economic Education* 9(1) p. 45

Chizmar, J. F. and Spencer, D. E. 1980 'Testing the specification of economic learning equations' *Journal of Economic Education* 11(2) p. 46

Hausman, J. A. 1978 'Specification tests in econometrics' *Econometrica* **46** pp. 1251–73

MacDowell, M. A., Senn, P. R. and Soper, J. C. 1977 'Does sex really matter?' *Journal of Economic Education* 9(1) p. 29

Mayer, T. 1980 'Economics as a hard science: realistic goal or wishful thinking' *Economic Inquiry* **18** p. 167

McKenzie, R. B. 1977 'Where is the economics in economics education?' *Journal of Economic Education* **9**(1)

Polachek, S. W., Kniesner, T. J. and Harwood, H. J. 1978 'Educational production functions' *Journal of Educational Statistics* **3** p. 216

Treyz, G. I. 1971 'Active programming and computer simulations by intermediate macroeconomic theory students' *Economic Education Experiences of Enterprising Teachers* **8** Joint Council on Economic Education, New York, pp. 80–2

Wetzel, J. N. 1977 'Measuring student scholastic effort: an economic theory of learning approach' *Journal of Economic Education* **9**(1) p. 34

A comparison between multiple regression and log–linear analyses as applied to educational data

Keith G. Lumsden
Margaret Cuthbert
Alex Scott

The Esmée Fairbairn Research Centre, Heriot-Watt University, Edinburgh

Much of the existing body of knowledge in economics education is based on empirical findings which in turn rely almost exclusively on multiple regression analysis. It is our contention that many of the 'not statistically significant' findings in economics education research are due to the unsuitability of multiple regression analysis when applied to large heterogeneous data sets. General linear modelling (GLM) has the promise of overcoming many of the restrictions and weaknesses of multiple regression analysis. The technique has been used to re-analyse research findings on the efficacy of innovative teaching techniques in economics on different types of students in various institutional settings.

Introduction

In the mid-1970s The Esmée Fairbairn Research Centre undertook a five-year study* to investigate the efficacy of innovative teaching techniques in introductory university economics courses. To assess these techniques, course packages in basic micro and macroeconomics were constructed, combining innovative and conventional techniques in different proportions. The conventional techniques included lectures, tutorials, essays, texts and readings. The new techniques included Teaching Information Processing System (TIPS)† (Kelley, 1968), cases, programmed learning and macrosimulations. During

---

*The study was financed by the Department of Education and Science and The Esmée Fairbairn Charitable Trust.
†TIPS comprises regular multiple choice assignments (surveys) which are computer marked and which provide fast feedback to both teacher and student permitting revision of study habits and teaching materials to meet specified goals.

the academic year 1979–80, over 2500 students studying first-year economics in these institutions sat a common three-hour final examination which consisted of 20 multiple choice questions (10 micro and 10 macro) to measure knowledge of concepts and simple to intermediate applications, and one micro essay and one macro essay to measure synthesis and evaluation.

The form and content of the common final examination were determined by a committee including representatives of each participating institution. To avoid any misunderstanding concerning examination content, detailed sets of course notes were provided to participating institutions. These notes, which reflected an Advisory Board consensus on which fundamental concepts should be included in any course purporting to teach basic economics, served as the basis of all the examination questions. A major innovatory feature of the common final examination, designed to produce a consistent measure of output, was the lack of choice of questions. Some institutions agreed to set the complete common final, others to include part of it as an obligatory section of their own final. Those institutions which could not agree to the obligatory nature of the common final were excluded from the analysis.

Table 1 sets out the number of students who sat each part of the common final under examination conditions. A total of 1032 students sat all parts of both micro and macro, i.e. the complete common final.

Agreement to set the common final was a necessary but not sufficient condition for generating a usable set of marks. Clearly the multiple choice test scores introduced no marker bias; to ensure that marker and institutional biases did not occur in the case and essay marks, all papers were collected and marked by a single experienced academic; the marks which he produced were used in the analysis without any alteration. Table 2 shows the degree of consistency between the marks of the regrader and the originals as revealed by the 28 correlation coefficients.

The consistency of the regrader also came in for scrutiny. A random sample of 180 scripts was drawn and regraded; the correlations between these subsequent grades and the regrades were: case 0.94, micro essay 0.77, macro essay 0.84. In addition there was no difference between the means of the

Table 1 Number of students sitting different parts of the common final

Output measure		Number of students
Micro	Essay	1935
	Multiple choice	1740
	Case	1254
Macro	Essay	1629
	Multiple choice	1483

Table 2 Correlation coefficients between regrades and original marks

Range of correlation coefficients	Number of correlations
0.40 – 0.59	9
0.60 – 0.69	12
0.70 and greater	7

All correlation coefficients were significant at the 99 per cent level.

regrades and the subsequent sample, and no evidence that there had been a significant change in standards during the protracted period of regrading.

Multiple regression analyses were carried out in which each measure of output was the dependent variable and in which student and course characteristics were the independent variables. Because statistical problems were encountered with multiple regression analyses, alternative statistical techniques, in particular log–linear modelling, were applied to a subset of the data.

This paper is concerned with an assessment of the relative strengths and weaknesses of multiple regression and log–linear modelling; both are subsets of general linear modelling (GLM), which includes a wide range of analytical techniques, each with its own comparative advantage. While data sets can be subjected to a variety of statistical techniques, the optimal choices, i.e. those which yield maximum information, often depend upon the structure of the data sets and the distribution of the error terms. Because of the success of the higher education experiment, and the demand by school teachers for the innovative techniques, a similar project* was initiated in the schools sector in Scotland; currently 100 schools are involved. The data for the schools project will be subjected to both regression analysis and log–linear modelling. The introduction of more general linear modelling to the schools project will, we hope, advance understanding of some of the complex relationships between inputs and outputs in this field as well as proving to be of importance for other researchers in education.

Preparing for the experiment

Two criteria were used in selecting innovative teaching techniques for the experiment. First, the techniques had to have the potential to be cost effective. Second, having met the first criterion, they had to have a high probability of being adopted by universities and polytechnics. Past research suggested that while videotaped and filmed lectures satisfied the first criterion they failed on the second, and consequently were not included in the study. TIPS, cases, programmed learning and macrosimulations, while not new to every institution of higher education in the UK, were not widely used. Where they were used, they tended to be supplementary to conventional teaching and were not well integrated into introductory economics courses. Each of these techniques had been used in courses in the US, and research findings had suggested they were cost effective; unfortunately, most of the research findings were institution specific, not consistent, and dealt with each technique in isolation. This was the first major study to attempt to assess combinations of these techniques over a substantial number of institutions.

The ideal research design involves constructing a matrix in which the axes consist of student, course and institutional characteristics, each cell in the

*The school study is being financed by the Scottish Education Department and the Industry Department for Scotland.

matrix containing sufficient observations to test the efficacy of various combinations of teaching techniques on different types of students in various educational settings. Since this theoretical ideal cannot be realized in practice, two 'second best' options present themselves.

The first involves limiting the institutional characteristics, i.e. choosing one or two institutions, and carefully monitoring each student to ensure that the data sets are complete in the restricted data matrix. There are two main problems with this approach. The first is that the findings in the experimental institutions cannot be generalized unless highly unrealistic homogeneity assumptions are made about the participating and non-participating institutions. The second problem is a practical one: it is difficult to ensure that test and control groups are separated when students in one institution, taking the same course, are subjected to different combinations of teaching techniques.

The alternative research design, which was adopted, involves choosing a representative cross-section of institutions for the experiment and making this sample large enough to ensure a data matrix of adequate size to facilitate statistical analyses. The disadvantages of this approach are twofold. First, the experiment cannot be closely monitored by the researchers. Second, missing observations which occur because of lack of close monitoring may be non-comparable with the data collected. Thus the data collected may be biased, e.g. students who consistently 'skip' lectures and tutorials and do not fill in questionnaires may have different characteristics from those on whom the analyses are carried out.

Having decided on the research design after weighing up the relative costs and benefits of the two approaches, a total of 26 pilot courses were run in seven institutions to solve logistic problems in the three years prior to the experimental year.

The experiment

During the academic year 1979–80, over 2500 students studying first-year economics in 19 universities, polytechnics and business schools were involved in the project. Because participating institutions tended to adopt one of three broad strategies concerning the innovative techniques, it was possible to measure the total and marginal costs of the 'new' courses in anticipation of the statistical analysis on the output. The three strategies were as follows:

1 The conventional course was radically altered; innovative techniques were substituted for tutorials and essays – 'complete substitution'.

2 Conventional inputs were reduced and innovative techniques substituted in varying degrees by different institutions – 'partial substitution'.

3 Innovative techniques were added to conventional courses – 'add on'.

In addition to the 'complete substitution', 'partial substitution' and 'add on' courses, three conventional courses were included as a basis for comparison.

The principal costs borne by institutions for the typical introductory economics course in universities and polytechnics consist of those associated with three lectures per week, tutorials of 10 students per tutorial per week, supervision, assignment and examination preparation and marking. Reasons for the continued existence of the standard introductory course are discussed elsewhere (Lumsden and Scott, 1985). Because the three strategies employ different amounts of high priced labour inputs, the pilot studies produced widely varying course costs; the average cost per student varied from £15 to £44, and marginal cost per student varied from £7 to £34 (1980 prices). On the assumption of positive marginal product of factor inputs, however small, adherents of the *status quo* would predict a positive correlation between course costs and course output.

The common final examination which was administered at the end of the academic year, together with student questionnaire responses, yielded several output measures. To relate course inputs to course outputs two techniques were used. First, each institution was ranked by its mean performance on each of the several output measures and compared with the input cost data. Second, multiple regression analyses were carried out in which each of the output measures was the dependent variable and student and course characteristics the independent variables. The most striking feature using the first approach was a lack of any connection between course inputs and outputs. For some measures of output the high resource input courses, i.e. the expensive ones, ranked highly; for other measures of output they appeared at the bottom of the rankings. Furthermore, the courses moved about in the rankings according to the output measure. It was clear that factors other than the measured course inputs were the main determinants of relative course outputs.

The regression analysis was intended to control for student characteristics and thus determine whether consistent rankings exist between the course packages. The first set of regression results did little to help answer questions regarding the relative cost effectiveness of the different course packages. In particular, the following results emerged:

1 The coefficients of the variables relating to course characteristics were unrealistic. For example, with the microeconomic essay score as the dependent variable, with a mean of 46, the following coefficients were estimated:

    using TIPS   (Yes = 1, No = 0)   +54.5
    using cases   (Yes = 1, No = 0)   −27.9
    using programmed text (Yes = 1, No = 0)   +27.3

These estimates were too large to be realistic.

2 Excluding two or three institutions from a regression altered the magnitude and sign of the coefficients of some of the independent variables significantly.

3 Excluding selected variables from the regressions, e.g. the textbook used, completely altered the coefficients.

The regression results were therefore unrealistic and unstable. Closer investigation led to two main conclusions:

1 Although this was a large-scale study in terms of the number of student observations and institutions involved, the number of observations on different courses was relatively small in relation to the set of variables required to represent each course package. In addition, because of the different course designs, each set of course-related variables was unique; that is, there was no precise duplication of course design between institutions. There were considerable differences in the means of the output variables between institutions (the microeconomic essay, for example, varied from 38.4 to 52.4); these differences were not eliminated by the inclusion of student-related variables, hence the unique group of course input variables was picking up the large institution differences in an unpredictable manner. Subsequent simulations using variations in the number of institutions and different specifications demonstrate that any number of different 'findings' can be generated from this data set.

2 The factors affecting learning within institutions depended on the individual case. For the new teaching technique on which the largest amount of data is available (TIPS), regression analysis was carried out between the percentage of TIPS surveys done and the output measures for each institution. Eleven institutions which used TIPS provided information on four measures of output, but in only two are the coefficients significant for all output measures; in three institutions, there are no significant coefficients for any measures of output. In six institutions, the coefficients are significant for essay marks. The coefficients themselves vary considerably in magnitude between institutions. While the number of observations is much smaller for students using cases and macrosimulations, similar findings emerge.

These two statistical problems – the instability of the course input variable coefficients and the unique learning effects within institutions – must raise questions about the validity of past research findings based on regression analyses, especially those relating to individual institutions. However, the most immediate question facing the research team in this project was what to do on the statistical front. The question was even more intriguing in the light of other non-regression findings which had emerged from the study. For example, responses to student questionnaires indicated that the majority of students was more concerned with passing the final examination than with maximizing examination marks, and that different students were utilizing the various teaching techniques in different ways. Thus complicated interaction effects relating to the way different students react to the techniques may help to explain the regression results. Another important finding, at odds with

Table 3   Correlations between the different types of examination

	Micro		Macro	
	Case	Essay	Multiple choice	Essay
Micro				
Multiple choice	0.11	0.18	0.43	0.18
	1254	1332	1483	1483
	(0.60)	(0.55)	(0.75)	(0.49)
Case		0.23	0.10	0.14
		881	1254	1032
		(0.61)	(0.53)	(0.55)
Essay			0.19	0.54
			1211	1211
			(0.47)	(0.74)
Macro				
Multiple choice				0.26
				1483
				(0.57)

Student correlations are followed by number of observations.
Numbers in parentheses are the mean estimated correlations of 100 UK academics.
All student correlations are significant at the 99 per cent level.

conventional wisdom, was the correlation between parts of the final examination. Table 3 shows these correlations, including the significantly lower than anticipated correlation between multiple choice and essay results.

These results suggest that different types of questions measure different aspects of economics comprehension, thus the interaction effects may differ according to the measure of output. Two additional factors motivated further thought on the problems. First, the regression results from the well-behaved variables – age, sex, number of A levels, A level/no A level economics and mathematics, etc. – reinforced past research findings, e.g. males perform better on multiple choice examinations than do females. In areas hitherto unexplored, the research produced new findings, for example, females perform statistically significantly better on essay examinations, *ceteris paribus,* than do males (Lumsden and Scott, in preparation).

The second factor was based on extensive casual empiricism gained from teaching courses using the new techniques, and observing the effects of the new techniques in the pilot institutions; the techniques apparently worked for many students, and it was felt that the multiple regression results did not adequately reflect the effects.

In an attempt to overcome these two statistical problems it was decided to investigate other techniques in the GLM range. The technique chosen, because of the structure of the data and the distribution of the error term, was log–linear modelling. The computer program used was GLIM (Baker and Nelder, 1978) and is described in more detail in the Appendix.

A comparison of regression and log–linear modelling

The analysis which follows describes log–linear modelling, and illustrates how it provides an alternative set of results and can identify important characteristics of the data which cannot be achieved using multiple regression.

To provide a clear picture of how log–linear modelling operates, the analysis will be carried out using only three variables: whether the student has A level economics, the percentage of the TIPS surveys completed and the institution attended. Further, this relatively simple model includes only those institutions where TIPS was included in the course package.

The model of student performance tested is

$$V_i = a + bA + cT + dI \qquad (i = 1 \ldots 4) \qquad (1)$$

where V_1 = Micro Essay Mark
V_2 = Macro Essay Mark
V_3 = Micro Multiple Choice Score
V_4 = Macro Multiple Choice Score
A = Student has A level economics (yes = 1, no = 0)
T = Percentage of TIPS surveys completed
I = Institution attended (yes = 1, no = 0 for each institution)
$a, b, c, d,$ = Parameters to be estimated

The results of multiple regression analyses of these data are presented in Table 4.

The regression coefficients reveal the relative magnitudes of the effects of the three variables on performance. For example, students with A level economics score on average 4.17 more than those without on the Micro Essay; the student doing 100 per cent TIPS surveys scores 5.00 more than a student doing 50 per cent (i.e. 50 × 0.10), and students attending Institution B score 9.5 more on average than students attending Institution I. It was found that no matter how many variables were included in the multiple regressions, the institution effects were relatively large. Since the institution effects were so important, it is of considerable interest to determine whether the estimated differences were due to the performance of all students in a particular institution being better or worse than others, or whether there were concentrations of particular groups of students within the institutions, such as the very good or the very poor. Such information is very difficult to extract using multiple regression, and in fact the data-dredging approach which it necessitates raises doubts concerning the validity of the significance tests.

Table 4   Examination performance as a function of selected variables

	Micro Essay	Macro Essay	Micro Multiple Choice	Macro Multiple Choice
Constant	34.45	30.54	7.12	5.02
A level/higher economics	4.17*	6.9*	0.186	0.46*
% TIPS completed	0.10*	0.162*	0.006*	0.01*
Institution attended: C	5.5*	4.1	−1.289*	−0.27
I	base	3.47	−0.008	
B	9.5*	−5.7*		−0.097
F	7.8*	1.8	−0.5*	
E	3.8	5.9*	−0.38*	−0.097
H	6.4*	7.85*	base	0.638*
A	5.3*	base	−0.42*	base
D	0.27			
G	−6.1*		−0.008	
J			−0.5*	
K				
R^2	0.29	0.10	0.23	0.21
Number of observations	1634	1329	1263	1007
Mean of dependent variable	46.4	42.4	7.2	5.8

*Statistically significant at 95 per cent level.
A blank denotes that the institution was not included in a particular regression.

Besides the practical difficulties of investigating the data in depth, multiple regression analysis is subject to drawbacks when analysing educational data; it is therefore extremely useful to have access to an alternative statistical technique which could provide corroborative findings. The main problems associated with multiple regression analysis are the treatment of interaction effects, non-linearity in the underlying data, and the behaviour of the error term. These are explained briefly below.

Interaction effects When significant interaction effects are omitted from the model, the estimates of the main effects will be biased and will not have minimum variance; in other words, the regression coefficients may have the wrong values and may appear to be statistically insignificant, which would not have been the case had the interaction effects been included. Furthermore, since the relationship between the interaction effects and the dependent variable may not be linear, the examination of partial correlation coefficients may not be an adequate screening test for the existence of interactions.

Non-linearity Multiple regression uses a well-defined functional form to relate the dependent variable to each exogenous variable. For example, in the model described by equation (1) the relationship is assumed to be linear; thus a 1 per cent increase in the percentage TIPS surveys completed leads to a 0.1 increase in Micro Essay Mark irrespective of whether the student has already completed 10 per cent or 90 per cent of the TIPS surveys. The reasonable hypothesis of diminishing marginal product of TIPS surveys beyond some point suggests that the linear regression coefficient must be treated with some reserve. It is possible to investigate different mathematical forms and compare the goodness of fit; while this approach is often useful, it is possible that the data do not conform to any mathematical form.

The error term An important assumption in multiple regression analysis is that the error term is normally distributed, and its variance is independent of the magnitude of the dependent variable; if this assumption does not hold the estimated regression coefficients may appear to be insignificant. A major characteristic of the multiple choice scores is their binomial nature: the responses to the individual questions generate a binomial distribution; the multiple choice score is the sum of the individual binomial distributions, therefore the distribution of the multiple choice scores may have certain binomial characteristics, including non-constant variance. The essay marks themselves may also have binomial characteristics, since marks for essays are awarded in large part on the basis of the number of valid points which the student has mentioned. While the magnitude of this problem cannot be calculated, the fact that it exists makes an alternative analysis desirable.

Log–linear analysis approaches both the data and the statistical estimation in a different way to multiple regression. The first main difference is that the data are not used in their raw form but are categorized; for example, essay marks on the scale 0 to 100 are not used, but instead are allocated to categories such as 0–30, 31–50, 51+. The different axes along which data are classified are called factors, and each factor is split into two or more levels. The data observed consists of counts of the numbers of observations falling into each possible combination of the levels of the different factors.

An example of categorical data is a group of students classified by sex and score in exam, giving the following table of counts:

| | **Exam Mark Band** | | | |
	1	2	3	**Total**
Sex				
Male	80	100	120	300
Female	140	110	95	345
Total	220	210	215	645

In this example there are two factors, Exam Mark Band and Sex; the first factor, Exam Mark Band, has three levels (1 = low, 2 = medium, 3 = high) and the second factor, Sex, has two levels (male and female).

The second main difference is that log–linear analysis describes and estimates the probability structure underlying an observed set of categorical data. One convenient way of presenting the results of a log–linear analysis is to express the fitted model in a relative odds formulation. Consider a simple model in three factors: Exam Mark (at three levels: low, medium, high), whether the student has A level economics (at two levels), and the percentage of TIPS completed by the student (at three levels: low, medium, high). Exam Mark is the dependent variable. The log linear results can be presented in a relative odds formulation, for example the probability of a student having a high mark rather than a low mark, given that he has A level economics and has completed a high percentage of TIPS. This can be written as

$$\frac{P(\text{Mark = high mark/student has 'A' economics and has high \% TIPS})}{P(\text{Mark = low mark/student has 'A' economics and high \% TIPS})}$$

This relative likelihood or relative odds of a factor being at level i, say, rather than level 1 can be expressed as a product of terms. The above expression can be written as

$$\frac{P(\text{Mark = high})}{P(\text{Mark = low})} \times \frac{P(\text{Mark = high and student has 'A' economics})}{P(\text{Mark = low and student has 'A' economics})} \times$$

$$\times \frac{P(\text{Mark = high and student has high \% TIPS})}{P(\text{Mark = low and student has high \% TIPS})}$$

The second and third terms in the product are the contributions to the relative odds of scoring a high rather than low mark of A level economics and high percentage of TIPS completed respectively.

The restrictive assumptions which are necessary for multiple regression analysis do not apply. First, all possible interaction effects can be taken into account, subject to there being observations in the defined cells. In the study, no cell had less than five observations. Second, no mathematical form is assumed between the categories, therefore the potential distortions arising from forcing the data into a linear form do not arise. Third, the assumption of constant error term variance is irrelevant. However, if the underlying assumptions of multiple regression analysis do apply, and if the model has been correctly specified in terms of interaction effects and the mathematical form is approximately correct, multiple regression and log–linear analysis will produce similar results, albeit in different forms. Indeed, in this instance, multiple regression may prove the better technique.

While log–linear analysis clearly provides a valuable complement to multiple regression analysis in that it can generate alternative findings and identify where the assumptions are possibly being violated, the technique itself is subject to certain drawbacks:

1 Categorizing the continuous variables raises problems. First, there is a loss of information. This may not be too serious a problem for the output measures, where there is a tendency to mark on the basis of fail, pass and merit; however, the within-category effects are lost for all continuous variables. Second, the results may be dependent on the categories chosen; for example categories 0–30, 31–50, 51+ may generate different results from categories 0–25, 26–50, 51–74, 75+. Sensitivity analysis was carried out in this study and it appeared that the findings were not greatly dependent on the categories; however, it cannot be concluded that this will apply in all cases.

2 It is necessary to ensure that an adequate number of observations is available in each cell for statistical analysis.

The results of the log–linear analyses are set out in Tables 5–8. The results for the three variables included in the regression analysis are discussed below.

Percentage of TIPS surveys completed   The contributions of the various factors to the relative odds of being in a high or medium mark group rather than having a low mark in the Micro Essay are given in Table 5. The first part of the table shows the contribution of percentage TIPS completed.

For students who had completed a low percentage of TIPS surveys the contribution to the ratio of the probability of being in the medium mark category to being in the low mark category was 0.68; the contribution to the ratio for being in the high mark category was 0.54. The ratios of the probabilities are significantly different from 1. This means that considering only the contribution of TIPS to relative probabilities, students who did a low percentage of TIPS were nearly one and a half times more likely to be in the low mark category than in the medium mark category, and nearly twice as likely to be in the low mark category than in the high mark category. For ease of exposition, the ratio of probabilities will be referred to as relative odds; the

Table 5   Log–linear analysis: Micro Essay (relative odds)

		% TIPS completed		
		Low	Medium	High
Micro Essay	Medium	0.68*	1.18	1.25*
Exam Mark Band	High	0.54*	1.00	1.84*

		'A' economics	No 'A' economics
Micro Essay	Medium	1.18*	0.85*
Exam Mark Band	High	1.29*	0.77*

		Institution								
		I	E	B	C	H	D	A	F	G
Micro Essay	Medium	0.76	0.78	0.98	1.65	1.97*	1.02	0.85	1.65*	0.36*
Exam Mark Band	High	0.60	1.40	2.00*	1.20	1.50*	0.30*	1.26	1.92*	0.38*

*Significant at 95 per cent level.

results could be expressed in terms of the actual probabilities but the relative magnitudes emerge more clearly when expressed as relative odds. At the other end of the scale the contribution to relative odds of being in the high mark category was 1.84 for students completing a high percentage of TIPS surveys and 1.25 of being in the medium band category; in other words, students who completed a low percentage of TIPS surveys were half as likely to be in the high mark category as in the low mark category, while students completing a high percentage of TIPS surveys were nearly twice as likely to be in the high mark category than in the low mark category, other things being equal.

The information conveyed by these results differs from the multiple regression finding that each additional per cent of TIPS surveys completed is associated with an additional 0.1 per cent on the Micro Essay mark. The log–linear results are consistent with the regression result in that they demonstrate the strong positive relationship between the percentage of TIPS surveys completed and Micro Exam mark.

Tables 6, 7 and 8, in which the output measures are respectively Macro Essay, Micro and Macro Multiple Choice scores, reveal a similar pattern: students who did a low percentage of TIPS surveys were much less likely to be in the high mark category than the low mark category for all measures of output, while students who did a high percentage of TIPS surveys were much more likely to be in the high mark category than the low mark category, other things being equal.

Table 6 Log–linear analysis: Macro Essay (relative odds)

		% TIPS completed		
		Low	Medium	High
Macro Essay	Medium	0.77*	1.05	1.24
Exam Mark Band	High	0.60*	0.87	1.91*

		'A' economics	No 'A' economics
Macro Essay	Medium	1.21*	0.82*
Exam Mark Band	High	1.37*	0.73*

		Institution						
		D	E	B	C	H	F	I
Macro Essay	Medium	1.10	0.65	0.54*	1.82*	1.77*	1.04	0.78
Exam Mark Band	High	0.80	2.46*	0.37*	0.97	1.28	0.72	1.50

*Significant at 95 per cent level.

Contribution of A level economics In Table 4 the A level economics regression coefficient was 4.17 for the Micro Essay, which suggested that on average students with A level economics scored 4.17 more on the Micro Essay than those without. This compares with the results in Table 5, which show that the contribution to relative odds of being in the Micro Essay high mark category for students with A level economics was 1.29, compared to 0.77 for students without A level economics. These relative odds contributions show effects of lower magnitude than those associated with students doing a high rather than a low percentage of TIPS surveys, i.e. the effect on the probability of being in the high mark rather than low mark category is less for having A level economics than for doing a high percentage of TIPS surveys.

The relative odds results in Tables 5–8 are consistent for the four measures of output; an interesting point is that the relative odds results for A level economics are statistically significant for Micro Multiple Choice whereas the regression coefficient was not significant at the 95 per cent level.

Institution effects The multiple regression results in Table 4 demonstrate that there are relatively large effects associated with individual institutions. However, it is only possible to draw conclusions such as, 'Students in Institution B performed on average 9.5 marks better on the Micro Essay than students in Institution I, holding other variables constant.' The regression approach to the analysis of institution effects using dummy variables gives very little scope for describing the different forms of institutional effect which may occur. As an extreme example, Institution A could have 50 per cent of its students score 100 per cent and 50 per cent score 0; Institution B could have 100 per cent of its students score 50 per cent. The means would be identical.

Table 7   Log–linear analysis: Micro Multiple Choice (relative odds)

		% TIPS completed		
		Low	Medium	High
Micro Objective	Medium	0.977	0.759*	1.35*
Score Band	High	0.75*	0.82	1.61*
		'A' economics	No 'A' economics	
Micro Objective	Medium	1.26*	0.79*	
Score Band	High	1.15*	0.87*	
		Institution							
		A	E	B	C	H	D	K	J
Micro Objective	Medium	1.52 0.67 0.95 0.52*1.10 0.99 2.10*0.89							
Score Band	High	2.00 0.67 0.84 0.23*1.10 0.95 1.87 1.97							

*Significant at 95 per cent level.

Four types of institution effect can be hypothesized and tested using log–linear analysis:

Type 1   The polarizing effect: a higher proportion of students both in the high mark and low mark categories

Type 2   The averaging effect: a lower proportion of students both in the low mark and high mark categories

Type 3   The overall negative effect: a higher proportion of students in the lower mark category and a lower proportion of students in the high and medium categories

Type 4   The overall positive effect: a higher proportion of students in the high and medium categories and a lower proportion in the low mark category

A negative regression coefficient provides much the same information as Type 3, and a positive coefficient much the same as Type 4; however, the Type 1 and 2 effects cannot be identified using regression analysis. The relative odds in Tables 5–8 show differences in institutional effects which may reveal a great deal about their teaching characteristics.

Institution B is of interest on the basis of the multiple regression results because it had the highest positive coefficient for Micro Essay, the highest negative coefficient for Macro Essay, it was equal to the base institution for Micro Multiple Choice (which was in turn the highest scoring institution), and it was equal to the base institution for Macro Multiple Choice which in turn had institutions both above and below. Inspection of the log–linear results reveals that for Micro Essay the relative odds of being in the high mark

Table 8   Log–linear analysis: Macro Multiple Choice (relative odds)

		% TIPS completed		
		Low	Medium	High
Macro Objective	Medium	0.86	0.95	1.20
Score Band	High	0.56*	1.10	1.60*
		'A' economics	No 'A' economics	
Macro Objective	Medium	1.20	0.83	
Score Band	High	1.40*	0.69*	

		Institution				
		D	E	B	C	H
Macro Objective	Medium	0.77	0.67	2.15*	0.63*	1.42*
Score Band	High	0.99	0.70	0.94	0.65*	2.35*

*Significant at 95 per cent level.

category were twice that of being in the low mark category; this suggests that in terms of the Micro Essay, Institution B is Type 1, in other words the high average level of performance revealed by the regression coefficient is due to a relatively high proportion of students in the high mark band and a relatively low proportion of students in the low mark band. The Micro Multiple Choice results in Table 7 show no difference in the relative odds between mark categories, suggesting that the main impact of Institution B is on teaching related to the Micro Essay. The low Macro Essay mark associated with Institution B is corroborated by the low relative odds of being in the high and medium mark bands. This suggests a Type 3 effect for macroeconomics teaching, i.e. students perform uniformly badly. A slightly different picture is revealed in Table 8, which shows that the relative odds of the medium mark category for Macro Multiple Choice are relatively high, but the relative odds of the high mark category are not. This suggests a Type 2 effect, i.e. that there is an averaging effect on performance.

Thus if the institution effect can be attributed to differences in teaching, this single institution reveals considerable differences in teaching performance between micro and macroeconomics, and to some extent between the types of learning implied by the essays and multiple choice tests.

A different story emerges for Institution C, which had a positive regression coefficient for Micro Essay, an insignificant coefficient for Macro Essay, and negative coefficients for both Micro and Macro Multiple Choice. For the Macro Essay, Institution C clearly appears to be of Type 2 with the contribution to the relative likelihood of medium to low essay mark being 1.82 (and significant), while the contribution to the relative odds of high to low essay mark is only 0.97. For the Micro Essay, there is a strong suggestion that Institution C is again Type 2; the contribution to medium to low relative odds is 1.65 (but not significant), while the contribution to the relative odds of high to low is 1.2. The relative odds for both Micro and Macro Multiple Choice strongly suggest that Institution C is of Type 3, i.e. a concentration of students in the low mark category. Here is an interesting example of an institution where students tend to produce average essays but are poor in multiple choice exams.

Each of the institutions can be analysed in this way, and while confidentiality commitments prohibit naming the institutions there is little doubt that the teaching faculty in those institutions would be able to provide informative interpretations of the results.

The 'best fit' models as described above only involve first-order relationships between the dependent variable and the explanatory variables. In arriving at this model, tests were carried out to see whether any terms should be included representing relationships between the dependent variable and interactions among the explanatory variables. (An example of such a situation might be if performance were related to particular combinations of A level economics and percentage of TIPS completed.) There were no significant higher-order relationships of this kind.

In one sense this may seem a negative result. However, the powerful model fitting capabilities of the log–linear approach mean that the possibility of higher-order interactions have been exhaustively investigated and positively excluded from these particular models. Thus the results can be interpreted with some confidence without the lingering doubt that there may be undetected higher-order interactions.

Conclusion

From these results it is clear that log–linear analysis has a contribution to make to educational research, since it adds insights to the findings of multiple regression. When the data from the Scottish schools study become available in 1986–87, both multiple regression and log–linear modelling will be utilized. Educational researchers in other fields might do well to note that this technique exists and that it may be an appropriate technique for analysing their data. There is considerable potential for using this technique, first to examine and describe the structure of a data set, and then to formulate hypotheses which can be tested on a fresh data set by the most appropriate technique in the general linear modelling range.

Acknowledgement

The authors are indebted to Allen C. Kelley for comments on an earlier draft.

Appendix: Some practical aspects of GLIM

Access to general linear modelling packages is improving all the time. GLIM is a computer package for the fitting of general linear models to quantitative, qualitative and mixed data (Baker and Nelder, 1978). However, the output from GLIM is not easy to interpret unless one is a trained statistician. Log–linear analysis is also available on SPSS release 9. Some computers may have difficulty in providing the space necessary to handle a large number of data cells, causing constraints on the number of interactions which can be investigated.

References

Baker, R. J. and Nelder, J. A. 1978 *The Glim System (Release 3) Manual* Numerical Algorithms Group

Kelley, A. C. 1968 'An experiment with TIPS, a computer aided instructional system for undergraduate education' *American Economic Review Proceedings* (May)

Lumsden, K. G. and Scott, A. 1985 'Public funding of universities: effects on economics 1 students' in G. Shaw and D. Greenaway (eds.) *Public Choice, Public Finance and Public Policy: Essays in Honour of Alan Peacock* Martin Robinson

Lumsden, K. G. and Scott, A. (in preparation) 'Sex and the economics student re-examined'

Empirical evidence on economic literacy in schools

Michael Watts

Director, Center for Economic Education; Associate Director, Indiana Council for Economic Education and Assistant Professor of Economics, Purdue University

Survey and multiple regression results are provided for a large, random sample of teachers and students in four grades (5, 8, 11 and 12). Over 200 classes in public and private schools in the state of Indiana were pre- and post-tested. Impacts of various student, teacher and school system characteristics on measures of student learning are estimated. Policy measures discussed include the effects of a separate economics course, teacher training in economics, and school system commitment to economics education as measured by participation in the national Developmental Economic Education Program (DEEP).

Introduction

Economic education programmes for elementary and secondary teachers have been offered on a regular basis in Indiana since 1954, and on a relatively widespread basis since the mid-1970s. For the past decade, intensive summer workshops awarding three semester hours of credit in economics have been offered annually in various parts of the state. At least 11 such courses have been offered each year in this period, reaching a total of several hundred teachers each summer. About 2000 Indiana teachers participate each year in credit or non-credit programmes sponsored by the Indiana Council for Economic Education (ICEE), offered by one of the 11 university Centers for Economic Education which have been established at leading public and private universities in the state, or by economics and/or education professors who co-operate with the ICEE to offer such programmes on campuses where no Center exists. While certification requirements for future teachers in Indiana are generally similar to those in most other states, the ICEE is one of the oldest, largest and most active state councils in the US, suggesting that economics training of teachers and students in the state might be more extensive than average.

Prior to 1983, however, there was no extensive state-wide data from Indiana or other states to support or refute such a claim. As Stephen Buckles of the University of Missouri once suggested in a useful over-simplification of the research and evaluation work in pre-college economics education published over the past few decades, the earliest studies focused on how much teachers learned in workshops and other specialized training courses while more recent studies usually examined how much the students of the teachers who received this training learned.* In other words, although a large and growing body of work has consistently shown that teachers do score significantly higher on standardized exams after training and that students of these teachers will also exhibit improved scores when classroom time is devoted to instruction on economics, little or no evidence apart from the national norming results on standardized tests in the discipline is available to suggest how widespread economics instruction and learning really is in the schools. Furthermore, there is scant evidence (apart from the 1981 Yankelovich survey and a dozen or so recent state surveys, which received little attention outside the states in which they were conducted) on the level of economics training of classroom teachers, and particularly on how much time is allocated to economics instruction at different grade levels and in key subject areas (Yankelovich, Skelly and White, 1981; Walstad and Watts, 1985).

In 1981, the ICEE set out to undertake a 'state-wide assessment' of economics instruction in public and private elementary and secondary schools to address these questions. A random sample of schools was drawn, stratified by enrolment size to ensure that small schools were not over-represented and that the geographical distribution of schools tested would closely reflect the distribution of the state's population. Approvals for testing were obtained from administrators of over 150 schools in the state; then classes (and thereby teachers and students) at these schools were selected at random.†

Testing was done in the four grade levels – 5, 8, 11 and 12 – in which key social studies courses (US history in grades 5, 8 and 11; government and/or economics in grade 12) are required for *all* students in the public and in most private schools. Like many states in the US, Indiana has developed guidelines listing basic economic concepts to be included in its elementary and secondary

---

* Buckles' comment was made as a discussant at the 'Evaluation' session of the 1983 annual meetings of the Joint Council on Economic Education and the National Association of Economic Educators, in San Antonio, Texas.

† Sampling classes rather than students does introduce the possibility of sampling bias resulting from intra-class correlations on the different variables studied. The large number of classes included in this project, coupled with the facts that these classes are required of *all* Indiana students, that 'honours' and Learning Disability (LD) classes were excluded from the survey, and that limited ability grouping apart from these two categories is observed in Indiana secondary schools, tended to mitigate this problem here. The descriptive statistics on the variables (see Table 8) do appear representative of Indiana students and classes in these grade levels. While it is, of course, preferable to take a direct sample of students, that procedure was not feasible given the constraints of this study.

social studies programmes.* These required courses represent the primary opportunities in the curriculum to meet these guidelines.

It was determined that it would be impossible to use nationally normed tests for the study, primarily because several major school districts in the state used, in 1981–82, class periods as short as 35–45 minutes. The nationally normed tests available for these grades each include 40 or more items and normally require at least 50–60 minutes of class time to administer. A panel of experts was therefore appointed to develop new test instruments for this study, which were field tested with over 1000 students from the state in the spring and summer of 1982.†

Pre-testing and teacher survey collection was completed in September and early October 1982; more than 5300 students from over 200 classes were tested. A total of 209 teachers completed surveys. Post-testing was conducted in late April and May of 1983. Given drop-outs, early graduation, transfers, absenteeism and re-scheduling of classes between the first and second term in secondary grades,‡ the total number of students post-tested fell to just over 4300 students. Research assistants provided by the ICEE administered all tests and collected background information on the students who were pre-tested, as well as their teachers. Background data on school systems was collected by the author from the Indiana Department of Public Instruction and other agencies, most notably the Indiana Farm Bureau, Inc. which regularly publishes information on Indiana schools and school districts (Indiana Farm Bureau, 1981).

Data from the project are reported below in two sections: the first reports descriptive statistics and other basic information from the teacher surveys and from student test scores and responses on different sections of the testing instruments. In the second section, the regression results on a simple model of student learning are summarized. Some conclusions and recommendations from the study are discussed in the final section of the paper.

Teacher background, classroom instructional time and student test results

Responses from the teachers provided information on their general academic training, their college-level coursework in economics (before and after graduation) and on how much classroom time they planned to devote to economics instruction during the 1982–83 academic year. On average, the teachers questioned reported 15.2 years of full-time job experience and had

---

* The Indiana guidelines were published and widely distributed in 1979 in *Social Studies: A Guide for Curriculum Development,* Samuel Shermis (ed.), Indiana Department of Public Instruction.

† Technical data on the testing instruments are available on request from the author.

‡ Especially important in grades 11 and 12, and reflected in the drop in sample size in these grades in Tables 6 and 7.

received their last academic degree, which for 90 per cent of the teachers was a master's or higher post-graduate degree, 12 years earlier. This pattern of responses was expected, and is generally observed across the US, as fewer new teachers were hired during the 1970s in response to falling student enrolments. The master's degree finding is probably somewhat higher in Indiana than in many states, however, because to maintain their professional licence Indiana teachers are required to earn an approved post-graduate degree within five years of receiving their baccalaureate.

Information on the economics coursework completed by all of the teachers in the sample is presented in Table 1. The teachers are divided into the four grades in which classes were tested in the study. No teacher taught more than one tested class so there is no overlap across columns, just as it would be rare in Indiana to find one teacher assigned to classes in more than one of these grades (with the possible exception of the grade 11 and 12 classes). The numbers reported in the table may be interpreted in a very straightforward way – 53 per cent of the grade 5 teachers had completed no college credit hours in economics, 22 per cent had completed 1–3 hours, and so on. The grade 12 teachers have been separated into two groups, labelled 'economics' and 'non-economics' teachers, to identify those who were teaching, or had recently taught, the one-term course in economics taken by slightly more than half of the students at this grade level in Indiana public schools.

Table 2 reports the teacher responses on how many years ago they had completed their last intensive course in economics, including in-service workshops. Table 3 shows how many teachers at each grade level had, in fact, completed such a workshop since beginning to teach.

The general picture that emerges from the data in these tables is a disturbing one. Except for the economics teachers, training is quite limited, with modal levels at what are usually *minimum* certification requirements at teacher training institutions. Moreover, the training was completed, on average, more than 12 years ago, suggesting a probable major deterioration in the human capital the teachers had acquired from their own economics courses.* Certainly economic issues and even important analytical concepts have undergone major changes in the last dozen years – for example, the stress on uncertainty and information costs in microeconomics; on the supply side, monetary policy and rational expectations in macroeconomics; and such 'new' issues as tax simplification, deficits, industrial policy, energy, educational reforms and high technology automation. The low levels of teacher training in economics raise serious questions concerning how well teachers can cover basic economic concepts long recognized in the discipline, let alone the more current concepts and issues.

This is not to suggest in any way that the Indiana teachers are less well trained than their counterparts in other states. A recent study suggests that they are, in fact, as well or even slightly better trained than teachers in other

---

*See the literature on 'lasting effects' of economics instruction – for example, Saunders (1970 and 1980). Much of this literature is summarized in Siegfried and Fels (1979, pp. 950–52).

Table 1 Teachers' credit hours in economics*

Credit hours	Grade level					
	5 (n = 51)	8 (n = 48)	11 (n = 54)	12 non-economics (n = 29)	all non-economics (n = 182)	12 economics (n = 27)
0	53%	21%	7%	7%	24%	0
1-3	22%	25%	26%	17%	23%	0
4-6	14%	25%	30%	41%	26%	15%
7-9	2%	8%	9%	10%	7%	7%
10-12	3%	10%	4%	7%	6%	19%
13-15	0	2%	4%	3%	2%	15%
>15	0	6%	9%	7%	6%	41%
No response	8%	2%	11%	10%	8%	7%

* Columns may not total 100%, owing to rounding error
n = 209

Source: From 'The Indiana Council for Economic Education's Statewide Assessment –
Summary Report No. 1: A Profile of Teachers' Michael Watts, 1983 (unpublished monograph)

Table 2   Number of years since teachers attended last economics course or workshop

Years	Grade level					
	5	8	11	12 (non-economics)	all grades (non-economics)	12 (economics)
0–4	10%	6%	17%	3%	10%	48%
5–8	14%	19%	11%	24%	16%	15%
9–12	12%	23%	7%	10%	13%	11%
13–16	22%	17%	17%	10%	17%	4%
17–21	20%	13%	17%	21%	17%	0
>21	20%	23%	20%	21%	21%	7%
No response	4%	0	11%	10%	6%	15%

Source: From 'The Indiana Council for Economic Education's Statewide Assessment –
Summary Report No. 1: A Profile of Teachers' Michael Watts, 1983 (unpublished monograph)

Table 3   Percentage of teachers who have completed a workshop on economics education

Grade level	Yes	No	No response
5	6%	88%	6%
8	10%	83%	6%
11	20%	69%	11%
12 (Non-economics)	17%	72%	10%
12 (Economics)	63%	33%	4%
All teachers	20%	73%	8%

Source: From 'The Indiana Council for Economic Education's Statewide Assessment – Summary Report No. 1: A Profile of Teachers' Michael Watts, 1983 (unpublished monograph)

states where similar data is available (Walstad and Watts, 1985). For example, the Indiana economics teachers have substantially more training than is given in other states; they also have more recent training, with almost half taking a course in the last four years. In general, however, training levels are not as high as some important early studies suggested would be required to implement effective economic education programmes at the pre-college level (Bach and Saunders, 1965).

Teacher responses to the question on classroom time scheduled for economics instruction also raise questions on how extensive, logically complete and systematically integrated the instruction that is provided will be. These data are summarized in Table 4; very little information is available on this issue from other studies, but what there is again suggests that the Indiana teachers' responses are typical (O'Toole, 1980; Yankelovich, Skelly and White, 1981, p. 45; Walstad and Watts, 1985).

Turning from this discussion of teacher inputs to the results of the student testing, average improvements of 18 per cent in grade 5, 13 per cent in grade 8, 6 per cent in grade 11, and 8 per cent in grade 12 were observed. Improvement here refers to simple percentage increases in the mean student scores on cognitive items between the pre- and post-tests. It is not unusual to find larger percentage increases for elementary and junior high students, since one additional year of school and life experiences is a relatively greater addition for them than for the older students. The reason for greater improvement by the high school seniors (grade 12) than juniors (grade 11) is almost certainly that a majority of Indiana students take an economics course in grade 12.

Unfortunately, these increases are not particularly large compared with earlier test results gathered nationally and in Indiana. The discussion guide for the national *Test of Economic Literacy* (Soper, 1979), published by the Joint Council on Economic Education in 1979, includes data that show improvements of 7–12 per cent comparing students' scores in grade 12 to

Table 4   Teacher responses on expected minutes of economic instruction per week

Minutes/week	Grade level					
	5	8	11	12 (non-economics)	all grades (non-economics)	12 (economics)
0	12%	6%	6%	15%	9%	
1–9	2%	15%	17%	5%	10%	
10–19	18%	27%	19%	15%	20%	
20–29	8%	8%	19%	12%	12%	
30–39	8%	13%	17%	15%	13%	
40–49	10%	6%	6%	2%	6%	
50–59	4%	4%	2%	5%	4%	
≥60<200	4%	6%	4%	12%	6%	
≥200						75%
No response	35%	15%	13%	17%	20%	25%

Source: From 'The Indiana Council for Economic Education's Statewide Assessment – Summary Report No. 1: A Profile of Teachers' Michael Watts, 1983 (unpublished monograph)

grade 11, where neither group of students had taken a course in economics. Grade 5 students with no formal instruction in economics scored 8–13 per cent higher than grade 4 students on the Joint Council's *Basic Economics Test* (Chizmar and Halinski, 1980). Summarizing these data on improvement rates, then, it is expected that scores on virtually any tests tailored for students in these grades would increase over the course of a school year even if little or no formal instruction on the subject being tested was provided. The average improvements reported here are broadly in line with that sort of increase in score – not with the gains that would be expected to follow formal and reasonably systematic instruction on a subject. The economics instruction that was provided, if any, did not significantly add to gains expected to result from normal maturation.

The mean pre-test score for the grade 12 students who would go on to take an economics course during the 1982–83 school year was slightly higher than the same score for the students who did not (11.4 versus 11.2). This difference was not statistically significant at customary confidence levels (0.05). The difference that does exist probably reflects the fact that college-bound students in Indiana are somewhat more likely to take the economics course; but it should be noted that many local school systems in the state require the course for graduation, including several large systems such as Indianapolis.

On the post-test the 'economics' group scored 9.2 per cent higher than the 'non-economics' group, and that difference was strongly significant (at the 0.01 level). However, on the 24-item cognitive section of the test this reflected an actual score differential of just over one question – not enough improvement to suggest that a one-semester course can, independently, guarantee a high level of economic literacy.

Comparing item-by-item responses for the two groups of students (see Table 5), there were five questions on the pre-test where a significantly larger proportion of the students who would go on to take an economics course than those who would not answered correctly. The five concepts/topics covered on those questions were: scarcity, opportunity cost, shortage, tariffs, and determinants of potential GNP. The 'non-economics' group scored significantly higher on two questions, which covered the concepts/topics of GNP and minimum wage effects on teenagers' wages and employment levels.

On the post-test, the 'economics' groups scored significantly higher on a total of nine questions. On three questions they maintained the significant advantage noted on the pre-test (on the topics of scarcity, shortages and determinants of potential GNP). On five topics (changes in supply determinants, productivity determining high wage levels, the economic role of profits, major spending groups in the economy, and the definition of money) a significant difference occurred where none was observed on the pre-test. In one case (the question on minimum wage effects) the 'economics' group improved from a significantly lower performance on the pre-test to a significantly higher rating on the post-test. The 'non-economics' group did not score significantly higher than the 'economics' group on any of the cognitive measures on the post-test. This does, at least, suggest that the economics course is having a positive effect on both definitional *and* reasoning/analysis understandings of the students.

Briefly summarizing the general areas of student strengths and weaknesses on these tests for all four grade levels:

1 Students understand microeconomics better than macroeconomics, especially in terms of principles and conceptual understanding as compared with institutional facts, though students are extremely weak on basic money and banking facts as well as concepts.

2 While certain microeconomic principles (e.g. supply and demand and gains from international trade) are understood as simple, logical statements by many students, an overall understanding of the effects of competition in a market *system* in leading towards socially beneficial outcomes and behaviour is not present. This shows up most directly in questions on the economic role and effects of government, and in some misunderstandings on tariffs. Without such understanding, the students obviously cannot analyse possible total (i.e. net) benefits of such policies and arrangements.

3 Students at all grade levels persist in thinking of opportunity cost as the monetary dollar price of a good or service, not the value of the best alternative forgone whenever an economic choice is made. This confusion may not be too serious in individual producer decisions (e.g. which job pays best), but it will be more serious in consumption decisions (e.g. what do I really have to give up to go to a movie or buy a car) and most critical in evaluating public policy decisions where there often are no clear or direct price signals (e.g. in comparing costs of pollution and pollution control, determining who finally pays taxes, evaluating long-run costs of inflation). Several other state and national reports which asked large samples of teachers what concepts they cover have noted that the opportunity cost concept is not one most teachers claim to teach (e.g. Yankelovich, Skelly and White, 1981, pp. 23–4), probably because of the limited training noted earlier, given that this concept tends to be covered only in formal economics courses.

4 On questions measuring students' attitude towards studying economics, they show that they are at least potentially ready to receive more economics instruction favourably. They believe that economics is important; they hope it can be presented clearly and interestingly.

Simple models of student learning and regression analysis

Regression analysis is a standard statistical procedure widely used by economists and other researchers to model relationships involving several variables and to test whether the impact of a particular independent variable is, *ceteris*

Table 5   Grade 12 correct responses (%)

	Pre-Test			Concept	Post-Test		
	With economics[a]	No economics	Total		With economics	No economics	Total
(1)	74**	68	71	Scarcity	79**	71	76
(2)	37*	32	34	Opportunity cost	41	36	39
(3)	59	56	58	Specialization and exchange	61	60	61
(4)	35	33	34	Technological changes/supply	34	36	35
(5)	64	65	65	Change in supply	67*	60	65
(6)	39	35	37	Wages/high output for workers	43*	36	41
(7)	69	67	68	Economic role of profits	71**	61	66
(8)	53	54	54	Monopoly	57	52	55
(9)	72	74	74	Mutual gains from trade	77	74	76
(10)	45	46	46	Self-interest/competition/invisible hand	54	51	53
(11)	42	39	40	Public goods/government	41	39	41
(12)	43	47	46	External costs	50	53	51
(13)	25	25	25	Cost/benefit framework	25	25	26
(14)	53*	47	50	Shortage	62**	53	58
(15)	61	61	61	Excise tax effects on price, quantity	69	68	69

No.	Item	Pre-Test		Post-Test	
		With economics	No economics	With economics	No economics
(16)	Minimum wage effects on wages, employment	78***	77	77	78
(17)	Tariffs	39	38	42	43
(18)	National output consumed by major groups	45	46	53**	44
(19)	Gross national product	50***	48	59**	49
(20)	Aggregate demand decrease	28	27	32	29
(21)	Determinates of potential gross national product	34	37	50**	33
(22)	Definition of money	23	24	38**	18
(23)	Creating money	44	44	46	48
(24)	Identifying an appropriate fiscal policy	23	24	26	26
	Mean	11.403	11.205	12.610**	11.544
	Standard deviation	3.422	3.473	3.799	3.502
		556	804	510	331

* Economics students significantly higher than non-economics students, 0.05.
** Economics students significantly higher than non-economics students, 0.01.
*** Non-economics students significantly higher than economics students, 0.05.

a This is the group of students who did go on to take an economics course during the school year – they had not completed such a course at the time the pre-test was administered.

Source: From 'The Indiana Council for Economic Education's Statewide Assessment – Summary Report No. 2: A Profile of Indiana Students' Economic Literacy' Michael Watts, 1984 (unpublished monograph)

paribus, in an hypothesized direction *and* significantly greater or less than zero. In other words, some dependent variable is expressed as a function of several independent variables plus an error term; coefficients on each of the independent variables are calculated by the regression program; and those coefficients are then evaluated as significantly different from zero (or not) using a *t*-test.

In this study, a general equation using pre-test scores as the dependent variable was estimated in each of the four grades, with a set of student and school system characteristics entered as explanatory variables. A binary was used to indicate the students' sex (1 = male), and percentile scores on standardized aptitude/IQ tests were entered as a measure of the students' general mental ability. School system variables included were enrolments in the school district (in log form) to measure district size and thereby specialization levels by teachers and in other school services; assessed valuation per student as a measure of the tax base of the district (i.e. one income constraint facing the district *and* a partial measure of average family wealth in the district); a 'poverty index' indicating the percentage of students in the district receiving government-paid 'free lunches' (i.e. another family wealth measure, particularly important as a control in urban districts with valuable business properties included in the assessment base variable discussed above, which might otherwise mask large numbers of poor families in a district); and finally a binary indicating whether the district participated in the Developmental Economic Education Program (DEEP) sponsored by the Joint Council on Economic Education nationally and, in Indiana, by the ICEE (1 = yes).* The pre-test equations are presented in Table 6. Only students with complete information on sex, aptitude/IQ scores and each of the school system variables were included in the regression analysis. Since the school system variables were not meaningful for private schools included in the study, students from those schools are not included in these data.

The pre-test equations indicate, as expected, that students with higher aptitude/IQ scores performed well on the economics tests in all four grade levels. The sex variable was also uniformly significant; many other studies have found that male students tend to do better on economics tests than females, particularly when no formal instruction has been provided (Siegfried, 1979).

Wealthier districts generally began the year with students stronger in economics than did poor districts, which is not surprising. The assessed valuation variable was positive in all grades and significant in three; the poverty variable was negative in all grades and also significant in three. The district enrolment variable was positive in all three of the secondary grade

---

* DEEP is a highly de-centralized programme in that each school district develops its own curriculum plan and implementation strategies. Some DEEP districts develop very detailed plans and carefully monitor implementation programmes; others do not, and are sometimes described as 'paper DEEP' in reference to the one-page form that must be completed and signed by a district representative and a state economic education officer before the district can be accepted into the DEEP programme.

Table 6 Pre-test scores as dependent variable (t statistics in parentheses)

Independent variables	Grade level			
	5	8	11	12
Student variables				
IQ/aptitude percentile	0.081 (20.182)**	0.079 (18.527)**	0.056 (14.794)**	0.067 (15.643)**
Sex	0.545 (3.073)**	0.617 (2.989)**	0.588 (3.011)**	0.521 (2.482)**
School system variables				
Log n enrolment	−0.048 (0.432)	0.312 (2.422)**	0.016 (0.104)	0.324 (2.189)**
Assessed valuation per student	0.000098 (0.930)	0.000042 (2.110)**	0.000021 (2.036)**	0.000037 (2.614)**
Poverty index	−3.117 (3.230)**	−2.118 (1.309)	−2.717 (1.746)*	−5.595 (3.243)**
DEEP	−0.040 (0.139)	−0.508 (2.432)**	0.150 (0.495)	−0.773 (2.505)**
Constant	5.537 (5.729)**	1.255 (1.099)	6.662 (5.155)**	4.717 (3.853)**
F	83.759	68.916	45.126	51.623
P	0.000	0.000	0.000	0.000
Adjusted R^2	0.333	0.361	0.269	0.295
n	994	721	721	728

* Significant at 0.05 level (one-tailed test).
** Significant at 0.01 level (one-tailed test).
Source: From Watts, 1985

levels and twice significant, which is consistent with studies which have found advantages to large size in these grades (e.g. Riew, 1966). The DEEP variable was negative in three grade levels, twice significant, suggesting that these districts began the school year with weaker students in terms of their economic understanding.

Table 7 presents the post-test equations, which include pre-test scores as one explanatory variable. This specification implies that the other independent variables will largely measure effects on the flow of student learning during the school year. As expected, then, both pre-test scores and the IQ/aptitude variables were positive and significant in all four equations. The student sex variable was significant only once, in grade 5, which is again consistent with many earlier studies which found that male students do not generally learn economics at a faster rate than females, even though they

Table 7   Post-test scores as dependent variable (t statistics in parentheses)

Independent variables	Grade level			
	5	8	11	12
Student variables				
Pre score	0.477 (13.606)**	0.382 (10.194)**	0.424 (7.654)**	0.387 (6.465)**
IQ/aptitude percentile	0.060 (11.686)**	0.063 (11.820)**	0.030 (4.302)**	0.048 (6.194)**
Sex	0.372 (1.927)*	−0.023 (0.109)	0.331 (1.058)	0.032 (0.096)
ECON	— —	— —	— —	1.163 (3.317)**
School system variables				
Log n enrolment	0.166 (1.279)	−0.252 (1.626)	0.455 (1.395)	0.237 (0.913)
Assessed valuation per student	0.000035 (2.949)**	−0.000017 (0.770)	0.000031 (2.018)**	0.000017 (0.576)
Poverty index	−0.599 (0.561)	−0.796 (0.430)	−7.091 (2.587)**	−2.053 (0.657)
DEEP	0.315 (0.914)	0.638 (2.746)**	−0.127 (0.205)	−0.058 (0.113)
Teacher variables				
Years from last economics course	−0.013 (0.654)	−0.108 (5.873)**	−0.022 (1.068)	0.026 (1.310)
Minutes of economics taught	0.0037 (1.012)	0.0086 (0.147)	0.0051 (0.602)	— —
Experience	0.028 (1.208)	0.112 (5.683)**	0.052 (1.343)	−0.014 (0.590)
Constant	2.324 (2.055)**	5.693 (4.504)**	0.916 (0.382)	2.161 (1.073)
F	78.925	69.439	19.539	19.274
P	0.000	0.000	0.000	0.000
Adjusted R^2	0.472	0.525	0.322	0.337
n	873	620	392	361

* Significant at 0.05 level (one-tailed test).
** Significant at 0.01 level (one-tailed test).
Source: From Watts, 1985

Table 8 Means and standard deviation of variables reported in Table 7

Independent variables	Grade level			
	5	8	11	12
Student variables				
Post score	11.030 (3.894)	10.606 (3.761)	11.212 (3.594)	12.155 (3.790)
Pre score	9.458 (22.940)	9.224 (3.442)	10.298 (3.214)	11.427 (3.273)
IQ/aptitude percentile	54.578 (22.940)	57.921 (24.137)	56.020 (26.106)	57.302 (26.060)
Sex	0.493 (0.500)	0.529 (0.500)	0.559 (0.497)	0.532 (0.500)
ECON	— —	— —	— —	0.512 (0.500)
School system variables				
Log n enrolment	8.415 (1.139)	8.551 (0.896)	8.829 (1.278)	8.841 (1.165)
Assessed valuation per student	25.364 (10.396)	23.172 (5.434)	23.785 (10.121)	21.774 (6.242)
Poverty index	0.174 (0.124)	0.155 (0.069)	0.162 (0.097)	0.159 (0.094)
DEEP	0.291 (0.454)	0.423 (0.494)	0.485 (0.500)	0.349 (0.477)
Teacher variables				
Years from last economics course	14.986 (8.060)	14.419 (8.646)	15.056 (8.938)	13.814 (9.109)
Minutes of economics taught	17.746 (28.925)	20.308 (21.153)	24.638 (20.022)	— —
Experience	13.002 (6.942)	15.052 (7.942)	13.707 (5.383)	17.928 (9.186)
n	873	620	392	361

Source: From Watts, 1985

begin with higher levels of understanding in many grade levels. The economics variable indicating grade 12 students who were in the one-term economics course (a binary, 1 = yes) was, as expected, positive and significant, but as discussed in the previous section, not so large as to suggest that the one-semester course can, independently, guarantee high levels of economic literacy.

Turning to the school district variables, enrolment is usually positive but never significant. Assessed valuation is positive in three grade levels, twice significantly so. The poverty index is always negative, but only once significant. Taken together, however, it appears to be important to capture the effect of the two wealth measures both in the pre-test 'stock' equations and in the post-test/'learning flow' equations. The DEEP binary is positive in the two lower grades and once significant; it is negative but insignificant in both grades 11 and 12. While some earlier studies have reported more favourable findings on DEEP (Walstad and Soper, 1982) and (Soper and Brenneke, 1981), it should be noted that those studies did not control for several of the factors included here, nor were they based on random sampling procedures.

Looking finally at the teacher input variables in these equations, the number of years from the teachers' last course in economics was negative in all grades except 12, which probably reflects the fact that the grade 12 economics teachers did tend to return for advanced training, refresher courses and workshops more frequently than the other teachers. It should be noted, however, that the variable was significant only once, in grade 8. Years of full-time teaching experience shows a similar pattern – positive in all grades except 12, but significant only in grade 8. Considered together, these variables offer some evidence of a trade-off between experience and years from last training in economics. The best of both worlds would be, obviously, an experienced teacher who returns periodically for higher level or even refresher courses in the subject.

The variable measuring planned minutes of instruction (based on the teacher survey responses described earlier) is not included for grade 12, where it is highly correlated with the economics variable discussed above. In the other grade levels, the measure was always positive but insignificant, perhaps because the measure did not matter given the poor levels of teacher training in economics discussed above, or because teachers could or did not accurately indicate the amount of time they actually devoted to economics instruction during the school year.

Some general conclusions and policy recommendations

The ICEE statewide assessment certainly has not answered all of the questions economic educators in the state would like to have answered. In fact, it raised many fundamental questions to be addressed in Indiana and, based on comparisons of the Indiana data with information taken from other state and national studies, by economic educators elsewhere as well. The questions include, for example, how well can infusing economics instruction into the regular curriculum in grades K–12, even with particular stress in such areas as social studies, be implemented as a comprehensive strategy given limited and dated teacher training in economics, and limited classroom time devoted to economics instruction. How can the impressive testing results noted in 'model' programmes and schools in Indiana and elsewhere be expanded to reach the great majority of, if not all, elementary and secondary students? What resources will be required to accomplish this, and what else in the curriculum, if anything, would be reduced or eliminated to make more instructional time available? How can we make the formal course on economics more effective? How can we best encourage, or perhaps require, more economics training for current and future classroom teachers?

In Indiana, given this new information on the problems facing economic education programmes in the schools, the decision was made to adopt a set of four policy recommendations, which were presented to the State Board of Education in 1984. These recommendations are:

1   a twelfth-grade economics course requirement for all Indiana students, to replace the local school system requirement and elective options that now reach just over half of all students

2   a requirement that all school systems develop and implement plans for formal economics instruction in grades K–12, so that this instruction will be infused into instruction in other subject areas

3   a requirement to meet minimum competence levels in grades 5, 8 and 12, measured on nationally normed economics tests for students at these grade levels or equivalent test forms authorized by the Indiana Department of Education

4   increased minimum certification requirements in economics for all future teachers – two courses (i.e. six semester hours*) for all elementary and secondary teachers, three courses (nine semester hours) for secondary social studies teachers, and seven courses (21 semester hours) for teachers with a minor in economics and any teacher certified to teach the separate course in economics (these requirements follow those established by a California task force in 1977 – Mackey *et alia,* 1977)

It is *not* likely that all of these recommendations will be adopted soon in Indiana; indeed some may never be implemented. The recommendations were certainly not put forward with the promise that their implementation would guarantee a high degree of economic literacy among graduates of Indiana schools, or that they would answer all of the questions listed above. Indeed, a majority of states have already passed one or more of these recommendations (though none have passed more than two, to our knowledge), and results in those states are still unclear (Brennan and Banaszak, 1982).

What the recommendations do recognize is that a far higher level of resource commitment will be required in Indiana to make economic literacy a

---

*A semester hour of credit is typically awarded by American colleges for each 15 lecture hours of instruction.

widespread, routine outcome of elementary and secondary education in the state; that proven instructional materials, training programmes and evaluation instruments and procedures are available and can be more widely employed if additional resources are made available; and that the *status quo* is unsatisfactory to those who believe economics education is important for all students, not just for those in model programmes.

Acknowledgements

Professors Peter Harrington, Phillip Saunders, DeVon Yoho and Dennis Weidenaar served, with the author, on a Steering Committee which oversaw the research project from which these results are taken and developed the test instruments used in the project. Partial financial support for the project was provided by the William B. Stokely, Jr., Foundation, Inc.; the PPG Industries Foundation, Inc.; and the Joint Council on Economic Education. Assistance in data collection was provided by the Indiana Department of Public Instruction. Any conclusions, errors or omissions in the paper are, of course, the sole responsibility of the author.

References

Bach, G. L. and Saunders, P. 1965 'Economic education: aspirations and achievements' *American Economic Review* **57** pp. 329–56

Brennan, D. C. and Banaszak, R. A. 1982 *A Study of State Mandates and Competencies for Economic Education: Update* Center for Economic Education, University of the Pacific, Stockton, California

Chizmar, J. F. and Halinski, R. S. 1980 *Basic Economics Test: Examiner's Manual* Joint Council on Economic Education, New York

Indiana Farm Bureau, 1981 *School Statistical Report* Indiana Farm Bureau, Inc. (Legislative Department), Indianapolis

Mackey, J. A., Glenn, A. D. and Lewis D. R. 1977 'Improving teacher training for precollege economic education' *Journal of Economic Education* **8**(2) pp. 118–23

O'Toole, D. 1980 'Economic education in Virginia's public schools' in *A Look at Virginia Public Education* Virginia State Chamber of Commerce, Richmond, pp. 31–40

Riew, J. 1966 'Economies of scale in high school operations' *Review of Economics and Statistics* **48** pp. 280–87

Saunders, P. 1970 'Does high school economics have a lasting impact?' *Journal of Economic Education* **2** pp. 39–55

Saunders, P. 1980 'The lasting effects of introductory economics courses' *Journal of Economic Education* **12** pp. 1–14

Shermis, S. (ed.) 1979 *Social Studies: A Guide for Curriculum Development* Indiana Department of Public Instruction

Siegfried, J. J. 1979 'Male-female differences in economics education: a survey' *Journal of Economic Education* **10** pp. 1–11

Siegfried, J. J. and Fels, R. 1979 'Research on teaching college economics: a survey' *Journal of Economic Education Literature* **17** pp. 923–69

Soper, J. C. 1979 *Test of Economic Literacy: Discussion Guide and Rationale* Joint Council on Economic Education, New York

Soper, J. C. and Brenneke, J. S. 1981 'The new test of economic literacy and an evaluation of the DEEP system' *Journal of Economic Education* **12**(1) pp. 1–14

Walstad, W. B. and Soper, J. C. 1982 'A model of economics learning in the high schools' *Journal of Economic Education* **13**(1) pp. 40–54

Walstad, W. B. and Watts, M. W. 1985 'Teaching economics in the schools: a review of survey findings' *Journal of Economic Education* **16**(2) pp. 135–46

Watts, M. 1985 'A statewide assessment of pre-college economic understanding and DEEP' *Journal of Economic Education* **16**(3) pp. 225–37

Yankelovich, Skelly and White Inc. 1981 *A National Survey of Economic Education* Phillips Petroleum, New York

Response   *Tony Halil*

Lumsden *et alia* have made an important and welcome contribution by identifying a class of statistical models known as 'linear models' used to model a wide variety of social and educational phenomena, and by their critical appraisal of the appropriateness of these models to their research data analysis. The prevailing notions of 'good scientific methodology' in social sciences have become synonymous with statistical inference, and by implication, therefore, research conclusions based on statistical analysis are the most desirable and valid. I do, therefore, welcome the general message of the paper, which is that statistical methods are useful but limited tools for the purpose of gaining knowledge. But I disagree with the criteria used to evaluate the regression model as well as with some of the statistical shortcomings ascribed to it.

Before commenting on some of the detailed points raised in the paper, it may be useful to establish a set of criteria that can be used to evaluate statistical models. The probability statements involved in testing a statistical model or hypothesis are of the form $p(M/D)$, that is, the probability of the model, given the data. The relevant statistical inference involves testing the 'goodness of fit' of the model (characterized by a vector of parameters θ), derived from and commensurate with the relevant substantive theory. The parameters of the model, θ, in this formulation, state the relations between the observed variables. In fact, θ should be specified such that it also includes parameters pertaining to the sampling structure (experimental design) of the observations as well as the measurement error of the observed variables. This assertion is based on the observation that the 'goodness of fit' of a model is based on the likelihood ratio, given by

$$\lambda = \frac{L(\hat{\hat{\theta}})}{L(\hat{\theta})}$$

where $\hat{\theta}$ is the maximum likelihood estimate of the parameters of the model without constraining or fixing the values of the parameters, and $\hat{\hat{\theta}}$ is the maximum likelihood estimate of the parameters when constraints or restrictions are imposed. The likelihood is, however, the probability of the data given the model (note the reversal), that is, $p(M/D)$; θ, therefore, ought to contain parameters on the sampling structure as well as the measurement error of the variables if the parameter estimates for the structural relations are to be unbiased and if the findings are to have any external validity. Failure to include these aspects in θ is a consistent feature of much that passes for statistical analysis in social sciences and inevitably leads to biased estimates of relationships and, subsequently, to inappropriate tests of statistical models or hypotheses. The three general criteria for evaluating models are:

1 commensurability of the statistical model with the substantive framework

2 representation of the sampling structure of the observations in the model

3 allowance for the measurement error of the observed variables

Having established the criteria for evaluating statistical models, perhaps the first question to be asked is whether the models employed in these authors' analyses do take into account the sampling structure implied by the experimental design. Unfortunately, they do not. The experimental design for the study generated a hierarchical structure for the observations, that is, outcome measures are nested within students, students are nested within classes/courses, courses are nested within institutions and institutions are nested within innovative techniques, while the statistical models are specified for students only. This is a particularly important consideration in educational research, in that its objects of study are hierarchically organized from pupils within classes within schools and within local education authorities etc. To their credit, the authors do recognize some of the problems arising from the hierarchical nature of the data as demonstrated by the arguments put forward in their remarks 1 and 2 above, but they think them to be pertinent to the regression model and not relevant for the log–linear model.

Turning to the more technical and statistical reasons for rejecting the regression model, namely, the unrealistic and unstable estimates obtained, the inability to cope with interactions and non-linear relationships, and the unreasonableness of normally distributed prediction errors: these reasons deal with issues of 'model specification' and their main concern is the commensurability of the statistical model with the substantive framework. With the exception of the distribution of errors, these objections against the regression model are unfounded, as explicated and amply demonstrated by Kerlinger and Pedhazur (1973). The estimation of the model parameters are, however, conditional on the model specified and the method of estimation used. Given that the regression models fitted are simple additive models with ordinary least square estimates of parameters, then what is to be rejected is not the regression approach but the models fitted. The inclusion of interaction effects and the use of generalized least squares estimation will be a positive step in the right direction.

The approach of regression modelling and log–linear modelling is the same, therefore the comments on model specification apply as much to multiple regression analysis as to log–linear model analysis. What is different in the two methods of analysis is the nature of the dependent variable. In regression analysis, the dependent variable is continuous, and required to be on an interval scale, whilst in log–linear model analysis, the dependent variable is either frequencies or proportions. I concur with the authors that the log–linear model approach is likely to produce more detailed description of group differences if the comparisons are to be made on the total score. The analysis on total scores, however, assumes that the responses on the test items are consistent with the ability estimate obtained from a total score. In addition, the log–linear model analysis would have been used to analyse the responses to each test item in order to check (1) whether there was consistency between test items and total score, and (2) whether the responses to test items were influenced by student characteristics, institutions, type of input etc.

I would summarize the above comments as follows:

1 The reasons for rejecting the regression model as unrealistic are unfounded, as interactions and non-linear relationships can be modelled successfully by using the regression model. The assumption of homogeneity of variances is specific to ordinary least squares estimation and can be overcome by using generalized least squares estimation.

2 The criteria for model evaluation if employed will lead to the rejection of the regression model as well as the log–linear model. The appropriate model for the data is the multi-level linear model.

3 The most informative use of the log–linear model in education would be within the context of latent trait modelling, that is, analysis of the factors influencing test item responses and the meaningfulness of the total test score.

Reference

Kerlinger, F. N. and Pedhazur, E. J. 1973 *Multiple Regression in Behavioural Research* Holt, Rinehart and Winston, New York

---

Response   *Barry McCormick*

These remarks concern the conceptual and statistical models that have been used to estimate the effect of various teaching programmes on economic learning, and focus on the papers by Chizmar, Lumsden *et alia*, and Watts. While each of these papers is of individual interest, their contents provide a direct reminder that a variety of models are presently deployed to study the contribution of teaching advances to economic knowledge, as it is usually defined. Although Watts is concerned with applications to school students rather than those at college, it remains striking that these three papers have no overlapping references or commonly agreed statistical framework. While diversity in an area is an indicator of quality if the important problems are inherently different or the data naturally present themselves in a way requiring distinctive statistical modelling (for example, with categorical dependent variables which limit the applicability of simple regression analysis), failing to interlace our experiments where it is possible must inhibit the construction of a coherent, robust, body of knowledge.

Watts offers an instructive assessment of the effects of various individual, school and institutional characteristics upon student test scores. The data base is an exciting one: a panel of over 4000 students, collected professionally, with tests administered before and after the economics instruction. He runs regressions on the pre-course, and on the post-course score conditioned on the pre-course score and exogenous variables. The results are numerous but occasionally disappointing – for example, planned length of the instruction has no impact on post-course scores, which Watts tentatively ascribes to either poor levels of teacher training in economics or failure to record the data accurately. This project might have benefited from a conventional panel data format leading to regressions of the 'change' in test score on the exogenous variables. To begin with it gets round the problem of errors in the score equation being correlated with the pre-score explanatory variable (so that least squares is inconsistent). It also avoids awkward questions such as, 'If the explanatory variables really do explain additions to knowledge, why does a pre-course score have a coefficient significantly less than one in the post-course score equation?'

The papers by Chizmar and Lumsden *et alia* both offer interesting studies of teaching innovations on undergraduate student performance, but have quite different frameworks. Chizmar writes down formal models of the allocation of time to studying economics and of achievement in examinations, which help anchor the argument. Lumsden *et alia* focus more on advancing a probabilistic statistical approach to modelling the implications for achievement – deserting traditional regression analysis. Chizmar's conceptual analysis of the allocation of time could be made more plausible by explicitly including choice of working hours (and thus perhaps the role of parental tuition gifts), rather than using a binary variable for working in an *ad hoc* way. At least the framework is there for such an extension. Lumsden's analysis, although searching in certain respects, suffers from the absence of a model of achievement, and leaves one wondering, for example, whether differences in the subsidiary university and A level courses might explain the large institutional differences found, and thus whether the regression analysis was not too hastily dropped for probabilistic modelling of artificially constructed discrete categories. If Lumsden appears to move unnecessarily from a traditional unifying statistical framework, I wonder whether the most serious difficulty with Chizmar's work is that more questioning within the context of an explicitly formulated model would be helpful. The empirical analysis of the time allocated to studying economics appears to be less encouraging than the full support inferred for the model really justifies, and it would have helped to know exactly what findings lead to rejecting the models.

Nevertheless, these are demanding criticisms of papers that exhibit, in turn, common sense with a super data set, useful formal modelling, and scepticism of mind towards conventional practice. While each paper takes matters forward in a distinctive way we must also hope that they help lead to the application of a more coherent and cogent methodology in this area.

Using the media in developing economics curricula

Alan Gregory

Senior Lecturer in Education, Monash University, Australia

The basis for school economics courses in terms of the economics
selected is examined. Economics is often justified for 'citizenship'
reasons, yet courses are derived from the 'discipline'. An experiment is
described which examines the media to see what economic concepts are
used.

Introduction

School economics is justified largely on the grounds of citizenship – of
enabling young people to be better able to understand and participate in their
society, in which the economic dimension is important. Courses in economics
are generally drawn directly from the discipline of economics itself. However,
if the citizenship aim is important, should other sources be used in addition to
the discipline to construct courses which might more accurately reflect the
kind of economics appropriate for participating in society today? This paper
discusses the results of an exploratory study of this question, carried out with
an analysis of a newspaper sampled over a year.

School economics – the citizenship aim

Economics for secondary school pupils is regarded as important in that it
helps illuminate issues that are at the heart of modern society. Economic
questions underpin so many of society's activities and problems – they are
unavoidable. 'Awareness', 'participation', 'understanding' are all terms used
to describe this social education dimension. The citizenship goal though is
argued in different ways.

Economics for citizenship conforms to the requirements Lawton had for
the *new* social sciences in schools, that they should primarily be socially
relevant, but also should possess structure, academic rigour and be capable of
imaginative teaching (Gleeson and Witty, 1976). It also forms part of
Lawton's cultural system, which he regards as the basis for curriculum

structure (Lawton, 1983). For a course to be *socially relevant* it needs to embody the best aspirations one can have in preparing pupils for the society of which they are a part.

While the economic dimension is not the only one, the potential citizen needs to understand that it is an important one, and one that is enmeshed with social and political questions. Economic issues also attract widespread publicity and controversy. Government policy decisions require an appreciation of the economic element. Economic events – be they involved with the problems of affluence or unemployment – have important personal implications as well as public ones.

The modern social-citizenship view is well expressed by Horton and Weidenaar (1975, p. 45):

> The aim of economics education is to improve our understanding of the world in which we live. Without this understanding we are frequently confused and unable to identify, analyse and interpret successfully the economic aspects inherent in so much about us.

They argue that in addition to enhancing personal self-esteem and rational individual decisions, a consequence will be better social decisions by the collective actions of citizens.

That economic education is regarded as essential for our young people to participate effectively in society is conveyed by the use of the term 'economic literacy'. Today the term 'literacy' has become attached to many subjects claiming a guaranteed place in the curriculum, particularly in the wake of the 'back to basics' movement.

But the term 'economic literacy' is not recent, having been used by the American economic education movement in the 1960s. The March 1964 issue of *Challenge* was devoted to economic literacy. Even the Australian proposal, APEL (the Australian Project for Economic Literacy, 1973), predated the current usage.

Some disagree with the citizenship justification. McKenzie (1976, 1977) feels it is based on the general welfare notion of the public good. To further the public good, students have not only to learn economics, but to retain it and employ it in their role as citizens. McKenzie cynically feels (leaving aside whether the economics which has been learnt has been retained) that individuals do not use such knowledge as they feel ineffective and have no incentive to do so. Some effort has to be made by individuals to retain and use economic knowledge in their role as citizens.

It is difficult to argue an exclusively intellectual case, for while those involved in economics teaching do feel our discipline offers a unique perspective, all subjects make similar claims. It cannot yet be proved that the intellectual skills economics develops are superior or more important than skills gained from other disciplines. Another justification is that economic education is of vocational value. This argument has been revived in recent times as economics is perceived to offer better employment prospects in a climate of high youth unemployment.

MacDowell *et alia* (1977) put a case for economics (coming from a perspective which examines the different performance of men and women in economics courses) based on the desirability for economic thinking in certain high status and well paid occupations. This career justification for economic education requires benefits to accrue to individuals from their taking economics. (The MacDowell study of 2000 US school students found sex-linked differences in economics learning first apparent in late secondary or early tertiary years.) So MacDowell's point argues a vocational argument for economics, particularly for women if they wish to enter certain occupations.

Wall's survey in Britain found 'that universities do not want to make A level economics a requirement for their economics courses' (1982, p. 107). Economists in Australian tertiary institutions would share this view and would see school economics serving the school leaver or those not likely to pursue tertiary level economics. However, a reservation expressed by one economics professor was that in periods when departments or faculties are competing for the best brains, school economics could help attract such students to tertiary economics. (Badly taught school economics could of course have the reverse effect.)

As Hansen (1977) has pointed out, economic understanding for citizenship or economic literacy has not been operationally defined. So there has developed the notion of some form of effectiveness. Effective economic education thus seems to require that pupils do not just learn, but *retain* and *use* that learning. One way to describe this effectiveness has been by the term 'economic efficacy'.

The notion of economic efficacy derives from that of political efficacy. Campbell *et alia* (1954, p. 187) define political efficacy as 'the feeling that individual political action does have, or can have an impact on the political process'. In other words, individuals' actions can have some political effect. Such efficacy would be lacking if individuals perceived their actions to be useless or to have no effect.

Wentworth (1976), applying the notion of efficacy to economics, defines it as 'the feeling that individual knowledge and economics actions does have or can have an impact on the economic system'.

Stigler (1983) queries the case for economic literacy. He requires to be convinced that it is more than something which is desirable, useful or even good, but that it is worth the cost. He argues that any subject which claims a special position must incorporate either some vital means of communication that necessitates everyone possessing it, or else a type of knowledge needed frequently and yet not better obtained from experts.

Part of the answer to Stigler is to decide what type of economics we are teaching in schools. Some forms of economics would, by Stigler's tests, be best purchased from experts. Is there then economic education which forms part of social communication which would be essential for all to have to undertake the duties of the citizen? So the demand for utilitarian economic education is not efficacious.

Wentworth's test of economic efficacy, which he developed from Easton and Dennis' (1967) measures of political efficacy, was adapted by Dunn, in an Australian study of elementary school children. Dunn (1983, p. 147) found that elementary school children had begun to develop attitudes concerning their roles in the economy, in other words a sense of economic efficacy, although he did not find any increase for grade 4 to grade 6. There was a positive relationship found between economic efficacy and socioeconomic status, although the relationship between economic understanding and economic efficacy was confused. The children in question indicated that the television was the main source of their economic knowledge, parents, newspapers and school being the next most important sources. Economic literacy, and the associated citizenship implications, remains 'the golden fleece of economics education' (Wentworth, 1976, p. 2) and while as with 'understanding' an operational definition remains elusive, there are clear moves for something more specific to the concern for utility, efficacy or effectiveness.

Course development

How are our courses/curricula in school economics determined?

Most courses are determined by education system examination boards or curriculum committees. Such committees of 'wise people' usually comprise teachers, educationalists and economists (tertiary and business). In Australia, such courses are typically determined by each state, and they quickly become enshrined in textbooks and other surrounding materials. Once established, such courses evolve rather than change drastically (Jesser, 1984).

National reports often play a significant role in assisting school systems and course committees. The Joint Council on Economic Education, from the National Task Force Report in the 1960s up to the latest edition of the *Master Curriculum Guide in Economics*, has played a major role in this regard in the US. Most countries have had such reports, as well as more general educational reports with consequences for economic education.

Special surveys or reports sometimes provide special insights. In the Australian context, Wilkes conducted a survey for the Australian Chamber of Commerce (Wilkes, 1978). This followed the methodology in Piper (1977) in *Essential Learning About Society*, and examined the views of various groups in the community about secondary school economics.

The groups in the survey consisted of young people who had recently left school and entered the workforce, teachers of economics and commercial subjects, members of the Chamber of Commerce, and contributors to the Australian Chamber of Commerce Economics Education Campaign. The young people surveyed were more in favour of an 'economics problems' approach, and least in favour of a 'comparative economic systems' approach. Teachers also favoured the 'economic problems' approach, but with more general agreement. But they did not favour an approach which incorporated 'specific vocational preparation'. Chamber of Commerce members favoured an approach which emphasized the private sector and, given their relative lack of response to the 'comparative economics systems approach', one might infer they meant the Australian private sector. The final group, which represented the contributors to the Australian Chamber of Commerce Economics Education Campaign, also favoured the 'private sector' approach but equally favoured the 'economic problems' approach. They were less inclined to isolate any one approach as being the least favoured one, attaching higher priority to most approaches than the other groups. The survey indicated support for a variety of approaches, with the 'economic problems' approach perhaps most favoured.

In terms of the topics which could be studied in an economics course, the survey found that both the young people and teachers agreed that the two most important topics to be taught in an economics class are 'the structure and operation of the Australian economy' and 'the economic role of the government'. The young people favoured least learning about 'Australia's population', and teachers were least in favour of teaching about 'inter-governmental financial relations'. The fact that the young people and teachers agree on the most important topics may not just be coincidental, since what ex-students feel to be important in a subject is usually determined by their own experience in the subject. The Chamber of Commerce respondents were more definite in their priorities, and preferred topics such as 'basic concepts and method of economics', and 'the structure and operation of Australia's economy', and least preferred 'intergovernmental financial relations', followed closely by 'Australia's population'. The final group agreed with the Chamber of Commerce members in their preferred topics but also added 'the economic role of the government'. They agreed with the teachers' and members' groups in least favouring 'intergovernmental financial relations'. Apart from those topics singled out as most and least favoured, the topics listed were generally deemed important and the survey again concluded that there is support for a large number of topics.

The survey's findings are useful in that they indicate the priorities the different groups attach to the different approaches to teaching economics and those topics that could be taught within these approaches. The overall trend appears to be one of moving away from a traditional approach with its set topics, to a less restricted approach of 'economic problems', against a setting of the Australian economy and the role of the government.

Given the exposure of citizens to economics analysis in the various forms of media, can we find some basis for school courses from this source? This would be in contrast to approaches based on the discipline, e.g. this is *the economics* that economists now tell us is currently focused upon, let's therefore select and simplify from this a socially related school economics.

Much of the work on the economics is based on 'structure of the disciplines' approaches such as expounded by Bruner in the post-Sputnik era of emphasis on the disciplines. The intellectual activity of the child was not seen as qualitatively different from that of the scholar. Many of these advocates

(including Bruner) now see such an approach as only part of curriculum.
Bruner in his 'Process of education revisited' (1971, p. 20) states:

> I would be quite satisfied with de-emphasis on the structure of knowledge, and
> deal with it in the context of the problems that face us. We might put vocation
> and intention back into the process of education.

However, the theories of the earlier Bruner prevail, for they suit the
approaches to curricula which are discipline centred, and which Eisner (1979)
would classify as the liberal education tradition of academic rationalism.
Bruner believes that teaching specific topics or skills, without making
students aware of their context in the broader structure of the subject, makes
it very difficult for the student to relate what has been learned to what will be
encountered later. Learning which does not include reference to the general
principles involved has few intellectual rewards. Knowledge that has been
gained without reference to the structure of the subject will be easily
forgotten.

The consideration that economics is a uniquely cohesive perspective fits
with the notion of structure. It suggests that it would not be so easy a task to
teach topics and concepts in isolation. However, conversely, some believe
that this means economics presents a major problem for learners to understand interrelationships of the various topics. Combining these efforts to
analyse what economics has to offer with the achievement of citizenship aims
has been a continuing quest of economic educators.

So, in trying to formulate a course in school economics there is the
discipline economics to draw on or cognitive frameworks like Bloom's, Taba's
or Gagné's, that make us twist our economics to such classifications, or
thirdly surveys of the opinions of groups in society. Another way of
illuminating our course development, and one that tries to derive an
appropriate economics for society, is to use the media. The media is a
powerful element in modern society and, whether we like it or not, economics
confronts all members of society, and strong viewpoints are presented and
assumptions made.

An adequate examination of economics in the media should include
television, radio, magazines, and a variety of newspapers. The study reported
here starts modestly with an attempt to analyse one newspaper. If we could
analyse what economics is in a media source such as a newspaper, the
question would then be, What economics would a person need to read and
understand that newspaper intelligently?

Newspapers as source materials

An interest in using an analysis of the media to assist in course development
had its origin in the appeal of the use of media as a teaching method
(Gregory, 1982).

Newspapers in particular can be a valuable teaching aid for the economics teacher.

Kelley (1983) suggests that the newspaper can be used as a most effective tool in the teaching of economics. He feels that the newspaper must be used actively in teaching. The value of such an approach lies in the opportunity to apply principles to the real world, to motivate students who can readily perceive its relevance, and to promote independent thinking in students. Newspapers may be used for set induction in teaching. The objectives of set induction for a lesson are:

1 to arouse interest and motivate the students

2 to encourage and promote student participation

3 to ensure students are ready and informed for the tasks that will follow

4 to achieve transfer from the introduction to the lesson and unit in general

Various teaching activities (questioning, demonstrating, lecturing, etc.) may be used to achieve these objectives. If a newspaper is used, then the introduction to the lesson may be a cutting, article, extract, document or cartoon whether current or historical, to provide a focus and arouse interest. The source materials approach of course refers to the use of a range of sources far wider than contemporary newspapers, which are the main concern of this article (Bell and Gregory, 1979). The students then work on the primary source material, questioning, discussing, analysing to elicit the underlying concept, principle or issue.

Because values are confronted directly, this can be controversial. The student is also exposed to emotional language and blatantly subjective viewpoints. The current newspaper obviously has special appeal in its relevance and association with issues which concern the learners.

Not only must students apply principles to the solution of real problems, but they must identify values, the logic of argument, and even question the capacity of economic analysis to provide an adequate answer.

Preliminary study

A preliminary exploration was made of this idea in the form of a two-week survey of a Melbourne daily newspaper, the *Age*, which caters for serious-minded readers. Two weeks in May 1983 were used, and the main current and political events of this period were listed separately. As seasonal factors were felt to be important, namely the national budget and release of various statistics (balance of payments, unemployment figures and so forth), it was recognized that any short period could not be representative. If we are to look at what economics in society is revealed by the newspaper we need to look at a representative period of time, and to examine the pattern over a year would seem desirable.

It was decided to exclude from this analysis the specialized business section of the paper, as the aim was related to what economics was contained in the general pages. The business pages would contain a large amount of economic material, and the general reader may or may not read this section. Given the purpose of trying to establish the economics required of an average reader of a reputable daily newspaper, it was decided to exclude the business pages. The business pages imply a specialist and perhaps more informed interest.

There are various forms of content analysis, both for newspapers (Holsti, 1968, 1969) and television (Gerbner *et alia*, 1978). Questions arose about the appropriate form of content analysis to allow for the position in the paper (was it a front page item, did it have a headline, how long was it?) to enable the concept to be weighted in some way. A front page item with a large headline on say the floating of the Australian dollar should receive an appropriate weighting in contrast to a small paragraph without a headline on the bottom of page 6 concerning the latest Treasury rate tenders. In both the exploratory and the main study these hopes did not come to fruition.

The process was difficult. The use of slogans and catch-phrases tended to distance the reader from the economics concept involved, particularly when several of these phrases were the journalist's own and not frequently used. Journalists also tend to use interchangeable labels for concepts, such as 'wage freeze', 'wage pause', which required the reader constantly to categorize such terms. Different journalists apply different terms to the same concepts, and give different definitions as well – definitions that are not necessarily wrong but reflect the viewpoint of the author. A final difficulty was some journalists' habit of linking concepts together as twin concepts. Inflation and unemployment are constantly offered this way, which perhaps is reasonable in policy or social terms, but which does tend to foster the belief that both concepts are interdependent and never mutually exclusive.

Having gathered all the economic concepts (in their many forms) from each newspaper, the next problem was to determine the pattern of distribution of those concepts throughout the newspapers as a whole. Most people tend to concentrate more on the first four or five pages and then move to the crossword, comic strips or sports pages, rather than deal with the extended articles further on. As it happens, the majority of economics concepts found were contained within the first five pages (60 per cent), with page 4 containing 18 per cent of all economics concepts, the highest individual page score. Given that most people read at least the first four to five pages, their ability to handle most of the articles will depend to some extent on their level of economic literacy. From page 12 onwards there was no individual page analysis, as it became specialized reading. Aside from the business pages, there was rarely any direct economics in the rest of the paper, although the analysis of job vacancy advertisements would be worth future examination.

The major surprise arising from this two-week exploratory study was the number of economic concepts involved: some 1700! Allowing for 'double counting' of a concept used a number of times in an item and for a generous definition of an economic concept to include many terms, the result was still surprising.

How then to cope with this long list? It was decided to group the concepts into headings or topics. The most popular categories or topics were the role of the government in the economy, and industrial relations issues. The headings or topics used were as follows:

1 *Basic terms and concepts* state of economy, economic problems, inflation, unemployment, public and private sectors, consumers, income

2 *Production and investment* producers, capital, production, competition, staff redundancy, investment

3 *Industrial relations* employer–employee relations, unions, labour organizations, wages policy, strikes, disputes, dispute settlement, awards, wage determination, cost of living, unions and government, specific unions

4 *The financial system* trade relations, imports, exports, international exchange, balance of payments, tariffs, protection, quotas, customs

5 *The overseas sector* banks, financial institutions, interest rates, money market

6 *The role of the government* budget, taxation, excise, indirect taxes, government expenditure, welfare, medicare, tax deductions, defence spending, budget deficit, income redistribution, economic management, wages freeze, monetary policy, government regulation, public authorities, state and federal government relations

The main study

The main study was made over the 1983–84 financial year. A random sample of 120 editions was selected from the year's papers, and a content analysis undertaken of the first 13 pages. The random selection gave a good spread of the year and days of the week.

The *Age*, a Melbourne-based daily, varies in size from 30 pages an issue to almost 200 pages for the Saturday edition, which includes a large classified advertisement section. However, the first 15 pages of the paper are generally consistent and are as follows:

Page 1	Main news stories and headlines
Page 2	News-in-brief summary News of the day column, television guide
Pages 3–10	General news, with an occasional full page advertisement; pages 6–7 are usually concerned with world news items
Page 11	Feature articles
Page 12	Letters to the editor, phone-in paragraphs from readers

Page 13   Editorial (usually covering two topics); main cartoon; one or two feature articles by regular journalists on current topics

Page 14   Arts

Page 15   Leisure living, computer items, special topics

A separate business section of between two and five pages is also a daily feature. This business section was excluded from the main study. As in the exploratory study, there was no significant direct economics in the pages outside of the first 13 and excluding the business pages.

The *Age* is 56 centimetres long by eight columns wide, giving 448 square centimetres per page (a size similar to *The Times* and *The Guardian* in the UK).

Economic concepts or terms were included at first mention in an article but not thereafter, to avoid the double counting effect revealed in the exploratory study. An attempt was also made to weight each item by the size of the article it was in, and by the headlines and position in the paper. This quickly proved impractical and had to be abandoned. Our simple analysis was laborious enough. Frequently economics items were in a political context and it was difficult to associate the concept with the size of the article or headline.

Economic concepts or issues were only included in the final tally if mentioned three times or more.

The term 'economic concept or issue' has been used generally. Economic definitions, terminology, ideas, principles, skills are used variously, and in many cases are used to mean what we call concepts, issues or items here. To take an example, a front page article discussing the state of the economy in the light of the release of quarterly national account figures on Friday, 30 March 1984 brought the following list of economic concepts and terms:

national economy	consumer confidence
economic recession	wages (real money)
national accounts	wages pause
industrial sector	retail sales
gross domestic product	rural recovery
'real' terms (implicit price deflator)	seasonally adjusted
private sector investment	lending to home buyers
private consumer spending	savings
company profits	economic growth
inflation	unemployment figures
budgets	

A number of these concepts were mentioned more than once – they represent rich fields for discussion in the classroom. People untrained in economics could not be expected adequately to understand the news item. For this day, there were 236 square centimetres of economics material on the front page.

As in the pilot study, the concepts were grouped under headings or topics, but the earlier list had to be expanded, since many more concepts and issues emerged. The headings/topics used are as follows:

1 Basic terms and concepts

2 Production, consumption and investment

3 Population and labour

4 Industrial relations

5 The overseas sector

6 Money and finance

7 The role of government

8 Comparative economic systems

The full results of this analysis are presented in the Appendix. It was surprising that economic indicators and the national accounts received sufficient mention for inclusion. Also enough items on other economies were published to justify a heading on economic systems.

The main economic items that dominate the year comprise industrial relations, especially strikes and disputes; the overall state of the economy and its regulation; and 'hip pocket nerve' items, such as the dole, pensions, taxes and welfare. This trilogy makes up the main media diet of economics. The outline of the items by headings or topic does not clearly convey the dominance of these three categories.

For the 120 editions sampled, we were able to calculate a column centimetre measure for the amount of economics material on each page. This is shown in Table 1 as the percentage of the space on each page devoted to economics topics.

Table 1   Column space devoted to
economic material*

Page	Per cent
1	23
2	1
3	19
4	15
5	9
6	7
7	6
8	2
9	1
10	7
11	12
12	9
13	16

*Data compiled from 120 issues of the *Age*
newspaper selected at random between 1
July 1983 and 30 June 1984.

The largest proportion of economics content (the business pages being excluded) was on the front page (23 per cent). The other major pages were general news item pages – pages 3 and 4 (19 and 15 per cent respectively), the editorial and feature page (9 per cent) and the other feature page (7 per cent). With page 11, mainly letters to the editor, the proportion (12 per cent) was not as large as expected. Allowing for advertisements on most pages, the proportions confirm the general impression of a significant amount of economics in the general pages of the newspaper. In item terms (avoiding double counting within an article, and excluding items not mentioned three times or more) there were 5546 from the 120 papers.

Conclusions

There are a number of difficulties with the approach suggested here. The form of content analysis used requires further development, in particular the 'weighting' question (size of article, position in paper, etc.) needs to be tackled. Of course a study needs to be made of a wider range of media sources – including not only the electronic media, but a wider range of print media. Dunn's findings (1983) suggest that television could be the most significant influence of all. What kind of economics would a tabloid or pictorial style paper provide? Egalitarian economic literacy would demand a more balanced picture. (Whitehead (1977) feels that the economics in certain papers may be negligible.) Journalists rely to a very large extent on the reader having more background knowledge in economics than they offer, e.g. in their discussion of the financial system there is much attention given to changing interest rates, but no hint given as to why they changed, but rather, what effects they will have. Also, in the process of credit creation, some aspects of the concept of the money supply are not adequately referred to, yet are so basic to an understanding of the whole field of finance. Another way of taking this would be to construct underlying concepts necessary for a proper understanding of the more visible concepts. Many of the concepts and terms will be manifestations of basic assumptions and underlying relationships. Concepts exist within social systems with values and special ways of functioning. Will the economy and the economic system that give rise to all these manifestations reveal itself?

What assumed knowledge underlies the economic concepts presented? Are there advance organizers, as Ausubel (1968) suggests, which are prerequisite for understanding certain concepts? Where does the economic concept presented come in Gagné's (1978) hierarchy of knowledge associated with it?

There are problems too with balance. The large list of items in the Appendix shows the dominance of items relating to government economic policy and industrial relations (especially disputes). There can be the menace of excessive contemporaneity. Do the items that touch our purses and affect our daily lives necessarily give us the best view of our economic world? Some issues have a short currency. Tax indexation was such an issue in the 1970s in Australia. Automatic tax indexation was introduced by the Fraser government for a few years, being abandoned when it was felt people did not understand it, and *ad hoc* tax cuts (at lower levels than with indexation) replaced it – an example of a lack of economic literacy in the Australian community. The student well versed in money and real distinctions could readily cope with tax indexation – stressing again the importance of concepts that underpin the issue rather than the issue itself.

The exercise does stress the importance of economics in the society in which our young people function. Economic issues do loom large in both quantity and range in the media. It is clearly important to understand this economics adequately, just to read the daily paper competently.

This study points to the desirability of illuminating economics courses by making them politically and socially related, and in the Australian context by concentrating on macro rather than micro economics. Our headings or topics provide the outline for a course, and while not surprising in itself, it is different in emphasis to the kind of outline derived from discipline-based or other perspectives. A socially oriented approach may be seen as more relevant and interesting to young people.

If economics for citizenship and economic literacy are our objectives, then this is a perspective well worth further study. The ability to read a daily newspaper intelligently could well be our definition of economic literacy.

Acknowledgement

I gratefully acknowledge the considerable help of my colleague, Anita Forsyth, in undertaking this study.

Appendix: Economics concepts derived – under headings from analysis of the *Age* newspaper*

(1 July 1983 – 30 June 1984, sample of 120 newspapers)

1 Basic terms and concepts

1.1	Economics			
	– definition	40	– economist	16
	– economic forecasting	8	– economy	32
1.2	Economy	90		
	– state of	41	– development	8
	– changes in state of	32	– socialism	10
	– growth	28	– recovery	43
	– free enterprise	13	– capitalism	9

*The figures give the number of articles or news items that involved these economic concepts over this period.

1.3   Economic problems   24
- recession/depression   40   – poverty   45
- inflation   65   – environmental   14
- unemployment   121

1.4   Sectors
- public   23   – rural/agricultural   36
- private   39   – manufacturing   17

1.5   Economic participators
- consumer   – employers association
- consumer association   – producers
- tax-payers association   – interest groups   6
- unions

1.6   Seasonal adjustment   10
- money and real terms   6

1.7   Economic 'commentators'/forecasters
- Economic Planning Advisory   – Institute of Public Affairs   4
  Council   – Organization for Economic
- Australian Bureau of   Co-operation and
  Statistics   9   Development   15
- Institute of Applied Economic
  and Social Research   6

1.8   Economic indicators   12
- consumer price index   25   – national accounts   5
- implicit price deflator   6   – retail sales   7
- unemployment rate of gross   – building approvals   6
  domestic product   38   – vehicle sales   9
- gross domestic product   8   – average weekly earnings   10

2   Production, consumption and investment

2.1   Production
- trade practices   4

(a) Producers
- sole traders, mergers,   – shares   30
  takeovers   3   – stock exchange   20
- business   9   – industry   51
- company   15   – restructuring   16
- shareholder   19   – monopoly/oligopoly   13

(b) Product
- measurement of   8   – surplus   3
- commodities   24   – manufacturing   17
- output   9   – rural production   25
- costs of   21   – retail/wholesale   21
- producer goods   3   – stocks   8
- profit   26   – resources   36
- efficiency   19   – productivity   15
- competition   21   – production   48
- markets   21

6   Money and finance

6.1   Financial institutions   24
    – tradings and savings banks   16
    – Reserve Bank   7

    – building societies   13
    – foreign banks   9

6.2   Money supply/volume of
    money/M_3 15
    – savings   16

6.3   Financial services
    – loans   24
    – credit cards   4
    – bankcard
    – overdrafts   19
    – home loans   11

    – mortgages   4
    – cheques   20
    – cashless shopping   6
    – liquidity   3

6.4   Monetary policy   21
    – interest rates   28
    – bonds/government bonds   11
    – deregulation of financial
      system   15

    – Martin Committee   3
    – money market   11

7   The role of government

7.1   Economic management and planning
    – economic objectives/policy/
      strategy   69
    – economic summit   19
    – treasurer/treasury   11
    – wages freeze/pause   8
    – trade-off   8
    – 'mini-budget'   3
    – government social priorities/
      values   16
    – industry development policy 29
    – monetarist approach   8
    – government regulation   21

    – Keynesian approach   4
    – state versus federal   20
    – fiscal/budgetary policy   41
    – 'wets'/'dries'   3
    – income (national income)   3
    – expenditure   4
    – decentralization   10
    – trade practice legislation   4
    – foreign aid   21
    – poverty line   12
    – standard of living   11

7.2   Budget   45
    (a) Revenue   48
    – tax/direct/indirect   69
    – PAYE tax   12
    – tax raising   49
    – tax concessions   22
    – tax on lump sum
      superannuation   31
    – sales tax   20
    – 'flat-rate'/proportional tax 12

    – regressive tax   3
    – progressive tax   5
    – capital gains tax   11
    – government charges   18
    – performance of government
      enterprise   10
    – government borrowing   12

8.5   China
      – state of economy   3   – trade   3

8.6   Japan
      – state of economy   3   – trade   4

References

Allen, D. I. 1979 'Learning models and teaching strategies in commercial and economic education' in A. Gregory (ed.) *Directions in Commercial, Economic and Legal Education in Australia* Victorian Commercial Teachers' Association, Fitzroy

Australian Commercial and Economic Teachers Association 1973 *Australian Project for Economic Literacy*

Ausubel, D. P. 1968 *Educational Psychology: A Cognitive View* Holt, Rinehart and Winston, New York

Bell, G. J. M. and Gregory, A. 1979 *Sources for Courses: A Handbook for Teachers of Economics* Victorian Commercial Teachers' Association, Fitzroy

Bruner, J. S. 1971 'The process of education revisited' *Phi Delta Kappan* September, pp. 19–22

Campbell, A., Gurin, G. and Miller, W. E. 1954 *The Voter Decides* Row Peterson, Evanston, Illinois

Dunn, G. N. D. 1983 'Economic understanding and economic efficacy of elementary school children' unpublished M.Ed. thesis, Monash University

Easton, D. and Dennis, J. 1967 'The child's acquisition of regime norms: political efficacy' *American Political Science Review* **61** pp. 25–38.

Eisner, E. W. 1979 *The Educational Imagination: On the Design and Evaluation of School Progress* Macmillan, New York

Gagné, R. M. 1978 *The Conditions of Learning* Holt, Rinehart and Winston, New York

Gerbner, G., Gross, L., Jackson-Beek, N., Jeffries-Fox, S. and Signorelli, N. 1978 'Culture indicators: violence profile' *Journal of Communication* Summer

Gleeson, D. and Witty, G. 1976 *Developments in Social Studies Teaching* Open Books

Gregory, A. 1982 'Using a source material approach in economics' *Economics* **18**(1) no. 77, pp. 27–9

Hansen, W. L. 1977 'The state of economic literacy' in D. R. Wentworth, W. L. Hansen and S. H. Hawke (eds.) *Perspectives on Economic Education* Joint Council on Economic Education, New York, pp. 62–3

Hocking, A., Gregory, A. and Wilkes, R. 1975 *Teaching Economics: A Guide to Investigating Economics* Longman Cheshire, Melbourne

Holsti, O. R. 1968 'Content analysis' in G. Lindzey and E. Aronson (eds.) *The Handbook of Social Psychology* 2nd edn., vol. 2, Addison-Wesley

Holsti, O. R. 1969 *Content Analysis for the Social Sciences and Humanities* Addison-Wesley

Horton, R. V. and Weidenaar, D. J. 1975 'Boosting payoffs for economics education' *Conference Board Report* April

Jesser, J. 1984 'Changes in the economics curriculum at year 12 level in Victoria' unpublished M.Ed. thesis, Monash University

Kelley, A. C. 1983 'The newspaper can be an effective teaching tool' *Journal of Economic Education* **14**(4) pp. 56–8

Lawton, D. 1983 *Curriculum Studies and Educational Planning* Hodder and Stoughton

MacDowell, M. A., Senn, P. R. and Soper, J. C. 1977 'Does sex really matter?' *Journal of Economic Education* **9**(1) pp. 28–33

McKenzie, R. B. 1976 'Politics learning and public goals education' *Frontiers of Economics* Summer

McKenzie, R. B. 1977 'Where is the economics in economic education?' *Journal of Economic Education* **9**(1) p. 9

Piper, K. 1977 *Essential Learning About Society: An Investigation into Learning for Social Competence* Australian Council for Educational Research, Melbourne

Stigler, G. J. 1983 'The case, if any, for economic literacy' *Journal of Economic Education* **14**(3) pp. 60–6

Wall, N. 1982 'University economics and school economics: the chasms and bridges' *Economics* **18**(3) no. 79, pp. 104–7

Wentworth, D. R. 1976 'Economic literacy and efficacy: suggestions for research' paper presented at annual meeting, National Council for Social Studies, November

Wentworth, D. R., Hansen, W. L. and Hawke, S. H. 1977 *Perspectives on Economic Education* Joint Council on Economic Education, New York

Whitehead, D. 1977 'Should economics be taught to all secondary pupils?' in T. K. Robinson and R. Wilson (eds.) *Extending Economics in the Curriculum* Routledge and Kegan Paul

Wilkes, R. E. 1978 *Economic Education in the Secondary Curriculum: An Evaluation* Australian Chamber of Commerce, Canberra

Wilkes, R. E. 1979 'Economic literacy: next moves in a long campaign' in A. Gregory (ed.) *Directions in Commercial, Economic and Legal Education in Australia* Victorian Commercial Teachers' Association, Fitzroy

Towards economics in an entitlement curriculum

Steve Hodkinson

Lecturer in Education, University of Manchester

One recent change in educational thinking in the UK is to regard economic awareness as an essential component of an entitlement curriculum for all school students. In this paper three aspects of this development are discussed. Where in an already overcrowded school curriculum is a place for economics to be found? How is an entitlement economics curriculum to be described? What are the implications for teacher training and how relevant are current initiatives?

Introduction

During the five secondary years, every pupil should study, on a worthwhile scale, history, geography, and, under whatever guise (which may in some cases be history or geography), the principles underlying a free society and some basic economic awareness. But choices will have to be made in years 4 and 5. Is it acceptable that any of these three elements can be dropped in these two years? (Department of Education and Science and Welsh Office, September 1984, paragraph 22)

In recent years in the UK economics education has been of increasing interest to educationalists, industrialists and those responsible for outlining national policies on the curriculum in secondary schools. The quotation heading this paper is the latest in a line of statements which refer to notions of basic economic awareness or economic literacy. It encapsulates many of the issues, problems and questions which confront curriculum development teams, local authority advisers and teacher trainers whose task it is to help teachers in schools to construct and shape an effective economics curriculum for the students in their charge. Three aspects of these problems are considered in this paper. First, the curriculum context dimension is investigated:

Where in the secondary school curriculum are programmes designed to promote economic literacy likely to be placed?
At what stages in the five years of secondary schooling are they likely to become available?

Second, the economic literacy dimension is examined:

How does existing UK work on the nature of economic literacy assist teachers to judge the worthiness of their efforts?

Third, the teacher training dimension is considered:

What are the implications for teacher training of a move towards school economic literacy programmes?
To what extent are the needs of existing and future teachers being met?

Curriculum context

Holley and Skelton (1980) recommended that the second stage of the Economics Education 14–16 Project* should be primarily concerned with the extension of economics as a separate subject ('core' or 'option') but that sufficient flexibility should be maintained to ensure that contributions could be made to the development of economics education through multidisciplinary social science/social studies courses or through the teaching of other subjects in the curriculum. Their emphasis on economics as a separate subject is based on predictions made by headteachers in a survey of schools in England and Wales conducted between 1976 and 1978. Those forecasts, with their emphasis on economics as a discrete subject, do not appear to have stood the test of time. Whilst there has been a welcome and significant increase in interest and involvement in economics education in recent years, statistical evidence clearly reveals that the explosive growth in separate subject examination economics at 16+ implied in Holley and Skelton's work has not materialized. Indeed, subsequent developments serve to illustrate the failure of the headteachers in the survey to predict the changes that would occur even in their own schools. They also highlight how thinking about the role of economics in the curriculum has changed since the mid-1970s when Holley and Skelton's work was carried out.

Signs that the climate of opinion was already changing by 1980 were evident in the views of the Economics Education 14–16 Project's Phase 2 development team. Ryba (1984, p. 144), for example, wrote, 'Accepting the current realities of schooling, we have been particularly concerned to formulate materials as capable of being used across the curriculum as within economics courses themselves.' Despite holding these views at the outset of its work, the

---

*The Economics Education 14–16 Project is sponsored by the Economics Association. Phase 1 (1976–78), based at Hull University, was directed by Brian Holley and was a major investigation into the extent of economics education 14–16 and the perceived needs of headteachers, teachers and their students. The results of the enquiries were published by the National Foundation for Educational Research in 1980. Phase 2 (1980–83) was directed by Raymond Ryba at Manchester University and was particularly concerned with the development of exemplar curriculum materials aimed at providing a basis for the extension of economics education across the whole ability range 14–16. These materials were published by Longman in October 1985.

development team must have been surprised at the variety of curriculum contexts in which economics was said to be taught when data was gathered on the use of Project materials in a network of pilot schools in 1981–82 (Ryba and Hodkinson, 1985). Since then, co-operative work with some 150 schools has served to reinforce the writer's view that economics is least likely to become available to all school students in single subject form.*

The Secretaries of State for Education and for Wales clearly recognize and support the development of economic awareness programmes in schools – their 1984 note emphasizes this. It is reasonable to infer, however, that their major concern is not with separate subject economics. Basic economic awareness programmes appear to be acceptable to them 'under whatever guise'. They particularly link such programmes with history and geography, and appear to see them go hand in hand with what they describe as 'the principles underlying a free society'. Guidance on curriculum context at national level is, therefore, far from clear. On the one hand, the possibility of an integrated humanities approach which encompasses elements of economics and political science is hinted at and, on the other, there is an assumption that economic awareness programmes can be taught through the medium of history or geography.

This 'confusion of curriculum possibilities' that exists for economic awareness programmes is in fact even broader than appears at first sight, for it has to be seen in the context of an education system whose tradition is one of local rather than national guidelines and, in economics, of local rather than national enterprise. Initiatives taken by individual local education authorities and individual schools within them are therefore vital pieces in the curriculum context jigsaw. In some local education authorities, where the government-financed Technical and Vocational Educational Initiative aims to reorientate the 14–18 curriculum for some students in a selected number of schools/colleges, economic awareness schemes are finding a slot in vocationally orientated business courses rather than in the traditional humanities subjects. In some other local education authorities, modular arrangements are in operation in which basic economic awareness is seen to be firmly established within general studies and personal and social education courses. Manchester Education Committee (1982), for example, in its document entitled 'A curriculum for today and tomorrow' provides a clear guideline to its schools on the need for economic awareness modules within contemporary studies and personal and social education courses. At the other extreme, however, many other local education authorities remain uncommitted even at the level of general statements of policy.

If it is accepted that economics education for all school students can and should occur 'under whatever guise' and that the individual and distinctive lines of development described above are to be supported, then curriculum developers and teacher trainers have to meet the challenge of ensuring that

*Phase 3 of the Project (1983–86) is a phase of activities in which a central team is co-operating with groups of local authority schools to introduce programmes of economic awareness across the ability range at 14–16 years. The writer is a member of the development team.

each line of development results in a curriculum in which the economics component is both 'worthwhile' and contains useful economic concepts and ideas.

This challenge is, however, only one part of the curriculum context problem, for the Secretaries of State point to the possibility of another and perhaps more significant longer-term development that must be faced. They ask whether it would be acceptable for economic awareness to be dropped from a student's curriculum at 14–16 years. Implicit in this question is the view that, irrespective of provision at 14–16 years, economic awareness programmes will be present in one or more of the first three years of secondary schooling. If such an interpretation is intended, then it represents a major development in government thinking on the role of economics in the curriculum. Moreover, it comes at a time when

1 current sponsorship of curriculum development in economics education is mainly aimed at 14–16 year olds

2 new initiatives in the 16–19 age range (Youth Training Scheme, Certificate of Pre-Vocational Education, AS levels) may lead to a switch of current resources and development

3 research and development on economics in the 11–14 curriculum in the UK has stagnated for almost a decade (the last major initiative was in Scotland in the early 1970s)

4 some writers have expressed the view that some aspects of economics may be beyond very young children (Henderson, 1985, p. 41)

5 the number of researchers engaged in economics education is low (a register of current research carried out by Whitehead in 1983 on behalf of the Economics Association indicated few researchers in a small number of institutions)

Such a development in national guidelines presents the academic community with a series of research and development tasks. Schools also face a major challenge if economics has to be seen as part of a mainstream entitlement curriculum and if continuity of economics experience has to be provided. In these circumstances, a decision to allow students to opt out of economics in years 4 and 5 could only be made in the knowledge that learning experiences at 11–14 years had met that entitlement. At the same time, traditional examination courses in economics at 16+ would assume their correct place as an extension/enrichment of that entitlement in contrast to being viewed as the entitlement itself.

It now seems likely that the decade of the 1990s will see all young people receiving an economics education as part of their general education. What form(s) it will eventually take and at which stage(s) it will occur remain far from clear. But it seems very likely that it will be the decisions of schools themselves which will frame the research questions and responses of curriculum developers and economics educators to the curriculum context problem.

Ready-made answers to the economics curriculum problems schools now face did not emerge from economics research and development activities in the 1970s. Indeed, Holley and Skelton (1980) did not recognize many of the problems as likely to occur. Moreover, whilst government seems to be firmly committed to the notion of economics education, it appears to be prepared to endorse the individual decisions of schools and local education authorities rather than to give firm guidance on the precise nature of its development.

Economic literacy

If the major thrust of development in the 11–16 economics curriculum in the late 1980s and early 1990s is towards the development of economic awareness components within a broad range of courses and not towards separate subject economics option courses for examination at 16+, then two major questions arise. What will be included in these programmes to allow schools to describe their 16 year old students as economically literate? What criteria are schools to use to judge whether or not their economics curriculum is 'of a worthwhile scale'?

   Much has been written and said about the school curriculum over the past 10 years and references to economics education are included in that literature (DES [Department of Education and Science], 1977; Economics Association, 1977; Hodkinson and Thomas, 1984; Atkinson, 1985). It is not the purpose of this paper to review these contributions in detail – that has been done elsewhere. Henderson, for example, shows himself to be less than satisfied with the statement by Her Majesty's Inspectorate (HMI) on the objectives of economics education (DES, 1977):

> It is hard to approve of this kind of muddle as a clear and useful set of objectives for economics education. If they were to constitute a starting point, all of the statements . . . would require rigorous analysis to prevent us from falling into the trap of teaching either rationality . . . or conformity to an existing order or notions of 'good' economic policy and behaviour not founded on (say) welfare economics. (Henderson, 1985, p. 36)

However, for a number of reasons it is important to discuss the usefulness of objectives set out in such documents as potential guidelines for teachers involved in the planning and teaching of economic awareness programmes. First, many teachers who are not trained in economics will be responsible for the economics curriculum and will require such guidance. Second, despite the fact that the Economics Education 14–16 Project, in co-operation with institutions, local education authorities and others, has established a growing number of potentially autonomous networks of schools which can work together on economic awareness programmes, many others will continue to work in isolation for some years to come. The majority of teachers will, therefore, inevitably rely on such published material, their own instincts or a mix of both. Moreover, whilst many general and social education courses recognize and emphasize general personal and social awareness and problem-solving skills as outcomes of the educational process, experience of working with such schools on behalf of the Economics Education 14–16 Project has led the writer to conclude that schools have much greater difficulty when asked to express their objectives in terms of the subject contexts in which such skills are to be developed. This latter problem may of course be particular to economics education because of its long association with an A level style education rather than with the mainstream of the 11–16 curriculum.

The main purpose of documents produced by HMI (DES, 1977) and the Economics Association (1977) is to discuss the contribution that a study of economics might make to certain areas of curriculum experience, that is to establish and justify the case for including economics in the curriculum of all young people. Their intention is to consider the broad objectives of economics education in the later years of compulsory education and not to provide specific guidelines for teachers as to the meaning of economic literacy. However, the Economics Association's document, for example, has come to be used in this context. Ryba and Hodkinson (1985, pp. 113–14) recommend it in these terms:

> Given the pressures on the curriculum, and the limitations on what can be attempted with the least able pupils, that minimum [level of competence] can only be related to the provision of access for all youngsters to a starter kit of knowledge, skills and attitudes, from which later development, whether in more advanced courses or in the 'school of life', can develop safely. That minimum level is what is meant by economic literacy. Of what does it consist? Obviously there are many different views. But the findings of the Economics Association's ad hoc committee on 'The Contribution of Economics to General Education' offers a carefully considered starting point.

Holley and Skelton (1980 pp. 186–7) are another source of advice to teachers on the economics curriculum at 14–16.

> The context of the economics element at 14–16 should consist of a blend of personal economics, commercial and industrial organisation, economic issues and basic economic concepts. The relative importance of each component should vary with the ability level of the pupil.

Their detailed recommendations provide what amounts to a course outline which might be seen to provide teachers with the basis for course planning.

Taken together these documents provide an awesome list of topics and concepts 'to be covered' or 'selected from' and of 'skills to be learned'. What they do not provide with any clarity or detail is the economics framework through which these topics can be investigated and the concepts and skills mastered. To some extent they address themselves to the less complex issues facing teachers – those of identifying themes, and listing topics, skills and so on. There is emphasis on product rather than process, on the outcomes of investigation rather than on the means by which it is carried out. There is, for example, little reference to a broader notion of economic literacy which would 'look at problem forming, problem setting, the questioning process, problem refining, analysis and solution . . . moving away from economics as a ready-made subject with a predetermined product and simple ends-dominated purposes and . . . towards it as something with which students and teachers are more speculatively involved' (Henderson, 1985, p. 40).

It seems clear to the writer that it is this latter notion of economic literacy that offers the key for teachers in schools. It releases them from the tyranny of content to be covered or described, a list impossible to be pursued in any meaningful way given the scarcity of available 'core' curriculum time for economics. Is it not possible that schools who use the lists described by HMI, the Economics Association and Holley and Skelton as a yardstick against which to measure the 'worthwhile scale' of their operations in economics may be tempted to conclude (and perhaps wrongly) that what they are able to offer falls short of what is either expected of them or deemed to be necessary? Is it not also possible that, in the face of this content emphasis, some schools will resort to description rather than analysis and to imparting knowledge rather than to problem solving; and thus incur the wrath of HMI and the Economics Association?

On the other hand, an approach to economic literacy which emphasizes the process of economic investigation and the procedures used by economists to analyse and interpret the economic system will capture for schools both the essence of the discipline and establish the criteria by which the scale of an entitlement economics education might be judged.

Such a development is not without its problems, as Henderson (1985, p. 41) points out:

> The view of the objective of economics education as being to understand the evolution and purpose of economics discourse is novel. There does not exist as yet . . . any considerable body of direct research into the nature of such discourse and problems pupils have in coping with it.

However, a literature which attempts to describe this broader view of economic literacy is beginning to emerge (Hodkinson and Thomas, 1984; Economics Association, 1984). In these writings, the purposes of economic awareness programmes are described as follows:

> In our view only those who grasp those economic facts – the meaning of the part they play in the system, the nature of their individual contribution and its effect upon the system – can be expected to cope constructively with its power and influence. If this is so, our students are entitled to expect their educational system to provide them with the means to attain that position. Economics education has a crucial role to play in this process, since it is only through an economics perspective that students can achieve sufficient objectivity to ensure a realistic scrutiny and evaluation of the economic issues and problems, experiences and policies, that confront individuals and nations. (Hodkinson and Thomas, 1984, p. 6)

Integral to the proposals is a questioning process, 'the economics perspective', which allows young people to enquire into the use of scarce resources by individuals, industrial, commercial and other groups in a country to achieve certain ends. National and international decisions about the use of scarce resources are also seen to be key contexts for enquiry. An example of a possible framework of questions is included in Appendix D of Linda Thomas's paper.

Using the questioning process used by economists as the framework by which resources can be devised and the information, concepts and skills required to investigate a problem or issue identified, is to view economic literacy as Keynes (1973) did, as 'a branch of logic, a way of thinking'. If accepted by teachers, such an approach provides a set of criteria which allows programmes of work at all levels of analysis to be planned (see, for example, Hodkinson and Thomas, 1984, pp. 11–18) – the purposes of economic literacy programmes are set out; the contexts for investigation are described (viz. any decision which involves the use of scarce resources); a problem-solving approach is recommended; and a framework of questions to structure that approach is provided. Henderson rightly warns that much more work needs to be done. However, such an approach does seem to offer a means by which young people will

> . . . be able to look at a single economic problem (at macro or micro level), to understand it and to be able to discuss it sensibly, to consider possible solutions and to weigh up the likely outcomes of each (and therefore its merits) in economic terms. (Northern Ireland Council for Educational Development, 1985)

Teacher training

Any major change in emphasis in the school curriculum requires a response from teacher training to ensure that it is carried into the classroom. Arguably, those who are currently teaching economics in schools are best placed to take on this new challenge. However, their number is few when set against the whole school population 11–16, their existing commitments many and the tiny flow of newly trained specialist economics teachers insufficient. (In 1985, for example, less than 100 graduates are being trained as economics teachers, and the proportion of these who will enter teaching is not known.) On the other hand, if it is accepted that economics education for all can and should occur 'under whatever guise', then an acceptance of the fact that it can and should be taught by teachers other than specialist economists is implied.

In the field of initial teacher training, the Secretaries of State for Education and the Welsh Office have recognized and accepted this situation. From 1986 all training institutions have been requested to ensure that all students following courses of initial training

> . . . have a basic understanding . . . of the relationships between the adult world and what is taught in schools, in particular, ways in which pupils can be helped to acquire an understanding of the values of a free society and its economic and other foundations. (Department of Education and Science, Circular 3/84, p. 9)

To what extent this request will have an immediate impact on initial training courses will depend on the energy and rigour with which local professional committees, HMI and the members of the government's accreditation council carry out their course inspections. The response in the writer's own institution has been encouraging and speedy:

1 to include 'economic and industrial awareness' in its programme of 'core' lecture studies

2 to plan for a professional 'option' course in 'economic and industrial awareness' which will be open to all trainees

3 to seek to strengthen its links with local schools so that all trainees have the opportunity to see economic literacy programmes in operation and to discuss them with teachers

4 to seek to strengthen its teaching staff so that its involvement in initial training (and in-service training) can be extended

Such plans will inevitably take time to come to fruition and additional resources to ensure effectiveness may be limited. Other institutions may be less well placed to respond quickly and, in those (the majority) where economics education is not well established, progress may well depend upon outside stimulus and examples of practice.

Whatever the pace at which this development occurs, the recognition by the Secretaries of State of the need for all teachers in training to be economically literate and to have an understanding of how school students can become so, is to be welcomed and supported.

To confine a discussion of teacher training to prospective entrants to the profession is to ignore the important fact that the vast majority of teachers who will be responsible for teaching the economic awareness component in the school curriculum are already teaching in schools. Theirs is an in-service training need with major implications for the allocation of resources to training. Moreover, if the economics curriculum is to be implemented largely by non-specialists, then training provision has to be both carefully developed and supported in the schools themselves. Just as achievement of the goal of economics education for all implies a shift for economics from the periphery of the curriculum to its centre, so must this change of emphasis be reflected in in-service teacher training.

Many local education authorities have recognized some of these implications and are working with groups like the Economics Education 14–16 Project, the Economics Research and Curriculum Unit at London University's Institute of Education and with industry and commerce. The 'Learning for a Changing World Project' is one example of co-operative effort. British Petroleum plc, in conjunction with the Economics Education 14–16 Project and the Careers Research Advisory Centre, has devised a three-year programme of activities within two local education authorities (Essex and Hertfordshire) which aims to establish the structures by which the local education authorities concerned can meet the economics curriculum and training needs of their schools and teachers. Inevitably, even if such a scheme were ideal it could only be partial, for the availability of resources for such activities (even in a major multinational company and on a 'pump-priming' basis) cannot be sufficient to meet the needs of the nation as a whole. Similarly, the Economics Education 14–16 Project, which has adapted the British Petroleum scheme in co-operation with a number of other local education authorities (some 11 in 1984–85) is unlikely to be able to reach out effectively to all local education authorities.

Such initiatives are partial for other reasons. It can be argued, for example, that their effects will be limited because outcomes are expected before process is established; that support for schools is too short-term and inflexible because it is concentrated in the initial stages rather than consistently and at a time when teachers, having accepted the need for change, are ready to plan its implementation; and that the course-based element (some six days maximum) is sufficient only for needs to be indentified rather than for training to be given.

Any general economic literacy training programme must go further than these initiatives. It must, for example, take into account the difficulties of implementation highlighted in this paper. It must tackle head-on the question as to what economic literacy means, as well as how activity-based approaches can be incorporated into teaching. It must recognize that schools face different constraints, have different starting points, and change at different speeds, and it must therefore be user-focused. It must include provision for longer-term school-based and effective course-based components so that teachers are given the time both for action and for reflection. It must support groups of teachers who can work together and share their classroom experiences because the constraints inside schools on effective curriculum development are recognized.

The incorporation of these and other features into a national economic literacy teacher training programme is a major long-term task and not one which can be carried out by a single project, centre or even a large multinational company. It is a task which can only be implemented by an effective partnership between government (which is responsible for policy and national resource use), local education authorities and their schools (which are responsible for the detailed implementation of the school curriculum and local resource use), the training institutions (who have expertise and training facilities) and industry and commerce (who recognize the need in principle and have resources for educational purposes). This is a challenge which will test the commitment of all with an interest in the future development of economics education.

References

Atkinson, G. B. J. (ed.) 1985 *Teaching Economics* 3rd edn., Heinemann Educational

Department of Education and Science 1977 *Curriculum 11–16: Working Papers by HM Inspectorate – A Contribution to the Current Debate*

Department of Education and Science and Welsh Office 1984 *The Organisation and Content of the 5–16 Curriculum: A Note by the Department of Education and Science and Welsh Office* (September)

Department of Education and Science and Welsh Office 1984 *Initial Teacher Training: Approval of Courses 1984* Circular no. 3/84 (DES) and Circular no. 21/84 (Welsh Office)

Economics Association 1977 *The Contribution of Economics to General Education*

Economics Association 1984 *Working Party Report on 17+* (published as an insert in *Economics* **20**(2) no. 86)

Henderson, W. 1985 'The objectives of economics education' in G. B. J. Atkinson (ed.) *Teaching Economics* 3rd edn., Heinemann Educational

Hodkinson, S. R. and Thomas, L. M. 1984 *Economics in the General Curriculum* Economics Research and Curriculum Unit, London University Institute of Education

Holley, B. and Skelton, V. 1980 *Economics Education 14–16* National Foundation for Educational Research, pp. 186–90

Keynes, J. M. 1973 *The Collected Writings of John Maynard Keynes, Vol. XIV The General Theory and After* Macmillan, p. 296

Manchester Education Committee 1982 'A curriculum for today and tomorrow' unpublished document

Northern Ireland Council for Educational Development 1985 'Suggestions for a minimum entitlement to, or attainment in, economic literacy/understanding' unpublished paper

Ryba, R. H. 1984 'The Economics Education 14–16 Project, Phase 2: The creation of the Project's exemplar materials' *Economics* **20**(4) no. 88, pp. 141–7

Ryba, R. H. and Hodkinson, S. R. 1985 'Economics for the 14–16 year old' in G. B. J. Atkinson (ed.) *Teaching Economics* 3rd edn., Heinemann Educational

Whitehead, D. J. 1983 *Register of Research and Curriculum Development in Economics Education* Economics Association

Assessment of achievement in economics

Linda Thomas

Lecturer in Education (Economics), University of London Institute of Education

New developments in economics education have coincided with a change in emphasis regarding the meaning of assessment. This paper provides an account of research work carried out at the University of London Institute of Education Economics Research and Curriculum Unit which aims to examine the role of new methods of assessment in economics.

Introduction

It has been argued by Satterly (1981) that there are

> two dominant approaches to the assessment and testing of children . . . a fundamental distinction between two types of practice which, though they overlap to a quite considerable extent, reflect different emphases in the measurement of performance and fulfil different assessment goals. These two approaches have come to be known as 'norm-referenced' and 'criterion-referenced' assessment and each is associated with a somewhat different type of measurement

In contrast, Skager (in Brown, 1980, p. 12) argues that

> the really important differentiating factors have to do with the function for which the test is to be used and the mode by which the test content is to be specified. Once this distinction is made, criterion- versus norm-referencing becomes a matter of type of score interpretation which is likely to be most useful. In many situations both types of interpretation are likely to be useful, whatever the mode of content specification.

Haladyne (in Brown, 1980, p. 13) also argues that a measure of achievement is neither norm referenced nor criterion referenced. It involves obtaining a numerical description (score) of a trait* (economic achievement) appertaining to an object (pupil) by using some rules (summing correct responses). The same measure then fulfils two functions because it provides information about how much of a trait an examinee possesses *and* information about the differences between examinees.

---

*Trait refers in this context to achievement rather than to personality or character.

The statements by Skager and Haladyne correspond with the position adopted in this paper. The distinction between norm-referenced and criterion-referenced assessment is not considered to be of great importance and the labels are avoided. The first section of the paper attempts to justify this stance. It defines the task of assessment as the provision of high quality information about achievement (attainment).* In the second section this definition is used to evaluate the information provided by the external examinations which are at present the main means of assessing economics attainment in England and Wales. In the third section the information provided by tests designed to measure *mastery* of a domain of knowledge is evaluated. Recent research work on psychological structures of understanding in economics and on the logic and structure of the subject are drawn on to challenge the usefulness of such information. In the final section the results of the preceding reviews are used to suggest that it may be necessary in future to think in terms of assessment which *describes* rather than *measures*, and that it may be useful to provide assessment materials instead of tests. Finally a research plan that was developed to conceptualize this task is described and progress considered.

The assessment of economics attainment

Brown (1980, p. 15) defines attainment tests as those which 'purport to measure pupils' attainment of something; they are not culture-free or content-free or concerned with dimensions of psychological traits; they are directed towards assessment of some particular knowledge or skills'. This definition implies that if tests of economics knowledge, understanding or skills are constructed from items which are related in some way to the content or objective with which the assessment is concerned then these tests may be classified as attainment tests. It also implies that it is always possible to interpret responses in terms of what the pupil knows or can do without reference to the performance of others. However, tests constructed in this way are not necessarily *good* tests of attainment. In order to be useful, attainment tests should ideally provide precise information about what pupils know, understand and can do, unambiguous information about what they cannot do and some information to aid diagnosis of causes of failure. They should therefore be designed to generate unequivocal responses which are interpretable in terms of specific knowledge, understanding and skills.

---

*For this paper these two terms are used synonymously.

External examinations

General Certificate of Education (GCE) and Certificate of Secondary Education (CSE) examinations in economics in England and Wales claim to be attainment tests designed to assess the achievement of particular knowledge and skills in economics. Examination boards provide a general statement of the behaviour and/or content on which the examination is focused.

The first draft of a joint O level/CSE examination syllabus in economics is contained in a consultative document produced by the East Anglian Examinations Board *et alia* (1983). The syllabus, part of which is reproduced in Appendix A, provides a detailed specification of the objectives of the examination. Further explanatory notes state that 'the syllabus is constructed in terms of objectives and these indicate the level of understanding required. "Define" is clearly a lower order activity than "examine", while "analyse" indicates the highest order of activity that candidates will be expected to undertake. It is intended, by this means, to indicate clearly the depth of treatment required.' Such specifications are a well-established method of syllabus presentation at A level. Other syllabuses refer to the list of content which is eligible for inclusion in test items arranged as a syllabus of familiar topics.

External examinations in England and Wales use a fixed time, written answer format. Pupils respond to essay, data response, stimulus material, short answer questions and multiple choice items without prior inspection. There is some variation at CSE where project or continuously assessed work may also be presented for examination but it occurs on a very small scale. Marking schemes provide rules by which the adequacy of responses are judged and each item is scored. Scores are summed in an agreed way and converted into grades which indicate a candidate's performance with respect to a general notion of attainment at, for example, GCSE* level economics.

The examination format

It is difficult to determine by inspection whether this format is an appropriate medium for testing the various things that pupils are intended to learn, although it may be argued that some practices are unlikely to be successful, e.g. the allocation of 35 minutes to an essay question to test one of the objectives of the Associated Examining Board (AEB) A level economics examination, 'planning, organisation and development of an extended argument in a logical way, the selection and marshalling of a range of facts, concepts and relationships into a coherent discussion' (AEB, 1984). If examination boards are serious in their intention to assess such skills it must surely be possible to devise a system whereby students may demonstrate the ability to research, to adapt existing ideas to new situations in a creative way

---

*The General Certificate in Secondary Education (GCSE) is to replace O level and CSE examinations at 16+. It is a new single system of examinations.

through a proper evaluation of their own work and to justify conclusions properly without the distractions of extreme stress and the constraint of memory.

Individual test items

It is also difficult to determine whether individual examination questions such as essays or data response items are an appropriate means of testing the various things that pupils are expected to learn. Scrutiny of the examination questions included in actual and specimen papers shows that all items in economics examinations are related in some way to the content or objectives with which the assessment of attainment is concerned. Thus in all cases individual pupil performances on test items are interpretable without reference to the performance of others. But what can be inferred about the type and quality of the information provided by such tests? In an analysis presented elsewhere (Thomas, 1985a) this question was divided into four parts.

> Does the information contained in the answers or references show whether or not the writer has given a successful answer? . . . does the information contained in the answers or responses show whether a writer who is judged as relatively unsuccessful has given a 'fairly good', 'competent', 'mediocre' or 'incompetent' answer? . . . does the information contained in the answers or responses convey much about what students know or understand? . . . does the information contained in the answers or responses provide any clues as to why students fail to give a successful answer?

Answers to these questions were obtained by referring to various reports such as the ones provided by examination boards and economics examiners. Comments made by Smith (1984), for example, were used to demonstrate the difficulty involved in obtaining an affirmative answer even to the first question. Agreement about placing an answer in the *successful* category is only reached by referring to an agreed marking scheme at A, O or CSE level.

In all other cases it was impossible to answer affirmatively. The unavoidable conclusion reached in the paper was that in view of the difficulty of ascribing 'any clear meaning to the responses and so to describe precisely what it is that the pupil knows or can do' (Brown, 1980, p. 15), individual items in GCE and CSE examinations rarely meet the criteria used to describe high quality information.

Composite scores

The procedure of adding up marks from different types of item to give a total score that purports to measure some general notion of economics achievement merely adds to the problem of interpretation. It has already been agreed that it is difficult to determine the meaning to be assigned to individual answers in terms of attainment of specific skills, understanding or knowledge. Unless questions test one and only one domain, it is almost impossible to predict the meaning of a score of 60 per cent or a grade C on individual questions. Composite scores or grades make matters worse. It is never possible to predict the meaning of a composite score of 60 per cent or a grade C on more than one question because an individual pupil's *responses* to different questions are not homogeneous (even if the questions possess *conceptual* homogeneity). Response homogeneity implies that for any given set of questions, any examinee either gets them all right or all wrong. Economics examinations do not conform to this specification. Some questions apply to content areas which are more familiar to pupils than others. Some questions are also more complex than others for reasons unrelated to economics achievement.* A further demonstration of the problems produced by the composite score arrangement is provided by Nuttall (1984, p. 6) when he suggests that 'in public examinations today . . . 100% on paper 1 and 0% on paper 2 is as good a performance and qualifies for the same grade as 0% on paper 1 and 100% on paper 2. I know I exaggerate, but there is a very wide range of possible performance that constitutes a typical grade 3 or a typical grade C at O level.'

Examination board response – new ideas in external assessment

Both GCE and CSE examinations in economics fulfil the purpose for which they were established – to facilitate selection by providing information which is assumed to predict future performance. But the case made above suggests that there is considerable room for improvement in the provision of other kinds of information. Moreover one of the more crucial problems identified is the matter of a composite score. Until this is tackled there is no incentive to improve individual items so as to increase their capacity to provide high quality information. The Secondary Examinations Council† has recently undertaken the task of constructing general criteria to allow interpretation of each of the grades in GCSE examinations to be made in terms of the attainment of specific skills, knowledge or understanding. It is possible to predict that the success of the exercise is conditional on its terms of reference. If it is to take place within the constraints of the present GCE and CSE systems the analysis contained here suggests that the exercise will be a futile one.

Another initiative of interest in this area is the exploratory work designed to produce *grade profiles* of pupils' achievements on various different aspects of an examination's objectives. One example of a grade profile is shown in Appendix B. Developed by Brookes (1984) from the original sequence provided by Frith and Macintosh (1984) this profile is devoid of any *content* specification. However, it represents a significant increase in the quality of the information provided for teachers, candidates and employers.

---

*Some examination questions demand greater computational, mathematical or linguistic skills than others.
†The Secondary Examinations Council has been set up to monitor and review present GCE A and O level and CSE examinations and to oversee the introduction of the GCSE.

Some examination boards have recently reacted in a very positive way to criticisms of their systems of assessment. The Northern Examining Association,* for example, is taking steps to develop a Northern Record of Achievement. This is intended to provide a wide range of information about pupils' achievements. Research is focusing on the notions of unit accreditation and credit accumulation in addition to the more familiar graded tests. These are described (NEA, 1984) as follows:

> the underlying idea is that, for both teaching and assessment purposes, the curriculum can be broken down into relatively small units. . . . As pupils work through the units, their progress is recorded and their success credited. . . . Units can be designed at different levels, the lowest level being accessible to all pupils. It is envisaged that the highest levels could be linked to the standards of the existing public examinations.

Very little of this research is concerned with economics but it merits some attention because it has the potential to offer an alternative form of assessment. However, any attempt to examine it in detail immediately comes up against the notion of *mastery* since as Nuttall (1984, p. 4) notes 'mastery is the important guiding principle'. It is therefore important to consider the meaning and purpose of mastery and to examine any implications arising from its use.

Testing a pupil's mastery of economics

The aims of tests designed to measure *mastery* are to provide diagnostic information, to serve the teacher who needs to make numerous quick decisions about the suitability of the work allocated to pupils in the classroom and to provide teachers and pupils with precise information about what knowledge or skills have been mastered.

Description

Tests which measure mastery are concerned to assess the achievement of knowledge, understanding and skills but they conceptualize that achievement in terms of specific groups of tasks that pupils should perform, the '. . . specific learning tasks on which students are to demonstrate performance at the end of the learning experience to show that they have achieved the instructional objective' (Gronlund, 1973, p. 10). Their advantages are clear since they aim to provide the high quality information that is defined here.

---

*The Northern Examining Association (NEA) is the title under which one GCE board, the Joint Matriculation Board, and the four northern CSE boards – the Associated Lancashire Schools Examining Board, the North Regional Examinations Board, the North West Regional Examinations Board and the Yorkshire and Humberside Regional Examinations Board – are working together to provide Joint GCE O level and CSE examinations, and the new single examination, the GCSE, which will replace the existing examinations at 16+ in 1988.

Gronlund (1973, p. 9) also claims that 'since achievement is reported in terms of specific learning tasks that each student has or has not mastered, the results are directly useful in instruction'. However, other implications exist which may hinder their adoption.

The behavioural model of learning   The practice of using educational objectives which are stated in terms of observable behaviour is rooted in the principles of behavioural psychology which studies learning only at its observable level. Skinner, for example, would be prepared to argue that the only meaningful goals of learning and teaching are those which may be stated in the form of observable behaviour. Thus instead of teaching a knowledge of economics, the aim should be to teach the behaviour from which such knowledge is inferred. Instead of teaching an ability to handle data, the aim should be to set up the behavioural repertoire which distinguishes the pupil who can handle data from the one who can not. It is possible to appreciate the usefulness of mastery tests without necessarily accepting behavioural principles but their origins limit their applicability to those areas of learning achievement which may be conceptualized in behaviourist terms. These may form only a small and relatively unimportant part of educational achievement. As Brown (1980, p. 25) points out, 'One might, for example, "master" the skills necessary to type competently and so be labelled a "good typist". . . . It is not so clear that "mastery" is relevant to learning that is concerned with understanding (of, say, the theory of evolution) or with appreciation (of, say Beethoven's works).' The concept of mastery is therefore unlikely to appeal to teachers who are unwilling to formulate their teaching aim in terms of a number of instructional objectives because they are more concerned to respond to pupil initiatives than to set preconceived targets. It is also unlikely to work in those cases where achievement is too complex to be defined in simple behavioural terms. Indeed, if the educational community becomes convinced that its use may persuade teachers to give priority to pupil behaviour that conforms to a narrow and often trivial specification of educational achievement and ignore other more important objectives, it may be rejected in its entirety.

Hierarchical structures   A less rigid interpretation of the behavioural learning model allows Gagné (1970), for example, to suggest that it is also appropriate to conceptualize the attainment of *complex* knowledge and skills in terms of mastery. The learning hierarchy approach assumes that learning proceeds from particular subordinate skills to more general skills and that it is always possible to break down complex skills or knowledge into a set of simpler capabilities. A learning hierarchy is revealed by using a process which asks, 'What would an individual have to do in order to attain successful performance on this task?' and repeating the procedure for each prerequisite mentioned. It therefore identifies all the elements of total performance in behavioural terms and allows even the most complex learning task to be perceived as a function of the mastery of a set of objectives presented hierarchically.

The Bloomian taxonomy   A different hierarchical specification forms the basis for another interpretation which permits attainment to be conceptualized as mastery. An example is provided in Appendix C to show how a general objective might be assessed at the different levels of the Bloomian taxonomy – knowledge, comprehension, application, analysis, synthesis and evaluation. The learning sequence in Appendix C is used to provide an operational statement of the behaviour and content on which the test focuses.

Evaluation

In order to evaluate the appropriateness of the information provided by tests of mastery in economics, it is necessary to consider the validity of the different attempts to conceptualize all attainment in terms of mastery since its high quality in itself does not guarantee its appropriateness. Evidence available from work in other subject areas is not encouraging. Brown (1980, p. 93) refers to work in French and physics to show that the notion of simple hierarchies is not supported by research findings. She quotes the results of language work carried out at the University of Stirling which show that 'diagnostic tests can be used to assess simple competencies, but beyond that global language competence involves new sorts of things; it is not just the sum of simple competencies or equivalent to mastery of the sections of work'. Dow *et alia* (1978) examine the minimum objectives required in teaching the behaviour of molecules in the solid state. They list eight objectives and conclude:

> Pupils have a fairly good knowledge of all . . . objectives, one at a time, yet they are not able to put all these attributes together as a single conception of the molecular behaviour within a solid. This ultimate synthesis into one concept is no doubt impossible because pupils do not really 'understand' why molecules within a solid should have any of these attributes – they merely recite what they have been told at the rate of one answer per question, drawing on the appropriate fact for the particular answer.

It is possible to find examples to show that the same phenomenon applies to some instances in economics. For example, it may be possible to produce a learning hierarchy to identify all the elements of a successful *elasticity* performance. But where would the pupil's understanding of the appropriateness of its use as a tool in certain situations appear in such a specification of performance? And how could this understanding be resolved in any sensible way into prerequisite* parts? Yet the kind of understanding that informs the student when to use and when not to use a concept and that eventually develops into an appreciation of the kind of analysis that is appropriate in different circumstances is crucial in economics. The assessment scheme in Appendix C may be analysed in the same way. Two open-ended test items are used to test the attainment of skills of synthesis and evaluation. It is possible

---

*Prerequisite is the term used to describe the action identified as necessary for successful performance.

to argue that these questions differ from lower level questions in the sense that they assess both the achievement of evaluation and synthesis with regard to the particular objective under examination and the achievement of a wider and deeper understanding of the purpose of economic analysis and of the nature of economic enquiry.

Recent work in two areas in economics provides more systematic evidence to support the claim that it is not valid to conceptualize all achievement of economics* knowledge, skills and understanding in terms of mastery.

Psychological structures The research study into adolescent pupils' understanding of some economics concepts which I conducted between 1979 and 1983 (Thomas, 1983) was concerned with the circumstances in which the word 'comprehension' might legitimately be applied with regard to individual concepts. By means of a close analysis of pupil behaviour it sought to expose the distinctive features of and indispensible conditions for comprehension of a range of concepts – their psychological structures.† The concepts chosen included wealth/income, money, costs, price, standard of living and elasticity. Tests were constructed and 237 12–16 year old pupils were interviewed individually in one-hour sessions conducted during ordinary school days. Two general conclusions are of interest in this context:

1 The study showed that tenacious commonsense *misconceptions* formed on the basis of early economics experience were already incorporated into pupils' conceptual repertoire. Although preliminary questions allowed pupils to demonstrate their mastery of the skills required to achieve an *economics* understanding, subsequent questions showed that they did not always choose to apply the skills when deriving an answer. Instead they often made use of the misconceptions which were also available to them. Mastery of component skills, in other words, was not shown to be a sufficient condition for economics understanding.

2 The study also allowed a conclusion to be reached about one of the general properties of the psychological structures of the various concepts. Each of the statements spelling out the necessary conditions for comprehension of individual concepts contained a reference to the particular perception which allowed pupils to concentrate on certain relationships and characteristics of task variables and to ignore the presence of others. Furthermore it was not possible to explain the existence of these essential perceptions or orientations in terms of any simple-to-complex sequence of learning hierarchies.

The logic and structure of the discipline Recent attempts to specify what it

*The use of the term *economics* is deliberate. It emphasizes that the knowledge, skills or understanding is related to the discipline of economics.
†Psychological structure describes the conditions that are necessary for understanding, in a logical sense, to occur. It is an orientation to a problem, a perception, rather than a behavioural prescription. Its origin is to be found in Marton and Dahlgren (1976) and its use is developed and extended in Thomas (1985b).

means to have a grasp of economics or to be able to reason in an economics way in a school context have sought to define and show what it means to have access to an economics perspective. Hodkinson and Thomas (1984) argue that 'access to the economics perspective – the means for objective analysis of particular situations, experiences and economic policies which involve a choice in the use of scarce resources – is derived from the use of a general theoretical framework to organise information and reflect on experience'. They further suggest that an operational specification of the theoretical framework – a procedural framework – facilitates its use as a means of organizing information and reflecting on experience. The authors provide practical evidence to support their claim that the procedural framework, reproduced in Appendix D, is recognizable in any valid piece of economics reasoning at any level and is both a necessary precondition for and an outcome of that reasoning.

This development implies that the first priority for teachers of economics is to promote the use of the procedural framework to explore situations that arise out of resource scarcity since this is the only way to ensure the effective acquisition of the intellectual, procedural and practical skills which are necessary to handle information, coordinate data, explore relationships and form concepts. It therefore also implies that attempts to conceptualize the attainment of economics understanding in terms of mastery of a hierarchically arranged sequence of skills are misguided.

A programme for research

The two systems of assessment described above provide two different contexts for formal testing of economics achievement but neither is completely satisfactory. Public examinations conceptualize attainment in a valid way but fail to provide information of a sufficiently high quality. Tests of mastery of specific behavioural objectives are capable of providing high quality information but their use is limited as a result of the way they conceptualize the achievement of economics understanding.

A radical reinterpretation may be necessary in order to resolve this dichotomy. McIntyre and Brown (1978) suggest:

> An alternative is to abandon the idea of measuring attainment. . . . The possibility of concerning oneself with attainment in some other way than by measuring is quite a difficult idea for us to entertain, since we have all become so accustomed to thinking about attainment in quantitative terms. Yet the concept of educational attainment does not in any way imply the use of measurement; it rather implies the making of qualitative judgements. . . . It is only because so many such judgements are required that some system of summarizing them has seemed necessary. Measurement provides one such system. . . . Given the problems which the measurement raises, among the questions we need to ask are whether it is necessary or useful to summarise judgements about attainment, and, if so, whether there are more satisfactory ways of doing this.

However, it is necessary to be cautious in taking such a radical step. It will still be necessary to conceptualize attainment, to identify the associated criteria of learning and to translate the criteria into operational form. In addition, the problem of devising sufficiently succinct summary statements of attainment in the different aspects of economics understanding must be solved. It is also necessary to deal with the problem of ensuring that pupil responses are systematically observed and interpreted by teachers and that the number of occasions which allow subjective reactions to pupils are minimized. Assessment *materials* rather than conventional tests are required so that assessment may occur in a relatively informal classroom setting. It is necessary to design materials to reflect the subject content and skills contained in normal classroom work but they must also be valid expressions of economics competence.

The research tasks described here are a response to the need to find out how to provide teachers with the assessment information they require in a systematic, relevant and *objective* way.

The research aims

1 to explore the problems of incorporating different forms of assessment into teaching

2 to obtain a set of procedures which recognizes and helps to solve the problems identified

3 to produce a set of criteria to enable teachers to devise, with confidence, their own assessment materials

Its intended outcomes are the provision of some assessment materials which exemplify the set of general criteria and the production of descriptive and evaluation reports to enable other interested people to have access to the processes involved.

The research tasks exemplify and provide the means to evaluate one particular course of action. A school-based element is incorporated at all stages in recognition of the danger involved in allowing abstract discussion of the meaning of economics achievement to dominate to such an extent that the products of research are far removed from the subject matter, skills and activities reflected in normal classroom work. Four major tasks are recognized.

The first task is to explore the problems involved in conceptualizing attainment and identifying criteria of learning in economics to obtain valid statements about what it means in general to attain economics understanding and to delineate the full range of conceptualizations and criteria which are compatible with the results of the process of exploration and specification.

The second task is to use the general statements of the meaning of attainment in economics to identify, select and combine different learning experiences into chunks of work. This process ensures that the conceptualizations of attainment in these specific contexts conform to the rules laid down in the first stage. It also serves to emphasize that assessment and learning activities are parts of the same whole.

The third task is to list specific criteria of learning for each module of work and since assessment depends on observation of overt behavioural indications of underlying knowledge, to provide behavioural interpretations of these criteria. In order to do this it is necessary to observe pupils as they interact with the learning experiences provided and to evaluate the validity of the observations in discussion with teachers.

The fourth task is to apply the criteria previously developed to construct assessment materials and use them to obtain information about pupils' attainments in these contexts. The process of evaluating the quality and validity of the information provided about attainment of general understanding and pupils' acquisition of specific knowledge and skills represents the final task for teachers and research team members. It allows the third aim to be achieved.

Review of progress

The notion of economics understanding, derived from the philosophical and psychological analysis of the meaning and nature of economic study, which is presented as an operational framework of procedures in Appendix D was used as a focus for the first task. As a result, economics attainment is conceptualized, in general, as *a synthesis of procedures and content*. The associated criteria of learning are identified by the following definition: *to achieve economics understanding in any context is to understand the nature and function of the relationships which anchor specific skills, concepts and information to a general framework.** In other words, the acquisition of specific skills is not sufficient to guarantee the attainment of understanding.

Modules are now being prepared in each of the four areas into which the whole range of economic experience has, for convenience, been classified: individual allocation of scarce resources; group/firm allocation of scarce resources; the state's allocation of scarce resources; the international economic system's allocation of scarce resources.

These modules are to be used in a group of schools in the London area in order to determine the specific activities, skills, concepts and knowledge which are required to *answer* the questions raised in the procedural framework and to provide operational definitions.

Conclusion

At this preliminary stage it is more appropriate to make statements about the kind of *questions* which the research programme may illuminate rather than about any of the *conclusions* which may eventually be reached.

---

*To understand the concept of average cost is to understand the way in which factor costs interact with output; to have an economics understanding is to appreciate that 'cost' is a model or system designed by economists to enable them to answer a particular set of questions concerning the allocation of scarce resources.

Some interesting questions concern the problems of providing useful information for teachers and ensuring accurate observation. The results of this work may also facilitate discussion about the relationship between the acquisition of particular skills, information and concepts and the attainment of economics understanding.

Appendix A: Assessment objectives

Source: From *Joint O Level/CSE Examinations in Economics* (Consultative Document), London and East Anglian Group, 1983, pp. 4–5

4   *Know the location of some major contemporary industries and understand the reasons for industrial location*

At the end of the course candidates will be expected to:

4.1   distinguish between the factors which may affect the location of an individual firm from those which may affect the location of an industry;

4.2   examine location factors in relation to particular firms and industries;

4.3   analyse the effects on the location of industry of changes in industrial structure over time.

5   *Understand the role of financial institutions and their importance for the economy*

At the end of the course candidates will be expected to:

5.1   explain the origins, nature, functions and importance of money;

5.2   describe and explain in simple terms the main functions of the major institutions in the money and capital markets;

5.3   describe and compare the different sources of finance available to varying forms of business organisation.

6   *Understand the structure of, and the reasons for, public revenue and expenditure*

At the end of the course candidates will be expected to:

6.1   describe the main components of central and local government income and expenditure;

6.2   examine the advantages and disadvantages of the main forms of taxation (including rates) both to an individual and to a government;

6.3   outline the methods of, and explain the reasons for, public borrowing;

6.4   examine the reasons for, and the changing nature of, public expenditure.

7   *Appreciate the forces, including government, which influence the price level, employment, income, output and economic growth*

At the end of the course candidates will be expected to:

7.1   define the terms 'inflation' and 'deflation' and explain how changes in the general level of prices can be measured;
7.2   describe the main causes and effects of inflation;
7.3   describe (in simple terms) the main factors which influence a nation's income and output;
7.4   describe and account for the main types of unemployment;
7.5   describe the nature of, and examine the desirability of, economic growth;
7.6   outline the main economic objectives and policies (including fiscal and monetary) of a government.

8   *Appreciate the importance of internal and international trade, and have a knowledge of relevant institutions*

At the end of the course candidates will be expected to:

8.1   explain the importance of internal trade;
8.2   outline the similarities and differences between internal and international trade;
8.3   explain the reasons for international trade and relate them to the principle of comparative costs;
8.4   examine the advantages and disadvantages of international trade;
8.5   describe and account for the various forms of protection;
8.6   describe the structure of the balance of payments accounts;
8.7   explain the forces which determine foreign exchange rates;
8.8   describe and examine the roles of the I.M.F., I.B.R.D., E.E.C., COMECON, G.A.T.T. and O.P.E.C.

9   *Be aware of the influences at work in the markets for factors of production, including the major institutions in the labour market*

At the end of the course candidates will be expected to:

9.1   define 'production';
9.2   explain the 'factors of production' which are combined in the productive process;
9.3   explain the term 'specialisation of resources' and examine the effects of specialisation;
9.4   examine the interrelationships between the market demand for, supply of, and price of, factors of production;
9.5   describe and examine the role of the major institutions within the labour market.

Appendix B: A grade profile

Source: From Brookes, 1984 (unpublished paper)

J. Smith: Economics A level, grade B

		Grade awarded
(i)	use of terminology	A
(ii)	knowledge of functions of organization and institutions	C
(iii)	knowledge of trends and sequences	B
(iv)	appreciation of classifications and categories	B
(v)	awareness of relationship between personal, local, national and international economic problems	D
(vi)	use of economic variables as tools of analysis	D
(vii)	use of economic measures	B

The grades awarded in each category are then explained in detail. For example, category (i) – use of terminology – merits a grade A. The grade is obtained over the following range of measures which are weighted to give the final A grade:

	Score	**Weight**
Short answer questions	75%	20%
Data response questions	85%	20%
Structured essay questions	72%	20%
Multiple data questions	78%	20%
Homework	65%	10%
Project work	75%	10%

Appendix C: An objectives hierarchy and learning sequence

Source: From Scottish Education Department/Scottish Central Committee on Social Subjects, Curriculum Paper 15 *The Social Subjects in Secondary Schools* HMSO, 1976

Objective:

'Pupil should be able to understand that there are links between one part of a production flow and another.'

Level 1 – Knowledge

Example test items:

A   When most goods are produced, which resources are used?
    (a)   natural resources only
    (b)   human resources only
    (c)   human and natural resources only
    (d)   human, natural and man-made resources

    OR

B   Name three types of resources used in the production process.

Level 2 – Comprehension

Example test items:

A   When goods are being produced the resources used in the process can be
    (a)   inputs only
    (b)   inputs at one stage, and outputs at another
    (c)   either inputs or outputs, but never both
    (d)   outputs only, because that is what production is for

    OR

B   How can a finished product from one factory be used as a resource in the
production of another finished product?

Level 3 – Application

Example test items:

A   When a forestry worker uses an electrically-driven saw to make planks of
wood, what resources are being used?
    (a)   the tree only
    (b)   labour only
    (c)   the tree and labour
    (d)   the tree, labour and man-made machinery

    OR

B   Classify and describe the resources employed by a farmer using a tractor
to plough his land.

Level 4 – Analysis

Example test items:

A

Using the diagram, it can be seen that
  (a) furniture production involves the use of human, natural and man-made resources
  (b) it is possible to make furniture without the use of trees
  (c) it is possible to use either men or machinery to make furniture
  (d) there are at least four kinds of resource required to make furniture

  OR

B What is meant by saying that a productive process becomes either more labour-intensive or more capital-intensive?

Level 5 – Synthesis

Example test items:

A The resources in a production flow
  (a) need not be linked together, because some are not needed
  (b) cannot be used in an alternative flow
  (c) are all linked together to produce goods and services
  (d) are all used up before the production flow is complete

  OR

B Is it necessary to increase the inputs of *all* factors of production in order to increase the output of goods and services?

Level 6 – Evaluation

Example test items:

A The most efficient production flow
  (a) takes least time to complete
  (b) involves fewest resources
  (c) achieves the highest returns for resources employed
  (d) involves least human effort

  OR

B How would you attempt to assess the efficiency of an assembly line production of motor vehicles?

Learning sequence

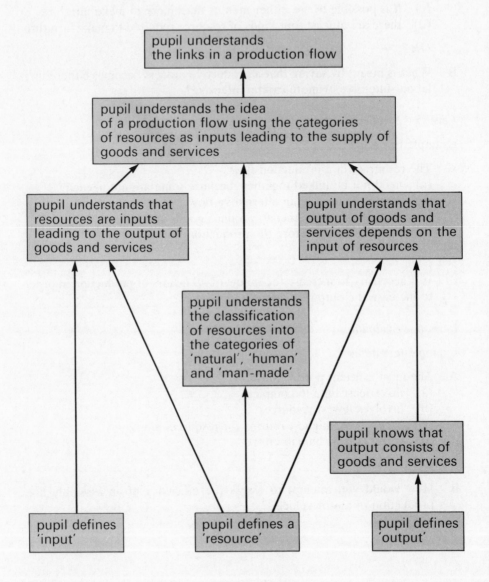

The learning sequence diagram shows how a pupil begins with definitions of basic terms and proceeds via classification and understanding of components and relationships to understanding of the idea of a production flow.

Appendix D: A procedural framework for economic literacy

Source: Adapted from Hodkinson and Thomas *Economics in the General Curriculum 14–18* Economics Research and Curriculum Unit, 1984, pp. 7–8

If scarce resources are used for a specific purpose what benefits are provided?

What costs arise from this use (of money, time, effort, etc.)?

Are the benefits greater than the costs for that particular choice?

Are other costs involved:

would an alternative use of resources have yielded more benefit?

is any other resource use implied?

are other people affected by the choice?

Are benefits real or perceived:

is sufficient information available?

do external pressures play any significant part?

Do real benefits exceed all real costs?

Are resources being used in the best way?

What does best mean?

References

Associated Examining Board 1984 *Examinations in Economics* p. 3

Brookes, K. 1984 'The assessment of economic literacy within programmes of general education in England and Wales' unpublished paper

Brown, S. 1980 *What Do They Know? A Review of Criterion-Referenced Assessment* HMSO

Dow, W. M., Auld, J. and Wilson, D. T. 1978 *Pupils' Concepts of Gases, Liquids, Solids* Dundee College of Education, pp. 4–19

Frith, D. S. and Macintosh, H. G. 1984 *A Teacher's Guide to Assessment* Stanley Thornes

Gagné, R. M. 1970 *The Conditions of Learning* 2nd edn., Holt, Rinehart and Winston, New York

Gronlund, N. E. 1973 *Preparing Criterion-referenced Tests for Classroom Instruction* Macmillan, New York

Hodkinson, S. R. and Thomas, L. M. 1984 *Economics in the General Curriculum 14–18* Economics Research and Curriculum Unit, University of London Institute of Education, pp. 7–8

London and East Anglian Group (East Anglian Examinations Board, London Regional Examining Board, University of London Entrance and Schools Examinations Council) 1983 *Joint O Level/CSE Examinations in Economics*

Marton, F. and Dahlgren, L. O. 1976 'On non-verbatim learning III. The outcome space of some basic concepts in economics' *Scandinavian Journal of Psychology* **17** pp. 49–55

McIntyre, D. and Brown, S. 1978 'The conceptualisation of attainment' *British Educational Research Journal* **4**(2) pp. 45–6

Northern Examining Association 1984 *A Northern Record of Achievement* p. 3

Nuttall, D. 1984 'Alternative assessments: Only connect' in Secondary Examinations Council (ed.) *New Approaches to Assessment* Secondary Examinations Council

Satterly, D. 1981 *Assessment in Schools* Blackwell, p. 46

Smith, P. 1984 'Question and answer' *Economic Review* **1**(4) pp. 19–23

Thomas, L. M. 1983 'An investigation of economics understanding among pupils aged 12–16 years' Ph.D. thesis, University of London

Thomas, L. M. 1985a 'Internal assessment' in D. J. Whitehead (ed.) *Handbook for Economics Teachers* 2nd edn., Heinemann Educational, in press

Thomas, L. M. 1985b 'The core of economics – a psychological viewpoint' in G. B. J. Atkinson (ed.) *Teaching Economics* 3rd edn., Heinemann Educational, pp. 47-72

An integrated economics education training model for teachers

Marie Wilson

Director, Economic Education Resource Centre, Vancouver, Canada

Studies have shown that students of teachers who have undergone
certain types of training exhibit greater increases in knowledge than
those whose teachers have not. The purpose of this paper is to outline
the development, testing and implementation of a fully integrated
economic education training model for teachers in the United States and
Canada. Films, print material and their accompanying training
programme are described for the reader.

Introduction

According to Hodgetts and Gallagher (1978), 'Despite its vital importance to
any real understanding of Canada, the study of the Canadian economic
system has never held a prominent place in our schools. Nevertheless, the
importance of this subject to all students who, in one way or another, are
going to be part of the labour force in a modern community, requires a
reassessment of the ways in which it may be studied in our schools.' Few
people would disagree with the efficacy of economics education, broadly
defined, yet it still remains true in 1985 that only one of the Canadian
provinces and slightly over 50 per cent of the states in the US have mandated
any form of economics education. In 1983, the Education Commission of the
States, the Task Force on Education for Economic Growth and the National
Commission on Excellence in Education all recommended that learning to
understand our economic system should be considered a basic part of
elementary and secondary education. While there appears to be a paucity of
empirical evidence documenting the reasons for the historical lack of attention paid to economics in schools, there does seem to be a general consensus,
both in Canada and the US, that teacher education programmes do not
require that participants undergo training in economics and related instructional methodology, regardless of what they plan to teach. Moreover, Frye
(1979) found that 10 of the 17 states at that time mandating the teaching of
economics did not even require economics teachers to take economics courses
or related instructional methodology courses for certification.

Although it is not the purpose of this paper to present a justification for economics education, it is important to mention that, since we live in a society where the public chooses to speak and vote on economic issues, those who are engaged in educating our students must be concerned with how intelligently they speak and vote. The virtue of the US and Canadian economic systems is the freedom of choice they offer. Economic choice is an important and basic element of any democracy. If educators are ill-prepared to impart sound economic knowledge, skills and attitudes, this does not bode well for the future of a democratic society. It was Alan Greenspan, former US Secretary of the Treasury, who noted that what is being taught in the universities today will determine national economic policy 10 years from now.

The educational background and training of teachers has significant implications for the teaching of economics and likewise any other subject. Holley and Skelton (1980) stated that, 'A number of recent research projects into the teaching of economics have been directed towards assessing the effects of the educational background of teachers upon the performance of their pupils. Results are as yet inconclusive. However, a number of investigations do suggest that the greater a teacher's expertise both in economics and in how to teach economics to his pupils, the more his pupils will in fact learn.' In addition, studies on teacher training have shown that training programmes are successful in improving not only teacher knowledge of economics, but also their attitudes towards the subject and methods of teaching economics. Moreover, teachers who have received training in economics and in the teaching of economics may be more efficient than those who have not in increasing student understanding of, and attitudes towards economics when they teach an economics unit in the classroom (Dawson, 1975; Walstad, 1982). Furthermore, testing of students whose teachers have been exposed to certain types of training in economics and related instructional methodology indicate larger gains in knowledge than students of those teachers who have not had such exposure (Highsmith, 1974; Cellini, 1983).

In outlining conditions necessary for learning, Vredeveld (1982) stated that

> . . . without the ability of the teacher to effectively transmit economic understanding, it is unlikely that learning will take place. As in the case of the student, the teacher must sense that economics is important or the teacher must have an interest in the topic. The teacher also should feel that there is a high probability of success in teaching economics, and instruction would be effective. Furthermore, a teacher must have a sense of his own ability to motivate the student and meet the conditions stated above for student learning. Finally, a teacher must not be intimidated by the probability of having a difficult time learning the subject and must have a strong sense that he can understand the economic concepts.

Specifically, this paper focuses on the development, testing, and implementation of an innovative approach to providing materials and training experiences for teachers in economics education.

Background and historical development

A primary goal of the Foundation for Research in Economics and Education (FREE), founded in 1970 by several economists at the University of California at Los Angeles, was to provide training for teachers in economics. The purpose was to assist teachers in becoming competent in explaining objectively economic principles and their applications so that they would be able to give analytically precise and unbiased presentations of how the US economic system operates. It was felt that one of the problems of economics education was inadequate instructional materials coupled with a lack of teacher expertise in the discipline.

'The People on Market Street' film series* was, therefore, created to teach secondary school students basic economic principles in an entertaining, value-free and intellectually satisfying way. Seven professionally produced and acted films take the viewer sequentially through the concepts of 'scarcity and planning', 'cost', 'demand', 'supply', 'market clearing price', 'wages and production' and 'property rights and pollution'.

'Market Street' is a community within whose boundaries lies an entire spectrum of economic circumstances – all the necessary elements to demonstrate the economic principles outlined. The characters in the films constitute a cross-section of individuals found in North America and are identifiable by all audiences. They do what people in the real world do: they compete for scarce goods, wait in line for tickets, buy less of a good when its price rises, and place different personal values on things.

Shortly after their release in 1977 by the Walt Disney Educational Media Company, the films achieved best-seller status in the educational market. First place awards in the Virgin Island International Film Festival and the International Film and TV Festival of New York testified to the films' high technical quality. Kudos from economists with political viewpoints as divergent as Paul Samuelson and Milton Friedman was evidence that the films were successful in presenting economic principles in a non-normative fashion.

Much of the subsequent development and testing of the films was undertaken by the Pacific Academy for Advanced Studies (PAAS) which was established by FREE to provide special instruction in the application of economic analysis. To ensure that the films would be used to their full potential, the PAAS created and tested the effectiveness of a co-ordinated implementation programme. The initial step was to write a series of guides, one for each of the seven films. Each guide is divided into two sections, one for the teacher and one for the student. The teacher section includes a synopsis of the programme, learning objectives, a glossary and an explanation of the principal concepts together with questions for discussion and suggested classroom activities. The student section contains worksheets for graphing practice, true-false exercises, short answer questions and pre- and post-tests.

*Information on availability may be obtained from the Pacific Academy for Advanced Studies, 1100 Glendon Avenue, Suite 1625, Los Angeles, California 90024.

The PAAS then designed a training programme to teach the microeconomic principles embodied in the films. The purpose was to provide an opportunity for teachers to experience first-rate instruction in economics while at the same time becoming familiar with materials and teaching strategies which could be used in their classrooms. It was felt that content and methodology could be combined effectively, a viewpoint supported by Senesh (1981) who has been quoted as saying, 'While working with children, I came to the conclusion that content and methodology are two sides of the same coin. They are inseparable. Each dimension reinforces the other and economic educators should possess competence in both areas.' The instructors were chosen for their expertise in, and commitment to economics education. With the development of the programme component, a fully integrated economics education training model thus existed – films, print materials and teacher training procedures.

Testing procedures and results

The 28 teachers who took part in the original pilot workshop in 1978 also participated in the testing project in 1979. The testing programme involved 2300 students in grades 7–12, aged 13–18, who were divided into three groups. The control group of over 449 students which did not view the films or receive instruction was used to verify that changes in performance on tests by experimental groups were not due to exogenous events such as maturation. The first experimental group consisted of 749 students who were shown 'The People on Market Street' films by teachers who had not received the PAAS training. The purpose was to measure the effectiveness of the films alone. The second experimental group was utilized to test the effectiveness of the fully integrated programme. In this group, 1115 students viewed the films and received instruction from PAAS-trained teachers. It was thus possible to determine the marginal effectiveness of the PAAS training by comparing the difference in performance between the two experimental groups.

The testing was carried out independently by the Education Research Council of America (ERCA), located in Cleveland, Ohio. The instrument was divided into two parts, the first of which was a 50-item multiple choice knowledge test which measured achievement on 20 different economic concepts. The second part of the test measured student reaction to 34 statements. By measuring the responses to these statements, ERCA was able to measure students' attitudes towards economics and market processes before and after the programme.

The control group showed no significant changes in either knowledge or attitudes. The first experimental group had post-test scores averaging 19 per cent higher than their pre-test test scores and a 9.6 per cent increase in their appreciation of the market system. The second experimental group almost doubled both of these gains showing average gains of 37 per cent and 18.3 per cent in knowledge and attitudes respectively (see Table 1).

Table 1 Average percentage increase in mean test scores

Group 1 Neither films nor training		Group 2 Films only		Group 3 Films and training	
Knowledge	Attitude	Knowledge	Attitude	Knowledge	Attitude
1.1	0.3	19.3	9.6	37.0	18.3

Source: After Baim and Tabbush 'Attempting to bypass the teacher: economics education films for high school students' unpublished paper, 1982

A closer analysis of the results by concept showed that the first experimental group had significant increases (at the 1 per cent level using a Chi-squared test) in 14 of 20 concepts on the knowledge test. Students in the second experimental group who received instruction as well as seeing the films, scored significant gains in all 20 concept areas at the 1 per cent level. Gains in all concept areas were larger than the 'films only' group.

With regard to changes in attitudes, the control group, exposed to neither films nor instruction, registered no significant change. Only grade 7 and grade 8 students (aged 12–14) in the first experimental group, who saw the films only, achieved statistically significant (at least to the 0.05 confidence level) attitudinal change. The specific areas that registered the largest gains were the operation of the free market economy, consumer sovereignty, and preference for the study of economics. Factors which did not register a significant change among grade 7 and grade 8 students were attitudes towards government regulation, middlemen and the profit motive.

The greatest change in attitudes occurred in the second experimental group. This change was significant to the 0.001 confidence level for all age groups tested. The most significant gains were recorded in specific attitudes towards the profit motive, the free market economy, and government regulation.

Baim and Tabbush (1982) summarized the results by stating that, 'While significant gains were recorded in most categories of the knowledge test by those who viewed the films, the most impressive gains were registered by students who were shown them by PAAS-trained teachers.' They concluded that 'teachers must be aware of and comfortable with the content of the film series to achieve maximum effectiveness'.

In recognition of the fact that PAAS-trained teachers utilizing sound support print and audio-visual materials had a significantly positive impact upon student learning, the PAAS proceeded to expand the programme to incorporate macroeconomic principles. The development of a separate guide, *The People on Market Street Guide to Macroeconomic Topics*, was undertaken to provide students and teachers with the required theory, applications and activities to understand the topics of money and banking, inflation, and employment and unemployment. A section of each unit relates the topics to the microeconomic principles embodied in the 'Market Street' films. In addition to the new guide, the training programme was expanded to two weeks, the second week being devoted to macroeconomic topics and issues.

Evaluation

Based on the aforementioned testing results there is little doubt that, in the short term at any rate, the programme is effective. However, it was deemed important to determine long-term effectiveness with respect to the attitudes and perceptions of participants.

Cellini (1983) undertook a study, the objective of which was to determine the effectiveness of the programme and its impact over time. The specific issues which she addressed included the extensiveness of the usage of the programme in the classroom, the relationship of the programme to non-economics courses, the perceived timeliness of the programme, the effectiveness of the programme over time and the merits and drawbacks of the materials. After having developed and pilot-tested a questionnaire, Cellini (1983) mailed 370 surveys to teachers who took the PAAS training in 1980, 1981 and 1982. Of these, 154, or 40 per cent, were returned, of which 150 were considered valid for analysis.

Responses indicated that most participants were experienced teachers: 77 per cent had taught for over 11 years. Only 8 per cent of respondents had taught for five years or less. The average years of teaching was 15.

The majority of respondents (60 per cent) taught grades 10–12, and the courses most often taught (see Table 2) were US history (42.7 per cent), economics (40.7 per cent), social studies (40 per cent) and government (30 per cent).

Table 2   Usage by courses taught

Courses	Percentage of total	Number
US history	42.7	64
Economics	40.7	61
Social studies	40.0	60
Government	30.0	45
World history	20.7	31
Geography	20.0	30
Consumer education	12.7	19
Business	10.0	15

Source: From Cellini 'PAAS program attitude study' unpublished study, 1983

In general the extent to which PAAS-trained teachers implemented the programme in their classes was quite high. Almost 50 per cent of the respondents indicated that they had applied information, skills and materials from the programme during all terms subsequent to their first training session. Approximately 81 per cent used the programme in at least half of the terms.

An examination of the teachers' reasons for attending the programme (see Table 3) showed that 88 per cent wished to update their knowledge of economics, 81.3 per cent wished to enhance their teaching techniques, and 78.6 per cent indicated that the programme offered practical application. Secondary factors were the payment of a fee for completing the course, and the fact that the programme carried college credit.*

With regard to the instructional materials, 92 per cent of the respondents considered them to be especially important. Approximately 87 per cent considered them 'to be very useful', and 69 per cent deemed them 'the best available'. These materials were also noted as being particularly useful for lesson preparation.

Of special note is the perceived usefulness of the programme to specific courses and grade levels (see Table 4). As one would expect, the majority of respondents considered the programme to be most useful in teaching economics, but consumer education, government, social studies, business and US history also rated highly. Responses regarding grade level indicated that the programme for teaching 17–18 year olds is most useful at the grade 12 level, and progressively less useful from grades 11 down to 6 in descending order.

The Canadian experience

In 1982, the Economic Education Resource Centre (EERC), a division of the Fraser Institute located in Vancouver, British Columbia, introduced a Canadian version of the programme in co-operation with the PAAS and the Office of Field Development, Faculty of Education, at the University of British Columbia. The University offered credit to participants.

The purpose of the Canadian programme was to present an opportunity for teachers to become more familiar with the discipline of economics and instructional strategies related to economics education. The objectives developed by the Economic Education Resource Centre were as follows:

A Participant

1 Through a knowledge of the nature and purpose of economics as a discipline, teachers will apply an economic framework in order to understand the key elements of the Canadian economic system.

---

*In the US and Canada, academic degrees are earned by accumulating a certain number of 'credits' or 'credit hours'. Courses which are assigned units of credit may be applied towards a degree.

Table 3   Reasons for attending PAAS workshop

	Percentages								Mean	Rank
	Disagree 1	2	3	4	Agree 5	No response				
Update knowledge of economics	2.7	1.3	6.0	18.7	69.3	2.0	100%		4.54	1
Fee offered	5.3	6.0	27.3	22.0	36.0	3.3	100%		3.80	4
College credit available	14.7	7.3	18.7	19.3	36.0	4.0	100%		3.57	5
Practical classroom application	2.0	2.7	12.7	31.3	47.3	4.0	100%		4.24	3
Enhance teaching techniques	2.7	3.3	11.3	30.0	51.3	1.3	100%		4.26	2

Source: After Cellini 'PAAS program attitude study' unpublished study, 1983

Table 4   Usefulness to courses and grades

	Percentages							Mean	Rank
	Not useful 1	2	3	4	Useful 5	No response			
Economics			1.3	4.0	87.3	7.3	100%	4.93	1
Consumer education		1.3	4.0	19.3	64.0	11.3	100%	4.65	2
Business		2.7	8.0	24.0	46.7	18.7	100%	4.41	3

Social studies		2.0	8.7	38.0	36.0	15.3	100%	4.28	4
US history		4.7	18.0	36.7	29.3	11.3	100%	4.02	5=
Political science	0.7	4.0	16.7	31.3	28.0	19.3	100%	4.02	5=
Civics		4.7	20.0	37.3	23.3	14.7	100%	3.93	7
Vocational education	1.3	8.7	24.0	22.0	24.7	19.3	100%	3.74	8
World history		10.0	26.7	26.0	21.3	16.0	100%	3.70	9
Mathematics	3.3	7.3	30.3	28.7	10.0	20.7	100%	3.43	10
Geography	1.3	12.7	32.7	27.3	9.3	16.7	100%	3.37	11
Philosophy	6.0	14.0	28.0	16.0	9.3	26.7	100%	3.12	12
English	13.3	29.3	24.7	5.3	0.7	26.7	100%	2.33	13
6th grade	8.0	16.7	30.7	14.0	8.7	22.0	100%	2.98	7
7th grade	2.7	10.0	28.0	24.0	16.0	19.3	100%	3.50	6
8th grade	0.7	6.0	25.3	26.7	22.0	19.3	100%	3.79	5
9th grade		2.0	13.3	30.7	33.3	20.7	100%	4.20	4
10th grade		1.3	10.0	26.7	43.3	18.7	100%	4.34	3
11th grade			2.7	19.3	63.3	14.7	100%	4.71	2
12th grade			2.0	8.7	76.7	12.7	100%	4.86	1

Source: From Cellini 'PAAS program attitude study' unpublished study, 1983

2 Teachers will analyse economic issues using basic principles and apply them to economics education.

3 Teachers will evaluate economics education as a means of teaching problem solving and decision making.

4 Teachers will analyse and evaluate instructional strategies and materials in the area of economics education.

5 Teachers will increase their skills in developing curriculum projects.

B Programme

1 To create a positive learning climate in which teachers and instructors will share their experiences and ideas.

2 To present the opportunities which economics education can offer to enrich the teaching/learning process, and to encourage educators to incorporate an economic perspective into their teaching when they consider it relevant.

3 To evaluate participant learning in economics education.

4 To evaluate the programme in terms of its effectiveness for delivering economics education to teachers.

A sample outline of one day's agenda is included in the Appendix. The course material was dealt with over a 10-day period with five hours of classroom time each day. A wide variety of teaching strategies was employed owing to the intensive nature of the programme. These included lecture, demonstration, simulation, films, discussion and guest speakers.

As in the US, the Canadian programme used 'The People on Market Street' film series and the seven microeconomic guides to 'The People on Market Street'. A Canadian version of the *Guide to Macroeconomic Topics* was developed by the Economic Education Resource Centre in 1984 since, owing to institutional differences between Canada and the US, the American edition is of limited use in Canada.

One hundred and three Canadian educators were exposed to training which was offered exclusively in the western province of British Columbia during the summers of 1982, 1983 and 1984. Of these teachers, 9 per cent taught at the elementary level, 90 per cent at the secondary level, and the remaining 1 per cent at the post-secondary level; 65 per cent were business education teachers, 26 per cent social studies teachers, 7 per cent taught mathematics and/or science, and 2 per cent were administrators or curriculum coordinators.

On the first day of each programme, the participants were given a pre-test. The test instrument was a 50-item multiple choice knowledge test which examined achievement on 20 different economic concepts. The same instrument was administered at the conclusion of the programme. The purpose of this procedure was two-fold: first, it permitted the instructors to assess quickly the entry-level knowledge of the participants, and second, it yielded a crude measure of gain in economic knowledge. The marks awarded to participants were based in no way on the pre-post scores, but rather on a formal examination.

While the Canadian programme has not yet been evaluated to the same extent as its original US model, participants' evaluations indicate that it has been highly successful and well received. An analysis of their responses to a questionnaire indicates several noteworthy items. First, teachers found the programme to be challenging, yet intellectually fulfilling. Second, they perceived the programme to be most useful in terms of practical classroom application. Third, the vast majority commented favourably on the relevance and quality of the films and printed materials. Fourth, and of extreme importance, there was unanimous agreement on the high quality of instruction throughout. In each case, the programme was taught by highly trained economists who had extensive experience in working with teachers. These individuals have not only a high degree of commitment to, but also expertise in economics education. There is no doubt that their talents contributed significantly to the success of the programme.

Conclusion

In recent years there has been a gradual increase in interest in economic education in North American schools as witnessed by state and provincial mandates, curriculum changes and a host of other evidence. The derived demand for various forms of teacher education programmes poses a challenge which has been addressed by a variety of organizations, institutions, and other groups and individuals.

The Economic Education Resource Centre in British Columbia adapted an integrated model which had been piloted, tested and found effective by the Pacific Academy for Advanced Studies in California. The three components of the programme – films, print material and teacher training – were utilized with certain modifications to accommodate the differences between Canada and the US. It is anticipated that the demonstrated long-term effectiveness of the programme in the US will also be evidenced in Canada, but this is yet to be documented.

During the summer of 1985, the Canadian programme will be expanded to universities in two other provinces at the request of educators who heard of its success.

There still remains a great deal of work to be undertaken to ameliorate the chronic problem of the lack of economics education opportunities for teachers. The programme described above is one approach which others may wish to consider.

Appendix: Sample outline for one day's activities

9:00 a.m.   Welcome and introductions
            Pre-test
            Positive versus normative economics – a mini-lecture
            and discussion
10:30 a.m. Coffee break
10:45 a.m. Scarcity and choice – mini-lecture
            Introduction to the film, 'Scarcity'
            Viewing of film
            Question and answer period on 'Scarcity'
            Demonstration lesson on how to teach the concept
            of scarcity to students
12:30 p.m. Lunch
1:45 p.m.   Opportunity cost and rational decision making – lecture
2:30-3:00 p.m. Simulated activity on decision making

References

Baim, D. and Tabbush, V. 1982 'Attempting to bypass the teacher: economics education films for high school students' unpublished paper presented at the Western Economics Association Meeting, Los Angeles, July 15–19

Cellini, H. 1983 'PAAS program attitude study' unpublished study submitted to the Pacific Academy for Advanced Studies, April 15

Dawson, G. G. 1975 'Economics curriculum development projects in the United States' in Norman Lee (ed.) *Teaching Economics* Heinemann Educational, p. 197

Frye, C. 1979 'An examination of statewide mandates in economic education and programs developed to implement these mandates' Master's Thesis, University of Central Florida at Orlando

Highsmith, R. 1974 'A study to measure the impact of in-service institutes on the students of teachers who have participated' *Journal of Economic Education* 5(2) pp. 77–81

Hodgetts, A. B. and Gallagher, P. 1978 *Teaching Canada for the '80s* The Ontario Institute for Studies in Education, p. 79

Holley, B. and Skelton, V. 1980 *Economics Education 14–16 (Phase 1 Final Report)* National Foundation for Educational Research, p. 78

Senesh, L. 1981 in S. Stowell Symmes (ed.) *Economic Education: Links to the Social Studies* National Council for the Social Studies Bulletin no. 65, p. 66

Vredeveld, G. 1982 'Some statements on learning theory in economics' unpublished statement prepared for the Learning Theory and Economics Conference, National Center of Economic Education for Children, Lesley College, Cambridge, Mass., April 18–20

Walstad, W. B. 1982 'Economics and learning theory' unpublished position paper prepared for the Learning Theory and Economics Conference, National Center of Economic Education for Children, Lesley College, Cambridge, Mass., April 18–20

Business studies and economics within a changing curriculum in Scotland

Barry Finlayson

Lecturer in Business Studies, Jordanhill College of Education, Glasgow

The paper attempts to indicate the significant changes that are taking place in Scotland to business studies and economics education in the light of national developments affecting the curriculum of pupils, the assessment of that curriculum and the process of teaching.

Background to the Scottish education system

The development and supervision of public sector education in Scotland is the responsibility of the Secretary of State for Scotland (SOS) who is directly responsible to Parliament. The provision of education is one of the duties of the nine regional councils and three island councils, which are known as local authorities. Thus a partnership exists between the department of government nationally responsible for education (the Scottish Education Department) and those regional bodies required by law to provide an education service in their area.

While the content and management of the school curriculum is determined by the local authorities and their headteachers, advice on curricular matters is available to the SOS through the Consultative Committee on the Curriculum (CCC). This body was established in 1965 and is responsible for a number of curriculum committees and the supporting Scottish Curriculum Development Service (SCDS). Together they promote developments in particular subjects and areas of education. Along with Her Majesty's Inspectors of Schools (HMI), the CCC is an important source of the curriculum guidance issued by the SOS to education authorities. Membership of the CCC includes a majority of educationalists drawn from a wide variety of backgrounds including universities, colleges, schools, and education authorities, and a small number representing the interests of parents, industry and commerce.

Pupils transfer from primary to secondary education at the age of 12 and almost all attend education authority schools with a comprehensive intake. A long tradition of comprehensive education has existed in Scotland particularly in rural areas. In addition, private provision of education does exist in Scotland through a small number of independent and grant-aided secondary schools and residential special schools.

The first two years of pupils' secondary school experience are regarded as an exploratory period during which their progress is observed. During this period pupils have a wide curriculum of many subjects so that they may identify their own particular aptitudes, abilities and interests. Most pupils are educated in mixed ability classes for the whole of this two-year period.

At the conclusion of their second year (S2), pupils are invited, with guidance, to make a choice of those subjects they will pursue in the Scottish Certificate of Education (SCE) examinations taken at the end of the period of compulsory education, namely at the conclusion of their fourth year in the secondary school (S4). The examinations are conducted by the Scottish Examination Board (SEB), a single statutory body set up in 1963 with responsibility for examining nationally all school subjects at ordinary, higher and post-higher grades. Some pupils may also combine certificate courses in certain subjects with school-devised non-certificate courses in other areas of the curriculum.

Almost half the number of candidates sitting ordinary grade examinations remain at school voluntarily beyond the statutory leaving age. The pupils have the opportunity of undertaking studies leading to the higher grade examination usually taken in S5 or S6. The more able candidates take four or five subjects and preserve a balanced curriculum, though obviously with less specialization than is possible at A level. The Certificate of Sixth Year Studies (CSYS) is also awarded by the SEB and is open to pupils who have normally taken sufficient higher grade subjects at the end of S5 and are contemplating further or higher education.

Courses of sixth year studies aim to promote pupils' ability to pursue independent study, usually through completion of a piece of research as a test not only of intellectual ability but of the capacity for personal study.

Introduction

The second half of the 1970s was a significant time of educational change in Scotland. Three important reports on secondary school education were produced in this period, the recommendations of which will not only shape Scottish education for the remainder of this century, but may also offer to many other educational systems throughout the world a curriculum and assessment model which some might find attractive.

The reports relate to three aspects of secondary education in Scotland. The Munn report (1977) considered the curriculum structure for pupils in the last two years of compulsory education, i.e. pupils aged 14–16 and in the third (S3) and fourth (S4) years of their secondary school experience. The Dunning report (1977) concerned itself with the assessment and certification of pupils in the last two years of their compulsory schooling, while the Pack report (1977) concentrated essentially on the importance of the teaching process and establishing in pupils motivation and a willingness to learn.

These reports and their recommendations have led to an acceleration of curriculum development of such proportions as to merit being described as a 'curriculum revolution'. Their recommendations have certainly influenced the future structure of the S3/S4 curriculum and assessment but the changes envisaged will inevitably have an influence upon the curriculum and assessment of pupils in S1/S2 and the nature of educational provision for those pupils in S5/S6.

The Munn report sought a curriculum for pupils in the last two years of compulsory education which provided balance, choice and flexibility.

A core of subjects was identified and optional subjects outside the core listed. As a result of consultation, a curriculum model for S3/S4 has now been laid out, underpinned by the principles of the Munn report and identifying seven modes as essential elements in the curriculum of all S3/S4 pupils (see Table 1). Core subjects are then associated with the appropriate mode, and

Table 1   A curriculum model for S3/S4

Key areas (modes) with minimum/maximum periods*	Core subjects	Some optional subjects
Linguistic and literary study 5/13	English	French German Gaelic Latin
Mathematical studies 5/9	Mathematics	Business studies Computing studies
Scientific study 4/16	Biology Chemistry Physics Science	Health studies Technological studies
Social studies 4/10	Contemporary social studies Economics Geography History Modern studies	Home economics Social and vocational skills
Creative and aesthetic activities 2/10	Art and design Creative and aesthetic studies Music	Craft and design
Physical activity 2/6	Physical education	
Religious studies and morality 2/6	Religious and moral education	

*Based on 40 periods per week.

Source: *Your Guide to the New Exams, Scottish Standard Grade (14–16)* BBC, 1985

optional subjects regarded as contributions to the appropriate mode are also identified.

The Dunning report envisaged an assessment structure appropriate to every pupil in the age group and providing certification at three levels – Credit, General and Foundation – and based upon what pupils could actually do. In other words, a criterion-referenced instead of a norm-referenced assessment system. In the area of assessment, secondary education in Scotland has the advantage of being administered through regional authorities with the Scottish Education Department setting broad policy guidelines and one examination body, the SEB, certificating pupils at the end of their school experience.

For the last 20 years the structure of assessment in Scottish secondary education has been based upon the ordinary grade examination taken by pupils at the end of S4 and designed for approximately the top third of the ability range. Pupils in S3/S4 and of less ability were therefore at a distinct disadvantage and found themselves either taking ordinary grade courses which were not appropriate to their needs or following the many 'non-certificate' courses offered by schools with no recognized certificate to work for at the end of the course. The level of motivation and behaviour difficulties manifested by such pupils was identified in the Pack report and attributed not only to the lack of suitable courses to meet their needs, but also to the learning and teaching approaches employed which were frequently better suited to the more able pupils. The early 1980s, therefore, seemed a propitious time to introduce a number of far-reaching changes into the curriculum of pupils in the last two years of their compulsory education.

In 1979 the Scottish Education Department initiated a feasibility study into the development of English, mathematics, and science courses at Foundation, General and Credit levels. At Foundation level, a significant component of internal assessment was envisaged, and at General and Credit levels the emphasis was to be on the external assessment of pupil performance to maintain national standards. Certification would be offered at grades 1–6, grades 1 and 2 equating with a Credit performance and grades 6 and 7 with a Foundation level performance. For each of the subjects concerned, the elements of the subject to be assessed were to be identified and criteria of performance set (i.e. there were to be grade related criteria – GRC). The mechanism to be used to develop such courses was that of the Joint Working Party (JWP) for the subject concerned with membership drawn in equal number from the national advisory body on the curriculum (CCC) and the national examination body (SEB). Each JWP was also to contain an HMI representative and supportive member from the SCDS.

The success of the feasibility study led the Secretary of State to initiate the Standard Grade Development Programme, a phased programme of development to convert subjects in the S3/S4 curriculum from ordinary grades to Standard grades at, in the majority of cases, the three levels – Credit, General and Foundation. This programme of development was planned to commence in 1982 so that by 1986 the majority of subjects in the curriculum would be offered as Standard grades thus enabling pupils of different abilities to undertake appropriate certificated courses in their chosen subjects.

Position of business studies in the Scottish curriculum

It is against this background of widespread curricular change and reorganization associated with the Standard Grade Development Programme referred to above that the role of business studies and economics in the school curriculum must be considered.

Firstly the term 'business studies' (BS) is used to describe that established group of subjects concerned with developing in pupils a knowledge and understanding of the operation of the industrial and commercial component of society. Through a study of secretarial studies, accounting and economics, the latter most commonly taught in BS departments, important life skills are developed and attitudes fostered. It is customary for schools with adequate staffing and pupil numbers to offer courses in the BS area to pupils at the beginning of S3, the curricular choice on the part of the pupils having been made at the conclusion of S2. As a result of a feasibility study into the teaching of economics in S1 and S2 undertaken in the early years of the 1970s (Scottish Central Committee on Social Subjects, 1978), which brought into existence a conceptually-based two-year course in the subject, a small number of Scottish secondary schools do offer pupils in those years a modest input of economics. Also, in a limited number of schools, other departments with the qualified teaching staff available, e.g. in modern studies, might offer economics to pupils where BS departments are unable to make their contribution.

Prior to the Standard Grade Development Programme, pupils could undertake ordinary grade courses in secretarial studies (which comprised typewriting, audio-typewriting, and office practice), accounting and economics, with a limited number of pupils also studying for an ordinary grade in economic history. Equivalent courses existed to allow deeper study for the award of higher grades usually taken by pupils in S5. Such higher grade courses, and indeed ordinary grade courses, have also attracted able pupils in S6 wishing to include an element(s) of BS in their school experience prior to further or higher education or before taking up employment.

For a number of years, those pupils completing a higher grade study in secretarial studies and economics in S5 have been able to undertake a deeper study of the subjects concerned through the completion of a CSYS course designed to extend knowledge and understanding and to promote further skill development prior to a career in industry or entry into a profession or university.

In addition to these contributions to the curriculum, BS departments have added specific inputs to school-based non-certificate courses for pupils not undertaking a full ordinary grade curriculum. Recently certain departments have been responsible for courses in keyboarding, money management and computer education, where the need has been identified and the resources made available.

Aims of business studies and economics in secondary schools

In 1982 the Scottish Central Committee on Business Subjects (SCCBS) identified a number of broad aims for business education in the secondary school (SCCBS *Starter Paper* 1982, paragraph 3.2). The aims set out were

1 to prepare pupils for entry into post-school society

2 to increase pupils' knowledge and understanding of the working of the modern industrialized society in which they live

3 to promote an awareness of the dynamic nature of society and the need for adaptability and change

4 to improve basic literacy and numeracy skills and to develop in pupils certain other social and life skills such as problem solving and keyboarding

5 to develop in pupils an orderly and systematic approach to their work, an ability to work with others, a willingness to consider differing viewpoints and ways of life, a concern for the needs of society and a respect for evidence as a basis for forming judgements

   In developing such a list of aims, the SCCBS took account of the general aims for secondary education as set out in the Munn report, Chapter 4. These were

1 to develop knowledge and understanding of the pupils themselves and of their social and physical environment

2 to develop cognitive, interpersonal and psychomotor skills

3 to promote the affective development of pupils

4 to equip pupils to cope with the demands of society and to develop social competence

   The business studies and economics curriculum can thus be clearly seen as going a considerable way towards supporting the aims of the Munn report.

Secretarial studies   The contribution which secretarial studies at ordinary and higher grades makes to the wider education of pupils is greater than many observers might recognize. It promotes the development of language skills and, to a lesser extent, numerical skills. Much of what is taught could be described as 'education for life'. A course in secretarial studies inculcates positive attitudes and, in particular, teaches orderliness and the need for organization in the execution of tasks. Inter-personal skills, manipulative skills, knowledge of equipment and machinery, the notion of quality and pride in one's work, initiative and self-criticism are all developed within secretarial studies courses. In addition, a keyboarding skill will be increasingly important for everyone as technological developments continue to pervade our lives. Also, from a vocational viewpoint, secretarial studies is a popular subject because most pupils and their parents believe that a course of this nature enhances employment prospects.

However, it is recognized that changes must be made to ensure that it is brought into line with modern office practice and techniques and to take account of the impact of new technology on work in offices. Of all the business subjects, secretarial studies is the one which must continually respond to the rapidly changing environment of the modern technologically-based office.

Clearly, developments like the word processor and electronic mail will have an impact not only on the work that goes on in offices but also on the employment of clerical and secretarial personnel. It is recognized that office staff of the future will need to be more adaptable and possess a wider range of skills, and it is this adaptability to change which should be taken into account when devising secretarial studies courses for the future.

Accounting   Ordinary grade accounting gives pupils an opportunity to use numbers in meaningful ways, to relate numeracy to real life, and to analyse information given in numerical terms. It gives pupils training in the skills of presentation and neatness and also offers an opportunity to come into contact with business documents and the basic principles of accounting. Accounting is an important aspect of business education but, where it is taught without thought for its context or its contribution to business activity, it is very much an isolated study with pupils having no greater understanding of how businesses operate than they did before embarking upon the course. Young people in the process of managing their own personal financial affairs must derive some benefit from a knowledge of accounting, and the ability to employ the skills the subject develops should support their approach to the more complicated personal financial affairs to be experienced as they progress through life, e.g. drafting, family budgets, choosing appropriate financial services and considering the real costs of borrowing.

Higher grade accounting can also claim to make a significant contribution to the general education of senior pupils, as it develops an appreciation of the importance of accounting generally as well as its more particular application to business enterprise. It includes a vocational element by providing a useful preparation for any pupil seeking a career in business or finance, and it also provides a sound foundation for those wishing to study the subject beyond school.

Economics   Everyone makes economic decisions every day and is influenced by the economic decisions of Government. All pupils should therefore be given an economics education to enable them to perform their functions as producers, consumers and voters. Currently in Scottish education, as we have seen, courses in economics tend to be offered as options for pupils to take at the conclusion of S2, although small numbers of pupils in certain schools may have the opportunity to undertake a study of the subject in S1/S2. At ordinary grade, courses in economics aim to

1 enable pupils to see economics as a dynamic social science of concern to everybody

2 provide pupils with an understanding of the basic economic problems which will increasingly face them

3 develop in pupils a capacity for economic reasoning and for logical expression of economic ideas based on a study of relevant data

(Scottish Certificate of Education Examination Board, 1973, p. 11)

At higher grade, while an understanding of economic concepts and principles is fundamental, the application of such understanding to the analysis of economic problems and an appreciation of the applicability and limitations of economic theory in contemporary society are also important skills and attitudes which are developed. In this way, higher grade economics makes a significant contribution to general education. It provides pupils with a means of understanding the economic aspects of their lives and, in addition, attempts to develop analytical skills as well as economic literacy and numeracy.

Business studies and economics in the Scottish curriculum: contribution, constraints and influences

The importance of business studies and economics in the Scottish curriculum is fully recognized. First, the Munn report recognized the importance of economics in a young person's curriculum by including it in the core of subjects recommended for S3/S4 pupils within the social subjects mode. Secondly, the report of the Education for the Industrial Society Project (EISP) stated (1983, paragraph 3.12) that *all* pupils should learn about economics, and recognized that although aspects of economics are currently present in courses of modern studies, geography, history and accounting, there was nevertheless a strong case for greater emphasis on the economic dimension of society in the curriculum. It was felt that the production of wealth and its distribution, the functions of labour, land and capital, and the causes of recession of unemployment were all vital to an understanding of industrial society; and concern was expressed at the paucity of understanding on the part of pupils about the nature of the manufacturing process from the processing of raw materials to the completion of the final product. It was felt that economics should be taught with the aim of helping pupils to understand more fully the nature of their changing industrial society and that means should be found to allow pupils to study economics either as a separate subject or as an essential complement to some broader course such as modern studies or business studies.

The EISP report also went on to describe the contributions that accounting and secretarial studies could make to an education for the industrial society. It also recommended that, while the vocational attractions of these subjects were powerful in influencing pupils to take the subjects up in S3, they also had much to offer to the education of the more academic pupils in the schools (paragraphs 3.20–3.23).

However, while recognizing the worthy contribution which business studies and economics make to the general and vocational education of young people, it must also be recognized that certain constraints continue to affect the development of the subjects in the Scottish secondary school.

First, the current situation of falling school rolls presents BS departments with a challenge made greater by the fact that pupils customarily opt to take up the subjects after making a choice at the end of S2. With no substantial presence in the S1/S2 curriculum and therefore no automatic 'follow through' on the part of pupils into S3 business studies and economics, the number of pupils opting to take the subject in S3/S4 must therefore be relatively small. At the end of S2, pupils (and there are now fewer of them) are faced with a choice of continuing with the subjects they have studied in S1/S2 or dropping certain subjects to take up a subject(s) in the BS and economics curriculum with which they are unfamiliar. A number of schools have attempted to make this choice more objective by offering pupils in S2 'taster courses' in BS and economics. Also a few BS departments attempt to secure some time on the S2 programme for inputs of their subjects. Such contributions usually include short keyboarding courses (either as discrete courses, or linked to computer appreciation courses) or inputs of economics.

The subjects do therefore compete in the market for young people at the end of S2 and such competition is bound to become more intense with falling school rolls.

At present an important committee of the CCC is examining the provision of education for pupils in the 10–14 age range with a view to making a number of recommendations. The SCCBS has made contact with this group to make a case for the formalizing of certain inputs of BS and economics in the first two years of a pupil's secondary experience. In addition a feasibility study mounted by the Scottish Central Committee on Social Subjects (SCCSS) entitled *S1/S2 Social Subjects Development Programme* (1984) makes a limited provision for *all* S1/S2 pupils to experience economics in a co-ordinated social subjects course where inputs of economics, history, modern studies and geography are co-operatively planned by the social subjects departments in the school.

The staffing position of BS and economics also represents a constraint upon developments. Three training colleges supply, after a one-year post-graduate course, BS and economics teachers for the schools. The Scottish Education Department recommends an annual quota of secondary teachers to be trained and the colleges allocate their numbers among the various secondary training departments. Throughout the 1980s, BS has been regarded as a 'shortage subject' where the demand for teachers has exceeded the supply. As a result, and particularly at a time when resources for education are scarce, many areas in Scotland, particularly Strathclyde and Central Region, have not always been able to recruit sufficient teachers to maintain an expansion of BS and economics in the curriculum.

Nevertheless, in spite of these difficulties the attraction of these subjects to pupils has resulted in no substantial fall in the numbers taking them at certificate level in schools. Their relevance to both general and vocational education has been recognized by pupils and parents alike and a further boost and recognition is currently reflected in the number of Technical and Vocational Education Initiative (TVEI) schemes operating in Scotland which include inputs from the BS and economics curricula.

Future position of business studies and economics

The restructuring of the secondary curriculum for pupils in S3/S4 is now under way through the phased implementation of the Standard Grade Development Programme referred to in the introduction to this paper.

Significant changes are taking place with the development, through Joint Working Parties (JWPs), of courses appropriate to and relevant for pupils of all abilities in the secondary school. The principal objective is to provide pupils in S3/S4 with a balanced curriculum through a structure of modes and courses and also to provide certification across the ability range, such certification being based upon pupil performance of tasks and processes against set criteria. Thus the aim of assessment of Standard grade courses is set firmly on a criterion-referenced system.

In addition to making the school experience of pupils as rewarding as possible, educators have a duty to prepare pupils for what will come after school. For most pupils, it must still be assumed that this means preparation for working life. It is estimated that almost half of all employees are engaged in commercial, clerical, administrative and executive work. There is, therefore, a clear case for schools providing a curriculum which includes education for business and administration. Indeed, the steadily rising proportion of economic activity which is devoted to the provision of services and administration has been matched by a huge expansion and development of commercial education at both school and post-school levels.

Whether the inclusion of business studies within the school curriculum leads to a conflict between general and vocational education is a controversy which still exists, although reactions to it are not now quite so pronounced. The distinctions between general and vocational education are becoming less clear and the notion that they are wholly contrasting styles of education is no longer tenable. There exists a continuum, at one end of which is an education entirely unrelated to future work and, at the other extreme, an education specifically designed to train a person to undertake one particular job. Between these two extremes, education contains both 'general' and 'vocational' elements and in Scottish secondary schools they can be found side by side and in varying proportions depending on the needs and demands of society, employment prospects, and the prevailing economic climate. While the vocational aspects of business subjects have a strong attraction for pupils, parents and employees, their contribution to general education should not be overlooked. If a study of any range of business subjects enables a pupil to earn a living, then it must be commended; if it also, or alternatively, helps to develop individual potential or contributes to aesthetic or moral development, that is equally commendable. The fundamental point is that teachers of business subjects should consciously retain a general education outlook even while teaching pupils for more specific purposes. Otherwise, there is a danger that in later life, the pupil's options will be unnecessarily restricted. Whatever else education achieves, it must have relevance and usefulness in preparing pupils for the 'business of living'.

The vocational incentive can be a powerful motivator for learning. If pupils perceive aspects of their schooling which (1) have relevance to the world of work and (2) are economically useful to them in later life and thus provide a vocational impulse for learning now, then such 'vocational' education is valuable. However, the state of the labour market for young people must always be considered, and if many pupils believe that there is little chance of obtaining a job, their motivation to work at school is decreased. This therefore suggests that the most appropriate education to provide for pupils is that which (1) develops a broad knowledge and understanding of the workings of a modern industrial society and (2) promotes the development of literacy and numeracy skills, introduces basic scientific knowledge and fosters social skills including punctuality and the ability to get on with other people. In summary, what is required is a broad general education, and business studies, through accounting, economics and secretarial studies, is clearly able to make a significant contribution to this objective.

With regard to the S3/S4 curriculum, the Standard Grade Development Programme sets out a pattern of new BS and economics courses to be offered to S3/S4 pupils from 1987 onwards.

Firstly a business studies course at Foundation, General, and Credit levels is to be devised. This course will be broadly based on office and commercial procedures and will take account of the new technological developments which are changing the nature of clerical work in industry and commerce. Such a course is intended to be attractive to both sexes, and will eventually replace secretarial studies at ordinary grade. It will have a place among the optional activities in the curriculum and will be designed to ensure coverage within a time allocation of 160 minutes per week over the two years S3 and S4. The course is further intended to broaden the curriculum in the light of the rapidly changing world in which we live. The Council of Europe (1982) declared that the school system should be designed to strengthen young people's knowledge of technology and that they should be provided with opportunities to acquire essential knowledge and skills to prepare them for working life. The impact of technology and the development of microcomputers have reinforced the view that schools should be providing opportunities for all pupils to acquire keyboard skills and a knowledge of information technology. The business studies course aims to fulfil these functions.

The place of the social subjects in the curriculum of the secondary school was confirmed in the Munn report and the recommendation of a social studies mode as an integral part of the curriculum for *all* pupils in S3 and S4 was endorsed in the Munn and Dunning reports, *Framework for Decision* (1982). The case for all pupils studying at least one social subject has therefore been accepted in order to achieve the aim to 'develop in pupils an understanding of the society in which they live and foster their capacity to make involved judgements on contemporary issues'. Moreover it is increasingly and convincingly argued that there is a need, during the period of compulsory education, for the preparation of all pupils for their roles as citizens, producers and consumers. Such preparation implies equipping pupils with the necessary knowledge and understanding of the functioning of society and with the process skills to enable them to be active and constructive participants in that society.

In *Framework for Decision* economics was recognized in its own right as capable of fulfilling the requirements of the social studies mode. At national level in Scotland, curriculum development in economics is undertaken by two central committees of the CCC, one of which is concerned with the social subjects and the other with business subjects. Thus economics is identified as both a social science and a business study and can be seen to contribute to the vocational as well as the general education of pupils. The vocational aspect is also highlighted by the development of TVEI, which also stresses the importance of inter-subject links.

Thus the importance of economics in the curriculum is recommended by the development of a Standard grade course in economics to be offered to pupils at General and Credit levels. The absence of a course at Foundation level does not support the view that such pupils would not derive benefit from such a course but recognizes that other courses, notably the multidisciplinary course contemporary social studies, offer elements of economics at Foundation level. However some pressure is likely to develop over the next few years in support of the provision of a full economics course at Foundation level. The aim of the Standard grade course in economics is to equip pupils with the process skills and the appropriate knowledge to help them understand more fully the economic dimension of their own lives and of society in general. Therefore the purpose of a course in economics should be to enable pupils to examine and tackle aspects of 'the economic problem' as they occur at various levels in and beyond their own community, and hence to develop in pupils economic literacy and numeracy.

The Munn committee made a strong case for courses, some of which might be of a multidisciplinary nature, which would broadly be oriented to the study of contemporary society and to the preparation for adult life and work. In addition comments on the Munn and Dunning reports had suggested that a curriculum of discrete subjects might not be the only or the best approach at Foundation level. Pupils who did not respond well to a subject-based curriculum should be offered, it was suggested, an alternative approach providing them with greater opportunity to explore themes relevant to their personal needs and interests. Therefore in 1979 the Government's Munn and Dunning feasibility study set about investigating the possibility of developing alternative or multidisciplinary courses dealing with health education, the preparation for adult life and work and an exploration and study of contemporary society, the latter two courses falling within the area of the BS and economics curriculum.

After preparatory piloting and consultation (Scottish Examination Board, 1983), the two-year multidisciplinary course Social and Vocational Skills (SVS) was introduced into the curriculum during session 1984/85 with certification in 1986 at Foundation and General levels. Pupils interested would opt to take the course at the end of S2 and the aim of their experience on the course would be to

1 develop practical, social, and vocational skills necessary for adult life such as competence in the management of time, money, basic equipment, and machines (the course would also aim for an achievement of competence in communication and interpersonal skills particularly relating to self, home and family, work, self-employment and leisure)

2 provide pupils with opportunities to apply their knowledge and skills in a variety of relevant social and vocational circumstances: personal life, the family, the wider community, the world of work and leisure

3 develop an awareness of the needs of others in the community

4 enhance personal qualities such as self-awareness, self-respect, confidence and initiative

5 foster a positive attitude to co-operation and teamwork

In many ways this course represents a revolutionary approach to curriculum design in Scotland in that no fixed syllabus of content is laid down. Being skills-based, a number of learning outcomes (skills) have been identified by the JWP responsible for its construction and classroom teachers are free to select appropriate content which will adequately develop the skills involved. Teachers design their own course and submit the course outline for moderation by the SEB. The course is also designed around inputs from different subject areas. While it is recognized that the subjects presently in the curriculum that can most immediately contribute their skills to the course are home economics, technical education, and business subjects, it is also recognized that other approaches could and are being developed. What has been recognized through piloting is the need for committed and interested teachers, whether they be from the subjects identified above or from quite different disciplines. Whatever team structure is chosen, the course is designed around a number of teachers who combine their own enthusiasms and interests.

A number of themes pervade the course – home, work, community – and through practically-based experiential learning, the skills identified can be developed. Teachers must be prepared to be flexible and adopt open teaching styles, often teaching life skills outside their own subject area.

A second multidisciplinary course with certain BS and economics inputs is the course intended for introduction in 1987 and entitled contemporary social studies (Scottish Examination Board, 1984). Set firmly within the social studies mode, this course, to be offered only at Foundation and General levels, seeks to develop an awareness in pupils of the social, economic, political, historical, and geographical dimensions of contemporary Scottish society. Designed around a minimum of nine modules, each lasting a minimum of 16 hours, the course seeks to use knowledge and understanding to promote the skills of enquiry, communication and critical thinking. The three modules for which syllabus content is prescribed deal with 'Scottish society', 'industrial studies' and 'the environment'. Three further modules covering the areas of study related to 'change in society', 'contemporary issues and problems' and 'contrasting society', will be taken by the course participants but devised by the schools. Schools will also be expected to produce a minimum of three and a maximum of six optional modules selected from new areas of study or based upon the six areas of study already covered. Where the latter is chosen, a different content base will be required from that used in other parts of the course. A team approach is recommended for the course with the social subjects specialists in the school combining to design their course and submit it for moderation. In common with all Standard grade developments, the course is designed around concepts and skills and involves practically-based learning.

The Munn report gave support to the idea of courses in S3/S4 that were shorter than the present two-year norm, a view also supported by the CCC who believed that such courses would be important not only in producing a greater degree of pupil choice and a wider span of interest, but would also allow greater flexibility in the construction of curricula to fulfil the modes of study. The attention which the Pack report drew to the exposure of S1/S2 pupils to a large number of teachers and the discontinuity of experience and relationship that such a situation produced, led that committee towards the view that the rotational timetabling of shorter but more intensive courses in certain subjects might go some way towards overcoming the drawbacks of longer two-year courses.

The curricular and educational attraction of short courses led the CCC to initiate a two-year development programme which sought to explore more fully the feasibility of short courses of the kind advocated by the Munn report, and of modular courses capable of being combined (clustered) in various subject or area of study patterns. Some 50 schools became involved, each responsible for devising one or more free-standing short courses. Modules/courses of 40 hours became the norm, and most of these were devised at

Foundation level but several were offered to pupils of average to above average ability. An overall evaluation of the short course programme was undertaken and published in February 1984 (Consultative Committee on the Curriculum, 1984).

In June 1983 the Joint Working Party Steering Committee responsible for the Standard Grade Development Programme, agreed to recommend that certain short courses should enter the development programme in Phase 3 and the Scottish Education Department Circular 1107 (1983) announced the intention to introduce short courses in association with two-year courses in computing studies, craft and design, and technological studies.

Against this background of a growing interest in a modular approach to course construction, the Government issued early in 1983, the document *16–18's in Scotland: An Action Plan* which laid out a framework of new courses based on a collection of learning units or modules, usually of 40 hours study, to replace present non-advanced further education (FE) courses in Scotland. This meant therefore that the non-advanced section of FE would replace their one-year and two-year courses with appropriate modules (short courses). It was noted that the first modules would be ready for teaching in FE colleges *and schools* by the beginning of session 1984–85. It was felt that the long-term strategy of modularizing the curriculum, giving credit in terms of competency gained, and working through a negotiated programme of modules towards an integrated curriculum and awards system which could be applied in both school and FE sectors, would materially assist in providing a coherent educational experience for the whole of the 14–18 age group and in turn this experience would relate meaningfully to the earlier and later stages of the lifelong educational process.

The development of the short course concept has much potential for the business studies and economics area of the curriculum by providing flexibility of choice for pupils and by offering them opportunities for extension and more detailed coverage of elements of existing Standard grade S3/S4 courses in the business studies and economics area. In addition, those pupils in S3/S4 not committed to the full two-year Standard grade BS and economics course(s), would have the opportunity of undertaking short modules if available. Such modules might include money management, keyboarding, personal financial services, enterprise for business, how firms work, and starting a small business. In this way non-specialist BS and economics pupils in S3/S4 would widen their educational experience without being locked into a full two-year course. Such courses might also be available to pupils studying full Standard grade BS and economics courses as a means of widening their experience. Appropriate guidance would ensure that their curriculum was correctly balanced across the recommended modes.

Two further developments in Scottish education are ensuring an important role for BS and economics in the curriculum. As a result of the recommendations of the report on the Education for the Industrial Society Project, the Scottish Education/Industry Committee (SEIC) with membership from education, industry and the trade unions was constituted in 1984 with the aim of 'keeping under review curricular matters in which there is a particular industrial interest and to draw such matters to the attention of appropriate project and subject committees of the CCC'. Within a wide-ranging programme of activities for the Committee, the following are of particular interest for the development of BS and economics.

Firstly, the SEIC has recommended that the issue of how increased economic literacy might be achieved within the curriculum should be pursued in conjunction with the SCCBS and SCCSS and the JWP on Economics, responsible for developing the Standard grade course. It is also hoped that, in conjunction with the S1/S2 Social Subjects Development Programme referred to earlier, a set of guidelines on economic literacy within the social subjects courses at this stage can be produced. The SEIC has also supported in principle the piloting in Scotland of the exemplar curriculum materials on economic literacy devised by the Economics Education 14–16 Project Economics Association. Also a module provided by the EISP in conjunction with Central Region and entitled 'Business Education' will soon be published either as a support material for the report of the JWP on business studies or as exemplar material for use with any putative short course covering 'education for enterprise'. Finally the SEIC believes that further consideration should be given to the stage(s) at which keyboarding skills should be taught and who is to be responsible for teaching them.

Secondly, BS and economics contributions are increasingly finding their way into the growing number of TVEI schemes currently operating in Scotland. The technical and vocational nature of such schemes guarantees a prominent place for subjects which cover the world of work, skill development, and vocational preparation. A knowledge of economics, secretarial studies, computing and accounting and the skills associated with these subjects must take their place on any TVEI-inspired course.

Conclusions

As this paper has shown, the second half of the 1980s will be a time of significant change in Scottish education which will affect all pupils in the age range 10–18.

The broad aim of such radical changes will be to improve the quality of education offered and to make the provision more appropriate and relevant in order that pupils may pass through the system and be better equipped with skills and knowledge to take their place in a rapidly changing society.

The Standard Grade Development Programme, with its emphasis upon a balanced curriculum and a pupil-centred, activity-based process learning model and designed to promote relevant skills through courses appropriate to the needs and abilities of the pupils concerned, certainly forms the main curriculum development thrust at present. The movement towards a form of assessment based on criteria is also firmly embedded in the Standard Grade

Development Programme and this criterion-referenced system is to be found in the modular provision proposed for students at post-16 level in non-advanced further education and in the schools, whereby programmes of study can be put together from a number of modules chosen to meet the needs of the users and the particular interests of the students. The emphasis upon pupil-centred activity-based learning and criterion-referenced assessment characterizes both the Standard grade developments and the post-16 developments. Thus meaningful articulation should result for pupils undertaking courses in S3 and S4 and moving on to continue their studies in S5 and S6.

Business studies has much to contribute to the general and vocational education of pupils in both of these major areas of development. Within the Standard Grade Development Programme, contributions have been identified through the courses business studies and economics. Opportunities also exist for inputs into multidisciplinary course provision within both the social and vocational skills and contemporary social studies courses. In addition potential contributions have been identified through the short course model where elements of business studies and economics could be available to pupils.

The curriculum of able students in the post-16 area can also be enhanced by taking higher grade courses in the business studies and economics field, while those students seeking a more skills-based and vocationally-oriented provision would find certain of the modules in business administration appropriate.

Increasingly it is also likely that inputs from the business studies and economics area will be offered to pupils in the earlier years of the secondary school.

In conclusion, teachers of BS and economics in Scotland are concerned about the future of accounting at both Standard and higher grades. The current proposals make no clear recommendations for the development of the subject for pupils in S3 and S4. A final decision on the future of accounting will be made when the nature of the Standard grade course in business studies has been established.

A matter of further concern relates to the difficult position that economics finds itself in at a time of falling school rolls when minority subjects attract relatively and absolutely small numbers of pupils and so result in the setting up of small non-economic teaching groups. Such subjects are often 'squeezed' out of the school curriculum and in a number of areas of Scotland economics finds itself in just this position.

Finally, unease also exists among teachers about the future of higher grade courses in the BS and economics area and the proposal made recently that the future of such courses should be considered by the appropriate JWP which would have the responsibility of deciding whether such courses should remain in the curriculum as full higher grade courses or should be replaced by appropriate modules under the post-16 developments. On balance, however, the future for business studies and economics should be seen as an optimistic one. Radical changes to the structure of business studies and economics in the secondary school curriculum are being planned and the final packaging of the curriculum input from this important area will, of necessity, be different from that currently present in schools. It is to be hoped however that the new structure which emerges will provide the balance, choice, and flexibility for pupils which the Munn report advocated and also will go a long way towards offering teachers enjoyable courses to teach which positively motivate students and enhance the learning process.

References

BBC 1985 *Your Guide to the New Exams, Scottish Standard Grade (14–16)*

Consultative Committee on the Curriculum 1984 *Short Courses: The Final Evaluation Report on the CCC's Short Course Programme 1982–83*

Council of Europe 1982 *Preparation for Personal Life and Life in Society* Council of Europe, Council for Cultural Co-operation

The Dunning report 1977 *Assessment for All: Report of the Committee to review Assessment in the Third and Fourth Years of Secondary Education in Scotland* HMSO

Economics Association 1985 *Understanding Economics* Longman

The Education for the Industrial Society Project Report 1983 *An Education for Life and Work: Final Report of the Project Planning Committee of the Education for the Industrial Society Project* Consultative Committee on the Curriculum

The Munn report 1977 *The Structure of the Curriculum in the Third and Fourth Years of the Scottish Secondary School* HMSO

The Munn and Dunning reports 1982 *Framework for Decision* Scottish Education Department

The Pack report 1977 *Truancy and Indiscipline in School in Scotland* HMSO

Scottish Central Committee on Business Subjects 1982 *Starter Paper* Consultative Committee on the Curriculum

Scottish Central Committee on Social Subjects 1978 *Economics in S1 and S2: A Feasibility Study* HMSO

Scottish Central Committee on Social Subjects 1984 *S1/S2 Social Subjects Development Programme: Draft 2* Consultative Committee on the Curriculum

Scottish Certificate of Education Examination Board 1973 *Accounting, Economics and Economic History: Ordinary Grade Syllabus and Specimen Papers*

Scottish Education Department 1983 *Circular 1107: Implementation of the Government's Proposals for the Reform of the Curriculum and Assessment in S3 and S4*

Scottish Education Department 1983 *16–18's in Scotland: An Action Plan*

Scottish Examination Board 1983 *Social and Vocational Skills: Report of the Joint Working Party*

Scottish Examination Board 1984 *Contemporary Social Studies: Report of the Joint Working Party*

Response   *Steve Hurd*

The papers reviewed here (Sumansky, Helburn, Moret and van Oosten, Gregory, Hodkinson, Thomas), reveal significant differences on the meaning of economic literacy. Sumansky describes the evolution of the US *Master Curriculum Guide in Economics: Framework for Teaching the Basic Concepts*. A structure of discipline approach is advocated for devising economics curricula, and the evolution of the 'Framework' has been characterized by an increasing refinement of concept specifications. Sumansky argues that designing model curricula does not work; defining the building blocks of core concepts does! The task of the next few years is to search for the quarks of economics, so that optimal learning strategies can be devised. The advent of the computer as an educational medium opens up 'prospects for defining optimal sequences for acquiring economic knowledge'. The latest, 1984, edition of the Framework gives as much prominence to a decision-making model as it does to concepts. The importance of students having a procedural framework within which to approach economic problems is highlighted, as is the acquisition of relevant numerical skills.

Hodkinson attaches even greater importance in courses to 'the process of economic investigation and the procedures used by economists to analyse and interpret the economic system'. He argues that courses in economic literacy should provide:

1 contexts for investigation which involve decision making in the face of scarcity

2 a problem-solving approach

3 a framework of questions to structure that approach

The notion of the procedural framework is explored further by Thomas: 'to achieve economic understanding in any context is to understand the nature and functions of the relationships which anchor specific skills, concepts and information to a general framework.' The specific framework offered resembles closely the social cost–benefit framework of welfare economics, with an emphasis upon allocation efficiency.

Helburn's paper offers a major challenge to the structure of discipline approach favoured in some of the papers. She argues that a discipline-centred approach inevitably supports the prevailing orthodoxy, which is currently dominated by the constrained optimization approach of neo-classical economics. Students should develop an awareness of the 'tentativeness of knowledge'. They must therefore be exposed to alternative frameworks, e.g. post-Keynesian and Marxian economics. Extending students' moral judgement is as important as their abstract reasoning powers.

This belief is echoed by Gregory, who argues that the goal in economics education is to 'improve understanding of the world'; and by Moret and van

Oosten, who emphasize the danger of elevating the learning of the 'frozen' language of concepts above students' actual understanding of economic problems.

Gregory questions the conventional Brunerian view that 'learning which does not include reference to the general principles involved has few intellectual rewards. Knowledge that has been gained without reference to the structure of the subject will be easily forgotten.' He argues that 'not only must students apply principles to the solution of real problems, but they must identify values, the logic of argument, and even question the capacity of economic analysis to provide an adequate answer.'

Moret and van Oosten accept the goal of developing conceptual under-standing, but argue that the use of correct terminology should not be emphasized too soon. In their view we should be more concerned with the process of learning. Courses should start with what students already know, and can express in their own language. They highlight the motivational benefits of starting a course from students' experiences and interest, and dealing with subjects that are practically useful in the future. The need to expose the economic knowledge which students bring to a course is supported by Thomas's finding that 'tenacious commonsense misconceptions formed on the basis of early economic experience (are) already incorporated into pupils' conceptual repertoire.'

In the UK in recent years there has been growing disillusionment with courses based upon teaching the 'facts of economics'. Interest has shifted towards identifying core concepts and procedures for approaching economic problems. This raises a number of important questions. Is content important at all? Does it matter whether the economist's toolkit is applied to shopping decisions, money management, production decisions, education and health care, energy, the Third World, or even understanding 'the economic basis of a free society'? Is more effective teaching of concepts in conflict with understanding the world? Does economics education have citizenship value? Is it a private or public good? How should the profession respond to the strong social pressures for particular forms of economics education?

Response   *Ron Wilkes*

The commonplaces of education, according to the intricate and cogent views of Joseph Schwab, are subject matter, the learner, the teacher and the milieu. These elements, as Schwab has demonstrated in his writings, are settings in which the relationship of theory to practice can be considered, tested and refined.

The papers under review (Sumansky, Helburn, Gregory, Hodkinson, Moret and van Oosten, Thomas, Wilson) are concerned, fundamentally, with processes of considering, testing and refining the relationship of theory to practice and each deals with more than one of the curricular commonplaces. As in Schwab's writings, the papers concentrate more on subject matter than the other basic elements. What economics to teach is the main theme, although there is diversity in the specific questions tackled, the writers' perspectives, the research methods and the conclusions.

Sumansky traces the lineage of the Joint Council on Economic Education's *Master Curriculum Guide in Economics,* an exercise that shows, through the increasing integration between content on the one hand and teaching strategies and learning theory on the other, an awareness of the important distinction that Schwab makes between subject matter and subject-matter-for-education. Subject matter from the discipline must be prepared if it is to be used effectively for education. Processes in such preparation need to be reported, explained and opened up to discussion, as Sumansky has done.

Subject matter, however, is itself a source of contention, as Helburn points out. The *Master Curriculum Guide* contains one version, a paradigm that is both orthodox and dominant and one that empirical analysis shows to be well established in textbooks. As Helburn points out, this leaves out not only other paradigms but also the dimensions and processes of debate between alternative schools of economic thought. The questions raised are fundamental. To what extent, one wonders, can the ideological considerations be separated from the scientific and the educational?

Gregory's approach to subject matter bypasses the disciplinary paradigms in favour of an investigation whose rationale links the citizenship justification for economics in schools with media usage of economic terms. His list of concepts has empirical support and the logic of their arrangement is open to examination. The suggestion that the ability to read intelligently the economic items in a daily newspaper could serve as a definition of economic literacy is a contentious statement on a popular theme and is likely to give rise to discussion.

Economic literacy, or basic economic awareness, is a theme taken up by Hodkinson in the context of recent centralized curriculum initiatives in the UK. His analysis highlights the difficulties not only of adapting subject matter (a similar problem to state mandates in the US) but also of preparing teachers for new developments of uncertain nature. Hodkinson's view of economic literacy appears to involve both substantive and syntactical structures from the economics discipline, but emphasis is strongly on the latter; on method rather than doctrine.

An educational model can influence strongly the selection, organization and presentation of subject matter; a proposition well illustrated by the work of Moret and van Oosten. One might ask which is the means and which the end; the three-level model or the economics? Apart from highlighting the relationship of subject matter and learning model, this paper emphasizes the importance of taking into account the needs and capabilities of the individual learner. In this vein, the relevance and permanence of learning are major issues raised by Moret and van Oosten.

In dealing with the topic of assessment of achievement in economics,

Thomas's paper is outside the immediate scope of Schwab's commonplaces. However, it is clear that assessment is pertinent to subject matter, teacher, learner and milieu. It is, moreover, a process that is adaptable and one in which the interplay of theory and practice has its own particular set of problems and challenges. Thomas's comprehensive coverage shows clearly the kinds of difficulties encountered in this sub-field of curriculum as well as giving a perspective on possibilities for improvement of education through improvement of assessment.

In Schwab's scheme of things, particular problems of curriculum involve all of the commonplaces even though such problems may be embedded most deeply in one of them. In the papers considered in this brief discussion, subject matter is a major, but never exclusive, concern. To varying degrees, learner, teacher and milieu are present. Perhaps it is the greater malleability of subject matter that makes it the most popular topic. However, we would do well to heed Schwab's warning against the hegemony of any one commonplace.

Among the necessary conditions for high quality economics education in schools are that teachers have knowledge of the subject matter and both expertise and enthusiasm in the use of available classroom materials. Wilson's informative report of an integrated training model for teachers raises important general questions about incentives for participants and the origin and organization of such programmes but also prompts more specific queries on methods of evaluation. More information about the test instruments used would help the reader to appraise the student results reported, particularly those dealing with increases in mean scores on an attitude test. A fuller reporting of statistics on students' results would also help. However, the brief report on participants' evaluations of the Canadian programme does suggest that it has been successful.

The research methods employed in this collection of papers are no less diverse than the questions posed for investigation. Of itself, this says nothing about the quality of the research, but it is a sign that curriculum research in economics education is in the healthy state of tailoring its methodology to fit its questions and not vice versa.

Response   *Angus Taylor*

Much of Finlayson's paper provides an interesting description of a model for curriculum change on a national scale as adopted by the Scots. A three-pronged approach through reviews of curriculum structure, of assessment and certification, and of the teaching process provides a potentially very powerful vehicle for the development of effective economics education. However, I wish to concentrate my comments on the potential of business studies courses for economics education. In doing so I am reacting to Finlayson's paper rather than criticizing Scottish initiatives. But first a word about economics education for all within this model.

The case for a degree of economic understanding for all is argued in the Munn report in making the case for a 'social studies mode' – the 'need . . . for the preparation of all pupils for their roles as citizens, producers and consumers.' Those are the key roles identified in the exemplar materials of the Economics Education 14–16 Project. However, the Scottish plan is for economics to be regarded as but one subject capable of fulfilling the requirements of the social studies mode. A basic education in economic understanding would be particularly well fitted into the multidisciplinary, modular courses being provided, whether that be social and vocational skills or contemporary social studies. One could envisage a school finding it possible to make such a course available to all at Standard grade – albeit at the appropriate level of certification.

What then might the role of business studies be in providing access to economics education in the final year of compulsory schooling? First we need to clarify a curriculum title which is growing in use, but where there are varying definitions. Finlayson gives evidence of this in describing the Scottish experience, where 'business studies' describes 'that established group of subjects concerned with developing in pupils a knowledge and understanding of the operation of the industrial and commercial component of society . . . through a study of secretarial studies, accounting and economics.' The English experience is that a dichotomy exists in the use of the title. Its traditional use in schools has been to describe courses in business skills (e.g. shorthand and typing), perhaps with a descriptive element of business organization (e.g. 'commerce'). Teachers of business studies so defined have had low status, and courses have been followed mainly by the less able girls. They have not provided any adequate source of an economic perspective and economic understanding. Such secretarial studies, invaluable though they no doubt are to children's education, would come into this category.

In recent years a GCE O level course in business studies has been developed which has a quite different emphasis, and this development is about to be reinforced by the inclusion of 'business studies' as one of the main titles for the new General Certificate in Secondary Education (GCSE), which becomes the main 16+ certificate from 1986–88. The Cambridge Board's O level syllabus included as specific aims 'to explain the role and purpose of business activity in the public and private sector . . . to examine how business is organised and financed . . . to consider what, why and how goods and services are provided' and to appreciate the interaction between business and government. For many of us this is providing a good vehicle for economics education.

The introduction of the GCSE will strengthen the presence of this approach to business studies within the curriculum in England and Wales – and this concurrent opportunity for economics education. All five of the new examining groups are preparing new syllabuses, and these must match national criteria laid down by the Secretary of State for business studies courses. The national criteria include five headings which are 'essential areas of study' in the core of a business studies course, these being: external environment of the business, business structure and organization, business behaviour, people in business, and aiding and controlling business activity.

Economics also appears as a GCSE title, and has its own national criteria. However, the argument being pursued here is that, in addition to economics education within a modular course taken by all, business studies provides a more likely vehicle within the optional courses provided in the British curriculum. There are a number of reasons for this.

The first group of reasons relates to the process of choice itself, particularly in the current educational and social climate. More students are likely to choose business studies than economics, and this, on anecdotal evidence, would appear to apply across the ability range. With job opportunities minimal for 16 year olds in many parts of the country, a sort of weak vocationalism operates. 'Economics' sounds academic; 'business studies' "promises" some applied benefits. It finds itself associated with other weak or general vocational subjects such as technology and information technology. The Technical and Vocational Education Initiative emphasizes business enterprises and also links it with these other subjects. The existence of post-16 BTEC courses further reinforces these developments.

Secondly, the business studies syllabuses provide a better vehicle for economics education through experiential learning than does the economics syllabus. Young people are responding to this approach and this affects choice. Methods of assessment more related to the real world become possible.

The Scottish developments described by Finlayson are exciting for teachers of economics and academics who concern themselves with economics education in schools because they illustrate the benefits of a national initiative on curriculum development as well as showing how a range of curriculum vehicles may need to be tried. However, for reasons I have just touched on, I am disappointed that it would appear that the opportunity to provide economics education through a business studies course as such has not been taken. An effective business studies course covers the three key dimensions for the economically literate student – as producer, as consumer and as citizen. It is an opportunity that the Scots might like to incorporate in their already challenging programme.

Index